Catholicism and Protestantism

A Cabana Chronicles Book

Conversations about God

John B. Bartholomew

John B. Bartholomew

Copyright 2019 by John B. Bartholomew

Catholicism and Protestantism

The Cabana Chronicles: Conversations about God

By John B. Bartholomew

Printed in the United States of America

ISBN 978-0-9961520-9-9

All rights reserved solely by the author. The author guarantees all contents are original and do not infringe upon the legal rights of any other person or work. Although much of the dialogue in this book is based on actual conversations, *The Cabana Chronicles* is a work of fiction. Any resemblance to statements made by discussion participants to statements made by persons, living or dead, is purely coincidental. No part of this book may be reproduced in any form without the permission of the author.

www.the-cabana-chronicles.com

Acknowledgments

This book would not have been possible without the input from all of my pastors, church elders and Christian friends, who have faithfully communicated the truth to me through their comments, sermons and classes. Dr. R. C. Sproul, Dr. A. Bernard Kuiper, Pastor Ron Shaw, Pastor Frank Vanlandingham, Pastor Nathanial Winkel, Pastor Harold Polk, Dr. Robert Branden, Dr. Voddie Baucham, Reverend Norman A. Shell, Pastor Brent Merten, Pastor Brad Fell, Pastor Roger Ruff, Pastor Duane Kirchner, Dr. Daniel Garland, Dr. Nabeel Jabbour, Dr.James Dretke, Dr. G. Kent Osteen and Dr. Bill Waddell, I thank you all. I particularly want to thank my Catholic *Facebook* friends, Micheal O' Fearghail, David McClelland, Ken Litchfield, Michael Zimmerman, and Christopher Lehe for their assistance in explaining the Catholic Church doctrine to me. I also want to thank Rick Roos, Mike Prieur, Charlie Harris, Thomas Scott, Ed Roper, Charles Leopardo, Stan Marciniak, Dennis Kautz, George Slakta, Elliott Lang, Tony Nash, and all other members of *The Cabana Chronicles Facebook Group* for their assistance in explaining Protestantism.

Last but not least, I thank my loving wife, Patti Lee Bartholomew, whose patience, suggestions and loyalty to the cause have served to support me in my endeavor to complete the *Cabana Chronicles* series project over the past fifteen years.

Book Contents

The Nicene Creed

The five *solas*

Authority in Christianity

Basis for the Reformation

Catholic Church tradition

The importance of Scripture

Introduction to Catholic doctrine

Apostolic tradition versus Catholic tradition

Motives and objectives of the Catholic Church

Discussion of invisible and visible church

Week Three

Sin

Seven deadly sins

Seven capital virtues

Vincible and invincible ignorance

The psychology of religion

The purpose of tradition

Oral tradition

Authority in biblical interpretation

Greek Orthodox Church

Protestant denominations

God's sovereignty and man's free will

The question of authority

The "Holy Father"

Week Four

God's plan of salvation

Antinomianism

The Order of Salvation

Unfolding revelation

The infallibility of the pope

Week Five

Sacred tradition

Purgatory

Works-based religions

Christianity, a designed religion?

Origin of Catholic traditions

Relativism

Indoctrination

The new pope's liberalism

Reasons for leaving the Catholic Church

Week Six

God's plan of salvation

Reasons for joining the Catholic Church

Peter, the first pope

Forgiveness of sin

Bible interpretation

Catholic rejection of *sola gratia*

The efficacy of Christ's atonement

Catholicism and Islam

Historic splits in the Christian church

Reason for number of Protestant denominations

Week Seven

Peter, the first pope evidence

Keys of the Kingdom

History of the papacy

Additional church history

Unity in Protestantism

Assertions of Catholicism

Essential differences

Discussion of Catholic tradition

Purgatory Revisited

Week Eight

Judgment Day

Indulgences

Forgiveness of sin

Celibacy

Sex scandal

Birth control

The sacraments

Baptism

Week Nine

Holy Communion

Confession/Penance

Marriage

Anointing the sick

Ordination

Confirmation

Veneration of Mary

Week Ten

Presentation of the Christian Reformed doctrine

Boice's four tenets of the Reformed doctrine

Summary and concluding remarks

CATHOLICISM AND PROTESTANTISM

Preface

"It seems to me that a man must be a

believer or seek some belief, otherwise

his life is empty, empty....To live and

not know why the cranes fly, why

children are born, why there are stars

in the sky....Either he knows what he

is living for, or it's all nonsense, waste."

From Chekhov's *Three Sisters*

Aristotle, the man considered to be the "father of philosophy," said there are three different ways to judge men's mode of living. Each mode differs in the degree of awareness of the experience of life.

The lowest level consists of people who are most easily satisfied with a life of mere day to day enjoyment. Often by necessity, they focus primarily on their own basic survival. Aristotle believed that the majority of people on earth are living at this level. He called the second level *the life of active citizenship*. People living at this level are satisfied with the pursuit of career, money, fame, honor and pride. He called the highest level of living *the life of contemplation*. This is the level requiring the most mental commitment. It is only at this level that we are motivated to really think about the real purpose of our lives. Socrates said the unexamined life isn't worth living.

This distinction of the three modes of living is of course, by its very nature, subjective. There are no arbitrary boundaries in place which separate them. And there are no restrictions to prevent people from moving from one level to another depending on the circumstances. It is therefore possible for a person to move up the ladder of mental involvement from one mode to another and many people do accomplish this feat as they mature in life. This is a welcome improvement to those people who recognize that something is missing in their lives, and they want to fill the perceived void.

We humans are religious by nature, and everyone has a set of beliefs that collectively make up what they call their religion. Most of us though don't give what we believe much thought. Surveys indicate that there are many people who confess that they may be living a life that falls somewhat short of their potential, but claim they just don't have the time or the inclination to do anything about it. Few of us take the time to think through what we believe and whether our beliefs can be supported and are worth retaining or whether they should be discarded for some other belief.

The ability of people to think introspectively, to lead a self-examined life, is a lost art in this day and age. People are content to settle for progress in the material sense but don't understand that only by questioning where we all stand on more important issues, do we truly move forward. In a chapter he wrote for John Piper's *The Supremacy of Christ in a Postmodern World*, Dr. David Wells said "Our conquest our external world seems to be in inverse relation to the conquest of our inner world. The more we triumph in the one, the less we seem to be able to hold together in the other." We must recognize how important the conquest of that inner world is to us; we must understand we have a basic need for real fulfillment in our lives and that to achieve this completeness, we need to recognize that we should engage in discussions of the more important issues in our lives.

We need to crave knowledge and clarity. We need to integrate the knowledge of others into our own by exchanging ideas and opinions with them. We need to use our good minds to formulate opinions about important matters, test the support of these opinions and discover the limitations of our fallible knowledge. Solomon tells us in Proverbs 27:17

that "As iron sharpens iron, so one man sharpens another." We can often learn about what we believe from what we find out we don't believe, and that is why discussions with those who oppose our beliefs are so constructive. We need to prioritize living a life of contemplation by seeking out others to talk to about what we believe and what they believe.

Philosophy has been characterized as a great conversation, and the same description would apply to theology, the father of philosophy. Valuable spiritual experiences can often come out of conversations revolving around these two important disciplines. Philosopher John Stuart Mill once said "Estimate the proportion of men and women who are selfish, sensual, frivolous, idle, absolutely common place and wrapped up in the smallest of petty routines, and consider how far the freest of free discussion is likely to improve them." Indeed this is exactly what I believe happened when we formed our little discussion group of "Winter Texans." We retirees met under a beach cabana on South Padre Island, Texas each season for three years to discuss philosophy, theology, and religion.

Most of us had had successful business careers which required our attention during those earning years so we had to wait until our retirement for the additional time to enable us to pursue that life of contemplation. We seemed to have reached that point in our lives when we had the time and the inclination to know more about what we believed, and how our beliefs compared to the doctrines of other religions. Believing that no day is lost on which some spiritual truth becomes clearer, we were motivated to meet on a regular basis to calibrate our spiritual compasses and put the priorities of life in proper order. We discovered that we now have that time to focus on the mental and the spiritual aspects of our lives. We understood that this is the very age when new horizons should be appearing and new doors opening. It almost seems as though our entire lives have led up to this point in time. We are motivated to once again pull those books off the shelf which address liberal arts subjects like theology, religion, philosophy, history, literature, and psychology and read them again, as though for the first time.

In our discussions of philosophy, religion, politics and theology, we discovered that we really enjoyed the experience of meeting together to discuss and debate such weighty subjects. Theology is important because it's important to understand what we believe. In fact, Christian apologist, C. S. Lewis, once said that he found the study of theology and doctrine more helpful in devotion than the devotional books. He said that "many who find that 'nothing happens' when they sit down, or kneel down, to a book of devotion, would find that the heart sings unbidden while they are working their way through a tough bit of theology with a pipe in their teeth and a pencil in their hand." Theologian Louis Berkhof wrote, "God sees the truth as a whole, and it is the duty of the theologian to think the truths after Him. Since, as another theologian, Dr. R. C. Sproul, said, we are all theologians, every Christian should endeavor to see the truth as God sees it. So then, the question is not whether we are theologians, but what kind of theologians will we be?

Introduction to the Cabana Chronicles Series

The Cabana Chronicles is a series of books addressing the subject of apologetics, the systematic and logical defense of the Christian religion as it is compared to several other world religions.

So, why is apologetics important? The Apostle Peter believed defending his religion was important when he tells us to always make sure Christians have an adequate explanation of why we believe what we believe. What was important in the first century is even more important now in this day and age. Dr. Peter Kreeft, in his introduction to his book, *Handbook of Christian Apologetics*, surmised that our "civilization today is in social crisis, intellectual crisis, and spiritual crisis. We do apologetics not to save the church but to save the world." Dr. Kreeft listed three reasons for the study of apologetics: It leads to faith for unbelievers; it builds up faith and aids love for Christianity for believers; and it engages in spiritual warfare.

Apologist Cornelius Van Til once said that "apologetics begins with dialogue. It is not a one way form of communication or a simple matter of proclamation." Since *The Cabana Chronicles* series is a record of the dialogue in our weekly debates, I believe the books in this series exemplifies what Van Til meant. As it was for Socrates, the argument is all. Indeed, throughout history, the dialogue literary style has proven to be a most effective learning tool because it translates thought-provoking concepts into the vernacular and encourages the reader to vicariously participate in the discussion taking place. It also allows for the expression of a variety of opinions in whatever is being discussed. Dr. Kreeft states that he loves the dialogue format. He tells us "an argument is valid if the conclusion follows necessarily from the premises. If all the terms in an argument are clear, and if all the premises are true, and if the argument is free from logical fallacy, then the conclusion must be true."

Philosophers who study epistemology, the study of how knowledge is obtained, tell us the three sources of man's knowledge are faith, tradition and reason. While each one of these sources is certainly utilized in the formulation of a person's beliefs to one degree or another, depending on the religion, one source of knowledge is typically emphasized over the other two.

*Other books in the series: *The Cabana Chronicles: Book One, Book Two, Book Three, The Foundation of Belief, The Religions of Secular Humanism and Christianity, Judaism and Christianity, Islam and Christianity, Mormonism and Christianity* and *Comparing Christian Denominations.*

Although much of the dialogue is based on actual conversations, The Cabana Chronicles is a work of fiction. Any resemblance to statements made by discussion participants to statements made by persons, living or dead, is purely coincidental.

Dedication

This book is dedicated to Charles "Chuck" Brookins.

JOHN B. BARTHOLOMEW

Catholicism and Protestantism

The righteous shall live by their faith.

A Faith is the substance of things hoped for,

the evidence of things not seen.

CATHOLICISM AND PROTESTANTISM

Week One

Bobby: It's good to be back under our old beach cabana to discuss religion again, eh? John, Darrel, Peter and Daniel, it's good to see you all back this year. In relating to your feedback from last season, our sessions will only be 45 minutes long this year instead of the hour plus sessions of the previous years. Is that okay with y'all?

Darrel: Sounds good to me. What are we going to discuss this season?

Bobby: I thought it would be interesting to compare Roman Catholicism to Protestantism. Here's a suggested outline of what I'd like to discuss in each of our sessions. Since I assumed this would be fine with you guys, I invited a Catholic friend of mine to be with us for our discussions. Say hello to Sonny Flynn, guys. Why don't each of you introduce yourself and tell Sonny a little bit about yourself to get acquainted.

John: I'm John Bartholomew. I'm a retired real estate appraiser. My wife and I have been coming down here to Padre Island from our home in the Vail Valley in Colorado since 1999. I have been a member of a PCA Presbyterian church and attended a Baptist church here on the Island during the Winter Texan season. I joined the Lutheran church in Eagle, Colorado and attend the Lutheran church in Port Isabel. By the way, Sonny, I've been recording our sessions each season and hope you don't mind going on the record, so-to-speak.

Sonny: Not at all, but why go to all that trouble?

John: I document our conversations in my series of books I appropriately call *The Cabana Chronicles.* Based on the interest in them so far, it seems as though there are actually some folks out there who are interested in reading about what a group of old guys have to say about philosophy, theology, religion and politics. The books focus on apologetics (the logical defense of the Christian religion) and comparative religion. I will also be able to provide you with a written transcript of the previous meeting which I can email to each of you every week for your review.

Bobby: Even though we should each focus on being good listeners, there will undoubtedly be times when we want something reviewed in a previous discussion. Daniel, you're next.

Daniel: I'm Daniel James. I have lived in the Rio Grande Valley for the past 20 years. I'm still working as a part time guidance counselor for the Port Isabel school district. I'm a Methodist. I attend church in Harlingen.

Darrel: I'm Darrel, Darrel Sanderman. I retired down here three years ago. I used to own a John Deere dealership in Arkansas. I've attended a variety of non-denominational churches for most of my adult life but they've always been reformed, Bible-believing churches. I'm not currently attending any church. I used to talk for a living so I always look forward to gabbing with you guys. I will say though that I've not had a good experience debating with Roman Catholics on *Facebook;* they are so defensive and testy about what they believe. Of course that can work both ways, I'm sure. Jewish intellectual Anthony Hecht once wrote that few things struck him with more force than "the profound and unappeasable hostility of Protestants and Catholics toward one another."

Sonny: I'm sorry to hear about that, Darrel; I hope you'll find me easy to talk to.

Bobby: I can vouch for Sonny; he's one of the good guys. Peter, you're next.

Peter: I'm Peter Cantrell. I'm a retired biochemist. I used to work with the FDA in Denver. I'm not a Christian. I call myself a secular humanist, an atheistic religion. I attend these discussions sessions to keep you guys honest.

Darrel: Yeah, right. Actually, I think Pete's here to learn from us because he knows there's Christianity and then there's all other religions; we pique his curiosity. What about you, Sonny; what's your background?

Sonny: As Bobby mentioned, I'm a Catholic and attend services at St. Mary's in Port Isabel. I'm a retired civil engineer from Chicago. By the way, before we go any further, I'd just like to point out for the record that we refer to ourselves as just "Catholics." Only Protestants refer to us as Roman Catholics. The word "catholic" means universal and that's what we are, the one true, holy and apostolic universal Church.

Darrel: I refer to you folks as Roman Catholics, "Romanists" or "papists" in order to emphasize your connection with the Roman church and the papacy, and why it's important to distinguish between the original, catholic or universal church and what the Catholic Church represents today. We Protestants don't accept the premise that you are the only true Christian church. I won't play what I call your "claim game" where no matter what any other Christian says, you claim you're the only true Christian church and the rest of us are heathens or heretics and have nothing to say about Christianity of any value. It makes it damn near impossible to have a productive discussion with any of you.

John: We should preface our discussion sessions by laying out some foundational info before we get into the details of what we each believe.

We know that every human being is naturally inclined to want to believe in something, even to worship something; you could say that everyone has a theology; the challenge is to have the right one. Which church we choose to support should be based on which one preaches and teaches what we know about our triune God and should not be based on any other reason. That's what we're meeting here to discuss.

As I see it, every human being has three main choices to make in deciding what to believe. We can choose to not believe in God at all; this is pure atheism, and it has several variations that are functionally the same as pure atheism like deism, agnosticism, Hinduism, etc. We can also choose to believe in a personal God, but presume the right to design him to fit what we want him to be like. That's the case with every other religion except Christianity. Lastly, we can recognize the existence of a personal, triune God who has inspired the writing of a book in which He tells us about Himself and how we are to relate to Him; that's Christianity. The book of course is the Holy Bible, and we are to understand that we are not only to believe this is God's Word, but we are to believe Him when He tells us how we are to relate to Him, and how He has insured our salvation. That's pure Christianity in the apostolic tradition.

We Protestants believe that Catholicism is a variation of the apostolic tradition. As Darrel just said, we do not accept the premise that the Catholic Church is the one, true church that represents the original Christian church based on the teachings of the apostles as Christ intended for it to be. Recall that I said that one of man's choices is to design a God after his own desire; well, I believe that the leaders of the Catholic Church have designed a church after their own desire, and I intend to prove that point in our discussions. Catholics adhere to a church that has over the centuries been successful in building a church institution whose worldly objectives are power, influence and wealth. As these discussions progress, I hope to offer evidence to support our statement.

Bobby: Okay then, I guess the battle lines have been drawn. As most of you know, I was raised a Catholic and attended Catholic schools. I am familiar with the Christian doctrine but rebelled against it. I guess I'm now a "none of the above" when it comes to declaring a religion. This is why I wanted to talk about various Christian denominations in these discussion sessions, particularly comparing Catholicism to Protestantism.

Sonny: I'm curious, Bobby, why did you leave your Catholic Church?

Bobby: Catholics dwell on sin and guilt. I came to the conclusion that I had been focusing on the Church's catechism, more worried about breaking the rules, anxiety issues for fear of going to hell because I missed a Holy day, missed mass last Sunday, or that I ate or drank too much, etc., etc. rather than focusing on the love of God and man. That's why I renounced the Christian religion.

Darrel: Tell me about it! My parents were Pentecostal; that's all I heard. Don't dance, don't smoke, don't drink, don't, don't, don't (fill in the blank) or you'll go to hell. But I would caution anyone who's experienced Christianity this way to not throw the baby out with the bathwater. Don't renounce Christianity; just find a Bible-believing denomination that doesn't focus on the negatives of legalism and fire and brimstone.

John: Yes, legalism is a trap. God makes his Law quite clear to us in the Bible; our churches can go wrong in stressing perfect obedience to God's rules and the rules added to His list by man. That's Judaism and Islam, not Christianity.

Christians know that God's law reveals we are sinners; that's one of its main purposes. Christianity is not so much a religion as it is a relationship, a relationship between God and man, and our inherent sin has destroyed our relationship with God because we know that God hates sin. We know that God is perfect and is just, and we are not; so we should know that we cannot possibly hope to repair the damaged relationship with God on our own by perfect obedience to His law and will. Sin exposes our unrighteousness and our need for a Savior to connect us with God. Our hope is based on our faith that Christ has done that; He has already repaired the relationship with God. Our faith motivates us to recognize sin and repent, which means to change our ways and not sin. As true Christians, we hope to become better people and please God to thank Him for what He has done for us in extending His grace, His unmerited favor to save us sinners.

Darrel: There are two different kinds of relationships, vertical and horizontal. By its very nature, all Christians must relate to our triune God vertically; we relate to our fellow humans horizontally. Our relationship to our church is also a horizontal relationship. Catholics exemplify this type of relationship in the unique way they connect with their church. As we shall see in these discussions, no other Christian denomination relates to its members the way the Catholic Church connects with its members. Such a horizontal relationship can serve to strengthen the vertical relationship with Christ, but it can also detract from where our main focus should be; on our vertical relationship with Christ.

Sonny: Our Church represents our relationship with Christ. I too once rebelled against the Catholic Church, but began to understand how it guided me to knowing the truth. I believe the Catholic faith to be perfect even though the Church is made up of human beings, and they make mistakes. My Church brings me closer to God.

John: We all have a core belief, a bias, and we bring it to discussions like this. This can't be avoided. Our prejudice, if you will, is deeply ingrained within us; and we always need to understand that these beliefs, these presuppositions, must always be taken into consideration as we attempt to pursue what's true. We aren't here to reinforce what someone else told us to believe; we're here to examine what we believe with an open mind, considering what others believe and comparing this to what we think we believe. In the end, it all comes down to what each of us believes is true. Over our lives, we have been indoctrinated by our parents, our friends, and society; you could say that our beliefs are traditions we follow out of habit. But there should come a time in every person's life for us to exhibit the courage and willingness it takes to examine what we believe and why we believe it; to put our beliefs to the test to determine whether they are true or not. Aristotle, the father of philosophy, believed that tradition was the weakest source of knowledge because it didn't require any thinking. Tradition actually stifles self-examination. It relieves people from the effort of thinking for themselves. Folks who mechanically repeat their presuppositions in a monologue of the deaf in these discussions won't get much out of them, and neither will any of the rest of us.

Peter: In this group, we challenge each other to think for ourselves, to examine what we believe and why we believe it. That's the examined life.

This can be very frustrating and uncomfortable for someone who just wants to find a choir to preach to or to sell us on some belief of theirs without ever having examined their beliefs enough to know why they believe it's true; but, according to epistemologists (those who study how we learn), discussing our beliefs with others has proven to be the best way to acquire and retain knowledge. Aristotle said that the pursuit of knowledge is man's ultimate objective.

John: Exactly. People have their various preconceived ideas and want to share them with others; they want to know that their ideas are well received; they want reinforcement and acceptance. We all have a very basic need to protect our self-esteem and like to believe that what we say is important. So, while our instinct is to talk to others, we should recognize how important it is to listen to what others are saying to us. When we listen to others, our influence in their lives is enhanced and relationships are strengthened. When people don't listen to what the other person is saying, a meaningful dialogue cannot take place, and neither party really gets anything out of it.

Daniel: Yes, for this reason, we must avoid yielding to our natural, prideful temptation to sell our opinion to each other and assume the other guy has nothing to tell us unless he agrees with us. I know I have to be careful about doing this. We need to resist assuming the other guy is always wrong and we are always right. We must avoid drawing a line in the sand and closing our minds to any opinion that doesn't match with our preconceived opinions. We must examine those preconceptions and ignore them if they don't make any sense.

Sonny: So, how do we avoid falling into this trap?

John: We need to approach this discussion introspectively, and use our good minds to examine our motives for belief and present opinions that we believe are the truth, not on what we want the truth to be. We must be sensitive enough to know when we are merely protecting our precious self-esteem and try to humbly listen to what the other guy has to say. We seem to be all pretty good talkers. We need to also become good listeners.

Daniel: I hope that all of you agree with me when I say that until we draw our last breath, we can continue to learn from each other. We need to focus on continuing to learn because the journey we call life is serious business.

Bobby: Our contentment in life depends on the choices we make. I saw a movie the other night called *The Words*. One of the characters concluded that it's much easier to make the choice than to live with that choice.

John: This is true, but it wouldn't be so easy to make the choice if we understood that all choices have consequences, and we need to focus on making the right choice.

Bobby: Sometimes the choices we make affect our entire lives. Actually, most of the choices we make can affect our lives. It's been that way with me.

John: You bet. There are consequences for every action we take and every word we utter both here on earth and in eternity. We need to understand our lives involve more than just the time we spend here on earth. We will live out our lives differently when we understand how we are living from God's perspective; and we know His perspective because we have the Bible.

Daniel: Yes, we do need to understand that what we do here on earth can certainly have eternal consequences. That's why it is so important to focus on what we are doing or plan to do and use our heads as well as our hearts to make choices that have beneficial consequences. We must surround ourselves with people who care enough about us to give us good advice. That's what good friends are for.

Darrel: Hallmark's new slogan is "Life is a special occasion." This is a one-time experience. We need to take it seriously; and we need to remember that we are supposed to enjoy life too. In the movie, *Auntie Mame*, Mame once said that life is a banquet and most poor bastards are starving to death. Our purpose in life is to glorify God *and enjoy him forever.*

Peter: I'm interested in how Christians connect with their church. I know your church is important to each of you guys so then what do Christians expect from their affiliation with their respective churches?

John: I want my church to present the gospel truth to us. The emphasis must always be on God's sovereignty, His grace, and on the authority of His Word.

Sonny: The purpose of the Catholic Church is the salvation of souls and that is the highest law of the Church; nothing goes above that law. The Church presents the truth as taught by the apostles and the early Church fathers.

Darrel: I contend that the CC doesn't present just the teachings of the apostles, but adds to those teachings by including the opinions of these early church fathers as dogma. As a result, the concept of God's grace is weakened by the addition of good works as a requirement for salvation. This false theology compromises God's sovereignty, creates guilt and discontentment by creating doubt that believers haven't done enough to be saved; hope is compromised. No true Christian church should ever give the impression works plays a role in our salvation; it's bad theology. Of course, some of our user-friendly, seeker Protestant churches have a problem understanding this concept too. Many of these churches de-emphasize the Bible, just as the Romanists have done over the centuries, and God's sovereignty cannot clearly be understood in relation to us if we don't believe the Bible is God's Word and what it says about his plan of salvation.

Bobby: You're talking about Catholic doctrine and theology, Darrel, and, as you can see from your outline, we're getting a little ahead of ourselves.

Peter: What about you, Sonny? What do you expect from your church?

Sonny: We Catholics believe that our Church is the one, true apostolic Church, the pillar and bulwark of truth (Catholic Church Catechism, par 171), the one representative of Christ's earthly Kingdom established here on earth (CCC 2105). In order to know the truth, it must be sought from the Church and only the Church. Most people believe it works the other way around, that we must seek the truth from the Bible and then find a Bible-believing church to attend.

Darrel: That is the way it works. Your church is full of itself. It claims for itself the authority (under the guidance of the pope (CCC 883, 895) to interpret Scripture (CCC 100), to reconcile sinners (CCC 1444), motivate people to believe in the gospel (CCC 119), to represent Christ (CCC 1548) and last, but not least, that it is necessary for salvation (CCC 816). And, there's more: CCC 2086 states that "all men may attain salvation through faith, Baptism and observance of the Commandments." This brings good works into the plan of salvation, a heretical concept we shall discuss in more detail later.

Sonny: I stand behind our Catechism. As sole authority to the truth, we expect the Church to tell us the true meaning of what the Bible is telling us, and we want what the Bible promises all true believers, to whit: Ministers who can forgive our sins in the name of Jesus; a healing rite for the dying and suffering; a true, physical connection with Christ through the Eucharist; heavenly intercessors to hear our prayers; Mary, the mother of Jesus, is to be considered the most blessed woman; contraception is intrinsically evil; sexual sins are transgressions that will keep one from gaining entry into heaven; celibacy is a good thing; the saints in heaven are alive and can appear to humans; salvation is not a sure thing.

Darrel: I'm a happy committed Protestant who believes in the theology of the Reformation and understands that, contrary to the way Catholicism is set up with its top down authority, my church's power flows up from its members who elect the Elders who lead them.

Sonny: We need an organized governing authority and a building that it uses for group worship. Our sacred tradition is equal to Scripture. In our Catechism of the Catholic Church (CCC 80), we are told that our sacred tradition and sacred Scripture are bound closely together and communicate one with the other; and CCC 81 states the Holy Tradition transmits in its entirety the Word of God which has been entrusted to the apostles by Christ the Lord and the Holy Spirit. As a result, our Church does not derive her certainty about all revealed truths from the Holy Scriptures alone; both Scripture and Tradition must be accepted and honored with equal sentiments of devotion and reverence (CCC 82).

Darrel: I'm aware that you believe your church relies on itself and not just the Bible to teach God's Word. Its man-made sacred tradition is nothing more than man's word on Christian doctrine and it has equal authority to Scripture. We go by God's Word, period! Paul states in 2 Timothy 3:16-17 "All scripture is given by the inspiration of God." In Mark 7:13 Christ says that we are not to "make the word of God of no effect through your tradition which you have handed down."

Sonny: When Paul says that all scripture is given by the inspiration of God, he isn't just referring to the Bible. In 2 Timothy 3:14, he states that we must remain faithful to what we've learned and believed, because we know from whom we learned it. Verses 14 and 15 point out the importance of both Scripture and tradition.

Darrel: We surely have no reason to believe that Paul's reference to what has been taught by the apostles wasn't recorded by them in the gospel accounts. Mark 7:13 records Christ's concern that the corporate church should not add to God's Word. As with his letter to the Laodicea church, his intent is to communicate the need for his church to repent for becoming confident in its outward prosperity while abandoning the one message that brings life to this lost world. A refusal to repent will bring Jesus' discipline on the church; hence the Reformation.

Sonny: Are you actually implying that the Reformation was the result of God's discipline?

Darrel: Do you Catholics even know your Bible?

Sonny: Of course I do. I was encouraged to read the Bible in growing up and am encouraging my children to read it as well. My six year old was given a Bible when I signed her up for her first year of faith formation.

Darrel: Well, we know from church history that this wasn't always the case. And, when you say you signed her up for "faith formation," this suggests the church will be supervising interpretation in a formative way; it implies the beginning of the indoctrination process. The Catholic Church wants to read the Bible to all its members, regardless of their age. It wants to control what it's saying so it can squeeze in its sacred oral tradition through its catechism. Christian liberty is stifled, and this is a spiritual tragedy because we cannot be sanctified apart from the Word. We are sanctified in order to be sent into the world with the gospel, just as Christ was sent into the world with the gospel (John 17:18).

Bobby: Define sanctification and Christian liberty, Darrel. You know our rules of engagement in these sessions. Define your terms.

Sonny: You guys actually have rules of engagement?

Darrel: Sure. We've been doing this for a couple of years now, and at our very first discussion session, we realized we needed to all agree on a set of rules that governed how we conducted these discussions for them to be most effective for us.

Bobby: As our discussion leader, my job is to enforce our rules. So far, our system has worked well. Our rules are pretty straightforward and make sense. Here they are: <u>Rule Number One</u>: Avoid a long monologue about what you believe; give the others a chance to respond and when they do, be a good listener. <u>Two:</u> Be civil to one another. <u>Three:</u> Quote only those experts who are recognized as credible to support an opinion. <u>Four:</u> Make sure we use terminology that is understood; use a definition, if necessary. We all obviously need to know exactly what we are talking about.

Darrel: These techie devices like my smart phone also give us immediate access to a number of different Bibles, a Websters,' "Nelson's Christian dictionary," and McKim's "Westminster Dictionary of theological terms."

So then, here's the definition of "sanctification" from McKim. It is "the process of being made holy and acceptable to God through the efforts of the Holy Spirit. The justified are renewed in the spirit and bear fruit of good works. Sanctification relies on God's preserving grace and the believer's perseverance in the faith. The process increases throughout our life but is never completed until our death."

The doctrine of Christian liberty is based on Paul's teaching as presented in 1 Corinthians 8-10, Romans 14 and the entire book of Galatians. It states that if Scripture (or truth legitimately deduced from it) does not address a particular doctrinal issue, the Christian is at liberty to decide what opinion to have on that issue.

Bobby: I know that the Catholic Church stresses its sole authority in interpreting God's Word for believers. I remember one of the Cardinals said that the Scriptures have only as much force as the fables of Aesop, if they aren't authorized by the Church.

Sonny: Well, the Catholic Church did give us the Bible after all.

Darrel: Yes, the Catholic Church was the only Christian church in the fourth century when the canon was organized. It documented those 27 books which were generally accepted as being part of the canon from the first century. But this doesn't mean your church should claim sole authority in interpreting God's Word just because it organized the Bible for us.

Sonny: There is only one Church. In our Catholic Bible, the word "church" is capitalized.

Darrel: The original Greek doesn't have capital letters, but the first official Catholic Bible was the Douray-Rheims translation in 1582, and "church" is not capitalized so I don't know what you're referring to.

Regardless, what you say is consistent with your assertion that the Catholic Church is the only Christian church. The word "church" is mentioned 80 times in the New Testament and it is never capitalized. There are also 40 references to the word "churches," so this would certainly indicate there wasn't intended to be just one Christian denomination.

John: The original texts do not capitalize "church" or pronouns referring to God. Capitalization designates a title, and, of course, this is why the Catholic Church capitalizes "church;" capitalization is obviously meant to designate that they are the one, true church.

Sonny: We Catholics maintain that the Catholic Church is the one, true church. It is not a Christian denomination. The Church stands alone, representing the entirety of the Christian faith. Where do you think the term was first used for the original Christian Church?

Darrel: Technically speaking, in the first century of its existence, the universal ("catholic") Christian church's leaders, Ignatius and Polycarp, disciples of the Apostle John, began to refer to the church as the *Catholic Church* with a capital "C." But it was never called the Catholic Church in the Bible. As is the case with "church," in every Bible except the Catholic Bible, whenever *catholic* is referenced it's designated with a small "c" not a capital "C."

Bobby: How did the Catholic Church become known as the Roman Catholic Church? Where did the name "Roman" come from?

Sonny: The Church of England, the Anglicans, gave us the name "Roman" Catholic in the 16th century, but we don't recognize the label. As I said before, there is no such animal as the Roman Catholic Church. Unfortunately many of our priests don't know this and call themselves Roman Catholics. To your second question, within the Catholic Church there are a number of individual churches, sometimes called rites. One of these is the Roman rite or Roman church. It includes most of the Catholics in the Western world. A Roman catholic is a Catholic who is a member of the Roman Rite. There are many Catholics in the East who are not Roman Catholics, such as Maronite Catholics, Ukranian Catholics, and Chaldean Catholics. These are all in communion with the pope, but they are not members of the Roman Rite, so they are not Roman Catholics. All rites are equal. They all teach the same faith; it is only local customs that are different among them. For your info, I'm a member of the Roman Rite.

Darrel: History records that before the papacy was formerly established, for the first 500 years, the leaders of the Catholic Church were called bishops. The concept that the Bishop of Rome would officially be called the pope gradually evolved and when Leo I (440-461 AD) had himself proclaimed to be the head of all the bishops and then lord of the whole church, some historians believe that he should be called the first pope in church history. Some other historians consider Gregory II, who was installed in 728, to be the first pope. But Gregory I, AThe Great," who was elected pope in 590 AD, is generally regarded by most historians as being the first actual bishop or pope of the church in Rome. Other historians believe this event occurred later in time.

Regardless of which Roman bishop was believed to be the first pope, historically, the papacy has always been an Italian institution, and historians conclude it actually evolved from the old Roman Empire and merely substituted the office of the pope in the place of the Caesars. Biblical interpreter, Henry H. Halley, called the papacy the Aghost of the Roman Empire come to life in the garb of Christianity." This is why we refer to the Catholic Church as actually being the Roman Catholic Church. Our objective in appropriately including the name *Roman* in your church's title is of course to distinguish it from the original Catholic church of the first century, and refute your church's claim to be that same church.

Sonny: The almost 2,000 year old Catholic Church is the one, true Church. It even preceded the Bible.

Darrel: Here we go with the "claim game" again. In stating this I'm assuming you mean that your church preceded the organization of our Bible, don't you?

Here's some more church history for you. As mentioned in the book of Acts, the followers of Christ early on became known as Christians. The name Christian, however, was never commonly applied to the church herself. In the New Testament itself, the church is simply called "the church." There was no reference to the Catholic Church or the Roman Catholic Church.

Sonny: The Bible doesn't refer to the trinity either, Daniel, but that doesn't mean the concept isn't a reality.

Darrel: The concept of the trinity is, of course, in the Bible. The concept of a single church of Christ claiming to sole representative of Christianity is not.

Sonny: I disagree with you; I'll prove what I say in our discussions. I mean to say that the Catholic Church did exist before the books of the New Testament were collected and the Hebrew Bible, which of course, had been written and organized by the Jews several thousand years before Christ, was added to produce the Bible we have today. This feat was accomplished through the Holy Spirit guiding the leaders of the one Christian Church existing at the time and for all time, the Catholic Church.

John: Just for the record, I should mention that there was no church organization at all before the Bible was actually written. Israel didn't have an organized church; they had the assembly of the people of God, the equivalent of Old Testament Israel. And, regarding the production of the New Testament, there are only two references in the gospels to the church, Matthew 16:18 and Matthew 18:17. In both cases they refer to a local gathering of followers of Christ. Soon after the church was formed (as recorded in the Book of Acts), the books that were to become the official canon were recognized and, of course, there was no Roman Catholic Church for several hundred years after that time.

Sonny: All the books to be included in the Bible and their order of inclusion were established under Pope Damasus I at the Council of Rome in 382 AD. This is why I say that our Church preceded the Bible.

Darrel: The "Catholic claim game" goes on. The historical facts don't support the Catholic Church's contention that it is actually that particular Christian church that preceded the formation of the Bible; and I intend to prove that statement in our discussions. Based on what we've already discussed about the history of the Roman Catholic Church, we see that the Roman Catholic Church wasn't even established as the entity it is today at the time of the formation of the canon. You can't dispute that fact because it's history.

To add to what John said, we know that church historians tell us the writings attributed to the apostles were circulating amongst the earliest Christian communities from the very beginning of the original, orthodox Christian church, which of course, as we contend, was definitely NOT the Roman Catholic Church. Paul's letters were circulating in collected form by the end of the first century. Justin Martyr, in the early second century, mentions the "memoirs of the apostles," the Gospels, and these writings were given equal authority to the Old Testament. The four Gospel canon was in place by the time of Irenaeus in 160 AD who directly refers to it. By the early third century, Origen of Alexandria may have been using the same 27 books as the modern New Testament, though there was still some question as to whether the books of Hebrews, James, 2 Peter and 2 and 3 John and Revelation should be included in the canon at the time. In his Easter letter of 367, Athanasius, Bishop of Alexandria, provides the earliest preserved list of exactly the same books that would later be acknowledged as the New Testament canon. So, although the initial development of the canon began in the first century, it remained for Athanasius to provide the leadership to organize the canon of books of both the Old and New Testaments.

My point is that no church should brag about doing what God expected it to do; I've said before that you Catholics are a boastful bunch, and you demonstrate that pride in your church, Sonny. We should never, ever presume that we owe anyone but God the credit for communicating his Word effectively. To presume otherwise is arrogance, even blasphemy.

John: We acknowledge that the Catholic Church did originally develop the canon of the Bible, but it also added seven extra books to that canon, 1,200 years later. Though what Catholics refer to as the deuterocanonical books have been around since the fourth century, it wasn't until the Council of Trent in 1563 in response to Luther objections to them, that they were officially considered to be part of the Catholic Bible. These books are part of fifteen books known as the Apocrypha, which means "secret or "hidden." These books themselves make no claim to be the Word of God, and Protestants consider them to be what they are, unnecessary add-on books. They vary in content, and some of them make inaccurate statements and statements that directly contradict the gospel (Sirach 3:3, 30, 12:4-7, Tobit 12:9, Wisdom 8:19, 20, for example), but, in general, they do provide us with some historical background.

It is important to note that these books were never received into the Jewish canon and were not considered as part of the inspired Scriptures by Jews or Christians in the early centuries of the Christian church. No New Testament author refers to any of them. Though Jerome included them in the Latin Vulgate, he accepted only the books in the Hebrew Canon, and that is why they were all correctly eliminated from the Bible during the Reformation when the Bible canon was restored to its original 66 books. In the Counter-Reformation, these books were elevated to canonical status at the Council of Trent which occurred from 1545-1563. The church was forced to do this in response to Luther's demand to exclude any thought of them as being Scripture. Sometimes these official church pronouncements were proactive, sometimes they were reactive. In addition, to date, no commentary has ever been written on either of the books of Maccabees, on Judith, or Tobit. This shows how little these books were considered by any of the fathers of the Christian church. The question before us is why did your church add these books to Scripture?

Sonny: I don't really know why the Church included these books in the Bible, John, and I've personally not read any of these deuterocanonical books. Maybe the Church believed they served some kind of ecclesiastical purpose. I do know they have historical support. Ancient testimony from the Jews in Alexandria, Egypt indicates that these books were part of the Old Testament Scripture. The Dead Sea Scrolls, those ancient Jewish tablets unearthed in 1947, also indicate that first century Jews used the Apocrypha alongside the accepted Old Testament writings. Scenes from the stories portrayed in the Apocrypha are on the walls of the catacombs in Rome where Christians hid from persecution. In addition, the Apocrypha was part of the Septuagint, the Bible of Jesus and the apostles. I just know that the Church has the sole right to determine which books are authoritative and which ones are not. The acceptance by some of our early church leaders like Augustine (he quoted 2 Maccabees 12:43) and three of our early church councils are a good reason for me to accept the Apocrypha as legitimate Scripture.

Darrel: I'm glad you mentioned Augustine because I intend to show you how his theology differs from Catholic Church theology during the course of these discussions. He is truly the "elephant in the room" for today's Catholicism, and many seem to recognize that reality because some of Augustine's theology has been ignored in modern Catholicism. Anyway, I suspect the Apocrypha is included in your Bible for the explicit purpose of including a passage like this one in 2 Maccabees 12:42-45 (referring to prayers for dead sinners) to support your concept of purgatory. Since there are no verses in the 66 book canon of the Bible that support this heresy, the Catholic Church needed to include a book in the canon that does support purgatory. As with most of your traditions, the self-serving motive of the church is obvious.

Sonny: First of all, Augustine did believe in purgatory, Darrel. He stated that it's not incredible to believe "that there should be some fire even after this life, and it can be inquired into and either be discovered or left hidden whether some of the faithful may be saved, some more slowly and some more quickly in the greater or lesser degree in which they loved the good things that perish, through a certain purgatorial fire." Second of all, there is biblical support; Hebrews 11:35 supports the concept of purgatory in referring to a better resurrection. Augustine also supported the authority of the Church when he stated, "We read in the books of the Maccabees that sacrifice was offered for the dead. But, even if it were found nowhere in the Old Testament writings, the authority of the Catholic Church which is clear on this point is of no small weight, where in the prayers of the priest poured forth to the Lord God at his altar the commendation of the dead has its place.".

Darrel: When we read sentences "not incredible to believe," "should be some fire even after this life.," "can be inquired into and either be discovered or left hidden" in the quote you gave us, his verbiage doesn't exactly communicate his ringing endorsement of the concept of purgatory. "Not incredible" just means it's possible; "should be" means it makes sense; "can be inquired into" leaves open the option of believing in it or not. He's only suggesting that there could be some sort of "purgatorial fire." He is being this vague because he undoubtedly recognized how purgatory compromised his belief in predestination by implying we get a second chance to cooperate with God's predestined choice of us to be saved.

Yes, Augustine did believe in predestination and credited First Corinthians 4:7 ("What do you have that you did not receive?") as his inspiration. He believed that God chooses to extend his saving grace to some (the elect), but not to all (bypassing the reprobate). He predestines some to eternal life, but leaves others in their sin to be justly condemned through their unbelief. In his response to Pelagius, he said that the sin of pride consists in assuming that "we are the ones who choose God or that God chooses us in his foreknowledge because of something worth in us," and he argued that it is God's grace that causes the individual act of faith. He said that the doctrine of predestination must absolutely be preached, so that he who has ears to hear, may hear."

Regarding Hebrews 11:35, in examining what the author is saying, we see it refers to events that occurred in 1 Kings 17:22 and 2 Kings 4:36, 37 where the souls of two children came back to Elijah and Elisha respectively. It's a real stretch to conclude these apparent miracles prove a purgatory exists, and nowhere in Scripture is a second resurrection mentioned. Are you familiar with Christ's story about the rich man and Lazarus in heaven (Luke 16:19-31) where there's only heaven and only hell; they aren't in purgatory. I see from our outline that we'll talk more about purgatory later on.

Sonny: Hebrew 11:35 verse also refers to events occurring during the Maccabean revolt which were recorded in 2 Maccabees; this supports the inclusion of at least the Book of 2 Maccabee in Scripture.

Darrel: To your second Augustine quote, it doesn't seem like he gave a ringing endorsement for the Apocrypha, purgatory, or, for that matter, even the authority of the Catholic Church either. When he declares that " the authority of the Catholic Church which is clear on this point is of no small weight," this could be interpreted to mean that some weight should or could be given. His language supports the historical fact that Augustine believed these were all elements of our faith that are not commanded or prohibited in Scripture so he simply went along with the presumption of his church that they should be biblical books. Theologians call such elements *adiaphora*, which means "not differentiable."

Yes, Augustine was a respected church leader and one of your saints, but he was also probably one of the most influential theologians in church history and had much more to say about the essential aspects of the Christian doctrine other than to simply deal with some of the church traditions he knew about in his time. In fact, it was Augustine who made it impossible for the church to ignore the subject of God's grace, an essential aspect of the Christian biblical doctrine.

Augustine died in 430AD, and there were only a few Catholic traditions like the inclusion of the Apocrypha, praying for the dead and purgatory he had to deal with. Of course, as church history reveals, there were so many more Catholic, extra-biblical traditions to follow after his death, and one wonders what he would have thought about each of them. I've read Augustine's books and I've read many books written about him and agree with many theologians that he would have rejected such Catholic traditions as indulgences, the infallibility of the pope, the rejection of the Bible as sole authority in our religion and many others.

Bobby: Why didn't the reformers recognize the Apocrypha as part of the Bible, John?

John: They were not officially recognized by the reformers because they believed they were unnecessary to the canon. The reformers believed they were accurate, but didn't believe these spurious accounts of Jesus' life added anything to the overall theme of the gospel. In his book *The Jesus I Never Knew*, Philip Yancey tells us the Apocrypha includes stories about Jesus making clay sparrows that He could bring to life with a puff of breath, and dropping dried fish into water which then miraculously starts swimming. They show Christ using his power to impress others, and therefore served more as a contrast to the actual Gospels in describing Christ's historical witness. Yancey calls them "second-century counterparts to modern comic books about *Superboy* and *Batgirl*."

Daniel: These books didn't even claim to be the Word of God or the work of prophets. They vary greatly in content and value. Paul E. Little, author of *Know Why You Believe*, said that some of them, like Maccabees, were probably written around 100 B.C. and are valuable for their historical content. Others are more characterized by legend and are of little value. Jerome included them in the Latin Vulgate but didn't consider them to be in the Hebrew Canon. They were not considered to be inspired Scripture by Jews or early Christians. This is evident from the writings of the first century historian Josephus and by Augustine. None of the New Testament writers quote any of the books of the Apocrypha.

Sonny: Regardless of what you people think about the Apocrypha, you have to agree with what Martin Luther said about our Church's important contribution to the Bible in organizing the canon. Luther said "We are compelled to concede to the Papists that they have the Word of God, that we received it from them, and that without them we should have no knowledge of it at all."

Darrel: If not the Catholic Church, then some other Christian church would have performed a function like this. We are meant to be a religion of the book. Luther was right in acquiescing to recognizing the Catholic Church's contribution to Christianity in its organization of the whole canon of the Bible; Christianity had its book.

During its first three centuries of persecution under the Romans, the churches necessarily organized, giving way to the control of bishops under one rule. Traditions developed as a consequence to replace the autonomous worship of local churches. In the fourth century, Constantine the Great saw an opportunity to unify the Holy Roman Empire and to control his people by replacing the old, pagan God with the God of the Christians. He appointed a group of church leaders and gave them the task of completing the Hebrew Bible to include the gospel accounts and the writings of the apostles because he believed in the triune God of the Christians and wanted to include this prophet who claimed to have been the son of the Jewish God in the mix. Thus this church council was formed and did their duty. It's not that Constantine was such a good Christian; he needed for this to happen to maintain control over the Holy Roman Empire. Rulers and the Church joined forces to keep their people compliant. As one cardinal said to the king, "If you keep them poor, I will keep them ignorant." Subsequent church councils were convened to keep adding whatever traditions were deemed necessary. The papal hierarchy was once and for all firmly established, and the church continued in its quest for power, political influence and wealth. By the 12th century the Roman Catholic Church had become the world's most powerful institution having the power to set up and depose kings, levy taxes, and confiscate property. They were doing just fine until Luther came along and caused the Reformation and John Calvin documented reformed theology in *Institutes of the Christian*

Religion. After that the Catholic Church lost its status as the official religion in most parts of the civilized world and the rest is history. God's purpose; God's timing; God's method to reveal His truth.

Sonny: We gave Christianity its book; but, that said, we don't place the emphasis on it as Protestantism does in its belief that it is the only authoritative source of knowledge of our religion. We do not believe Christianity was meant to be sourced entirely from some book to begin with; the proper role of the Bible is to compliment the Church and its mission; it was never meant to replace it.

Darrel: Right. The organized Catholic Church now needed a place for its self-proclaimed purpose, to indoctrinate believers to embrace it. The mission of the Catholic Church is exactly what we Protestants question. What began as Christ's mandated mission, to disciple others, transitioned into a self-serving mission of attainment of wealth and power through implementation of dogma which convey traditions not in the Bible. So then, it tells folks the Bible isn't that important anyway, and that it knows what God wants to say because Christ appointed the church to be sole authority on earth for the Christian religion, blah, blah, blah. I find it ironic that the church that gave us our Bible is the very church that denigrates its authority. It's like your church is saying, here's the Bible, but there's more to Christianity than just this book. The canon was just one of the first of many, many more arbitrary traditions to come; stay tuned.

Sonny: I'm not going to comment on that, Darrel, but there are several points in Peter's summary that are false. **1.** Constantine didn't seek a new religion. He simply made Christianity legal to practice. This is called the Edict of Milan. **2.** Christianity wasn't even established as the official religion until after Constantine. **3.** Constantine didn't orchestrate the replacement of paganism with Christianity; the majority of people were already Christian when Christianity became the official religion. It may seem to unbelievers like you that Christianity wouldn't have even survived if Constantine hadn't made it the official religion of his empire to control the masses, but this simply isn't historical fact.

Darrel: But Pete's right about the history of the Catholic Church and its connection with the Holy Roman Empire. Did you know that historians consider the Holy Roman Empire to be a restoration and Christian continuation of the ancient original Roman Empire? It's true.

Christians should know that we are to be separate from the world, and our church should always be separate from state (civil government). Everything of course is under God's sovereignty, and civil government is his other kingdom, but, for now, God does not intend for his church to assume the role of civil government. In Matthew 4:8-10, Christ rejects Satan's offer to give him the kingdom of the world.

Daniel Deutschlander, author of *Civil Government, God's Other Kingdom*, states: "Christ is King; he rules over two distinct kingdoms in very different ways. He gives each its proper work and the tools for carrying out that work. He has placed us by the gospel in the kingdom of the church; he has placed us by physical birth in the other kingdom. He accomplishes his will in both kingdoms."

Throughout its history, the Catholic Church has ignored God's Word on this subject of separation of church and state. From the time of Constantine when Christianity was recognized as a religion and emerged from its underground status in the 4th century, the Roman Catholic Church began to assert its authority and gradually became deeply rooted in and intertwined with the history of the Holy Roman Empire; and since the Holy Roman Empire was the dominant political system for most of central Europe and Italy for nearly 900 years (962-1806), religion became more and more intertwined with the state as the Roman Catholic Church worked in conjunction with the Empire to represent the unity of all Western Christian states within a single, unified structure as the secular counterpart. You could even say that and to this day, the Catholic Church remains a living relic of the Holy Roman Empire. Now, that's an institution!

Sonny: That's an inaccurate presumption, Darrel the Catholic Church in this day and age certainly doesn't have the power it once had.

Darrel: No, it doesn't rule as it once used to rule, but, as a relic of the old Holy Roman Empire, Catholics still pay homage to their church as though they considered it to be like an empire. It seems your church yearns for the good, old days, and, based on your prideful claim that you gave Christianity the Bible to assert your false claim that your church of today is the original and only Christian church, you've proved my point.

My point is that this authoritative claim to be his only church which is to proclaim its importance as an intermediary between its followers and him is clearly not what Christ intended for his church to become. Jesus came to serve, not to be served, and he expects his church to follow his example. He expects his church to proclaim the gospel and not to aspire to worldly power that does not serve Christ's purpose. No Christian church is to become an institution in acting like civil government in asserting such governing authority over its flock as the Catholic Church does. Deutschlander states: "For the church to expect to rule in this life is to set aside humiliation for glory. That's not the will of Christ; it's not the pattern he set for the church on earth. Worldly power is for worldly governments; lowliness, humility, and suffering in imitation of the Savior are for the church as she follows in his footsteps." This is why I find it impossible to accept the premise that this Catholic Church represents the only Christian church Christ intended for us; it is the exact opposite of his intentions for his church.

Bobby: When the Catholic Church claims to have organized the Bible in the 4th century, I assume it's referring only to the New Testament canon, right? After all, the Jews obviously had their Hebrew Bible centuries before Christ appeared on earth.

Sonny: Yes, but the Hebrew Bible was organized differently than ours, and we reorganized the Hebrew Bible books into Christianity's Old Testament; so this is exactly why our Church gave Christianity its Bible.

Daniel: I would use a better word to describe what the Catholic Church actually gave Christianity. The Catholic Church identified the canon dogmatically. Dogma is different than doctrine; doctrines are explanations, even suggestions; dogma is mandated doctrine, a belief which all Catholics are expected to embrace and obey. A dogma cannot be defined without an existing doctrine.

I say the canon was identified dogmatically to indicate that, over the years, the process of identifying the canonical limits was more organic and involved the worship of the Catholic Church. This is where we Protestants depart company from our Catholic brothers and sisters in Christ. It is not our intent to use God's Word for any other purpose than to know God's truth.

John: I should also point out here that the canon wasn't dogmatically formed by some group of church leaders who sat around the table and arbitrarily selected certain books from a variety of writings. The Christian church has considered the canon of the Bible to be complete and closed to any new additional writings by anyone since that time. No revelation has been given to us since the first century which merits or warrants inclusion in the canon of Holy Scripture. Even if another of Paul's letters was discovered, it would not be included.

Darrel: Another factor to consider is this issue of the actual translation of the Bible that is being used. Virtually all of the modern Bibles are based on translation of two dubious Vatican sets of manuscripts by two men, Hort and Westcott published in 1881. They relied heavily on the *Codex Vaticanus* which was essentially written by Origen and published in the 5th century. Critics believe these translators gave too much weight to the *Codex*, and we should in fact note that they only released their work after it was approved by the Catholic Church. And, of course, I think we can assume that their text referred to the Catholic Church in capital letters. Anyway, the original manuscript of the *Codex* is kept in the Vatican library. The Catholic Church wouldn't allow their purported, ancient manuscripts to be examined and compared to the other manuscripts when the KJV was translated in the 17th century. The Hort and Wescott "translation" is really what Catholics refer to as proof of scripture authority. These translators also followed the work of Origen in Alexandria, and Origen is known to have not believed Scripture as being divine; he actually had a habit of changing the text to satisfy his beliefs. Nonetheless, even with all the tampering, 95% of the known texts agree, the books Catholics added (the Apocrypha) notwithstanding.

Daniel: Yes, you are right, Darrel. Although the Catholic Church considered Origen to be a heretic, they did end up adopting some of his beliefs centuries after his death. We know that Origen adored the Scriptures and wrote commentaries on many books. In fact, he is considered to be one of the most influential scholars and exegetes of the Bible. He was very transparent with the textual difficulties between different manuscripts; he actually offers the Old Testament in six translations. He referred to the writings as "holy scriptures" and believed they are authoritative. The issues at hand concern textual issues (manuscripts, wording, sections of Scripture) and translation. The field of textual criticism is very technical and translating is not as straightforward as we would like it to be. The initial KJV had over 8,000 textual notes. No doubt there are some bad translations. Thankfully, Jesus Christ built His church, poured out the Holy Spirit at Pentecost, and we need to know that the Scripture was written by the Spirit of God, and has a meaning that may not always be apparent at first sight, but works its way into the hearts and minds of true believers over a lifetime of study and analysis.

Sonny: But you Protestants don't have an authority to direct you in your understanding of God's Word. We do. You believe you can just take it up and read it and somehow learn what it says without any guidance from a trusted authority.

Darrel: Trust me, I'm a bishop?

Sonny: I know you're being facetious, Darrel, but we believe we have to trust someone in authority for us to understand God's Word. The Bible is a complicated book, and it's extremely important we understand what it is saying to us. We shouldn't trust ourselves to understand the meaning of

Scripture. We need that strong, credible, trustworthy authority to guide us.

Darrel: Well, we Protestants don't require some church to be the sole authority in our lives. This of course is exactly why there is no church called THE Protestant Church. We see that as an advantage because we need not be challenged to serve two masters. Unshackled from any one particular church's thought-control and man-made traditions, we are free to trust in God that he is able to guide us in our understanding of what he is saying to us. Jesus told us he was leaving us with the Holy Spirit for such a purpose. Every true Christian has the anointing of the Holy Spirit, so we do not require the help of people who hold some high church office and claim to be more anointed than we are. The Catholic Church reminds me of Orwell's *Animal Farm*. Remember the sign the ruling pigs put up which said, "All animals are equal, but some are more equal than others.

Sonny: Jesus left us with His Church in giving the keys of the kingdom to Peter. He is the rock and the Church is built on the rock. Peter was our first pope.

Darrel: There's no mention of Christ designated just one church called *the Catholic Church* in the N.T. Whenever a Catholic asks me who received the keys to the kingdom, I answer that loaded question by replying that the keys of the kingdom are God's gift to his people to continue on with what Christ taught the apostles. Christ is the cornerstone (Ephesians 2:19-22), and he build his church on what Peter had just confessed in Matthew 16:16 when he identified Jesus as "the Christ, the Son of the living God." All who faithfully preach and teach the gospel are able to exercise them under the authority of Jesus Christ. That's what Augustine said. In his 26th sermon, he referred to Christ when he stated, "I will build my church upon myself who am the Son of the Living God. I will build it on Me and not on thee." Peter certainly doesn't indicate he is the cornerstone in his letters. See 1 Peter 2:4-8.

It's like you people have to start right out by giving us your credentials to establish your church's credibility. You vicariously rely on the assumed credibility of your church in an effort for your opinion to be credible. I'll warn you right now, Sonny, this approach isn't going to work for these discussions. You're not preaching to the choir, nor are you discussing religion with a bunch of seekers. We're all informed, well-educated Christians in this group and expect to discuss our respective beliefs with an open mind. We don't get away with just pointing to what our church says and calling it good; we think on our own in this group.

We also require evidence for our opinions. So then, please show me the verse where Jesus clarifies there will be just one visible church he trusts will be the keeper of the flame of apostolic teachings. No Catholic I've ever asked this question of has come up with a definitive verse proving their premise. We'll talk more about this when we take up a discussion of your claim that Peter was your first pope. Peter was nothing more than a witness, a special spokesman of the divine truth revealed to him by God.

Sonny: You are voicing your own opinion, Darrel, but you can't know all the apostles taught because you belong to a denomination that has no apostolic roots. The Catholic Church proceeds from the apostles and hence knows all that the apostles taught.

Darrel: All Bible-believing Christians are grafted onto the root of Christ, and that means we are all able to understand the apostolic teachings; Christ left us with the Holy Spirit to make sure we understand God's entire Word.

Sonny: Christ left us with His Church, and it is therefore the Church which believes first and so bears, nourishes and sustains my faith. The Church's faith precedes, engenders, supports and nourishes our faith.

Darrel: More memorized mantra from your vaunted catechism. You imply your Church is God.

Sonny: In a manner of speaking (which I'll explain later), I wouldn't deny that, Darrel.

Bobby: It all has to do with authority, right? The authority of the Catholic Church vs. the authority of the Bible by itself; but I think they seem to connect and Sonny has a point about the church authority being necessary for interpreting the Bible. The Bible is hard to read and understand. Are we not discouraged from leaning on our own understanding? Isn't it necessary to be able to rely upon a visible, tangible authority here on earth to guide believers through the Word of God?

John: Of course authority is important. Jared Wilson of the Midwestern Baptist Theological Seminary said that "God has embedded a dynamic of authority and submission into the creation order itself. There is, of course, the sovereign God's authority over all His creation, but there is also a structure of authority and submission endowed by God in the fabric of nature, the family, the church, and even society. Rightly ordered and administered, this structure nourishes us and glorifies God." My point here is that the church is mandated by Christ to *rightly order and administer* the Word and sacraments to nourish us and to glorify God, man's chief purpose in life. The contention of Protestantism is that the Roman Catholic Church does not serve this purpose.

To your second point, Bobby, the Bible does say that we're not to rely on our own understanding, and that's not what Protestantism advocates. Acts 5:29 tells us we are to rely on God, the Holy Spirit, for our theology not on man. We are to rely on the Holy Spirit, for guidance in understanding God's Word just as the Bible tells us in 1 John 2:27 and Acts 5:29, and that spirit guides us to attend a Bible-believing church which preaches and teaches the Word and motivates us to study the Word utilizing what godly theologians have written in interpreting meaning for us. Reading and studying God's Word seems like a daunting exercise, but God is not a God of confusion and His Word is not hard to read. The gospel accounts, in particular, with the exception of Luke who was a physician, were not written by a group of educated people who wanted to show how smart they were, they were written by common, uneducated people who wrote in the language of the common man. Although it's best if every Christian understands theology is important, we don't need to be theologians to read our Bible nor do you need a church to tell us what it means. That said, it's best to know as much as you can about what you believe, and that's why R. C. Sproul once said we should all be theologians.

Sonny: We rely on our Magisterium to interpret the Bible.

John: Which in turn relied on theologians to guide it in interpreting Christian doctrine. Were the early church fathers not theologians? Was Augustine not a theologian?

Bobby: So then, how would you recommend a person begin to read the Bible on his or her own?

John: Great question! I recommend the following sequence: Begin by reading the first nine chapters in Genesis. Then read Exodus 20 and follow that up with Deuteronomy 28. That should introduce most of the Old Testament's main characters, the history of the Jews and God's plan of salvation. You can then jump ahead to the gospel accounts and read the entire Book of John. Then read the entire book of Romans and finish up with Paul by reading 1 Corinthian 15. Finish up with Revelation 21 and 22.

Sonny: Some say Luther wanted to do it on his own; he wanted to form his own religion.

John: Luther and the other reformers did not want to replace The Catholic Church with The Protestant Church. I quote his introduction to the 95 theses: "Out of love for the truth and from desire to elucidate it, the Reverend Father Martin Luther, Master of Arts and Sacred Theology, and ordinary lecturer therein at Wittenberg, intends to defend the following statements and to dispute on them in that place. Therefore he asks that those who cannot be present and dispute with him orally shall do so in their absence by letter. In the name of our Lord Jesus Christ. Amen." Does that sound like Luther wanted to establish his own religion? I think not.

If you were to read through these 95 theses, you would see that they refer to the man-made traditions initiated by the Catholic Church over the centuries. They focus on the power of the pope, purgatory, and indulgences. At the time of their posting, Luther still affirmed the authority of the papacy and had not yet given up on the Catholic Church. He just wanted to rid Christianity of these man-made traditions he listed in the 95 theses and go back to placing all the emphasis on the Bible as our sole source of knowledge about God, and motivate Christians to read and learn on their own. All Christians were encouraged to read the Bible, and thanks to Gutenberg's invention of the printing press soon after Luther nailed his 95 theses to the church door, the Bible became available to everyone. It was written in Latin at the time, but Luther translated it into German.

Daniel: Yes, Christianity is a religion of the book, the Holy Bible, and it only makes sense that Christians should all be encouraged to read a book we consider to be the Word of God for ourselves. It is sad that a Christian denomination, any Christian denomination, would want to usurp that individual responsibility and intentionally discourage its members to avoid reading it. From beginning to end, all prophecy in the Bible finds its fulfillment in Jesus Himself. Each Old Testament prophet whets our appetite for Jesus, and this is exactly why every Christian needs to consistently read the Bible for himself, and a Christian church should encourage us to do so. God's Word leads us to God's Word incarnate, Jesus Christ, and we must each read this for ourselves and meditate on this truth (Psalm 1); we must not just solely depend on our church to read it to us as a parent would read to a small child and interpret it for us.

Sonny: Although, as I said before, we read our Bibles, it is important to note that despite our reverence and dependence on the Bible as the inerrant world of God in matters of faith and morals, the Christian faith, as our Catechism states in paragraph 108, is not a "religion of the book." The Catechism states that "Christianity is the religion of the Word of God, not a written and mute word, but incarnate and living." We must share the fact that the Sacred Scriptures fit in with the Sacred Oral or

Apostolic Tradition, as if they were both "flowing from the same divine well spring and coming together in some fashion to form one thing, and move toward the same goal." The Bible is used to build up our faith and turn our hearts to Christ and His bride, the Church. (See Ephesians 5:22-23).

Darrel: In other words, the Bible is to be supplemented by Catholic tradition and is incomplete without it and without its official interpretation of what the Bible says to us.

Sonny: Yes, as the Church is led by the Holy Spirit. We believe the Holy Spirit is the true interpreter of Scripture, but neither the inspiration of Scripture or prayer to the Holy Spirit guarantees its accurate interpretation by each individual Christian.

Darrel: The Holy Spirit communicates with individual believers quite well, Sonny, without having to go through some man-made church authority as a middle man. You just have your church's word on it that its sacred oral tradition is the apostolic tradition and flow from the same well spring. We don't accept your middle man's role in relating to our Lord. The fact that you people need that middle man and we don't represents our differences. Reading the Word for ourselves is incredibly important. That's what 2 Timothy 3:16, 17, 1 John 5:13 and Deuteronomy 12:32 tell us.

John: Dr. Dennis E. Johnson, professor emeritus of practical theology at Westminster Seminary California, tells us that by "paying attention to a particular Bible passage's original occasion, genre, and purpose, we honor the God who spoke His Word in history, in human language, and in a rich complex of contexts: the first recipients' cultural background, their place in redemptive history (Old Testament or New), their spiritual experience, and the figures of speech and types of literature they used. The better we understand these contexts, the better we grasp what God is saying and what He intends to do in us through each passage. And when we see the change that God intends this text to accomplish in our thought, emotions, and actions, we are discovering what the Bible means." When Catholics limit their interaction with God's Word to just what their church determines is important in Scripture and what it interprets the meaning to be, they are limited in their discovery of what the Bible means.

Darrel: Protestants believe that we are free to read the Word on our own and interpret its meaning, just as the Bible encourages us to do. That's what John 5:39, 14:26, Romans 15:4, and 1 John 2:27 tell us. We're helped in interpretation by the Holy Spirit.

Sonny: A spirit can be a bad spirit too, Darrel. This is why it's important we have a Church which prevents evil spirits from leading us astray.

Darrel: I think it's ironic that this is the very church that leads you astray of the Word with its added, extra-biblical traditions. We'll discuss those in detail later on. The papacy wanted its followers to remain ignorant of the Word so that it could slip in its tradition and retain its influence and control of believers. With the Catholic Church, it's all about power. Halley said that the papacy is "a political machine that got control of the Christian church."

John: The Catholic Church wanted to retain sole power in interpreting the Word of God. But, as I said, Gutenberg's press made the Bible available to the masses, and the jealously guarded secrets of the Word of God were made available to all who could read.

Darrel: Of course many people were illiterate, all the more reason for the Catholic Church to act as sole interpreter of the meaning of Scripture. But it was very concerned about the increase in literacy over the centuries and the availability of the Bible for the laity's use. It wanted to jealously guard its usurped position as the sole authority of God on earth. In his Word, God revealed the existence of his internal church which consisted of Christ's true believers that includes the saints living on earth and all the elect from the beginning of the world. This particular concept had its roots in the theology of Augustine, ironically, one of your Catholic saints.

Sonny: As a Roman Catholic bishop, Augustine followed the Eucharist and the other traditions of the Catholic Church. We would not honor him as a Doctor of the Church and a Saint if his views were not in keeping with our traditions.

Darrel: Well, we know from church history that Augustine didn't have to deal with very many of them, certainly not the number of them in your church in these times. There were only four traditions Augustine was aware of: The prayers for the dead, the sign of the cross, the veneration of the dead saints and the Mass as a daily celebration. As I said before, all the other Catholic traditions were added after his death in 430 AD. We also know that he was ambiguous on at least three out of the four of them; I suspect he may have had a premonition and introduced the concept of the invisible church to differentiate Christ's church of the elect from what he viewed as the very visible Catholic Church in his life.

Bobby: Define invisible church.

John: Yes, I believe it is important from the beginning of these discussions to differentiate between the visible and the invisible church.

Augustine described the invisible church as being headed by Christ and consisting of the elect. Its beliefs and precepts were based strictly on the teachings of the apostles as recorded in the New Testament, and by reference, in the Old Testament as well. Protestant theologian Dr. R. C. Sproul explained the distinction between the two terms this way: "There is a distinction to be drawn between the church as people see it and as God alone sees it. This difference is the historic distinction between the 'visible church' and the 'invisible church.' Invisible doesn't mean that no part of it can be seen, but that its exact boundary is not known to us. Only God knows (2 Timothy 2:19) which members of the earthly congregations are inwardly born again, and so belong to the church as an eternal and spiritual fellowship. Jesus taught that in the organized church there would always be people who seemed to be Christians, not excluding leaders, who were nevertheless not renewed in heart and would be exposed and rejected at the Judgment (Matthew

7:15-23, 13:24-30, 36-43, 47-50, 25:1-46). Two different perspectives doesn't mean there are two churches, one visible on earth and another hidden in heaven; the terms "invisible" and "visible" are therefore used to describe two distinct aspects of the one church.

The original church was very much visible as a physical entity, and its purpose was, and is, to represent the invisible church, the beliefs of the elect in preaching and teaching the gospel and administering the sacraments. This visible church of course split into a number of factions as it grew, some of them remaining true to the original apostolic, biblical doctrine and some not. And I might point out here that every member, by definition, of the invisible church is saved; this is of course is not necessarily the case with members of the visible church. Christ speaks of this distinction in Matthew 7:21-27, 13:24-30 and 24:29-51. Suffice it to say that we belong to the church as an eternal and spiritual fellowship. Jesus taught that in the visible church there would always be people who seemed to be Christians, not excluding leaders, who were nevertheless not renewed in heart and would be exposed and rejected at the Judgment.

There's so much more to talk about if we want to get into the particulars of Augustinian theology in general, of course, and I hope to do that when we formally present our reformed doctrine later on in these discussions. Yes, Augustine was a Roman Catholic, as you say, but that's because that was the only Christian church in the fourth century; but his theology was reformed enough to have influenced Calvin and Luther in documenting the theology of the Reformation. Calvin once said if he weren't a Calvinist, he'd be an Augustinian. Yes, indeed, your Saint Augustine believed in every one of the five points of the doctrines of grace; in fact, Calvin used Augustine theology as a basis for his belief in what constituted reformed theology.

Sonny: You're claiming Augustine as a Protestant? Nonsense. You Protestants cherry pick his quotes to support that ridiculous idea. His quotes indicate he believed in the bread as the body of Christ and the wine as His blood; he stressed the importance of Mary, "a Virgin conceiving, a Virgin bearing, a Virgin pregnant, a Virgin bringing forth, a Virgin perpetual. Why do you wonder at this, O man?" He also believed in apostolic succession. "If the very order of episcopal succession is to be considered, how much more sure, truly and safely do we number them (the bishops of Rome) from Peter himself, to whom, as to one representing the whole Church, the Lord said, 'Upon this rock I will build my Church, and the gates of hell shall not conquer it.' Peter was succeeded by Linus, Linus by Clement...In this order of succession a Donatist bishop is not to be found." The first thing Peter did was to implement apostolic succession as Paul referred to in Ephesians 2:20.

Darrel: In regards to Ephesians 2:20, Paul refers to "members of the household of God (i.e. the Christian church)" and the *teachings of the apostles* as its foundation with Christ being the cornerstone in whom the whole building, being fitted together, grows into a holy temple in the Lord. In whom we are also being built together for a dwelling place of God in the Spirit." He's not establishing the papacy.

In regards to Augustine's support of some of your church dogma, as a bishop, he may have acquiesced to some tradition, but, in the essentials, his theology was clearly Protestant. When we discuss his theology in more detail, you'll see what I mean. I invite you to read *Confessions* or *City of God* and see if you can't pick up on Protestant theology or just google "Augustine and Calvinism" and read what pops up. The reformers patterned their reformed theology after his theology. I quote what John Calvin wrote" "Augustine is so wholly with me, that if I wished to write a confession of my faith, I could do so with all fullness and satisfaction to myself out of his writings." Calvin referred to Augustine on one out of every four pages in his *Institutes of the Christian Religion.* As I say, Calvin referred to himself as an Augustinian and credited the great theologian for his doctrines of grace that form the basis of the theology of the Reformation. Throughout our discussions, I will be presenting a number of quotes from Augustine that support he was the initiator of reformed theology.

We know that Augustine introduced the concept of an invisible church and distinguished it from the visible church in *City of God*. In regards to his belief in apostolic succession, that concept was destroyed when the Emperor Diocletian killed all the authorities that could claim to be successors to the apostles.

You may recall that a man named Pelagius was opposed to Augustinian theology in the 4th century, and their debates ended when the church's condemned Pelagianism as heresy. The concept of man wanting to be God, however, will never go away, and, in the 17th century, we see the concept revived by Jacob Arminius in his Remonstrance which was subsequently judged to be heresy by the Synod in 1619.

Sonny: Yes, I know what you're talking about; I think you could say that the Catholic Church is divided between the Augustine/Aquinas concept and the Arminian school of thought. Some of our Churches lean towards Augustine, Aquinas, others lean more towards Arminianism. It's the same with Protestant churches too.

Darrel: Sure, I understand; heresies like Arminianism plague both of our denominations; but, as we shall see later on when we talk about God's plan of salvation, all Catholics are united in their Arminian belief that our good works count towards our salvation.

Sonny: Yes, we are united in our understanding of God's plan of salvation, and I hope to prove that the Catholicism of Augustine is indistinguishable from the Catholicism of today.

Darrel: You can't do that, Sonny, because Arminianism is a rehash of Pelagianism (like semi-Pelagianism), and we know that Pelagian was the heretic who opposed Augustine's theology. The theology of the Roman Catholic Church is not Augustinian theology as we see when you admit to an Arminian/Pelagian concept of God's plan of salvation. Luther simply took us back to the theology of one of your most revered saints, Saint Augustine. Catholics don't either know or want to think about the difference between what Augustine believed and what their church now believes, but an elephant in a room can't be ignored or dismissed. Ironically, based on your church dogma, it is Augustine's antagonist, Pelagius, who should replace Augustine as a Catholic saint because it is Pelagius who first defined your works-based theology.

Daniel: Long before the Roman Catholic Church had compromised the Bible's authority by adding man-made traditions which prompted the Reformation, heretics had attempted to lead Christians astray from the Word. Pelagius was just one of many heretics in opposition to Augustine's belief in the doctrines of grace. Throughout the history of the Reformed Christian church, such heretics have challenged our beliefs.

Sonny: Well, regardless of what Augustine believed in, there is no invisible church; there is only the visible church, the Catholic Church.

Darrel: It wasn't just Augustine who talked about the invisible church. Pope Pius XII declared that "the Church has two aspects, a visible and an invisible one." You people ignore your own saint and one of your pope's statements and instead emphasize the visible aspect of the church founded by Christ as you have just indicated.

Sonny: The Catholic Church is the mystical body of Christ.

Darrel: In the 20th century, more focus was placed on the Catholic Church as a supernatural organism with Pope Pius XII's proclamation that the Church was the *Encylical Mystici Corporis Christi* (the mystical body of Christ). In Catholic doctrine, the one true church is the visible society founded by Christ, namely the Catholic Church with global jurisdiction under the bishop of Rome.

John: The Reformation was really all about emphasizing the invisible, internal church over the visible, external church to illustrate how far the visible Catholic Church has stayed from its moorings. The add-on traditions were not biblically supported. Jesus would always appeal to the Word, not some tradition. "It is written." The Roman Catholic traditions had undermined the true doctrine of the historical faith of Christianity, and the Reformation was nothing more than the attempt to restore that original doctrine.

Sonny: The Catholic Church began as an apostolic institution. Traditions were practiced long before a completed Bible, and were not invented by the Church. If we define tradition as a truth not included in the Bible, we have to label our Church's production of the canon of the Bible as a tradition. Nowhere in Scripture does it say what books should be in the Bible, right? All Christians rely on this tradition, and, if the canon is accepted by all and believed to be divinely inspired, what makes it the only acceptable, divinely inspired, unwritten tradition? So I say that the traditions of the Church were not add-ons to Scripture; they simply defined and correctly interpreted Scripture to declare doctrines and dogmas on faith and morals. The Holy Spirit has been given to the Church to protect it from error.

Darrel: Yes, by this definition, the canon could be considered to be a tradition; but that understanding does not imply the authenticity of all the add-on traditions that came after the organization of the canon. The floodgates apparently had been opened, and the divinely inspired tradition of the canon was followed by the man-inspired traditions to come later like purgatory, veneration of Mary, seven sacraments, etc. were the result. Luther particularly objected to the tradition of indulgences.

Sonny: Reforming corrupt Church practices, as Luther challenged, is sometimes necessary (as is happening today with the priest sex scandal), but Luther did not work it out within the system and eventually became a heretic and Protestantism was born. Luther's Reformation was an attempt to destroy the Church. Some even say he wanted to be pope.

John: I've read a lot of books on and by Luther, and I know that the last thing he wanted to do was to destroy his church; after all, he was an ordained monk and very devout. He agonized over his inability to obey God to his satisfaction. Here's his quote in my Kindle: "I pray you leave my name alone and not to call yourselves Lutherans, but Christians. Who is Luther? My doctrine is not mine: I have not been crucified for anyone...How does it then benefit me, a miserable bag of dust and ashes, to give my name to the children of Christ? Cease, my dear friends, to cling to these party names and distinctions; away with all of this, and let us call ourselves only Christians, after Him from whom our doctrine comes." He wanted to reform from within, and that's why he came up with those 95 theses as points of discussion. The Reformation happened because the Catholic Church rejected all his appeals for them to even discuss his issues with them, much less change its ways.

Darrel: How could the Catholic Church just ignore Luther's objections when they, of all people, should know precisely what traditions they had implemented over the centuries and that this monk, Luther, just might have a point in opposing some of them? They knew damn well what they had accomplished in creating a Christian institution, and it suited them just fine. They certainly had no intention of letting this upstart monk destroy what it had taken centuries to accomplish. Aren't you Catholics the least bit curious about why your church acted this way?

Sonny: Modifications to our Church discipline should come from within, not by some revolution.

John: Luther was not a revolutionary. He wanted reform, and as a monk, he was coming from within the church. He tried to reason with them in requesting a discussion on the 95 theses he nailed on door of the Castle Church in Wittenberg. The Catholic Church ignored his request to debate his 95 theses. Theologian H. Richard Niebuhr once said that "Most Christian revolutions come not by the discovery of something that was not known before. They happen when somebody takes radically something that was always there." That's what Luther and the other reformers did. They wanted to focus on restoring something in Christianity that had always been there since the church's beginnings: the teachings of the apostles and divesting Christianity of all the baggage the Catholic Church had added on over the centuries.

Darrel: The ability of people to think introspectively, to lead a self-examined life, is a lost art in this day and age. I would challenge any Catholic to try and understand what it means to lead an examined life and at least give some thought about what Luther had to say. Do you really believe Satan was working through Luther to destroy your Church or, considering the enormous historical and spiritual impact of the Reformation, could it be that God sent his angels to motivate Martin Luther to reform Christ's church?

Sonny: Luther may have thought he was divinely inspired, but Satan has the power to use people as tools to destroy God's Church. Why would any man believe he needed to oppose the traditions the Church had taken centuries to develop?

John: Luther was a very devout Catholic, and we know he had his doubts he was doing the right thing in opposing his own church. He once asked himself, "Do you mean to say that all the previous teachers knew nothing....?" He was concerned that he was showing pride in believing he was the next interpreter of the Holy Ghost in these last times. This is why he initially just wanted to discuss the issues he had with the Catholic Church. Several years later, after the pope had excommunicated him, he apparently had become convinced of his purpose in leading the opposition to what he saw the Catholic Church had become.

Daniel: And the Reformation was the necessary result to heal the church. Aren't you people curious about what the reformers opposed in your church? Would it at least be possible that these brave Christians might have had a point about which of these man-made traditions needed to be eliminated or modified to accommodate to what God wills in His Word? Obviously the powers that be in the Catholic Church must have recognized the Reformation as being a threat to its powerful position or it would have done as Luther wished and convened a council to address his concerns. The Reformation's focus on returning to what God's Word taught encouraged people to read the Bible on their own, and the Catholic Church perceived that to be a threat to its influence. Through the reading and understanding of Christ's own prayer in John

17, the invisible church composed of God's true saints remained unified. Christ's prayer was answered.

Darrel: Catholics, of course, refer only to certain special super-Christians as saints and make a big deal out of confirming sainthood on someone, but Protestants know that all believers are saints, by definition. Peter is addressing his fellow Christians when he says in 1 Peter 2:9-10 that we are a "chosen generation, a royal priesthood, a holy nation." Paul also refers to all "those who have been sanctified in Christ Jesus, saints by calling" (1 Corinthians 1:2). Luther said that "Not only are we the freest of kings, we are also priests forever, which is far more excellent than being kings, for as priests we are worthy to appear before God to pray for others and to teach one another divine things. As saints, we are citizens in the Kingdom of God and should have a clear understanding of the nature of position. Exodus 19:5 states all believers are considered to be "a kingdom of priests."

I would recommend every Christian pick up the Bible and read and study it on a daily basis. Its unfathomable depth challenges us to pursue God's truth over our entire lifetime. In my experience, the majority of Christians doesn't seem to know the Bible as well as they should or could. This seems to be particularly true for Lutherans and Catholics. Christianity is a religion of the book, not some church, and it goes without saying that church tradition must never interfere with any Christian reading the Bible for ourselves.

How well do you know your Bible, Sonny?

Sonny: I know enough, Darrel, to say I agree that we are a chosen generation, a royal priesthood and all baptized are saints, but there is a difference in that Paul calls those who have gone before us "saints in light." These, are those "super Christians" that we honor. They are the "cloud of witnesses (Hebrews 12:1) who have preceded us into the glory of God. We are but saints on a journey; they are already there. We have this knowledge on the authority of our Church, which, from the beginning, has acted as our only authority to the Scriptures and the many things about God that are not written down in Scripture.

Darrel: Of course it would be ideal if we all could actually rely on just one authority here on earth that clearly communicated God's truth to us, but we can't; that isn't the role any church was, and is, to play in Christianity. God plays that role in giving us his Word and the Holy Spirit to guide us in our understanding of that Word.

So then, when it comes to earthly assistance in understanding theology and our religion, it's all about trust, and trust became an issue from the get-go. Almost from the very beginning of the Christian church, apostasy began to creep in; we can see this for ourselves when we read the quotes of the early church fathers from 100 AD on. A good book to read on this subject is *A Dictionary of Early Christian Beliefs* edited by David Bercot. The apostasies began with the Judaizers, a false cult that infiltrated the first churches Paul planted in Galatia, and he expressed his concern in Galatians 1:6-9. They were followed by the Gnostics and so on. Actually, come to think of it, your Roman Catholic doctrine is similar to the legalistic beliefs of the Judaizers, These new Christians wanted to retain the legalism of their former Jewish religion by adding works to faith for our right standing before God. This is the direction the Roman Catholic Church has pushed the original church along over the centuries, down, down, down the road of apostasy. That's ironic, isn't it? Here the Roman Catholic Church lays claim to being the first Christian, apostolic church, and it turns out it is the first church of apostasy. Heresy and apostasy continued over the centuries.

Bobby: Yes, when I was a Catholic, I believed there was a good, true Church at one time in Rome, but soon after Constantine legalized Christianity, the Church came under pagan influence, and it was poisoned with all these man-made traditions.

John: There are several stages of apostasy. Apostasy is a falling away from or renouncing the Christian faith. Jesus talked about this subject in His letter to the six churches in Revelation. The first step is the love of Christ is forsaken. Next is false teaching is tolerated. Sin is tolerated and death of the apostate church is imminent. The last step in apostasy is when Christ is actually replaced. As we go through these discussions, I intend to prove how the Catholic Church has yielded to these five steps.

Sonny: Have at it. I'm here to explain where you guys get it wrong.

Daniel: Church history is my hobby, and I know that, from its beginning, the original Christian apostolic church (as it was initially presented in the book of Acts) did indeed experience apostasy from its beginning as some people rejected the apostolic teaching. Paul started out his letter to the Galatians chastising them for "turning away from Him who called you in the grace of Christ, to a different gospel." Paul also said that "there are some who you trouble you and want to pervert the gospel of Christ." This sounds like heresy, which is defined as a view contrary to the official teachings of the church. In other words, it would involve any teachings contrary to the apostolic ministry.

Paul concludes his warning by stating that if he, or any of the other apostles, "preaches any other gospel to you than what we have preached to you, let him be accursed."

Darrel: Ironically, it is the Catholic Church that curses people who don't accept its false doctrine. They do this in their papal and council pronouncements. Canons 9 and 12 of the Council of Trent comes to mind where the church states that no one is truly justified by faith and that the person who doesn't accept this dogma "let him be accursed."

Sonny: Faith alone is not taught in the Bible. James refutes it in James 2:24 when he states we are not justified by faith alone. That's why Luther didn't want the book of James to be included in the New Testament canon.

John: Since this statement seems to contradict what Paul says in Ephesians 2:8, and God is not a God of contradiction, we must assume that when he referred to faith, James was referring to our intellectual assent to certain truths, not our faith in Christ. In other verses, James refers to it as "demonic" (2:19), "useless" (2:20), and "dead" (2:26). Luther concluded this, and that's why he acquiesced to including the book in the canon.

Darrel: Isn't it obvious that Catholics take James 2:24 out of context to back its false teaching? And, it's ironic that the very man Catholics believe is their first pope, Peter, warned about false teachings; Paul also tells his audience that the way to recognize false teachings is to discern whether they are man-centered or God-centered. "Do I now persuade men, or God, or do I seek to please men? For if I still pleased men, I would not be a bondservant of Christ." This verse illustrates the difference between us; Catholicism is governed by a church centered on man vs. a reformed church centered on God.

King Solomon spent more time building his own house than on building God's house, and his own house was twice as big as the Temple. And, of course, Solomon eventually fell into apostasy as had the entire nation of Israel done many times in their history. And the same thing happened in the history of the Christian church. From its very beginning, two versions of Christianity emerged in parallel over time: the apostolic and the apostate. Both streams of Christianity have been operating side by side for nearly 2,000 years. The apostolic churches represent the teachings of the original apostles which were to have been taught to faithful followers from the beginning who are pledged to teach them to others. This is what Paul is telling Timothy in 2 Timothy 2:2. The members of these churches have been hated and persecuted by the world. The apostate churches represent a falling away from the gospel; that's what the word "apostate" means. The members of these churches are loved by the world. They are known by their false teaching, their forsaking of Christ, and their tolerance of sin. The last step in apostasy occurs when Jesus is no longer part of the church. It is my contention that the Roman Catholic Church is yielding to apostasy and intends to offer evidence proving my conclusion during the course of these discussion sessions.

The Catholic Church has yielded to those five steps of apostasy. In these discussions, we shall expose the reality that the Catholic doctrine is very different from Protestant doctrine. We will support this conclusion by comparing and contrasting each and every one of Catholicism's main tenets of belief with the teachings of the apostles.

Sonny: Our history gives us credibility, Darrel. Jesus said the gates of hell would not prevail against His Church and we've been here from the beginning.

Darrel: Antiquity may be a useful marketing tool for you, but age doesn't necessarily connect with credibility; and I might add that your Catholic Church of today hasn't been around as long as you would like folks to think it has. It is the result of yielding to apostasy over the centuries; your church hasn't exactly aged like fine wine that gets better as it ages. The Catholic Church has become more like vinegar as it has aged.

Sonny: Names are important today, but even more important centuries ago. The early Church was initially referred to as "The Way," but soon after, in post-apostolic times in the third century, the Church did acquire a proper name to distinguish itself from these early apostate churches like the Essene community at Qumran. The name the Church acquired when it became necessary for her to have a proper name was the name by which she has been known ever since then: the Catholic Church. Constantine unified the twelve bishops into one Catholic Church.

Don't you think it makes sense that Christ founded a singular organization? There's no evidence in the Bible that God ever sanctioned multiple organizations of followers. Believers were always led by a single earthly representative who communicated one set of rules, one dogma for them to follow whether it be Noah, Abraham, Moses, or Peter.

Darrel: It does make sense that Christ would establish just the one church, and he did: he entrusted the apostles to teach God's Word through a visible church that reflected the tenets of the invisible church founded on him as its foundation. There is no biblical reference to appointing one of these apostles as the leader of one Christian church.

Sonny: If the early followers of "The Way" had not designated a single authoritative leader, confusion and apostasy would have resulted. Arguments among believers had to be adjudicated by a leader who had sole authority to do so. Yes, the reformers had some legitimate issues to discuss, but we can see what happened, how splitting away from the mother Church resulted in the formation of many, many Protestant denominations with many different interpretations of the doctrine of Christianity. Our Church can trace its history back to the first century AD, and Jesus said the gates of Hell cannot overcome it.

John: Christ is referring to the invincibility of his church established by the apostles which claims Him as its founder and sole authority. The CC focuses on itself as it proclaims to be the only visible representation of Christ's church. It minimizes the concept of the invisible church to compete with the gospel message. In its history, visible churches may come and go and change with the time, as the Catholic Church has done, but the tenets of the invisible church remain true and secure. The authority is God's Word; the representatives of that Word originally were the apostles who formed a church based on their teachings; the leaders of those churches were to continue to teach in the apostolic tradition. We Protestants believe we are one under the leadership of the apostolic teachings which are very clearly presented to us by God himself in his Word, the Holy Bible. We do not accept your Catholic Church as our authority because we believe it distorts and misrepresents these apostolic teachings. We distinguish between the original church founded on the apostolic teachings, and the Roman Catholic Church, founded on the teachings of the magisterium, a self-proclaimed group asserting sole authority over the Christian religion.

As the Catholic Church began to slowly and methodically become apostate over the centuries in relating to man's need for more emphasis on the visibility of an invisible church and Savior and his need to depend on one authority for God's truth, it began to focus on its own, self-serving need to attain and retain power, influence and wealth. There is no date in history we can point to and say that is when the Catholic Church turned into something it was never intended to be. Rather than failing all at once, it began to drift from about 300 AD when it changed significantly from a simple organization to a top-down hierarchy; from salvation being based on grace alone, as Augustine believed, to adding good works to God's grace as a requirement of salvation; from a straight-forward faith based on the Scriptures alone to a religion based on superstition and man-made, extra-biblical traditions and rituals. By the sixth century, the mainline churches had become decrepit. Regardless, God preserves the invisible church of the elect despite what man does to his visible church. The Reformation needed to happen under God's providence; it necessarily carved out the debate Luther had introduced. Although it split the visible church into two main denominations: Protestant and Catholic, the split did not affect the invisible church of saved believers which Luther and the other reformers believed was not being truthfully represented by the visible Catholic Church.

Sonny: Christ did not establish an invisible church on earth, it was visible and it was the Catholic Church. The Reformation split the Christian Church. Christ intended for His church to be built upon Him and the other apostles to provide us with an earthly authority to maintain the Christian religion. I don't care what Augustine said about some invisible church, we make no distinction between visible and invisible; our visible Church IS the invisible church; it is a visible manifestation and has an authoritative branch to serve the people. It is rooted in the spiritual precepts, commands, beliefs and practices ordained by God. One authority we can trust for truth is necessary; trusting in us can result in believing a lie.

Darrel: In its transition into an industry over the centuries through the centralization and synchronization, your visible church compromised the purpose of our religion.

Bobby: Well, it's time to end our very first session of the year. Y'all come back now.

Week Two

Bobby: So, gentlemen, let's start today's session by getting into the details of what Catholics believe, okay?

Sonny: I hope you guys don't mind me inviting an additional person to be a member of this group. I brought along a friend from Church. When I told him about our group, he asked me if he could come. Is that okay with y'all? His name is Ray, Ray Artemis. He's a retired plumber.

Bobby: It's fine with me, the more the merrier. I'm Bobby.

Darrel: Welcome to our little group, Ray. I'm Darrel, this erudite senior citizen to my left is John; next to him we have our token atheist, Peter, and Daniel here rounds out our group.

Before we begin with you guys presenting your doctrine, for Ray's benefit, he needs to know we do not accept the premise that there is any other authority in Christianity but the Bible; please don't use your Catholic Catechism to make your points. We also don't consider your Catholic Church to be the original Christian church either so if you would, please don't keep saying that over and over again as some of you people are in the habit of doing in these intra mural discussions. If we can possibly hope to get anything out of these discussions with you guys, it's important you understand that you can't just stand on ceremony and keep repeating this claim that you are a member of the one, true Christian church and treat us as heretics. If you insist on promoting your church in this way and close your mind to discussing theology and Christianity with us, we may as well call it quits now and go surf fishing instead of engaging in some dialogue of the deaf. People have core beliefs, preconceptions about life, and are often anxious to share those core beliefs with others. It can be a monologue that goes on seemingly forever or a dialogue of the deaf like we sometimes see when all these talking heads on some TV program like *Hannity* shouting at each other at the same time. This rule relates to our rule of being civil towards one another. We need to recognize we're meeting together to learn from each other and listen to what the other guy is saying before we respond with our opinion.

Sonny: Before we begin, I want to clarify that I didn't come here to force my belief on anyone. I came to educate you Protestants on what we believe. Fulton Sheen once said that "There are not over a hundred people in the United States who hate the Catholic Church. There are millions, however, who hate what they wrongly believe to be the Catholic Church, which is, of course, quite a different thing. These millions can hardly be blamed for hating because 'Catholics adore statues;' because they 'put the Blessed Mother on the same level with God;' because they say 'indulgence is a permission to commit sin;' because 'the Pope is a Fascist;' because the 'Church is the defender of Capitalism.' If the Church taught or believed any one of these things, it should be hated, but the fact is that the Church does not believe nor teach any one of them. It follows then that the hatred of the millions is directed against error and not against truth. As a matter of fact, if we Catholics believed all of the untruths and lies where were said against the Church, we probably would hate the Church a thousand times more than they do."

John: While Sheen is painting us all with a broad brush, yes, I personally believe that Catholics actually do some of the things on his list. The objective of these discussions is not only for us to hear how you Catholics can explain what many of us do not accept, but that you hear us out for the reasons we oppose some of what you believe.

Sonny: I look forward to our discussions. I don't necessarily believe all Protestants are heretics and do think that we sometimes paint Protestants with the broad brush, and tend to harshly criticize them for their lack of understanding of the Christian doctrine, but personally I believe they serve a useful purpose in God's plan in loving Jesus as much as we do and evangelizing and bringing in many seekers who would otherwise not accept Christianity. As a Catholic, I believe of course that the only visible church is the Catholic Church and that is the Church all who call themselves Christians should support.

Darrel: Is it any wonder Protestants dislike Catholicism based on this last statement of yours; no one likes a proud person, and every Christian should hate the sin of pride. I don't doubt that you're a fellow Christian, Sonny; it's your church's claim to be the first and only Christian church I do not accept. Nowhere in the gospel accounts does Christ ever indicate his church would be built through just one visible church which would one day connect with the Holy Roman Empire. No visible church, denomination or organization is the true church because the bride of Christ is not an institution, and it is not meant to be one; it is instead a spiritual entity made up of those who have by grace through faith been brought into a close, intimate relationship with Christ. That's what Paul tells us in Ephesians 2:8-9. The church fathers were motivated to promote the Catholic Church as an institution, and your Catholic Church of today is just that, a corporate institution of Christianity.

In the Bible we see that the local or visible church is nothing more than a gathering of professing believers who meet together on a regular basis. The visible church consists of members of the invisible church, an unspecified group of individuals (Philippians 3:6, 1 Timothy 3:5) who share a belief in Christ; this is a spiritual entity with Christ as its head. They have been called out of the world and set apart for the Lord, a universal group of people whom God has elected to know Christ. The word "church" is never used in the Bible to describe a building, a denomination or any type of organization. As Christians, we know our relationship is with Christ, not some church.

Anyway, I'm glad you believe we Protestants have some use, Sonny. Your superior attitude notwithstanding, Protestants indeed did and still do serve a useful purpose in God's plan; we derailed the Catholic Church from its objective of being God to all Christians. We wrenched Christianity from out of its firm grasp and took it back to what it was supposed to be from the beginning. This was surely in God's plan or the Reformation wouldn't have succeeded as it did. It's all in God's providence.

Sonny: We Catholics tend to view Protestantism as being a kind of "Christian-light" denomination, an entry level into the full communion we enjoy as Catholics. If a Protestant later chooses to mature in their faith, they join up with us for all of the sacraments which promote a most full communion with God. The process of maturing takes time; the Catholic Church is almost 2,000 years old, Darrel, and your oldest Protestant denomination, Lutheranism, is only 500 years old.

Darrel: Yes, the Christian church of the apostolic tradition was restored 500 years ago, and it took us all the way back to 33 AD, thank God. As you and Ray formally present your Catholic dogma to us, keep in mind you'll have to offer more proof of your credibility than just repeating the mantra you're church is the original Christian church. In regards to history, although the Christian church in Rome was established in 40 AD, the actual Roman Catholic Church of today was not founded in the first century; historians differ on whether it was founded in the eleventh century or even later on. There are also other churches that can claim to be the original church. The Coptic, Kerala, Armenian, Assyrian, Eastern Orthodox denominations can also claim to trace their roots back to the original church. The Jacobite Church and a couple of very minor groups in the Near East have truly ancient roots as well.

The Christian denominations created by the Reformation (Lutherans, Baptists, etc.) had a definite point in time when they were founded, and of course cannot claim to be truly ancient churches. However, it is debatable whether the history of a church or denomination is the key or even an important factor in whether this is a church which most completely follows the teachings of the apostles. The point I want to make here is that it is by faith of the apostles, not ordination lineage, that establishes the Christian church. One's pedigree doesn't determine the true church. The Pharisees had a great pedigree and an Abrahamic succession, but they were whitewashed tombs and the brood of vipers according to Christ. We could even make a strong argument that pedigree is an impediment, just as it was for the Pharisees, not a point of strength. We need to keep in mind that Christ wants us to worship him in spirit and in truth and the church that gets that right is truly God's church.

We believe the Catholic Church of today is at best a mere shadow of what it once was 2,000 years ago. We must recognize that the true church is the bride of Christ (Revelation 21:2, 9:22:17 and the body of Christ (Ephesians 4:12, 1 Corinthians 12:27). It cannot be contained, walled in, or defined by anything (which includes some concept of "apostolic succession") other than its love for Christ and its dedication to him. The true church is, as C. S. Lewis said, "spread out through all time and space and rooted in eternity, terrible as an army with banners."

The Reformation occurred for a good reason, and, if you aren't even curious about why it had to happen, what can we discuss with either of you? We ask that you keep an open mind or we may as well call it quits right now. We can't have an effective dialogue with an indoctrinated person. This is not what we're about here. We're interested in having an open, free-spirited discussion with you Catholics which will serve as a good learning experience for all of us. That's what this group is about. We all get to express our opinions, and each of us tries to keep an open mind. For example, that means you folks don't just summarily dismiss Protestantism as a heresy as you've been instructed by your church to do, and we won't do that to you guys either. These discussions are all about arriving at the truth, and that requires evidence to support opinion and since I assume we can all agree that the Bible is our source of God's truth, that big, black book is our evidence. We're to also not only think about what we believe, but examine why we believe it.

Sonny: We are not indoctrinated. Why won't you accept the reality if it's true? All truth and grace are conveyed by God through His Church. Our almost 2,000 year old Church is our only source of truth.

Darrel: And we say that all truth and grace are conveyed through God's Word, the Holy Bible.

Ray: We don't accept that premise, Darrel.

Darrel: Why not? We both believe the Bible is God's Word, right? Oops, I forgot what you said before about those sacred traditions of yours.

Daniel Ray, we're here to exchange opinions with emphasis on that word "exchange." In my experience, Catholics seem indoctrinated in what they're told to believe and indoctrination closes the mind. Catholics tell me they aren't usually interested in any of my opinions because I have no authority, but I hope you and Sonny can keep an open mind or we may as well dispense with these discussions right now before we go any further. The fishing's good this season, and I'd rather be doing that if we're just going to preach to each other.

Darrel: What do you expect from these discussion sessions, Ray? You should know that we crave knowledge and clarity in this group, and encourage you to express your own opinion, and, when possible, support it with concrete evidence. Common sense works well with us too. We don't do well with closed-minded people who don't or can't contribute their own opinions. Hell, even our Muslim guy last year opened up with us, and we really had a great season of discussions with him.

We need to integrate the knowledge of others into our own by exchanging ideas and opinions with them. We need to use our good minds to formulate opinions about important matters, test the support of these opinions and discover the limitations of our fallible knowledge. Solomon tells us in Proverbs 27:17 that "As iron sharpens iron, so one man sharpens another." We can often learn about what we believe from what we find out we don't believe, and that is why debates with those who oppose our beliefs are so constructive. We need to prioritize living a life of contemplation by seeking out others to talk to about what we believe and what they believe. Are you on board with this objective?

Ray: Of course. Sonny filled me in on this group's objective, and that's why I accepted his invitation to join you people. It's been my experience with discussing Christianity with Protestants that you have many pre-conceived notions about Catholicism that I'd like to try and clear up as well.

Bobby: We are here to express our personal opinions, and we have our simple rules of engagement. Basically, we are to be good listeners, provide credible evidence for our opinions, and clearly define our terms; of course we're also to be civil to one another.

John: And bring your Kindle or Nook, iPad or smart phone to the next session, Ray. With these wonderful electronic devices, we can immediately access the internet to quickly find the expert we want to quote to support some opinion we want to present to the group in our discussions.

I really like the rule of engagement that mandates we be good listeners. Jesus was a good listener. Remember the incident when He spoke with the Samaritan woman at the well? We Christians should remind ourselves that we are to love our fellow man, and listening is a way of loving. When we either totally ignore what a person is saying to us or just pretend to be listening, we're not showing our love for our neighbor. Only in paying close attention to what someone is saying can we understand a concept from their perspective. Other people's perspective can be extremely educational in finding out the truth; as Aristotle said, truth should be our main objective in this life.

Daniel: We are so inclined to be talkers sometimes it doesn't even matter if someone's even listening. My son-in-law will often just wander around the room talking to himself, seemingly not caring whether anyone's listening to what he has to say or not.

Peter: I think it's important to control our inherent bias so we can keep an open mind. You can't be a free thinker if your freedom is bound up with some core bias. Who knows, we just might learn from listening to the other guy enough to consider ditching some of our old beliefs if they prove to be unreasonable and unworkable and simply not true.

Darrel: That didn't seem to work the past several years with you, Pete. You're still an atheist in spite of our best efforts to help you see the light.

Peter: That's because I'm a skeptic, Darrel, and a hard sell. I think we all need to be skeptical about what others say to us. We need to test their truth claims and test what we say we believe. We should always try to use common sense in our discussions. Remember our discussion group motto, "Just Make Sense!"

Daniel: Yeah, listening provides a direct connection with people, and that's what we're here to do: connect with each other. And because listening creates space for someone else to talk, it shows them that their opinion matters; they matter.

John: Sometimes the most useful conversations I've been involved in are the ones where I've hardly said a word. People who take over the discussion and pontificate in some monologue are demonstrating to me that they can't get out of themselves. They seem to be on a mission to promote their self-importance. Come to think of it, the word "pontificate" comes from Catholics, and I have to confess, Ray, that I've encountered this problem time and again in my *Facebook* discussions with Catholics. Your people just seem to be so defensive about your church; it's hard to talk about any important doctrinal issues without you guys taking what I say as some kind of an attack on your church.

Darrel: In my discussions, I've rarely had a Catholic try and make some point by beginning the sentence with "I believe." Their attitude is "this is the way it is." It's a damn pronouncement, not an opinion.

Ray: Opinions are susceptible to error. Our Magisterium is our authority.

Peter: What, pray tell, is a magisterium?

Sonny: The Magisterium is the church's authority or office which is supposed to establish teachings. Its purpose is to maintain the integrity and unity of the faith and to keep Christians united in one body. Its authority is vested uniquely in the pope and the bishops, under the premise that they are in communion with the correct and true teachings of the faith. Sacred scripture and sacred tradition make up a single sacred deposit of the Word of God, which is entrusted to the Church. The Magisterium is not independent of this, since all that it proposes for belief as being divinely revealed is derived from this single deposit of faith.

Darrel: I'm familiar with the role your magisterium performs, Sonny. You people always defer to what I call your "Magisterium Masters."

It wasn't always this way in the Christian church. Many centuries ago the role of the overseers did not in any way resemble the papacy of today's Catholic Church. Ignatius of Antioch, an early church father, rejected the notion that bishops had any authority to dictate matters of faith or practice beyond their respective diocese and to teach anything that was not based on the teachings of the original apostles. In spite of his warning, as the centuries rolled by, the Catholic Church morphed into a political institution, and its magisterium began to view itself as the sole authority in the Christian church, handing down edicts and dictating dogma which bound the conscience of believers and insured the loyalty and compliance with the will of Rome.

We Protestants don't believe any one body of people like this is legitimate or necessary to tell us what to believe and how to believe. Such offers to help aren't always helpful, and, where power and wealth are involved, as is the case with your church, helpful help is not the case. For me, it's the equivalent of my five year old grandson offering to drive me to the airport. He isn't able to do it. But, unlike your church, at least I can say his intentions were good in trying to help me. We have God himself to explain his Word to us in the Holy Spirit, and I know I can trust that his intention is good. On the other hand, we should suspect that any self-promoting church authority like your magisterium has its own self-serving interest at heart in asserting its authority.

Ray: The almost 2,000 year old Catholic Church is the one true holy and apostolic Church. It dates back to the time of the Apostles as described in Acts 1:20-26. We consider Protestants, by definition, to be a heretical denomination because they have rejected the authority of the Catholic Church. A Protestant is not a member of the Catholic Church; therefore a Protestant is not a member of the Mystical Body of Christ.

Darrel: I agree with you, there is just the one Catholic Church; it's not holy and it's not apostolic.

John: There is just one true Christian and apostolic church and it is "catholic" in the sense that it is universal. We've already discussed that subject with Sonny before you joined our group. I'll bring you up to speed.

Soon after it was formed, the Christian church began to be referred to as the "catholic church" because it was universal, and, as you may know, "catholic" means "universal." So then, in this way, you could say that the "catholic church" was the only Christian church of that name at that time. Over the centuries, as the church grew, it designated itself to be The Catholic Church. It remained this way until the early 1500's when the Christian church split into Catholic and Protestant churches. While history records that your Catholic Church can trace its roots back to that first church in name, as the changes that took place over the centuries in church doctrine (which prompted the Reformation), your church drew further and further away from the doctrine of that original Christian church. I intend to offer evidence to support my contention.

So, we see here that age, in and of itself, is not the criterion to identify the one, true church of Christ. For this reason, we Protestants will not accept your premise that the Catholic Church of today continues to represent that original church founded by Christ which was to preach, teach and practice the teachings of the apostles; and we certainly won't accept the premise that the papacy represents some kind of apostolic succession. According to Scripture, an apostle can only be a person who was "one of the men who have accompanied us during all the time that the Lord Jesus went in and out among us." The notion that the apostles themselves had the authority to make someone into an apostle is ludicrous and a complete misunderstanding of Acts 1. God alone made His apostles, and to imply He had anything to do with the appointment of such bad, un-Christian popes over the centuries like Stephen VI, Sergius III, Anastasius III, John XII, Urban VIII, Leo X and Alexander VI (to name but a few), is blasphemous. These men are evidence of the reality that Catholicism does not share the same spirit as Christ intended for his church. Your church left that church centuries ago.

Sonny: We are the same church today as we were originally.

Darrel: You really don't know your church history very well if you believe what you just said, Sonny. We intend to prove that your church is <u>not</u> the same church as our first century Christian church because of all the add-on, extra-biblical traditions your church has seen fit to create over the centuries.

In every discussion I've ever had with Catholics, they will preface most every response by saying they are the one, true church established by Christ as described in the book of Acts. In constantly repeating this mantra, they are of course proving my accusation they are indoctrinated because that's what indoctrinated people sound like.

The assertion of that position is obviously very important to them because they believe it establishes credibility for their church's assumption of sole authority in our religion. This is not historically or theologically supported, and that is why I have an aversion to this assertion.

It's not enough though to arbitrarily continue on with the presumption that you are the original church when it's obvious how far you have strayed from the church founded on the teachings of the apostles. When we get into the history of the Christian church dating back to the original, we will see how from the beginning, things began to go terribly wrong. Luther believed that Satan used your bishops to design and implement these add-on traditions which were incorporated into actual church doctrine and served to draw the church further and further away from its original beliefs and purpose. He even called the pope the Anti-Christ.

Sonny: That's a ridiculous label to pin on the pope.

Darrel: Yeah, well, some historians call Gregory II, "Gregory the Great," the first pope, the head of the church, and you should know that, in the sixth century, it was he who first stated that whoever would declare himself to be the "universal priest" or the "head of the church" would be the Anti-Christ. Since many popes since then have declared themselves to be the head of the universal church, of course, the reformers were only following the lead of the first pope in referring to the papacy as the Anti-Christ.

Sonny: The Catholic Church is the Christian Church; it is not a Christian denomination.

Darrel: We of course believe that the Reformation created the Catholic Church denomination. You'll have concede that reality if you expect to have a real intra-mural discussion.

Sonny: We're going to defend what we believe, Darrel. I am a Catholic because I seek the truth, and the Church has the authority to teach. Open your mind to her truth, her authority to teach and the promises Jesus made about her.

Darrel: We'll respond to each of your pronouncements in these discussions, Sonny, and I hope you will keep an open mind to what we have to say and not just focus on Catholic apologetics when you should be practicing Christian apologetics. The authority you assert to gain credibility implies your leaders or magisterium has a direct pipeline of communication with God, and that we Protestants are left adrift relying on our own opinion. Well, your magisterium consists of men with opinions and just because you assert their authority which they proclaim to have doesn't mean what they say is somehow to be considered as a more authoritative opinion than any other Christian's opinion who's been educated in our belief.

Sonny: Then the question becomes, how are we to interpret the Word? The Bible is not an easy book to read or understand. Without a guide, you can't be sure you know what the Bible is saying. Our Church is our guide.

John: First of all, yes, there are biblical passages that are more difficult to understand, but, generally speaking, God intends for His Word to be understood by even uneducated people, and the Bible is written in everyday language; it's therefore a relatively easy read. We make the mistake of assuming that every verse in Scripture must be interpreted or deciphered as judges must interpret the law. We must understand we are to take the Bible's meaning normally and there is no need to overthink what is plain and apparent. Paul certainly follows this advice in his communication with the churches he founded in his clear and explicit teaching from Scripture as a solution to division in the early church. He expresses this objective in 1 Corinthians 4:6. "Now these things, brethren, I have figuratively applied to myself and Apollos for your sakes, so that in us you may learn not to exceed what is written, so that no one of you will become arrogant in behalf of one against the other." I believe that is exactly what the Catholic Church has done in representing itself as the only authority on the meaning of God's Word.

We believe the Bible is so clear on the basics of salvation that a person of normal intelligence who carefully reads God's Word can discern the essential gospel. We call this the doctrine of perspicuity, or clarity, of Scripture. Advanced education is helpful but is not required. The doctrine of perspicuity recognizes that not everything in Scripture is easy to understand. Some passages are more difficult to understand than others, but we don't need some church to fill in the blanks, because we can refer to the more clear verses to explain the less clear verses, assuming

God is not a God of confusion. We must recognize that a number of literary styles are used in the Bible, and we are to take the Bible normally, which means we take it literally when it's obvious that God intends for His Word to be taken literally, and understand when a metaphor or some other literary style is being used.

Second of all, in interpreting its meaning, we are to understand that God's truth does not come to us apart from the Apostolic testimony as recorded in the Bible. No human teacher who claims an anointing that is different in kind than what the Spirit gives to us is to be trusted. We must rely on the Holy Spirit to guide us in doing this correctly. When we encounter passages that seem confusing to us, we need to utilize other more clear verses to explain the confusing one, assuming God is not a God of contradiction whose intention is to confuse us. And of course we can also utilize commentaries written by brilliant theologians like Augustine, Aquinas, Luther and Calvin to help us with our understanding of Scripture. This is why we are able to accept the individual responsibility of forming our own opinions of God's Word, relying solely on the Holy Spirit to guide us in our knowledge of what God is saying to us.

Darrel: Of course, your church would like you to believe it's impossible to know God's Word without its help, but it isn't true. Your church wants to be in charge of every aspect of your connection with God. In *The Bondage of the Will*, Luther said, "I have thus far hounded the Pope, in whose kingdom nothing is more commonly said or more widely accepted than this dictum: 'the Scriptures are obscure and equivocal; we must seek the interpreting Spirit from the apostolic see of Rome!' No more disastrous words could be spoken; for by this means ungodly men have exalted themselves above the Scriptures and done what they liked, till the Scriptures were completely trodden down and we could believe and teach nothing but maniac's dreams. In a word, that dictum is no mere human invention; it is poison sent into the world by the inconceivably malevolent prince of all the devils himself!"

The Bible is our only authority, and most of its content makes plain sense and can be easily understood. When the Bible makes plain sense, seek no other sense.

Ray: Sure, but whose plain sense? You Protestants are your own authority in understanding the Bible. How can you be so sure you know what God says?

Darrel: Plain sense means what it says. Its content can be easily understood by anyone with common sense. The Bible is a reasonable book presenting a reasonable theology, and we are to use our God-given reason to understand its content.

Ray: What seems reasonable to one guy may not seem reasonable to another, right?

Peter: Wrong. Aristotle described the universal rule of logic that applies in all arguments.

John: And theologian, A. A. Tozer, reminds us that logic is universal. God is a God of reason so he has implanted in every human being the ability to reason.

Peter: This ability to reason should be prioritized. If we understand that what we believe is usually based on what we inherited from our parents or subjected to in our society, that's tradition, the weakest source of knowledge.

Ray: Says who?

Peter: Says Aristotle. Using references like this, Ray, is an example of rule number one: Recognized experts in the field of knowledge we are discussing is the strongest evidence you can offer to support your own opinion. A disciple of Plato's, Aristotle is universally recognized as the father of philosophy. He should have credibility.

Ray: So, what does the great philosopher believe is the strongest source of knowledge?

Peter: Hey, don't knock philosophers, Sonny; didn't your Thomas Aquinas consider himself to be a philosopher? Augustine too.

Sonny: They considered themselves to be theologians.

John: These two disciplines cross over, Sonny. In *Summa Theologica*, the "philosopher" Aquinas kept referring to was actually Aristotle. So, there you have it; Aquinas gave Aristotle credibility and so should we.

Peter: According to Aristotle, there are three sources of knowledge: Tradition, reason and faith. We've already discussed the weakest of these, tradition. Tradition is the weakest because it's used as a shortcut to thinking; it saves time and effort to do no thinking on your own and to believe only what your tradition sets out for you to believe. The Catholic Church sets down your traditions and you follow them. Period. The less a belief system prioritizes its tradition, the more credible it should be. The strongest source is reason because it involves deductive reasoning, the gold standard in the thought process in establishing the ultimate degree of certainty. If some aspect of what we believe doesn't stand up to critical analysis, this should create doubt, and we should be prepared to discard that belief in favor of a more reasonable one. That's what having an open mind means to me.

Darrel: As the D.A. said in a *Law and Order* episode, "For all you know you don't know anything." We utilize these three sources of knowledge to try and learn and they can interrelate. All three can be involved in formulating an opinion. We Christians of course believe that faith is the most reliable source of knowledge. We all seek the truth, and God is the truth.

Ray: Although our correct understanding of the Bible comes from our tradition, our belief is based on faith, not tradition and not on reason. Faith in our God, the God who is truth, is the strongest source of truth.

Darrel: Faith is tradition when it's blind faith arising from indoctrination.

Daniel: A true, saving faith in Christ is not just based on God's revelation as presented in His Word, the Holy Bible; it's a living thing. We Christians are enabled by God through our conscience to focus on our faith as we go through this life. Paul tells us in 2 Corinthians 4:18 that we are not to look for things that are seen but to the things that are unseen. This is because the things that are seen are transient, ephemeral, but the things that are unseen are eternal.

John: In his *Institutes of the Christian Religion*, John Calvin defined faith as "a firm and sure knowledge of the divine favor towards us, founded on the Truth of a promise in Christ and revealed to our minds and sealed on our hearts by the Holy Spirit." God has enabled Christians to understand that the very fact that we have our faith is evidence of our belief that Christianity is the truth, the only truth.

Sonny: As a Catholic, I don't place much stock in what John Calvin says, of course, but I can certainly agree with that statement. God has enabled us through the Church to know the truth. Paul says this in Ephesians 3:10.

Darrel: Yes, in Ephesians 3:10-12, Paul states that God's intent is to make known his manifold wisdom through the church, but the "c" in "church" is a small "c" which means he's not referring to any one particular visible Christian church, but he's referring to the invisible church of Christ. In 1 Corinthians 14:33, Paul refers to "all the churches of the saints" not to just one church or one group of super-Christians designated to be saints by some church. Hebrews 10:14 states that through the one sacrifice of Christ, we have been made holy; we have been made saints.

Bobby: Why are you a Catholic, Sonny?

Sonny: I'm a Catholic because the Church represents the only truth for me; but, of course, that's a standard answer so I'll expand on that by giving you the same answer Catholic theologian G. K. Chesterton gave. The Catholic Church "is not only larger than me, but larger than anything in the world; that it is indeed larger than the world...I consider it in its capacity of a guardian of the truth...There is no other case of one continuous intelligent institution that has been thinking about thinking for two thousand years. Its experience naturally covers nearly all experiences; and especially nearly all errors. The result is a map in which all the blind alleys and bad roads are clearly marked, all the ways that have shown to be worthless by the best of all evidence: the evidence of those who have gone down them."

Darrel: Well, if we inserted the word "Christian" for the word "Catholic Church," I would certainly agree with what Chesterton said in giving my reason for being a Christian. Christianity is the only truth, and our churches are supposed to support that truth in their teaching, preaching and encouraging the reading and studying of God's Word. Christianity is larger than us, larger than anything in the world and it indeed is the guardian of truth. But when Chesterton starts talking about the CC as an intelligent institution that covers all experiences and errors, he has promoted the purpose of the visible church to a level I do not accept and do not require. G. K. obviously bought into Catholicism's claim that it alone represents the one, holy and apostolic Christian church.

Sonny: We maintain that Catholicism and Christianity are one and the same.

Darrel: That's an arrogant and false assumption. We Protestants subscribe to the same Christian creed as Catholics, the Nicene Creed and its abbreviated version, the Apostle's Creed; each was developed by our church fathers. But, apparently the Catholic Church wasn't content with the Nicene Creed as it was developed at the Council of Nicaea in 325 because, in 1565, Pope Pius IV added traditions imposed at the Council of Trent. The pope listed the seven sacraments which were necessary for "the salvation of mankind, though not all are necessary for everyone" (whatever that means). He reiterated everything the Council of Trent had affirmed in opposition to the basic tenets of the reformers like Luther. He reiterated the practice of transubstantiation in the Eucharist, which we'll get into later on in these discussions. He reaffirmed the Catholic belief in Purgatory, and specified the relics to be venerated. He affirmed that, outside of the Church, no one can be saved. This is heresy.

Sonny: No, it's not! We believe, as Chesterton believed, that the Church has provided us with "a map in which all the blind alleys and bad roads are clearly marked." The Nicene Creed had to be restated in order to differentiate what our Church believes and what Protestants believe. At one time it was used by theologians as an oath of loyalty to the Church and to reconcile converts to the Christ, but it is rarely used these days.

Bobby: Does that mean you don't accept the Nicene Creed anymore?

Sonny: We accept the Nicene Creed with the modification added by the pope.

Darrel: These modifications exemplified by Pope Pius IV's addition to the Nicene Creed, exemplify what I call the *yeah, but* routine inherent in Catholicism. *Yeah*, Catholics say they believe in the Nicene Creed, *but* they have added these modifications to it. The Apostle Paul talks about this *yeah, but* in Catholicism in 2 Corinthians 1:15-20. He says that "Our word to you has not been Yes and No." Verse 20 states, "For all the promises of God in Him are, Yes, and in Him Amen, to the glory of God through us." So, in its blatant attempt to establish and maintain a purpose for itself in the lives of its followers, the Catholic Church ignores what Paul is saying here and amends the biblical Christian doctrine to make room for itself. We shall see many more examples of these "yeah, buts" as we get into what Catholics believe.

Sonny: It all comes down to authority, the Church vs. the Bible. We believe in the sole authority of the Church. We believe in the Bible as an authority, but we also believe in the sacred tradition of the Church.

Darrel: Luther believed that all truths are found in the Bible. He believed that the Bible was the sole source of normative, infallible apostolic revelation, and that all things necessary for salvation and concerning faith and life are taught in the Bible with enough clarity that the ordinary believer can find them there and understand the Christian doctrine. He questioned the need for extra-biblical traditions and particularly opposed the tradition of indulgences. The Reformation was the result. He believed in the five *solas,* one of them being *sola Scriptura,* the Bible alone is our only authority for our belief and each of these *solas* defines our belief which is supported in that Bible.

ASola" means Aonly" in Latin. The five *solas* are: *Sola fide* (only through faith are we saved), *sola gratia* (only through God's grace), *solus Christus* (only through Christ), *sola Scriptura* (Scripture is our only reference for our belief) and *soli Deo gloria* (to God alone be the glory). Examples of biblical support for each of the *solas* are found in Ephesians 2:8, Colossians 1:15 and Romans 8:34, Romans 15:4, and 1 Corinthians 10:31.

Sonny: We do believe in Christ alone; we believe in giving all the glory to God; but we have a different understanding than you do of *sola gratia* and *sola fide*; and we surely don't believe in *sola Scriptura.* With so many different versions of the Bible, and so many ways to interpret what it says, we can logically conclude that the Bible was only meant to complement the Church and its mission; it was never meant to replace it. G. K. Chesterton said that "The Bible by itself cannot be a basis of agreement when it is a cause of disagreement; it cannot be the common ground of Christians when some take it allegorically and some literally. The Catholic refers it to something that can say something to the living, consistent, and continuous mind of which I have spoken; the highest mind of man guided by God." You people have those 30,000 different denominations, each one established after the Reformation (Lutherans in 1517, Anglican in 1534, Presbyterian in 1560, Baptist in 1605, Methodist in 1744, to name the main ones) and each one offering a different take on what the Bible means; and that means that some of your Protestant churches differ in their understanding of the other four *solas.* There are so many of your denominations, we can't know what a Protestant believes.

Darrel: Yes, we have many denominations, but all Bible-believing Protestants who accept reformed theology are on the same page in their belief in the five *solas.* And when they were formed is not relevant because each one that preaches and teaches the theology of the Reformation in the true tradition of the apostles represents the original Christian church. The unity in Protestantism is based strictly on the theology of the Reformation as stated in the Canons of Dort in 1618-1619. This is the Protestantism we will be presenting in these discussions. The Protestant doctrine we hold to and will discuss and defend is the belief of the churches of the Reformation, the doctrine based only on the apostolic teaching as summarized by the five *solas* derived from Scripture. Just as you are unified in your belief in the Catholic theology represented to you in your church dogma, we are unified in our understanding of the biblical theology of the Reformation.

Ray: Whether or not those who ascribe to the "reformed theology" are unified in their beliefs, so what of it? Who, other than those involved, are likely to know exactly what those beliefs are?

Darrel: We are all involved, or should be involved in knowing the belief that unifies us. A true faith is an intelligent faith, as Calvin once said, and that means that, regardless of which denomination we belong to, we are united under the banner of the theology of the Reformation. We stress union with Christ over union to some church denomination; it is our faith in the Word of God that unites us. (Galatians 3:27). Any other human distinction in this life is comparatively negligible to the union God's people share. We must not allow distinctions to disrupt fellowship among Christian because, in doing so, we rebuild the barrier Christ tore down and submit to Satan's desire to divide us.

I'm looking forward to disclosing in these discussions just exactly what the theology of the Reformation is and comparing it with what you and Sonny believe. What we believe about Christianity and what you Catholics believe will indeed frame these discussions this season. As with all our discussions, we're after the truth here.

Knowledge of our respective theologies is a challenge for Protestant churches and your Catholic Church as well. We at least have our Bible as our only source of knowledge while you have your masters of the magisterium defining what you are to believe as expressed in your 752 page Catholic Catechism. It's no wonder that many Catholics aren't as unified as you would like to believe; knowing and understanding every one of those requirements in your legalistic catechism is a daunting task. As a result, in my experience, many of your people are confused and uniformed of what their church wants them to believe.

Ray: You have your Bible, but it's not enough. *Sola Scriptura* relies on the assumption the canon we organized includes everything God wishes to say to us. The Catholic Church relied on our Sacred Tradition to give us the Bible.

Darrel: The CC denigrates *sola Scriptura* by saying it organized the Bible as a man-made tradition, and this therefore entitles it to go on adding more man-made traditions.

Ray: Nowhere in the Bible does it say that the Bible is to be considered as God's only Word.

John: You are correct. Although 2 Timothy 3:16, Acts 17:11, 2 Corinthians 4:6 and Mark 7:6-7 have typically been cited as support verses, they don't directly refer to this concept; and you are correct in saying the Catholic Church resorted to oral tradition which had determined the organization of most of the books in the canon before the Catholic Church documented it; and of course, the OT was attested to by God Himself when Christ so often states in the gospels "It is written." Since we believe the canon was as inspired by the Holy Spirit as each book in the canon was so inspired, then we have to conclude that this is the only truth God wishes to convey to us, *regardless of where it came from or how it was organized.* We therefore must consider it to be the only written proof we have of what God wants us to believe.

Sola Scriptura has often been misunderstood and misapplied. It is supposed to be understood as our one source of evidence we can always rely upon to support what we believe. Unfortunately, some have used *sola Scriptura* as a justification for a "me, God, and the Bible" type of individualism, where the church bears no real authority, and the history of the church is not considered when interpreting and applying Scripture. That's wrong. The church is of critical importance and the Bible and the church should both be viewed as the tools God uses to connect us to Christ. Lutherans call the Bible a means of God's grace, a way He extends His grace to us.

I want to emphasize that the authority of the church should always be considered and respected, and God's church can be used by the Holy Spirit to guide and direct us in interpreting his Word. Just because we don't have the need you do to rely on just the one authoritative source of knowledge you believe to be true, doesn't mean we presume we are to interpret Scripture autonomously and not refer to the various opinions of respected theologians like Augustine, Aquinas, Dr. R. C. Sproul, Charles Spurgeon, and Oswald Chambers and apologists like C. S. Lewis to help us understand what God is saying to us. Dr. Michael J. Kruger, professor of the New Testament and Early Christianity at Reformed Theological Seminary in Charlotte, North Carolina, said that many Protestant "churches today are almost *ahistorica*l, cut off entirely from the rich traditions, creeds and confessions of the church. They misunderstand *sola Scriptura* to mean that the Bible is the only authority rather than understand it to mean that the Bible is the only infallible authority. Ironically, such an individualistic approach actually undercuts the very doctrine of *sola Scriptura* it is intended to protect. By emphasizing the autonomy of the individual believer, one is left with only private, subjective conclusions about what Scripture means. It is not so much the authority of Scripture that is prized as the authority of the individual."

Sonny: This is what we Catholics say too. We respect our church fathers but defer to our Supreme Pontiff because he, by virtue of his office, possesses infallible teaching authority when, as supreme pastor and teacher of all the faithful, he proclaims with a definitive act that a doctrine of faith or morals is to be held as such. (CCC 891). The pope is our visible representative of the invisible Christ. He is therefore considered to be infallible when he's speaking *ex cathedra*, from the chair.

Darrel: Protestants, of course, don't accept that authority because we believe that no human being is infallible except for Jesus Christ, and he is the only head of the Christian church which represents his body. The man you are insisting is your first pope didn't get off to a very good start as he denied Christ three times, did he? This pope of yours proclaims tradition and Christ objected to the Pharisees doing this. In Mark 7:13, He stated that the Word of God was not to be made "of no effect through tradition which has been handed down." This is why we believe that *sola Scriptura* is such an important aspect of the Christian belief. Catholics replace the five *solas* with one, *sola Catholic Church*.

Sonny: Our Church protects us from heresies like Protestantism.

Darrel: If we presume that the Bible is God's Word and that he, in the form of the Holy Spirit, guides us in understanding his Word, we believe *sola Scriptura* protects us from heresies like Catholicism that defer to the word of their Catholic Church. Through our knowledge of Scripture, we can recognize false doctrine. You are simply told by your church what is to be considered false doctrine.

John: The value of *sola Scriptura* is that it protects us from unorthodox, heretical beliefs introduced by churches that do not follow the apostolic teachings documented in the Bible. It also "protects us from overcorrecting and raising creeds and confessions or other human documents or ideas to the level of Scripture" as we believe the Catholic Church has done. Dr. Kruger warns that "we must always be on guard against making the same mistake as Rome and embracing what we might call 'traditionalism,' which attempts to bind the consciences of Christians in areas that the Bible does not. In this sense, *sola Scriptura* is a guardian of Christian liberty. But the biggest danger we face when it comes to *sola Scriptura* is not misunderstanding it. The biggest danger is forgetting it."

Darrel: The Reformers did not see themselves as coming up with new doctrine; they understood their mission was to recover something very, very old, the true religion of Christianity Christ had intended it to be; something the church had originally believed but had later twisted and distorted.

Ray: The reformers intended to start a new religion. Luther wanted to establish "Lutheranism."

Never fear because Martin Luther and the good guys are here to straighten out what they believed had become of Christianity, You believe that for 1,500 years the Catholic Church was foundering in ignorance until the great reformer came along to reinvent the faith in accordance with his own taste and the prevailing philosophies of the day.

The Reformation was a rebellion, plain and simple. There has always been a spirit of rebellion in man from the get-go. We are inclined to hate authority. Luther wanted to destroy the Catholic Church and establish his own church.

John: Luther stated he had no intention of doing that and discouraged the use of the name "Lutherans." You're correct is saying man is by nature a rebel against authority, but the Reformation wasn't a rebellion against Christianity and God, it was a reformation of the Christian religion. Luther was a Catholic monk and knew Scripture tells us to submit to authority, but not when that authority requires us to distort the Word of God; and therein is the reason Luther and the other reformers opposed the Catholic Church. They believed the Church required them to believe things and do things that violated the Word of God.

Ray: No. The Reformation was what it was; a disaster for Christianity.

John: The Reformation was a preservation of the Christian religion; it was a disaster for the Roman Catholic Church. In breaking up the powerful hold the church held over its members, it caused a return to the Christian religion of the apostolic teachings; it put Christianity back on its Christ-centered track. There would no longer be just some huge, man-made, powerful church organization consisting of self-appointed and self-serving individuals who tyrannically ruled over their religious domain with an iron hand. The Catholic Church, of course, knew what they had to lose, and that's why they were so aggressive in their condemnation of Luther and the other reformers.

Darrel: Right. It certainly isn't any wonder that they had Martin Luther scheduled for execution. Off with his head to shut him up!

Daniel: Luther and all the other reformers believed that the Bible was God's inerrant and infallible Word, and that it only made sense to rely solely on what our creator told us than to rely on anything a man or some organization would tell us about the truth. The reformed Christian churches are defined by the creeds like the Apostles Creed, the Nicene Creed, and, most particularly the Westminster Stands, the Belgic Confession, the Heidelberg Catechism, the Canons of Dort and the Augsburg Confession, all of them taken directly from the Bible; and we are also defined by the other four *solas* of the Reformation.

Ray: The reformers designed a new religion.

John: Not so, Ray. Dr. Kruger says that "The Reformers were not innovators but excavators."

Darrel: Luther was brilliant; Calvin was brilliant; simply ignoring the opinions and contributions of these learned Christians and dismissing them as heretics is counter-intuitive, and just plain obtuse. In my experience in discussing theology and religion with Catholics, they've proved to be both stubborn in their defense of their vaunted church and stupid in not wishing to open their minds to learning anything else about Christianity but what their church has told them to believe. Their natural spirit of inquiry is stifled through indoctrination.

Daniel: But Catholics are surely smart enough to recognize the authority of Scripture, right? Don't Catholics have that in common with Protestants?

Darrel: *Yeah*, Catholics believe in the Bible as an authority; *but* they also believe in their church tradition as an authority.

John: We object to what we call "traditionalism" of your church, Sonny. When we get into discussing each of them in detail in the next few sessions, I hope to provide evidence to support the Protestant claim that it is Catholicism that has left Christianity, and it is Protestantism that has brought it back. I hope to use only the Bible to prove my point so that's why it's necessary to talk about how we both understand its authority. Our discussions won't be productive unless you agree to respect the authority of the Bible.

Sonny: Yeah, I do respect the authority of the Bible, but...

Darrel: See there, it's just as I said; another "yeah, but."

Look, man, can't you see that biblical authority has to be our premise to continue discussing our two denominations? From what I know about you Catholics, you don't regard the Bible as your sole authority because your church has squeezed itself into the picture. You've also indicated that your church doesn't encourage its followers to express their personal opinions; you must always defer to your church. Your church frowns on you people thinking on your own because they want to maintain their sole authority in your spiritual life. Their opinion is the only opinion that counts.

Ray: How many times must I state that our Magisterium is our authority? Its opinion is the only opinion that counts. Do you want us to believe that the likes of heretics Martin Luther and John Calvin are more trustworthy than the Magisterium?

Darrel: Only Catholics regard this magisterium of yours to have any credibility. Because this anonymous group of "super-special" Christians tells you that Calvin and Luther are heretics, you must believe them or be excommunicated as Luther was. But, in simply dismissing the man who used to be one of your own as a heretic and dismissing the man who wrote the most definitive description of the biblical Christian doctrine in the history of our church as a heretic, your church is being unreasonable. You should know that even Calvin's detractors recognized the credibility of his monumental effort in writing *Institutes of the Christian Religion*. Open-mindedness and objectivity in search of clarity require this deference to him and other theologians you Catholics arbitrarily label as heretics because your church tells you they are.

John: I can tell you, Ray, some Lutherans believe John Calvin may have been a heretic too, but Luther didn't. We should all keep an open mind.

Sonny: What are you guys implying?

Darrel: In most discussions I've had with Catholics, they seem to always defer to what their church has to say; we Protestants aren't so indoctrinated we simply accept whatever opinion our church has regarding our Christian doctrine. I personally consult a variety of resources that help me in understanding the meaning of God's Word. Our Protestant churches don't make authoritative pronouncements from the pulpit or "ex cathedra." We believe we are enabled by the Holy Spirit to exercise more of our own initiative in understanding God's Word and in maintaining our connection with Christ.

Sonny: Spirits can be misleading. We recognize that there are three Spirits from whom we may receive prompting: The Holy Spirit, the Spirit of truth (1 John 4:6), the human spirit within each of us. (1 Thessalonians 5:23, Hebrews 4:12), and the evil or demonic spirit which comes from Satin, the spirit of error. (1 John 4:6). Only the Church can be trusted to convey the right spirit.

Darrel: But the church is comprised of men who can be misled by the wrong spirit, right?

Sonny: For almost 2,000 years, the Church has earned our trust.

Darrel: Well, there were some reformers in the fifteenth and sixteenth centuries who had trusted the Catholic Church but began to believe that the wrong spirit had taken hold of their church and was guiding every Christian down the wrong path to the truth, away from the purity of the gospel message. Martin Luther believed that his Catholic Church had changed and strayed from the apostolic teachings and its purpose. The reformers risked their very lives in opposing the church institution. They believed the time had come to take back their religion that had been hijacked by the church for its own use.

John: Luther was a brilliant and devout monk who wrestled with his sinful nature daily. He realized he could never please God no matter how hard he tried. When he understood the true meaning of God's grace from reading his Bible, he was relieved of his guilt in not being able to satisfy a holy and righteous God.

Darrel: The key phrase here is "reading his Bible." Luther understood that he could and should enjoy a one-on-one relationship with God and his revealed Word, and trust in the guidance of the Holy Spirit to interpret what God is saying to us in his Word. We understand that it takes a whole Bible to make a whole Christian; it is the lens through which we view all of life. Only by reading our Bible consistently and continually will we develop the faith habit of looking through the appearance of the thing to see the reality. In my experience in talking with Catholics about the Bible, they seem to shy away from reading the Bible on their own, and tell me they prefer to have it read to them in their worship service. We Protestants trust ourselves to read the Bible without having to rely upon our church to tell us what God is saying to us in his Word. That doesn't mean we don't utilize our pastors to guide us in interpreting God's Word and to provide us with good Bible study instruction and resources; it means we don't arbitrarily consider our church to be the sole authority in our spiritual lives.

Sonny: You can't trust your own uneducated opinion in studying the Bible. It's just your opinion.

John: Yes, what we believe we know is our opinion; actually most everything any of us know, everything we've learned, is derived from someone's opinion, including the opinions of your church leaders; the challenge is to be discerning enough to know when someone is speaking God's Word to us or attempting to mislead us. Ironically, it was your arbitrarily assigned first pope, Peter, who actually warned us about following false doctrine and to exercise discernment. I say again, the Holy Spirit provides us with the ability to discern.

Darrel: Actually, at one time in its illustrious history, the Roman Catholic Church prevented its members from reading the Bible. This means the vaunted church can interpret Scripture in any way they see fit depending on its objective.

Daniel: You're kidding, right. The Church actually did that?

Darrel: Yes. The Bible was forbidden to laymen by the Council of Valencia in 1229.

John: The reformers believed they could trust themselves through the spirit to read and interpret Scripture on their own. Luther said that Scripture knows no "masters, judges, or arbiters." It knows "only witnesses, disciples, and confessors."

Darrel: The Catholic Church's objective, of course, was to continue to be that "master, judge and arbiter" in the lives of its members. Luther challenged that authority.

Daniel: Yes, I know that, for many, many centuries, the Catholic Church has convinced its members they can't do it without them, in my experience, Catholics don't know their Bible very well; this may be because they have never been encouraged to read it independent of their church's interpretation.

John: This is very sad because the study of Scripture is a means of enjoying deeper communion with our triune God. Lutherans call God's Word a means of grace.

Sonny: We study our Bibles daily.

Darrel: Really? When do you do your daily devotions, Sonny, in the morning (which I prefer) or at bedtime each night? What does studying your Bible mean to you? What Bible study guide do you use?

Sonny: We derive our Bible study by attending daily Mass.

Darrel: So, you're making my point for me. You're telling us you don't feel comfortable to read and study your Bible unless you're in church having the Bible read to you by one of your priests. Your church of course is like a parent to you people so I guess that doesn't surprise me; after all a father reads books to his children.

Sonny: I'm making my own point, Darrel; we don't study the Bible without church guidance; nor should we.

Darrel: I asked about your daily devotions, Sonny. Are you saying you go to Mass each day?

Sonny: Well, no, that's impossible for most people, but we can if we want to. I go on Sunday.

Darrel: Well then, since you don't, of course, go every day; I guess that means you don't study your Bible daily.

Sonny: Darrel, I take your point, but I don't see the necessity to study my Bible daily.

Darrel: So much to learn from the Word, so little time, my friend, so little time.

John: Lutherans believe that God administers His grace through His Word and the sacraments. As Psalm 1:1-2 states, "Blessed is the man who walks not in the counsel of the ungodly, nor stands in the path of sinners, nor sits in the seat of the scornful; But his delight is in the law of the LORD, and in His law *he meditates day and night*." To me, this means we must resolve to delight in the law of the Lord every day. Christians should know our focus is on Christ, and so we are motivated to meet Him every day. The Bible is His book; it is all about Him.

Darrel: John-boy, you had better check with the Catholic Church authorities before you tell us what this verse means to you. After all, it's just your own opinion.

Sonny: I know you're being sarcastic, Darrel, but you do bring up a good point. We must always be certain to study our Bible under the auspices and guidance of our Church to insure we are receiving the truth.

Bobby: Okay, let's get back on track here. We're about half way through our session here and these guys haven't even formally presented what Catholics believe. Let's do that.

Sonny: Here are several handouts which will help in explaining who we are and what we believe.

Darrel: Handouts already? Wow, you came prepared, Sonny.

Sonny: Yes, well, I believe in being prepared for discussions like this.

As you can see from the first handout I gave you, we believe the Church is One. (John 17:1-26, Romans 12:5, 1 Corinthians 10:17, 12:13). The Church is Holy. (Ephesians 5:25-27, Revelation 19:7-8). The Church is Catholic (Matthew 28:19-20, Revelation 5:9-10). And the Church is Apostolic (succession). (Ephesians 2:19-20).

Daniel: Let's respond to each of these points: The Christian church is indeed one and it is holy; it is also catholic, with a small "c" which means it's universal. What do you mean though that the church is apostolic succession?

Sonny: When Christ told the apostles to establish his Church (which we believe of course is the Catholic Church with a capital "C"), He was actually establishing the papacy at that time and all the popes to follow Peter, our first pope. This established a succession of Church leaders who were to adhere to the teachings of those original apostles. Ephesians 2:19-20 provides support for our belief.

Daniel: No, I don't think this verse does that, Sonny. When we examine what Paul is telling us, he is only referring to all "members of the household of God," not some papacy or popes or bishops. "Household of God" means all followers of the apostolic church which is to be holy and one. Christ was speaking to all of the apostles and He meant for His church to be universal and the apostles understood it this way; but the Catholics inserted themselves into that position and capitalized the "c" to graphically illustrate their claim that they are that universal church, that ONE universal church. The verses given to us to support this contention, Matthew 28:19-20 (urging followers to make disciples of all nations) and Revelation 5:9-10 (referring to all kings and priests of God to reign on the earth), are obvious examples of how Catholics stretch biblical verses to support such an arrogant statement. Just read those verses and you will all agree with me.

Ironically, in its assertion it is the original, apostolic church, in establishing itself as its own entity, it has separated itself from the original church. The Catholic Church has implemented traditions which only serve to weaken the apostolic tradition.

Ray: What do you mean by "apostolic tradition."

Darrel: <u>The apostolic tradition is the only genuine, God-ordained tradition in Christianity</u>. When Paul commended the church in Corinth (1 Corinthians 11:2) for maintaining the traditions he had delivered to them, and asked his followers to stand firm and hold to the traditions they were taught in 2 Thessalonians 2:15, he was referring to beliefs that were taught to them by the apostles as presented in the Bible. He referred to these apostolic teachings as the traditions of our Christian doctrine which he had communicated to them. The Catholic Church tags onto these verses, presuming Paul was referring to its man-made, biblically unsupported traditions like purgatory. In Matthew 15:3, Jesus condemns traditions that contradict God's Word, and in Mark 7:9, he distinguishes the difference between human tradition (as presented in the dogma of the Catholic Church) which we should reject and apostolic tradition, which we must accept. When the Bible refers to traditions, it's referring only to the apostolic tradition based on the teachings of the apostles. The original Christian church is the church based only on the apostolic teachings with Christ as its foundation.

Ray: Only warped history and anti-Catholic historians would tell you that the traditions of the Catholic Church were added to the Church after the Church gave us the canon.

Darrel: Not so. I intend to prove that the majority of your traditions were additions to the teachings of the apostles over the centuries.

John: He has a point, Ray. Catholic Church history tells us that these various traditions of yours such as purgatory and indulgences, veneration of Mary, the Mass, extreme unction and affirmation of seven sacraments, canonization of dead saints, celibacy, transubstantiation and the forbidding of the cup to laity, confession to a priest, and infallibility, and other rituals and traditions of your Catholic Church all came into being after the Bible's canon was organized? I have a list here and I'll just read a few of your traditions that were instituted over the centuries along with the date of the official pronouncement.

Mass was adopted as a daily worship celebration in 394 and attendance was made obligatory in the 11th century; celibacy was decreed by Pope Boniface VII in 1079; confession to a priest and the dogma of transubstantiation were instituted by Pope Innocent III in the Lateran Council in 1215; the doctrine of the seven sacraments was affirmed in 1439; Pope Pius IX proclaimed the dogma of papal infallibility in 1870 in the First Vatican Council, and so on and so forth. So then, by definition, all of these papal pronouncements were considered to be "extra-biblical;" they were added to Scripture. Of course, the Bible clearly states we are forbidden to add to or take away from Scripture. See Deuteronomy 4:2, 12:32, Revelation 22:18-19. In Matthew 23:4, Christ speaks of not wishing for anyone to bear such a burden. This concept refers to the importance of believing the Bible alone is sufficient for all truth (2 Peter 1:3).

Sonny: The traditions were based on what Christ and the apostles said but weren't written down, and they were there long before they were declared official by the Church Councils. Usually the Church doesn't state that which everyone agrees with so the official recognition dates vary. Anyway, these sacred oral traditions were communicated by divine revelation, from the dawn of human history to the end of the apostolic age, as passed on from one generation of believers to the next, and as preserved under divine guidance by the Church established by Christ. The transmitted revelation, our sacred tradition, more technically also means that part of God's revealed word is not contained in the Bible.

Darrel: This concept of course allows the Catholic Church to add to what God had apparently omitted from his Word. This is blasphemy! This is exactly how your church was able to support some of the more pagan traditions like purgatory, etc. But these traditions weren't followed until the Catholic Church required its followers to officially believe in them through some edict issued by some pope or church council. Don't you find it interesting that these traditions began to be made official in the eleventh century when history records the Roman Catholic Church really began as that entity?

For the record, church councils can serve two purposes, one good and one bad. The Bible is self-authenticating, and a church council does good when it recognizes the authority inherent in the books themselves. On the other hand, a church council does bad when it competes with the authority of the Bible and adds traditions to Scripture. Catholic Church Councils of Ephesus, Verona, Lateran Council, Constance, Florence and Trent (my personal favorite) were convened over the past 1,600 years for the sole purpose of adding traditions to the Bible.

John: Good point, Darrel. Over the centuries, the Catholic Church became more and more about itself than about Christ.

Human beings are naturally religious, and that instinct is expressed through religious rituals; but, when the religion becomes more about the rituals (the orthopraxy) than the orthodoxy, the religion becomes more about itself than about the pursuit of truth. As contemporary theologian, Dr. R. C. Sproul, once said in *Tabletalk* magazine, "Christian theology tends to focus more on getting our beliefs right than on enforcing adherence to a set of religious rituals." Protestants focus on theology more than on ritual.

Bobby: Okay, so let's talk some more about these Catholic traditions.

Sonny: Our Church-ordained sacred tradition is the apostolic tradition. By this I mean that sacred tradition was communicated to us by the apostles who handed it down by the spoken word of their preaching, by the example they gave, by the institutions they established.

Darrel: How did the apostles receive this tradition?

Sonny: From the lips of Christ, from His way of life and His works, or from the Holy Spirit. Sacred tradition and sacred Scripture make up a single sacred deposit of the Word of God, and is, at the very least, considered to be equal in authority to the Bible and, even greater than the Bible because the Church came before the Bible.

Darrel: Regardless of when you claim the Catholic Church was officially established, it wasn't until 1545 when the Council of Trent officially declared that Catholic tradition is of equal authority with the Bible. It doesn't matter when you say the concept was thought of, we only have your official declarations to go by. Can you see a pattern here? First your leaders perceive that they want to add something to God's Word to serve their own interest, and then later on they finally get around to making that concept official so Catholic believers would be required to accept it as church dogma. Luther and the reformers were on to the self-serving motive of their Catholic Church, and questioned what the church could really settle about Christian doctrine that Scripture had not settled first. The chicken came before the egg.

Sonny: I only know that our sole authority really has always been the Catholic Church. God left us a Church to guide us and not the Bible. The Church includes oral tradition that was not included in the Bible.

Darrel: In 1 Corinthians 11:2, Paul refers to what he and the other apostles had taught in their writings which of course later became part of the canon of the Bible. What the apostles said orally was recorded in the gospel and in their own writings. There is no reason to want to include oral tradition known only to the Catholic Church because we are to consider the Bible sufficient. The only reason the CC refers to oral traditions is to support its extra-biblical traditions like purgatory, veneration of Mary, the rites of the priesthood, etc. Once we step outside the words written by the apostles, we enter the world of hearsay. That's how heresy originates. Don't you know that Jesus and the apostles constantly appealed to the Bible as the final authority? Of course you do, yet, as you have stated, the true objective of the Catholic Church is revealed in its false claim to being the authority even over the Bible.

Ray: You're jumping to the wrong conclusion, Darrel! First of all, there is no evidence of Christ instructing His disciples or the apostles to document everything He said to them, and, in fact, the Bible says that most of what Jesus said isn't in Scripture; there are several verses in the Bible that tell us it does not represent the entire Word of God. In John 21:25, the Apostle says that "There are also many things that Jesus did, which if they were written one by one, I suppose that even the world itself could not contain the books that would be written." Very little of the thousands of hours of preaching from the apostles is in the Bible. To presume that all we need is in Scripture when Scripture never says so is not really defensible. The Word of God does not cease to be the Word of God because it was never written. The oral word is preserved and protected by the Spirit, and the Word of God in its oral form, has the full force and power and authority like what is written in the Bible. In chastising the Ephesians for misbehaving, Paul refers to the oral traditions they had previously received when he writes, "You did not so learn Christ in this way! These oral traditions are to be followed as the word of God.

Second of all, there is biblical support for adding tradition to the Bible. In 1 Thessalonians 1:5, Paul states the gospel came to us not only in word, but in the power of the Holy Spirit. In 2 Corinthians 10:10-11, he refers to teaching that is not included in his letters, but that tradition which he will reveal when he sees the members of the Thessalonian Church. The Apostle John refers to what he will tell believers when he sees them that he hasn't included in his letters.

Darrel: Of course there were oral teachings, but we must presume they are consistent with what the apostles communicated in their letters. The traditions of the Catholic Church are not consistent with the content of the letters and the gospel accounts as I shall prove in these discussions. Furthermore, you should note that neither John nor Paul referred to your Catholic Church to be responsible for adding tradition that they didn't include in their letters to the Christian churches. They said they would do that in person. No, your church took it upon itself to tell us what was not written in the Bible, to claim what it believed these apostles said, or should have said, to the church. Doesn't this cause you to question your church's motive in doing this? Can't you see how the Catholic Church is acting in its own self-interest by claiming sole authority over your spiritual life?

Sonny: None of us can know all that the apostles taught, Darrel, but that isn't what we're saying. We are saying that the sacred tradition was communicated to us through apostolic succession. This tradition is interpreted authentically solely by the Magisterium of the Church, that is, by the pope, as the successor to Peter and by the bishops in communion with him. It is therefore incumbent to obey the Church Magisterium which possesses the succession from the apostles, those who have received the infallible charism of truth, according to the good pleasure of the Father.

Darrel: Okay, so I hear you saying that this oral tradition wasn't written down by the original apostles but by your popes and magisterium which claimed to be successors to Peter in the apostolic tradition? Man, it just keeps getting deeper!

Sonny: Yes, what you just said is exactly what one of our first church fathers, Ireneaus, told us to believe. In the second century, Irenaeus said that "True knowledge of Christianity can only be obtained in the doctrine of the apostles and the ancient constitution of the Church throughout all the world, and the distinctive manifestation of the body of Christ according to the successors of the bishops, by which they have handed down that Church which exists in every place, and has come even unto us, being guarded and preserved without any forging of Scriptures, by a very complete system of doctrine, and neither receiving addition nor suffering curtailment in the truths which she believes and it consists in reading the word of God without falsification, and a lawful and diligent exposition in harmony with the Scriptures, both without danger and without blasphemy, and above all, it consists of the pre-eminent gift of love, which is more precious than knowledge, more glorious than prophecy, and which excels all the other gifts of God."

The Catholic Church is THE Church of the Apostles. The extra-biblical traditions of Catholicism go along with the Bible itself. If you have only the Bible as your source of knowledge of the Christian religion, you don't have all the teachings of Christ and the Apostles. It's very simple: The extra-biblical traditions are Sacred Apostolic Traditions. Christianity has never been just about what's in the Bible. The Church guides us in our understanding of our religion. Our journey is to find out what happened to all the teachings from Jesus and the apostles that were never written down.

Darrel: Our life long journey is to know as much of the meaning of what was written down as we can know as we grow in holiness through our sanctification. There's no biblical support for oral tradition or apostolic succession; and I'm going to prove it to you.

Sonny: Documents written by the apostles were collected by local churches, copied and preserved; they were given the same high respect as the Old Testament Scriptures. Over the course of several centuries, different lists were put forth as to what documents were fit to be read in the Mass. The four gospels were unanimous from the get-go, as were most of the letters attributed to Paul; other documents like 2 Peter, 2 and 3 John, James, Jude, Hebrews, and Revelation were more controversial. The Scriptures were not completed in the canon until we accomplished this task 1,500 years after the events occurred. Before being committed to writing, there were Oral Traditions which were already believed and practiced, and these constitute the dogma of our belief as much as the Bible itself. They are not all included in the Bible but are considered to be God's revelation. You could say then that the Bible is an apostolic tradition of the Catholic Church. The Bible doesn't specify what books are to be included in it, so that's an example of a tradition not mentioned in the Bible, right?

John: I'm not sure how you're trying to make this connection, Sonny. We had the O.T. canon before your church gave us the entire canon, Old and New Testaments, and Christ of course did refer to a number of Old Testament books in the gospel accounts. We believe God inspired the canon of the Bible in the same way He inspired the authors of the books to write down His Word. The canon therefore is not an appropriate example of a tradition just because it wasn't directly specified in the Bible. It seems your church was evidently inspired by its production of the canon to produce more of what it considered to be oral traditions not referred to in Scripture. Thanks for the canon, but you can leave the rest.

Sonny: Okay, I'll give you another example of an oral tradition. The prophecy in the book of Matthew that the coming Messiah shall be a Nazarene is oral tradition. Jesus relies on the oral tradition in recognizing Moses' seal of authority. This reality is not described in the Old Testament. Referring to John as the beloved disciple is an example of oral tradition, so are the teachings of the Blessed Trinity and Christ's human/ divine nature.

Darrel: This reference to John as the beloved disciple is in the book he himself authored (John 10:29, 20:2 and 20:24). Using this verse to illustrate some oral tradition that isn't mentioned anywhere else in Scripture is a real stretch, Sonny.

Sonny: Okay, what about when Paul relies on the oral tradition of the apostles for his statement in Acts 20:35 where he tells people they must support the weak? He also relies on oral tradition not recorded anywhere in Scripture when in1 Corinthians 10:4, he refers to a story of the church fathers being "baptized into Moses in the cloud and in the sea, drinking of that spiritual Rock that followed them and that Rock was Christ."

Darrel: In the Old Testament, God is often described as the Rock, and Israel is described as having forsaken God, the "Rock of his salvation."

Sonny: Well, what about the verse in Ephesians 5:14 where Paul is obviously relying on oral tradition in quoting an early Christian hymn, "awake O sleeper rise from the dead and Christ shall give you light?"

Darrel: Paul is probably referring to Isaiah 60:1 where the prophet says "Arise, shine, for your light has come!" Paul is reiterating what he said in 2:1-10 about being dead in sin. When your church uses a verse like this to somehow prove the existence of oral tradition that is not recorded in Scripture, your suspicion of its motives should be aroused, Sonny.

Sonny: Really? Well, how about when the author of Hebrews relies on the oral tradition of the martyrs being sawed in two. This is not recorded in any of the books of the Old Testament.

Darrel: I agree with you on this one. According to tradition, the prophet Isaiah did die in this way; but, even if you provide an example of an oral tradition, if any of these oral traditions contradict the written word as most of the alleged oral traditions your church has added to the Bible do, then, as Christ said, the Catholic Church is "setting aside the commandments of God in order to keep your tradition." (Mark 7:9). When doctrine contradicts what the Bible does say to us, it is to be rejected. Peter warns us about this in his second epistle. Please think about why your church wants you to believe this, okay?

Sonny: It isn't that our Church wants us to believe in the oral tradition; it's that we all must believe in them for the sake of the survival of the Church. You said so yourself that, from its beginnings, the teachings of the apostles were being subjected to apostasies, and it was necessary to establish one Catholic Church headed by successors to the apostles who were obliged to tell the gospel truth. How do you suppose it was possible that the Church could have persisted for so many centuries if it didn't represent itself to be the sole authority of belief and instill church dogma? It would not have survived if it had limited itself to simply enforcing the teachings of the apostles as they had been written down.

Darrel: In saying that the add-on, biblically unsupported traditions were necessary for the survival of the Christian church, you are admitting that, in pursuit of its own self-interest, the church invented the dogma it felt necessary to impose to maintain its influential and powerful position in the civilized world.

Sonny: I'm saying that the dogma was supported by oral tradition and was necessary for the Church to continue to exist and pursue the great commission.

Darrel: God preserves his Word and his church; he surely didn't need for your people to design their own religion based on dogma they believed was necessary to preserve their own self interests. It's obvious this is what has happened because there's no indication that Peter would have successors who were to assume leadership of the Christian church and present what basically amounts to continuing revelation from God for purposes of preserving his church. Irenaeus merely was laying the groundwork for his church's conquest of the Christian church.

Sonny: There is biblical precedence for apostolic succession. Acts 1:21-26 describes how the apostles acted quickly to replace Judas. Paul describes the apostolic authority that had been bestowed on Titus and urges him to act decisively in this leadership role.

Ray: Yeah, do your homework on early Christian writings. The testimony of the early Church saints is deafening in its unanimous assertion of apostolic succession. Far from being discussed by only a few, scattered writers, the belief that the apostles handed on their apostolic authority to bishops and priests was one of the most frequently and vociferously defended doctrines in the first several centuries of Christianity. I refer you to Acts 1:15-28, 1:20, 1:22, 6:6, 9:17-19, 13:3, 14:23, 15:22-27, 2 Corinthians 1:21-22, Colossians 1:25, 1 Timothy 3:1, 4:14, 5:22, 2 Timothy 1:6, 4:1-6, 2:2, Titus 1:5, Luke 10:1, and 1 John 4:6. Without a doubt, authority is transferred by the Sacrament of Ordination. The word "apostle" means "one who was sent," and only a clergyman ordained in by an apostle, or their correctly ordained successors, can receive, and pass down authority.

Darrel: Apostle refers only to the earliest, closest followers of Jesus. The key phrase you use here is when you referred to a "correctly ordained successor." Of course, you're referring to your belief in apostolic succession; but we know from Scripture that Christ didn't refer to such a process of succession of the apostles; he intended for the apostolic tradition to be handed down from one generation to the next, of course, but the actual church offices of pope, bishops or priests were not mentioned in the gospel accounts; and, another thing, if you review those early Christian writings, you will see a very gradual transition from writing about Christ to writing about the Catholic Church; this is the last step in apostasy.

If you step back, Ray, and examine objectively what you just said about the presumed authority of your Catholic Church and these extra-biblical traditions of yours, you'll see how this looks to those of us who have not been indoctrinated to believe what you believe. You Catholics insist on the premise that your church is the only Christian church and that Peter was your first pope, and that the teachings of the original apostles were supplemented by traditions revealed to popes in succession from Peter because they too represented the Church with the keys to the kingdom; and you consider these traditions to be equal to, or greater than, the authority of the written Word of God, I'm not sure how we can have an open discussion with you because we don't accept that premise. If, on the other hand, you are willing to open up your mind, shrug off the mind-numbing burden of what you have been told by your church to believe and be willing to at least entertain what we have to say to you about your denomination, these discussions won't be just a waste of time for all of us.

John: Even though I know none of us Protestants have much of a chance to convince any Catholic who is satisfied with his or her belief to renounce what you believe and swim on over to where the water's clearer, I'm here to learn from you Catholics; and I want these discussions to prompt you Catholics to learn from what we have to say, to think about what you believe and why you believe it, to think outside the box, to focus more on our wonderfully unique religion instead of on your church institution; to avoid disproportionately focusing your major effort on promoting your version of Christianity with its organization and traditions and focus on Christ. Hebrews 3:1: "Therefore, holy brothers, who share in the heavenly calling, fix your thoughts on Jesus, the apostle and high priest whom we confess." We need to understand we, both Catholics and Protestants, share in that heavenly calling.

Sonny: I came here to teach you Protestants about Catholicism; but that doesn't mean I'm not willing to listen to what you all have to say about my religion.

Darrel: Sure, but I think we should have the opportunity to ask questions or make comments about each issue you present right after you've presented it. Otherwise, I'll lose track of what I want to ask you unless I take copious notes.

Bobby: I think that's a good way to proceed. It's the procedure we've observed in past sessions.

Darrel: Okay then, this is what I have to say in response to what you just said about us not knowing all of what the apostles taught.

Since the Bible tells us that there is much that Christ said that was not recorded in the gospel accounts, yes, it's certainly possible that no one, not even a Catholic, can know all of what the apostles taught. But, we must trust that the New Testament tells us all of what God wants us to know regardless because the writers of Scripture were guided by God to say what he intend to say in his Word. Do you agree with that?

Sonny: Yes, but I also believe that the Church was given the authority to continue to teach what the apostles taught because it too was inspired by the Holy Spirit to report the truth.

Darrel: Well, since some of your traditions clearly contradict apostolic tradition and God is not a God of contradiction, this should suggest that your church was at times inspired by another spirit than the Holy Spirit. Luther thought that your church was being used by Satan to further his objective of destroying Christianity. We must remember that Luther was in the trenches of the turmoil of the times and was an eyewitness to what the Catholic Church had become. The add-on traditions imposed by the Catholic Church on the Christianity in the apostolic tradition over the previous 1,500 years strongly suggest an ulterior motive other than presenting the truth.

Sonny: And what would that ulterior motive be, Darrel?

Darrel: Are you really so naïve you can't suspect that the Catholic Church just might have had a very worldly, secular motive of attainment of wealth, power and influence over people's lives? This is so damn obvious to anyone not indoctrinated into your denomination.

The church consists of human beings, of course, and we humans are instinctively inclined to want to attain and retain control. We want to be our own authority. Over the centuries, the Roman Catholic Church has dominated civilizations. It was inseparable from the State. I just finished reading Ken Follett's *The Pillars of the Earth*, a historical novel about the position of the Catholic Church in the middle ages. The author dramatically describes the balance of power between the monarchy of the State and the monarchy of Catholicism during this period of time. His depiction of the Catholic Church's immense power and influence over people's lives results in a highly engrossing narrative which I recommend everyone read.

The Catholic Church developed two standards of authority; the Bible and its traditions. The first was of God's origin, the other of human origin. Luther protested by stressing *sola fide*, by faith alone, and that dealt them a mighty blow; but when he also stressed *sola Scriptura*, he threatened to rock them to their very foundation because it undermined all of their traditions and thus threatened the authority of the Catholic Church which the traditions were designed to embolden. Luther and the other reformers encouraged Christians to think for themselves, to not rely on some powerful, human authority like the Catholic Church; we were to rely on the Word alone for our authority. No man, no church, no organization, no pope could impose the burden of obedience on believers in Christ; we are accountable only to God's revealed, written, absolute, unchanging Word as our guide. The Reformation made it possible for believers to be free from the authoritarian rule of the Catholic Church.

Sonny: Well, as you people seem so fond of saying, the reformers threw the baby out with the bathwater, and, as a result (according to the *Christian Sourcebook*) there are approximately 20-30,000 denominations, with 270 new ones being formed each year. As evidenced by the TV evangelists, self-proclaimed theologians, preachers, and teachers who are proclaiming a false and twisted doctrine like the "prosperity gospel," denial of the true presence of Christ in the Eucharist, and dogmas on Blessed Mary, each of your denominations has a different understanding of the Christian doctrine. Unity in Christianity is rooted in the truth. In discarding Catholicism, you created chaos.

Darrel: TV evangelists don't usually speak for the reformed theology that unites us. Your church proclaims itself to be the sole authority and forces your allegiance to its proclaimed dogma for fear of eternal damnation to prevent the chaos, right? It looks good on paper to have just the one authority, but not when it results in the truth being sacrificed on such an altar of authority.

Sonny: Martin Luther was concerned about the monster he'd created. In referring to all the denominations that spun off from the Reformation he stated, "This one will not hear of Baptism, and that one denies the sacrament; another puts a world between this and the last day; some teach that Christ is not God, some say this, some say that; there are as many sects and creeds as there are heads. No yokel is so rude but when he has dreams and fancies, he thinks himself inspired by the Holy Ghost and must be a prophet."

Darrel: Luther of course was concerned about heresies developing in Protestantism, just as he had seen develop in Catholicism. Yes, we have our different denominations and that is because with us, it's not all about the "Church" as it is with you folks. When Jesus prayed for unity in John 17:20-21, he was not referring to an organizational or bureaucratic unity of some church like yours. He is praying for unity in truth, love, and mission. Just as he and his Father are united in truth, love and mission. As Christians unite around the truth, love one another and work together to make disciples, the world will know that Jesus is the full revelation of the Father. Luther was certainly familiar with this verse in John and what Christ was saying, and that is why he was frustrated that this splitting away from the one dominant church would undoubtedly create disunity.

Sonny: Hiliare Belloc, author of *The Great Heresies*, stated that the reformers "weren't as much concerned to set right the evils which have grown up in the thing to be reformed as filled with passion and hatred of the thing itself...its essential, its good, that by which has a right to survive."

John: Its survival was, and is, indeed important to the Catholic Church, and I believe that the corporate institution it had become was more concerned about its survival, its retention of its power and wealth, than it was about addressing any of the 95 concerns that Luther posted on the church door. Luther didn't intend or desire to start a revolution against his Catholic Church. Yes, he was a passionate and outspoken man, but he did not hate his church; he was simply expressing his frustration over some of its traditions and maligning the fact that his church had strayed from depending on the Bible as Christianity's sole authority for truth.

Darrel: In my experience, many Catholics don't know very much about what their church teaches, much less what we believe. Unless you have either attended different Protestant denomination services, studied up on Protestantism by reading a book like John's *Comparing Christian Denominations*, they don't know what they're talking about.

Ray: Your various denominations don't know what they're talking about because you have no unifying authority. All of your denominations are man-made institutions that Christ never started or supported which are in fact in contention with His one, true and original Church. We are all meant to be in one faith, under one and singular authority and if that authority is corrupt, God will clean it up using faithful men and women within the system of ecclesial and civil authority to purify the Church. We receive the life of faith through the Church; she is our mother (CCC 169). There is one true church, the Catholic Church, which was founded by the apostles, and that is us. There are not two, true churches.

Darrel: The Catholic Church had floated away from its apostolic moorings, and reform was required to get it back to the dock. God used faithful men like Luther and Calvin to restore Christ's church. Unity is achieved through our unified belief in what God's Word is saying to us, not through allegiance to some self-proclaimed church. We are not to sacrifice truth on the altar of unity.

Sonny: I'm not challenging you Protestants spirituality and your love of God. I believe that most of you are sincerely trying to live out the gospel truth as it has been taught to you by your various denominations; but, therein lies the rub. You're all being taught something different and there is no one authority over all that governs what is taught about Christianity. You Protestants have no accountability.

Darrel: We are of course accountable to God and responsible for correctly understanding his Word. We don't need to depend on one, self-proclaiming, self-centered visible church institution for us to understand the doctrine of the invisible church of Christ's elect.

Every Catholic maintains the false claim that their church is THE church. I know it's hard to visualize the invisible church of believers because it's a concept and not a visible thing. Catholicism's appeal is to those who want to put a face on God, and the Catholic Church gives them that face. Catholics are people who are attracted to the history, the pomp, sacred traditions, trappings and rituals of the Catholic Church, and they want an authority in their spiritual life. We don't need to have Christ and Christianity made visible to us by a church; that doesn't make us heathens or heretics.

Ray: This "invisible church" is a false tradition from Protestants during the Reformation.

John: That's not true. As I said before, Augustine recognized it as a reality and, since he is a Catholic saint, both Catholic and Protestant should recognize its existence. It's not a new concept at all; and it certainly isn't a "tradition;" it's a concept that describes a reality.

Darrel: One church, two aspects. When we look at our Christian church, we should see the invisible church standing before the visible church. Regardless of what denomination a person belongs to, the visible church should never block out our vision of the invisible church. Catholicism inserts itself in between man and God.

We believe that the Christian church with Christ at the head is indeed the family and flock of God, His Israel, the body and bride of Christ, and the temple of the Holy Spirit. It is not one visible church which calls itself the Catholic Church.

The New Testament teaches that the church is the fulfillment of the Old Testament beliefs, hopes and patterns which are brought to fruition by Jesus Christ. Theologians tell us that the church exists as the church militant (those who are still on earth) and the church triumphant (those who have died and entered glory). When I just referred to visible churches in the plural, I was referring to the church as it appears in its local congregations here on earth. Each of these congregations is a representative of the universal church of God as He has willed it to be built in the original, apostolic teachings and tradition. According to Paul, the one church universal is any church denomination as represented in each of its local congregations. In this regard, the church on earth is one in Christ, despite the great number of local congregations and denominations. It is holy because it is consecrated to God corporately, as each Christian is individually. It is catholic (meaning universal) because it is worldwide. Finally, it is apostolic because it is founded on apostolic teaching. In summary, I can only conclude that there is the invisible church, of which there is only one, and the visible church, of which there are many; one church, two aspects, two perspectives, God's and man's. To God, there is just the one church, the church He founded through Christ, the church that has only him as its bride and body consisting only of God's elect: the invisible church. This doesn't mean there are two churches, one visible and another hidden in heaven, but one church only known perfectly to God and known imperfectly on earth. There is a great overlap between both categories; many of the members of the invisible church are indeed members of the visible church, but the reverse is not necessarily the case.

Bobby: It's time to call it quits for today. See y'all next week.

Week Three

Bobby: Okay, let's get started. I recall from last week that we were discussing the invisible church. Any more thoughts on that subject before we move on with our agenda?

Darrel: I'm beginning to wonder if you Catholic people are teachable. Even when we talk about a concept one of your most respected Saints has put forth, you deny its presence.

Ray: I was just going to ask you the same question, Darrel. Why don't you tell us what you've learned from us so far, and then we can determine whether you're teachable?

Darrel: You teach Catholicism, which may or may not have much to do with the subject always at hand in these discussions, Christianity. We are the elect and know we are guided by the Holy Spirit to understand our belief; we trust that our Creator has the power to directly communicate with us, as he has from the beginning of time. God doesn't need a man-made institution to connect to us and teach us his Word. He communicates to members of the invisible church of his own design. Jesus states in Acts 1:8 that "you shall receive power when the Holy Spirit has come upon you; and you shall be witnesses to Me in Jerusalem, and in all Judea and Samaria, and to the end of the earth." The spirit gives the apostles power to witness the gospel truth to the world. No one person is given this responsibility. The church was founded on these apostolic teachings and must remain true to them. Since the Catholic Church became an entity unto itself, it became apostate because it left the original authority of the apostolic church. The Protestant churches which were established by the Reformation in the theology of the Reformation, represents a reversal of this heresy, a return to the church the apostles established in the first century.

The true Christian church consists of those who trust in Christ, not the ecclesiastical, top down organization of your Catholic Church with its popes, bishops and priests. Your church is visible, very, very visible, and that's its intention. From its earliest beginnings, the Catholic Church began to assert itself more and more into the lives of its followers as it grew in influence, power and wealth; it became the only authority in defining Christian truth and compels obedience to its traditions, dogma and decrees. How can you ignore what Paul warns in Colossians 2:20-22 about "submitting to decrees?" And, in Matthew 15:6, Christ warns about "invalidating the Word of God for the sake of your traditions," and again in verse 9 where he says that such men "worship me in vain as they teach as doctrine the traditions of men."

Can't you people see that your popes and the rest of your officials are just sinful men who are violating what these Bible verses are saying to us? And this bogus claim that your popes represent some succession of the apostles is unsubstantiated in Scripture. Sure, Peter played a special role as an apostle, but he certainly wasn't thought of as their leader or the head of the new church because such clerical distinctions were foreign to the Word of God. Interpretation of Scripture is not the sole prerogative of any man or organization; the meaning of Scripture is made clear by the Holy Spirit to those who are enlightened of Christ and approach God's Word in a spirit of humility and teachableness. So then, the question is, are Catholics willing to learn from people who don't share their belief or their church affiliation?

Daniel: Support for Catholic theology and the Catholic Church is based on one claim: the Catholic Church is the only Christian church; it claims there is no invisible church.

It's obvious to me that the reason the Catholic Church asserts there is no distinction between the invisible and visible church is because the concept of the invisible church confuses its objective of declaring itself to be THE one, true, visible Christian church, THE ONE authority and proclaims that all other Christian denominations are heresies. The reformers were sensitive to the number of traditions the papacy had imposed on the doctrine of the original church and emphasized the existence of the invisible church to contrast its precepts with what the visible Roman Catholic Church had become over the centuries and why the Reformation was so necessary.

Ray: Luther attempted to destroy the one church in an effort to prioritize this mysterious invisible church. If Luther was right, why isn't everyone a Lutheran?

Darrel: For the same reason, we aren't all of any one denomination. God didn't proclaim that there would be just one denomination which represented the Christian church. As I said before, from a human standpoint, that would have been the ideal situation; but, from its beginning, the Christian church began to drift from the teachings of the apostles. Paul didn't set up a Catholic Church, he set up Christian churches in these regions, and he sent them letters to prevent them from drifting away from the gospel.

Ray: Okay, I'll bite, what good is an invisible church?

John: The invisible church sets the standard for the visible church. When the visible church is in synch with the invisible church, man sees things from God's perspective. The invisible church is the true church because it consists of true believers; it represents what the visible church ideally should be. In reality, however, all members of the visible church may not be true believers. This is what Augustine was referring to when he made the distinction between the visible and invisible church. We need to understand what God's church looks like from His perspective, not man's.

The invisible church with Christ as its head should always be before us as we go about the business of achieving the purpose on earth of the visible church. We should always stay focused on the precepts of the invisible church and understand that the purpose of the visible church is not to usurp the concept of the invisible church, but is to serve as the structure and organization that enables us to worship our triune God, to study and preach the Word of God, to administer the sacraments and for fellowship with other believers. As I said before, one church: two perspectives. We need both; our challenge is to keep them in balance. As with most important things in life, it's all about the balance. No visible church should ignore its obligation to reflect the invisible church, and we should not be so focused on the concept of the invisible church, we neglect our connection with our visible church.

Darrel: I'll say this again: There is one invisible church and many visible churches which represent the invisible church in truth and in spirit. Had God wanted there to be just one visible church on earth, there would have been just the one church; his will be done; but he didn't. I refer you to Acts 9:31 where Luke talks about the churches throughout all Judea, Galilee, and Samaria as having peace and being very enlightened. "And walking in the fear of the Lord and in the comfort of the Holy Spirit, they were multiplied."

Ray: Last week Darrel asked whether we Catholics are teachable; well, I ask the same question of you Protestants. Let's go over the handout Sonny passed out last session and see if you are teachable.

Darrel: Indoctrinated believers, like yourself and all other Catholics I've communicated with, are not open-minded because they are restricted from thinking on their own; they are taught to go to their church in all religious and spiritual matters. As we get further into these discussions and discover more and more about what Catholics believe and why they believe it, I have no doubt that we won't see that the extra-biblical traditions the Roman Catholic Church has embraced have absolutely no biblical support and were never included in the apostolic teachings. I hope to prove which Christian denomination is the heretic. I will prove your church's claim to be the original, apostolic church to be false.

Ray: And we welcome the opportunity to dispute that opinion and prove you all wrong. Everything we need to know is in our Catholic Church Catechism (CCC).

Bobby: Yes, in reviewing these handouts Sonny passed out, I see much of what I was taught in my Catechism classes. In addition to the Catechism, the Mass is the "authentic" summary of Catholic dogma. As Pope John Paul II said Catholics consider all this dogma "the sure norm" for teaching the faith. The Catechism is 752 pages long and you can see for yourselves how complicated Catholicism is. They have an explanation for everything!

Sonny: Yes, and that's what the Church is supposed to do; provide answers. Some of these answers are in the Bible, some of our tradition is written down, our sacred tradition, and some of it is not. The part that is not written down is our larger tradition and that records the community's experience of God or more specifically of Jesus Christ. It's unfolding.

It is revealed to us as "unraveling revelation" from our Magisterium to enlighten us with further knowledge. This is not new dogma; there's been no new dogma since the Apostle John died; the dogma proclaimed by the Magisterium is provided to enhance our understanding of what has been already revealed.

Darrel: This concept of unraveling revelation, considering popes to be descendants of the original apostles, interpreting oral traditions and so forth obviously gives your church a license to say anything it wants to say about Christianity, Sonny, and that's exactly what it does. Don't you see that? No Christian church is supposed to fill in the blanks God <u>intentionally</u> left in God's Word with their own traditions just to provide answers to questions God did not address in his Word. The Bible clearly states that God retains knowledge he doesn't choose to share with us, and we must not try and put words in his mouth, okay? In looking at these handouts which tell us what Catholics are taught in catechism, it's obvious there is dogma like listing the Seven Deadly Sins that is unique to Catholicism.

It's also obvious that the Catholic Church goes into all this unbiblical detail in an attempt to fulfill its self-serving interest by being the ultimate, sole authority in the lives of its followers. A Catholic has to go to his church as the sole authority for anything spiritual. Catholics have no other choice because the Catholic Church has made the dogma so complicated, <u>it's created a need for itself</u> as the only source of explanation of its own dogma. Of course, inquiring minds want to know so then here comes the masters of the magisterium of the Catholic Church to the rescue. If it doesn't know the answer, another church council will be convened, and an answer will be forthcoming by decree based on more unraveling revelation of tradition. The unraveling revelation is actually unraveling inspiration as the Catholic Church is inspired from time to time to provide more answers to its followers' relevant questions and concerns.

Daniel: As I look this list over, there just seems to be a lot of descriptive details about sin.

Sonny: Yes, Catholicism focuses on explaining sin. Our Church has historically recognized that there are these two different forms of sin: Mortal and Venial. Mortal sin is a deliberately intended act that is so serious in its nature, that it constitutes a radial rejection of Christ and His sacrifice for us, and ruptures our relationship with God. It cuts off a person from God's grace and takes us out of the state of salvation. Venial sin, on the other hand, is an act that, while sinful and harms our relationship with God, is not so serious that it takes us out of a state of grace. Such a sin does not formally entail destroying our union with God.

Darrel: There is absolutely no biblical support for dividing sin into these two categories, Sonny.

Sonny: See 1 John 5:17 where the apostle tells us that there is a sin not leading to death and a sin leading to death. "All unrighteousness is sin, and there is sin not leading to death." The sin leading to death is a mortal sin, and the sin not leading to death is a venial sin.

John: Well, since we know from Scripture that none of the sins of the true Christian leads to death except the sin of blasphemy of the Holy Spirit or to a person's stubborn refusal to accept the gospel, that must be the sin leading to death John is referring to. There is no mention of mortal or venial sins in God's Word. In its context, we see that in this verse, John is referring to the sin of ignoring God's Word as He describes how our sin separates us from Him and our subsequent need to repent and accept His offer of forgiveness.

Darrel: This division of degree of sin is another example of how Catholicism has yielded to apostasy. In claiming there is one type of sin that is not so serious that they take the sinner out of a state of grace, it minimizes sin. The Bible tells us that all sin is bad; they all offend God. The only two types of sin the Bible addresses are those sins which are outwardly committed when we do something to violate either God's law or the law of the land, and the secret sins which are the inward hatred, envy, covetousness and other attitudes that God forbids but that our neighbors cannot see. Regardless of how you try and categorize sin, the point is that all sin is bad, and if we intend to grow spiritually, we must prioritize putting all of our sins to death.

Daniel: I see there are four sins crying to heaven for vengeance. **1.** Willful murder (including abortion). **2.** The sin of Sodom. **3.** Oppression of the poor. **4.** Defrauding laborers of their wages. There are six sins against the Holy Spirit: **1.** Presumption of God's mercy. **2.** Despair. **3.** Impugning the known truth. **4.** Envy at another's spiritual good. **5.** Obstinancy in sin. **6.** Final impenitence. And finally, on the subject of sin classification, there are nine ways of being accessory to another's sin: By counsel, by command, by consent, by provocation, by praise or flattery, by concealment, by partaking, by silence, by defense of the ill done. Whew! It must be impossible to keep all these distinctions straight. It sure seems that there are a lot of terms used that I don't fully understand.

Sonny: To be honest with you, there are a number of them on this list that are confusing to me too. But, my priest knows what they all mean, and I rely on him to know which category my sin fits into in my confession to him.

Darrel: Ah, yes, another job for the church leadership; it creates a job for itself. Of course the priest also knows which is the proper penance and indulgence associated with the particular sin, right? Wow, no wonder even Luther had issues over this routine. Of course, we know that one fine day he read Romans 1:17 where Paul quotes the prophet Habbukuk,"The righteous shall live by their faith," and the rest was history, as they say. Luther understood that we don't obtain righteousness before God by following all the rituals and traditions and obedience to all these rules and observing the appropriate penance, we are declared righteous by our faith in the value and meaning of Christ's atoning sacrifice, and do not need to follow the church's required procedures.

Daniel: We're not done yet with Sonny's list. Following an explanation of the types of sins is a listing of the Seven Capital Virtues that are necessary to overcome the Seven Deadly Sins. I'll just read the list: The virtues are: humility, generosity, chastity, meekness, temperance, brotherly love, and diligence; and the Three Theological Virtues are faith, hope and charity and the Four Cardinal Virtues are justice, prudence, fortitude and temperance. The Seven Gifts of the Holy Spirit are wisdom, understanding, fortitude, counsel, knowledge, piety and fear of the Lord. Of course, every Christian should be familiar with the Twelve Fruits of the Holy Spirit Paul mentions in Galatians: charity, joy, peace, patience, kindness, goodness, long-suffering, mildness, faith, modesty, continence, chastity. Then we have the Seven Spiritual Works of Mercy, to admonish the sinner, to instruct the ignorant, to counsel the doubtful, to comfort the sorrowful, to bear wrongs patiently, to forgive all injuries, to pray for the living and the dead. Then there are the Seven Corporal Works of Mercy: To feed the hungry, to give drink to the thirsty, to clothe the naked, to visit the imprisoned, to shelter the homeless, to visit the sick and to bury the dead. And, last but not least, the Seven Sacraments are listed: Baptism, confirmation, Holy Communion, (the Eucharist), confession, marriage, Holy Orders (ordination) and anointing of the sick (Last Rites). There are also the five precepts of the Church: **1.** Attend Mass on Sundays and on holy days of obligation and rest from servile labor. **2.** Confess your sins at least once a year. **3.** Receive the sacrament of the Eucharist at least during the Easter season. **4.** Observe the days of fasting and abstinence established by the Church. **5.** Provide for the needs of the Church. Even though some of the items on this list are not biblically supported, I'm sure all Christians would agree on the truth and importance of the tenets in this list. The issue I have with it is that all these requirements evidence that

Catholicism is much more legalistic than Protestantism; even the hint of legalism must be avoided; we are to emphasize the gospel over the law.

John: I recall you saying before, Sonny, that the way you worship is the way you believe. Well, I say that what one believes, one acts on. A person's actions should be consistent with their stated beliefs, and so the challenge for every Christian is to be charitable, faithful, joyful, peaceful, kind, humble, good, long-suffering, to comfort the sick, forgive others, feed the hungry, pray for the living (not the dead), exercise justice, mercy, prudence, fortitude, and temperance, etc. The items on your list that reinforce biblical principles are of course good for all of us to read and follow. The problem though with such a list is that it indicates a focus on doing these good works as a necessary requirement for good standing in the Catholic Church and implies that such good works are indeed a necessary aspect to being saved. In defining two types of sin, categorizing certain virtues as being cardinal virtues, defining what gifts are from the Holy Spirit, listing the spiritual works of mercy and so on, Catholicism is presuming on God's Word because none of this dogma is mentioned in Scripture. We can all appreciate the focus on being virtuous, but we must remember that works are a product of our salvation, not a requirement and your catechism can be misleading in that regard. Secular Ben Franklin compiled such a list and resolved to practice a different virtue on his list each day of the week. He finally gave up in frustration. It's either in your heart to automatically practice virtue or it is not.

Although Protestants of course are certainly aware of the fruits of the spirit, the virtues that Paul lists in Galatians, we presume a Christian will be virtuous because it is not only consistent with what we believe, but obedience is really our only option if we actually possess a true, saving faith. We believe that *we act, therefore we are*. Catholics, like all other works-based belief systems believe *they are because they act*. Protestants believe that practicing these virtues defines who we are, the elect who have been chosen to be saved. The acts don't save us. Big difference!

Sonny: When we practice these virtues listed, we prove ourselves worthy before Christ.

Darrel: We don't have to prove anything to Christ. He knows who are his, and he knows what's in every person's heart. Although we owe him everything, it isn't like we have some debt to pay off. That's what Mormons believe; that's bad company.

John: We Protestants believe that the whole point of the gospel is that Jesus died for the unworthy, for sinners of all kinds. The Bible tells us that while we were yet sinners, Christ died for us. That is the good news of the gospel. So then, we should know that we need not make ourselves worthy before Christ, and even so, we lack the ability to act worthy anyway. You know that the Bible tells us we are all sinners and unable to act right before God; we can therefore not make ourselves worthy even if we were able to consistently practice each and every one of the virtues your catechism lists.

Ray: Have any of you ever talked to a priest about this?

Darrel: I would rather hear from the consumer, like you Catholics, than from a salesman for the product; and anyway, I don't trust a salesman who has to sell his product or be fired (ex-communicated) to tell me the truth. His job is to sell the church objective in promoting its importance by developing dogma through man-made tradition that addresses man's need to follow a strong leader, to be a member of some exclusive club and to be partially in charge of his own salvation. He promotes the church as being the sole authority to be trusted in order to seal the deal.

Yes, we should fear for our salvation in the sense we recognize how important it is to understand our real role in God's plan of salvation, but we should fear more the Catholic Church and its heretical doctrine because it's the wrong theology. Catholicism focuses on the church over the gospel. That's been my contention all along in these discussions.

Ray: How would you know, Darrel? Have you ever been to a Mass?

Darrel: Many, many years ago. The service is liturgical and I like that.

John: So do I. Lutherans conduct a liturgical service too.

Ray: We believe that to miss Mass is committing a mortal sin

Darrel: Well then, I would assume the majority of Catholics have committed a mortal sin then.

Look, man, the Catholic catechism is so complicated, it's impossible to pay heed to all of what it requires for a Catholic to be considered devout. Even your "super-Christians," your clergy, screw it up from time to time. But, of course, the Catholic Church knows this. In organizing the catechism and its requirements and dogma, the Catholic Church creates a use for itself; followers have to keep coming back to it to stay on the catechism track. It has made room for itself. You thus have no time to read any books about Christianity. I'll bet you've never even read Augustine's *City of God* or Aquinas' *Summa Theologica*. These are theologians who are Catholics (the only Christian church in their day) and you even call them saints. Remember when I said that their beliefs are actually more Protestant than the Catholicism of today?

Sonny: I doubt that, Darrel. And how would you know? Have you read these books?

Darrel: Yes, I have. In fact, I've read many of the books John has listed in his bibliography on his *the-cabana-chronicles.com* website. I assume you just have the one book, your catechism, listed in your bibliography. When would have the time to do anything else?

Bobby: Remember to be civil to our guest, Darrel. Mocking people isn't polite. Remember that you're all supposed to be Christians, right? Who's the real enemy here?

John: Paul states in Ephesians 6:12 that we do not "wrestle against flesh and blood, but against principalities, against powers, against the rulers of the darkness of this age, against spiritual hosts of wickedness in the heavenly places."

Bobby: Good quote. In fact, this second handout Sonny gave us points to a number of similarities between what Catholics believe and what Protestants believe, does it not?

Daniel: Yes, and, in fact, that is why we consider Catholics to be our brothers and sisters in Christ. The question is do you consider us to be brothers and sisters in Christ? What about you, Sonny, do you consider us Protestants to be brothers in Christ?

Sonny: Believe it or not, I've never been asked that question. I'll take a rain check on my answer if you don't mind. We'll see how the discussion goes before I can give you a definitive answer.

Darrel: I see; it depends on whether we meet your conditions or not, eh? Why don't you accept us as fellow Christians, Ray? Do you think we heretics are saved?

Ray: You have to be a Catholic to go to heaven. The Church clearly teaches that there is no salvation outside the Church. The Catechism teaches there is no salvation apart from Christ and His One, Holy, Catholic, and Apostolic Church. Those who are invincibly ignorant concerning this truth will not be culpable for this lack of knowledge before God. These people have the real possibility of salvation even if they never come to an explicit knowledge of Christ and/or His Church.

Sonny: We can't say for sure, of course, what God will do for those outside the Church, so it's best not to presume to judge. We can only hope and pray that God will have mercy on them.

Darrel: We all need God's mercy, but we understand his grace and believe what the gospel tells us, that salvation is through Christ and him crucified, not the necessity of belonging to any man-made institution.

John: This term you used, Ray is new to me. What is "invincible ignorance?"

Ray: Invincible ignorance is applied to those people who, through no fault of their own, do not know the gospel of Christ or His Church, but nevertheless seek God with a sincere heart, and, moved by grace, try in their actions to do His will as they know it through the dictates of their conscience. These people may achieve eternal salvation. Vincible ignorance applies to those people who have a reason to believe that what the Catholic Church believes is God's requirement and he or she ignores that reality. This is ignorance for which a person is responsible. I refer you to Romans 2:14-15 and John 15:22.

Daniel: So then, I assume we Protestants fall into that vincible ignorance category, right?

Ray: Yes; but it's not too late to return to the fold.

Darrel: As Christ gathers his sheep, the papacy gathers its goats.

Daniel: We Protestants have confidence in God's invincible favor, His amazing, undeserved grace in Christ. We have a good reason to believe what the gospel teaches, and we believe that is our only qualification for our salvation. Of course, we aren't obligated to fit some church institution into our spiritual life. As with almost every aspect of their doctrine, the Catholic Church adds itself to the requirement, just as Ray has stated in adding the words "or his Church" meaning of course the Catholic Church.

Ray: All I can say is that the condition of vincible ignorance only applies to those who know that the Catholic Church is the true Church, not to those who don't know that this is who we are. These people are suffering from invincible ignorance; they are ignorant through no fault of their own.

Daniel: I of course know your church, but I don't believe it's the true Christian church; so then, am I saved or not?

Ray: No.

Sonny: Does one need to be a Catholic to be saved? No. Does one need to be a member of the Body of Christ to be saved? Yes.

Daniel: But of course, you have both said that the Catholic Church represents the true body of Christ, so then, that means you agree with Ray's answer; you're just being more polite.

I believe we are saved through our belief in the invisible church of Christ; you believe we can only be saved through our allegiance to THE visible church, which you are convinced is the Roman Catholic Church. Am I right?

Ray: Yes. But, as I say, anyone who knows we are the true Church and rejects us is damned; most people don't know this.

Daniel: Did you know that Mormons believe you have to be a member in good standing of their church to go to the highest heaven? The same belief is expressed in Islam. No mosque, no possibility of ever getting to know those 99 virgins in paradise.

John: It seems like Mormons have taken some of their doctrine from Catholicism. They believe that their church is the only true church and that salvation can only come through them. Jehovah's Witnesses believe this too. Mormons also believe in additional sacred scripture, apostolic succession, use images in their churches, have accumulated great wealth and power and believe in good works to earn salvation. We Protestants consider false religions like Islam and false cults like Mormons to be our contrarian indicators. As Christians, we should understand that salvation only comes through Christ, not some particular visible church. Even though, Catholics have been indoctrinated to believe that their church has some unique, mystical connection with Christ, that shouldn't inspire their leaders to damn everyone who isn't a Catholic.

Daniel: I don't think that's not what these guys are saying. I think they're implying we need to somehow recognize that they are the one, true Christian church, and then, if we still reject their claim, we will be condemned.

Darrel: Sure, sure, their focus is on what we know about Catholicism, but I wonder what these guys really know about what we Protestants believe.

Ray: We know you are heretics. I'm just not sure how deep that runs until we get further into these discussions of our respective doctrines.

John: Well, you should know that we consider you folks to be the ones who have opposed the doctrine of the original church, but we still believe you are our brothers in Christ because we know you believe Christ is God and He is our savior.

The actual beliefs of the original, apostolic church will serve as the ultimate gold standard for what the Christian church is meant to be. That was Christ's intent, and that should be our objective. So then, as we compare our Protestant beliefs to the beliefs of the original apostolic church in these discussions, we hope to provide you with evidence which backs our claim that our reformed, Bible-believing Protestant churches represent a restoration of the beliefs and doctrine of the original, apostolic church Christ mandated be established, and that it is indeed your church whose beliefs have drifted away from the apostolic teachings.

Darrel: Jesus faced the same dilemma we face now with the various churches John addressed in the book of Revelation. Like the Catholic Church, these churches had, in one way or another, all gone astray to some extent and John records Christ's reprimands to them. In the first century, it was some of the Jewish religious leaders who opposed the apostolic teachings. They believed they were the guardians of God's Word, and that the Hebrew Bible was subject to their interpretation. This new group of religious zealots was considered to be heretical. But Jesus addressed their belief and claimed to be the authority by stating the three simple words he used to respond to Satan's temptations: "It is written." These words appear over 90 times in the New Testament. He claimed the authority over them in stating that they were "mistaken, not understanding the power of God and the Scriptures, " thus nullifying the Word of God by their traditions, and asking them "Have you not read?" We can only know the incarnate Word of God by reading the written Word of God that was given to us by the apostles of Jesus who wrote of Christ with the inspirations and guidance of the Holy Spirit. Luther's intention was to remind the Catholic Church that Christ was the authority and not them.

Ray: Christ gave the authority to the Church through its leaders who succeeded the apostles.

Darrel: Not so. Your church appropriated the authority Christ intended for the Christian church.

John: We can see here that it really comes down to the question of authority in interpreting what the Bible is saying to us about our religion.

Darrel: I am no expert on the psychology of authority, but it sure seems to me that many of those people raised in the Catholic tradition who do not reject it are people who have a psychological need for authority; they prefer some institutional authority figure to tell them what to believe. They also prefer ritualistic rules and regulations to follow.

Sonny: You're speculating, Darrel. What are you a psychologist?

Darrel: Of course not; although I will say that I majored in psychology in college and it is a hobby of mine. There is a psychology of religion. Human behavior is important in every aspect of our lives, every belief we have, every reason we have to believe what we believe.

John: Actually, Darrel's right. There are psychological as well as philosophical and theological reasons why people choose one Christian denomination over another. In the case of Catholicism, some psychologists do refer to the relationship between church and members as an example of a classic co-dependency. The Catholic Church organization is determined to promote itself as an indispensable authority in the lives of its followers; it discourages private interpretation of the Bible and has developed traditions designed to further its cause.

Psychologist, Carl Jung, a disciple of Freud's, talked about man's "craving for ritual and tradition." Catholicism's elevating the priesthood to a sacrament, advocating the need for the church to be an intermediary in prayer and in administration of Holy Communion, performing the "sacrament" of the Mass, requiring priests in hearing member's confession, dispensing indulgences and penance, and performing last rites, etc. are all examples of its extra-biblical, add-on traditions. I want to talk more about each of these traditions later on in our discussions.

Darrel: Throughout its history, such traditions have also served Catholic Church in marketing Christianity to the uneducated and impoverished folks who aren't focused on leading an examined life who need a more graphic and visual illustration of our religion to best understand its meaning. Most people in the world don't lead an examined life and most people in the world are followers who depend on authoritative leadership to know what they believe to be true; and many people just don't want to grow up and take the initiative in understanding the Bible and theological concepts. Catholics seem to just stop learning after they've been indoctrinated in Catholicism through their catechism.

Theologian Karl Barth once said that the two greatest sins were sloth (referring to spiritual laziness) and pride. In Catholicism, it's obvious from these discussions your pride is showing. You show your sloth by refusing to exert the effort <u>to grow up in your faith.</u> It takes work to learn more and more about our wonderful religion as we progress through life in our sanctification. It seems Catholics need a church to be their parent.

People don't seem to want to grow up. We live in a society where folks want to delay the process of maturing into adulthood; those on welfare treat their government like a parent, and Catholics relate to their church in the same way. You people have your church family with your priests you call "Father" and the ultimate title for your pope, "Holy Father" and, of course there's also "Mother Mary," right?

Ray: Yes. Our mother is our Church. Our Catechism (CCC 1367) states that "No one can have God as Father who does not have the Church as Mother."

Darrel: You're an adult, Ray, why would you need a parent to take care of you? And besides, remember that Christ said that if we are to be worthy of him, we should focus more on him than on our parents. (Matthew 10:37). Your church's insistence on a co-dependent, family relationship with its members is in direct opposition to what Christ said in Luke 14:26 and Matthew 10:37 when he said his disciples are to leave their families to follow Him. In Luke 14:26, he even used the word "hate" your families and follow me. So then, it's time to grow up, man, and leave your parental church and follow Christ.

Protestantism is a more mature denomination because it encourages independence and personal responsibility. We're mature enough to handle our Christian liberty. Catholics need to be dependent on their church, relying on some authority to do your work for you to read and understand God's Word. You either agree with the church interpretation or you are damned as a heretic and anathema. As I say, it's slothful to remain immature and delegate all religious authority and responsibility to some church masters of the magisterium to read and interpretation of God's Word to you. Pride rears its ugly head when you assert that your church is the only Christian church when the rest of the world merely sees it as another Christian denomination. Ironically, Catholics are limiting themselves in the pursuit of truth as they pridefully assert that they, and they alone, possess it.

Ray: Nonsense! We certainly recognize our duty as Catholics. If the rejection of Protestant's personal interpretation of Scripture is prideful and slothful then that's what we are, and that applies to you people as well because you pridefully reject our Church's dogma.

Darrel: It isn't prideful to oppose what we believe is bad theology, Ray.

So you have a duty to perform the rituals and obey the traditions of your vaunted church; this is how you make yourselves worthy to Christ. Duty for us Protestants means our duty to glorify God in practicing a doctrine solely based on his Word. R. C. Sproul once said that all Christians should be theologians; we should all know God. That should be our only duty. Catholics prioritize obedience to church dogma over learning the true theology of the Christian religion. This is not what our God wants us believers to do.

Ray: That's ridiculous! Our almost 2,000 year old Church tells us what God wants, Darrel. Protestants have all these denominations each telling their followers what God wants.

Darrel: Back to that approach again, eh? Yes, we have different denominations, but only those which preach and teach biblical doctrine are credible. All others are false. We seek God's truth, and won't let a church get in the way of accomplishing our objective.

John: Over the centuries of its existence, the Catholic Church has designed its own theology to meet the wants of man. As I said before, we should choose a church that supports our theology and not base our choice on anything else. The theology is the steak, traditions, rituals, and architecture of buildings are the sizzle. While they're important, they should not be the determining factor in our choice of which church denomination to support. Catholicism appeals to those who treasure traditions because traditions are a short-cut to knowledge. The church appeals to our natural inclination to want our good works to be of some value; it appeals to those who are interested in art and architecture; it appeals to those who want to enhance their emotional experience in their connection with Christ through its pomp, and the emotion in experiencing the Eucharist; it appeals to our natural inclination to want a second chance (purgatory). The Catholic Church addresses these natural concerns of ours by adding to God's Word, and they get away with it because the majority of Catholics I've attempted to discuss theology with don't know what their theology is nor what the Bible tells them about the theology of the apostolic teachings.

Darrel: Good point, John. Yes, Catholicism gives its *theologically-challenged* followers all they want. As we have said, most people are followers and want a strong, authoritative leader to guide them, the Catholic Church gives them the papacy and a hierarchy of special, saintly, churchy leaders, with presumed sole authority and infallibility; it even makes the ordination of such individuals a sacraments, as though it was ordained by Christ; followers are given a father figure in the pope and a mother figure in this strange veneration of Mary, the mother of Jesus. As we go along in these discussions and learn more and more about Catholicism, we should keep this psychological aspect of this denomination in mind. We should be skeptics in looking at the motives for the Catholic Church and the motives of its loyal followers, and hopefully, you two Catholics will be motivated to see it this way.

Sonny: There's a psychology to Protestantism too; fallen man is a born rebel. The reformers rebelled against the Church, and you continue to rebel now.

John: The reformers rebelled against what the Catholic Church had become, and we continue to follow their lead. We Protestants practice what C. S. Lewis called "mere Christianity." No "yeah, buts," just straightforward faith in Christ without the necessity of a church authority telling us what to believe. We know we are purified through the sacrificial atonement of Christ. Period.

Daniel: But "mere Christianity" doesn't leave any purpose for some church to claim for itself. If Christ is all that's necessary for salvation, where does that leave the Catholic Church? In asserting itself as sole authority and sole requirement for our salvation. It's like "Father knows best" making "Room for Daddy," as Darrel said before. Throughout its entire history from almost its very beginning, the Catholic Church has devised these sacred traditions and continuing revelation to find a way to make itself useful and important to its followers. In addition to giving folks parents, it gave them Christ himself through the usurped authority of their pope whom they call "Vicar of Christ; "vicar" means substitute.

John: There's actually a philosophical component to what the Catholic Church has done with the Christian religion. The philosopher Georg Wilhelm Friedrick Hegel taught that God is constantly evolving and that his last and most important evolution is in the state itself. God is in the state. As we know, in its history, the Catholic Church and the state were one and the same, and, as Darrel said before, as a relic of the Holy Roman Empire, the Catholic Church still represents itself to be like a state which is to be revered by its followers who still pay homage to their church as though they considered it to be like an empire. You Catholics have provided evidence of this reverent connection with your church in every remark or statement you have made so far in these discussions. In referring to itself as Christ's substitute, it is implying the state and God are all but identical and that believers should look to it and it alone for their very salvation. That's pure Hegelian reasoning.

Sonny: You guys have each attacked my Church from a variety of angles. John brought up the psychological aspect of weak people wanting a strong leader, a church that plays to men's desires and emotions; Darrel has attacked us from a historical perspective, claiming we gradually transitioned into an institution over the centuries, and our Church has abused its power and influence; and then John tacked on this philosophical component with the reference to Hegel's belief. Daniel, you have chimed in with references to our assumed lack of contentment and our need for parents. But, you people have overlooked that the Catholic Church was the only Christian church until the sixteenth century and therefore was singularly responsible for preaching the gospel which addressed man's <u>need</u> for salvation. Give it some credit.

John: Point well taken, Sonny. But, if the Catholic Church had just stayed the course and continued to be the light for God's truth instead of creating a papacy and sacred, unbiblical traditions, the Reformation would not have been necessary, and the Christian church would be the stronger for it.

Darrel: If the Catholic Church had just let the Apostle Peter be; if it had just left Mary be; neither of these folks ever aspired to the position and purpose your church has designated for them. If your church had just let the Bible remain the one, true authority of our religion, we would all be better off. When it strayed, it necessitated the division that Satan loves.

Bobby: When I was a Catholic, the Church was our sole figure of authority. Under threat of excommunication and hell itself, we were required to attend Mass on a regular basis. We were required to confess our sins to a priest at least once a year. We were also to pray to the Virgin Mary to offer our prayers to God. We were required to depend on the Church for forgiveness of our sin, for administration of the sacraments for worship in the Mass, for effective prayers, and for interpreting the meaning of Scripture; and the Church depends on its members to attend worship service, tithe, and basically depend on them as the ultimate authority as it enjoys all the advantages that such influence and power offer.

Darrel: Correct. That's what we've been saying; it's what a classic co-dependency looks like.

Sonny: We need the church in order to receive the life giving sacraments that emanate from its central form of worship, the Mass. Nowhere else can I obtain these spiritual benefits.

John: We rely on our church to administer the sacrament of baptism and Holy Communion too, but, from what you've indicated in these discussions so far and from what I have surmised from my many conversations with my Catholic friends, Protestants have a different relationship with their churches than Catholics have with theirs. We know that we're to attend church on a regular basis to worship God, to hear the Word, to pray, ask for forgiveness of our sin, to fellowship, and to receive God's blessing on us through the sacrament of Holy Communion. We know we are to be regular attendees because we need for our church to be our constant companion for the whole journey of our life. We are the family of God and our deep commitment to and active participation in the church is nonnegotiable. A pastor of mine once told me that the likelihood that a member of the visible church is also a member of the invisible church of Christ is not as great as the likelihood that a member of the invisible church will also be a member of a visible church which represents that invisible church. The difference is that we are not mandated to follow rules, traditions, and rituals to make ourselves worthy to Christ. Our connection with our churches is motivated by our inherent desire to worship our God in truth and in spirit. Catholics connect with their church out of obligation and a need for authority.

Bobby: I left the Catholic Church because I couldn't accept the authority and the legalism and all the traditions.

Ray: You shouldn't have done that, Bobby. Now you're on the outside looking in.

Bobby: Into what? Some fricken abyss of confusion and discontent? I am relieved of the burden of following all the rules and regs imposed by the traditions, rituals, ceremonies and going to Mass every day of the week or feel like an outcast before God and man.

John: Luther left the Catholic Church he obviously remained a Christian, a more pure, biblical form; you threw the baby out with the bathwater and became an agnostic.

Ray: In desiring your freedom, you have become enslaved to sin, Bobby. You need to return to the authority of the Church to guide and direct you in your spiritual life and serve as your defender against Satan's power.

Bobby: Thanks for being concerned about my spiritual welfare, guys, but I'm here to learn, not to be chastised or reprimanded. As I say, that's the main reason I left the Catholic Church.

Darrel: As John implied, the Catholic Church needs you more than you need it, Bobby. You can join a Protestant church and be guided in the truth.

John: I'm not so sure the relationship between the Catholic Church and its members represents a classic co-dependency, Darrel, but I do believe that Catholics place an inordinate amount of trust in their vaunted church as their sole religious authority. Such allegiance can serve to distract us from our main purpose, to glorify God. We Protestants claim Christ is the authority in interpreting God's Word. We base our claim on the Bible which reveals to us that Jesus told his followers he would leave an interpreter, the Holy Spirit, to continue to interpret God's Word. This belief is consistent with what Jesus said in John 16:13-15: "When the Spirit of truth has come, He will guide you into all truth; for He will not speak on His own authority, but whatever He hears He will speak; and He will tell you things to come. He will glorify Me, for He will take of what is Mine, and declare it to you. All things that the Father has are Mine. Therefore, I said that He (the Holy Spirit) will take of Mine and declare it to you." We believe the Bible is God's only Word to us, and the Holy Spirit has not only guided the New Testament writers in preparing the new written revelation that would take its place beside the Old Testament, but will also interpret the meaning of Scripture; the Bible is our only authority. James 1:5 tells us that if we believe we lack wisdom, we are to pray to God to receive it and He will give it to us.

Sonny: We of course believe that Christ gave authority to the Church to teach God's word.

Darrel: And does God's word include your made-up traditions too?

Sonny: Yes, but they aren't made-up. They were revealed through our Church and, as I said before are considered to be equal in authority to the Bible because they are all based on apostolic teaching and inspired by the Holy Spirit.

Darrel: Really? I'm sure you know that none of the apostles ever referred to any of these traditions of yours.

Sonny: Not everything has been recorded in Scripture. There were those apostolic teachings and traditions that are oral and not recorded in the

Bible, and there are some that were written in the heart of the Church by the Holy Spirit.

Darrel: Which means, of course, that your Catholic Church has granted itself open license to come up with any tradition it wants to introduce into the Christian religion on its own churchy authority, right? It can make up its own beliefs which may or may not coincide with what the Bible is saying to us. Trust me, I'm your bishop? Is that so different than the way cult leaders connect with their followers? Trust me, I'm Joseph Smith.

Ray: That's ridiculous to compare us with the Mormon religion.

Darrel: Is it really? You have your vaunted, revered Catholic Church organization; Mormons had Joseph Smith; you have your Church as your sole authority; Smith represented the same to the Mormon followers; you have your traditions; Mormons have theirs. I could go on and on, but I think I made my point.

Sonny: Mormons and other false religions and cults do not have the Holy Spirit's guidance through the leaders in our Church because they don't even believe in the triune God.

Daniel: Good point. Christ said in John 14:26, that "the Counselor, the Holy Spirit, whom the Father will send in my name, will teach you all things and will remind you of everything I have said to you." Mormons and other cults who don't understand who Christ really is can never be in commune with the Holy Spirit who was sent in His name. This same spirit Christ referred to guides all Bible-believing Christians; the difference is that we believe the Holy Spirit guides us individually. There is no individuality in Catholicism; everything goes through the church.

Ray: Our Church functions as the Holy Spirit; the Spirit communicates with our Magisterium.

Darrel: Protestants don't elevate our church to such a status; nor should we; there's no biblical support for us to do that. Our church doesn't act as a substitute for God for us. We don't need it to do that for us. You people apparently do. Your church won't just settle for being a conduit for guidance from God; it wants to be seen as the sole authority on what you're supposed to believe. I think the most damaging and most heretical tradition your church has added to your version of the Christian doctrine was when the Council of Trent in 1545 affirmed that all these traditions were to be considered as equal in authority to the very Word of God, the Holy Bible. Your church had its chance to get it right and blew it, man. Instead of dumping the extra-biblical stuff, it supported its apostasy.

Sonny: This is important, so please pay attention. You Protestants display a wide variety of different doctrines, and each claims to believe in the teachings of *sola scriptura*, the idea that we must use only the Bible when forming our theology; but there is so much more to Christian theology than the Bible. When Christians separated from the Catholic Church, they deprived themselves of the rich traditions of the Church and exposed yourselves to all sorts of different doctrines because you have no one authority besides your Bible; and we know that the Bible can be interpreted in many different ways. This is why you people have formed so many different denominations. This diversity of Protestant doctrines stems from the doctrine of private judgment, which denies the infallible authority of the Church and claims that each individual is to interpret Scripture for himself. This Christian liberty of yours has led you astray of the truth.

Darrel: One authority is best only when it's infallible, and yours is fallible because you vaunted church veered away from the teachings of the apostles in implementing its own traditions many of which contradicted the teachings of the apostles. At least one Catholic publically protested this "Doctrine of Papal Infallibility" issued by Vatican I. Nineteenth century British historian Lord Acton stated that he could not accept this declared dogma, and that "we are to judge Pope and King unlike other men, with a favourable presumption that they did not wrong. If there is any presumption it is the other way, against the holders of power, increasing as the power increases. Historic responsibility has to make up for the want of legal responsibility. Power tends to corrupt and absolute power corrupts absolutely."

Catholicism has had a negative effect on history. On the other hand, Protestant Christianity has had a positive effect on our history. The idea that people should be ruled by words inscribed on paper and not by men's pronouncements comes from our doctrine of *sola Scriptura;* the idea that citizens should be governed by those chosen by them from among them (electing elders and deacons) and not by some pope comes from our concept of Christian liberty. The idea that there should not be a royal, privileged class is directly related to our concept of all believers as saints and priests.

Catholics mean to discredit the value of "diversity," but the flip side is that it can strengthen our belief in the truth because opinions are tested and the truth will out. Your reference to diversity reminds me of a somewhat similar word I've used when I refer to the Catholic Church, the word "diversion." We believe in the infallibility of the Holy Spirit to guide us in our understanding of God's Word and see the Catholic Church as diverting its members from the gospel truth in the pursuit of its own interests. Our diversity is unified under the Spirit's guidance which insures we will always be on the same page in knowing God's truth as expressed in the theology of the Reformation.

Sonny: It is you Protestants who are subject to being led astray of God's truth. Your own individual self-interest acts as a diversion from knowing the gospel truth. That's what Peter is saying in 2 Peter 1:20 when he rejects private interpretation. He tells us the first rule of Bible interpretation is to understand that no prophecy of Scripture is a matter of one's own interpretation. A significant feature of this heresy is the attempt to pit the Church against the Bible, denying that the Magisterium has an infallible authority to teach and interpret Scripture. Augustine once said, "For my part, I should not believe the gospel except as moved by the authority of the Catholic Church."

John: I remind you that Augustine was a bishop in the only Christian church existing in the fifth century, and he wasn't referring to all your traditions because most of them were added after he died. He is not saying the Catholic Church has the authority to <u>create</u> Scripture, just to act as a trusted guide in interpreting Scripture just as Darrel said before when he surmised that our church should always be used as our guide to interpreting God's Word. That said, I believe you have brought up several points that I think should be addressed, so let's take them one at a time to avoid confusion. Regarding your comment about Peter warning not to rely on private interpretation, when we read a few verses before 2 Peter 1:20, Peter warns us not to follow "cleverly invented stories," and "to pay attention to the word of the prophets, as to a light shining in a dark place," we should recognize what your Catholic Church has done to our religion by adding all those sacred traditions to God's Word as spoken through the prophets. Unless you are telling us we need to consider your priests, bishops and popes as prophets, and I don't think you would even try to make that presumption.

Regarding your reference to the number of Protestant denominations, we've already responded to that comment; however many there may be, those that claim to believe in the five *solas* and adhere to the creeds are, by definition, <u>reformed and unified</u>. You could say that while all Reformed churches are Protestant, not all Protestant churches are reformed. There is obvious unity in the Reformed churches.

Sonny: But you're always squabbling with each other over doctrine.

John: As I said before, Protestants are more democratic and less authoritative in our church organizations, and this is a good thing because it encourages an open mind in believers.

Sure, there's some differences of opinions among our reformed churches but, most of them involve "majoring in the minors" over what constitutes the true reformed doctrine. Theologian Dr. Keith A. Mathison says, "the debate over the meaning of the word *reformed* is a wonderful opportunity for those on all sides to dig deeper into Scripture and into the riches of our theological heritage which exercising the charity and patience encouraged by that heritage itself."

Sonny: The Catholic Church is your Christian heritage. Believers were Catholic before they became Protestants. Can't you see that?

John: Again with the "we came first" routine. Sure, this was the reality when there was only the one Christian church, but, as we've said before, over the centuries, the Catholic Church has shirked its responsibility to represent the invisible church of Christ; in its pursuit of its own self-interest, it blew Christ's mandate. It left us, not the other way around. When I look at what the Catholic Church has become over the centuries and study its beliefs and organization, I see why Martin Luther and the other reformers risked their lives to oppose a church in need of reform; a church that needs to be brought back to that original Christian heritage as defined by the teachings of the apostles.

Sonny: Yeah, brought back to your 30,000 Protestant church denominations.

Bobby: But don't Catholics have a variety of different churches? In catechism class, I was taught there was the Armenian Catholic Church, the Belarusian Catholic Church, the Ukranian Greek Catholic Church and so on. I believe there were over 20 of them, right?

Sonny: The Catholic Church is one body composed of ecclesial communities, a multitude of local or particular Churches; but they are all in full communion with Rome.

Darrel: I'm sorry, did you just say "Rome?" I thought you didn't want to be identified with Rome.

Sonny: In this instance, I wanted to distinguish between the Roman Catholic Church and the Greek Orthodox Church.

Darrel: Yes, what about the Greek Orthodox Church? Your church split into two groups when the Eastern Orthodox Church (aka the Greek Orthodox Church) was formed in 1054 and of course split again with the Reformation. The Greek or Eastern Orthodox Church is the third largest Christian denomination after Roman Catholics and Protestants and is concentrated in South and East Europe.

Sonny: One major reason I'm not Orthodox is due to their difficulty in defining what makes them the One True Faith (whereas we Catholics have the Roman Church and its bishop as the mark and measure of unity and uniformity of doctrine, just as Christ promised). But they still hold to many essential aspects of the apostolic faith, especially the Eucharist. You could say they're not bound by a common organization or head but rather by a common faith, but an imperfect one because they aren't connected with the One Holy Catholic and Apostolic Church. Their separation from Roman Catholicism was primarily over their rejection of the supremacy of the pope.

Daniel: I am somewhat familiar with the Eastern Orthodox doctrine. It acknowledges some of the traditions expressed in the Roman Catholic Church. For example, while the deification of the Virgin Mary is certainly not the dogma it is in Roman Catholicism, nonetheless it is approved. They accept all seven sacraments of Romanism, and intercession for the dead, another Roman Catholic tradition which has absolutely no biblical support whatsoever, is also common. It doesn't accept the concept of purgatory or the Immaculate Conception. Generally I would say that although some of the Roman Catholic traditions are not accepted, most of them appear to be acceptable to Orthodox Catholics even if they are not actually prioritized in their doctrine. They're renowned for their liturgy. I would conclude that they are more similar to Protestants than to Romanists.

Darrel: So, basically, the reason these denominations are separate is the Orthodox Church wanted to split off from Rome and the papacy.

Sonny: Correct. Orthodox Catholics are like misguided so I think when a person talks about Roman Catholics, he's basically talking about all Catholics. Our Church split over power and politics; we basically share the same beliefs.

Darrel: Did you just say the Catholics split over power and politics? We've been saying that your church is all about power and politics and now you confirm that with this little history lesson. Protestants split over theology; you guys split over greed. Can't you see that?

Sonny: As I said before, your Protestant churches split into so many different denominations. We are just the one apostolic church, the Church given the keys of the kingdom. We need to have just one authority for knowledge of truth.

Darrel: But only if we can trust it to tell us the truth. We trust only God, the author of truth, to tell us the truth, and he does so through his Word. Your magisterium presumes to speak for God, but it consists of sinful men. The CC's centralized rule may seem practical, but its man-made dogma competes with and confuses God's truth in his Word. The practical solution isn't always the best when it comes to the pursuit of truth.

Regarding this "keys" thing again, the giving of the keys is a metaphor which could either symbolize opening the door of the kingdom to the Jews and proselytes and later the Gentiles (Acts 10), or it could also specify that the apostles are foundational to the church; they have been given binding and loosing powers or "keys," which lock and unlock doors. The apostles open the kingdom to those who share Peter's confession and exclude those who not receive their testimony to Christ. (10:14). Through them Jesus reveals His own world of Kingdom authority. The apostolic foundation of the church is laid in the Bible, the written Word of God. By the way, we don't consider the number of Protestant denominations to be relevant to attaining God's truth. You keep coming back to this comment because you believe your CC offers just the one authority and that's a good thing. Of course, we're not structured the way your church is, we're more independently organized, but, in reality we are all in full communion with the doctrine of the Reformation. These Protestant churches that were formed then represent the apostolic teachings and are therefore all unified under one "holy, catholic (with a small "c) and apostolic church regardless of whether they call themselves Lutheran, Methodist, Presbyterian or some non-denominational church. And, like your different "communities," our different denominations differ only in the non-essentials.

Ray: How do you determine whether a difference is essential or non-essential?

John: I define essential and non-essential as Dr. R. C. Sproul defined them. He said that an essential difference interferes with our very connection with Jesus Christ; non-essentials are those issues that, if lacking, do not prevent our union with Christ. The elements of our faith that are not commanded or prohibited in Scripture are non-essentials and, as I said before, these elements are called *adiaphora* by theologians. Paul refers to these in 1 Corinthians 6:12. We should ask ourselves whether we would go to the cross to support any particular element of our doctrine; if we would not, it is a non-essential. In the non-essential things, we have the liberty to follow our consciences under the Word and the Spirit. We certainly shouldn't let them divide us as Christians.

Darrel: Well, I believe that our understanding of authority in interpretation of Scripture is an essential difference.

John: Would you go to the cross to support your understanding of God's plan of salvation?

Darrel: I don't think so; but I would go to the cross to support my belief in Christ as my savior.

John: Exactly; that's an essential, and we are in agreement with Catholics on this point.

Darrel: I see what you mean; but, whether it is an essential difference or not, I believe our difference in who we regard as our authority in interpretation of God's word is critical.

Let's take this verse Sonny mentioned before, 2 Peter 1:20, for example. Sonny believes his church's association with the Apostle Peter as its first pope somehow gives it permission to be sole interpreter of Scripture;

we don't see it that way at all. Catholics, of course, have one rule in Bible interpretation: The vaunted "church" says, blah, blah, blah. But it makes more sense to follow these two rules: **1.** Use Scripture to interpret Scripture. Assuming God is not a God of contradiction so we can use the more clear verses to interpret the meaning of the less clear verses. **2.** Interpret the Bible normally; that is, we should always choose the explanation that appears most obvious to the way most people would normally interpret the verse. Okay, so, with these rules in mind, let's see what the apostle Peter is saying here.

This is probably one of those verses in the Bible which, if the Catholics hadn't tried to use it to explain the Catholic Church's assumption of sole authority for interpretation of the Bible, we would have had no problem in understanding what it means.

We've said this before, but you guys just don't seem to understand how your church makes room for itself, creates a need for itself to make itself useful in the spiritual lives of its followers by arbitrarily designated itself as sole authority and discouraging people from even reading their Bible, much less try to understand it. As I said before, the Bible really isn't that difficult a book to understand. No authority is necessary to interpret Scripture, in our concerted opinion; and, if you could possibly overcome your indoctrinated aversion to private interpretation and participate in our analysis of what this verse really means, you might just learn something you didn't know before. That's what we're here to do.

So then, let's see if there might be an alternative explanation to the meaning of this verse. If we look at this particular verse in context, we see that it represents a continuation of Peter's concern about the reliability of Scripture itself, and not the authority of those who interpret it. That issue comes up later in 3:16. In the present context, Peter is arguing that the prophetic testimony in Scripture comes altogether from God. This includes not only visions from God, but words used to describe and interpret the meaning of them. Using the accepted best method of using Scripture to interpret Scripture, we refer to Daniel 8:15-19 and Zechariah 1:9 where both prophets receive an explanation from the

Holy Spirit through an angel for a vision they each had. Verse 21 goes on to reiterate that the Holy Spirit is the source of prophecy, enabling the prophets to speak and write as God's representatives. Second Timothy 3:16 and 1 Peter 1:10-12 make the same point which is to trust only in the guidance of the Holy Spirit in interpreting the meaning of God's Word.

Sonny: At the risk of repeating myself, the Catholic Church is inspired by the Holy Spirit.

Peter: You are saying that you believe the Catholic Church is the prominent authority for your denomination, right?

Sonny: We are not a denomination, Peter. We are THE Christian religion. We are the Christian Church; and, to answer your question, yes, the Church is our sole authority for the truth.

Darrel: Theologian Charles Spurgeon once said that "whatever a man depends upon, whatever rules his mind, whatever govern his affections, whatever is the chief object of his delight, is his God." Since we began these discussions with you about your religion, you have referred to your church many, many times; your church is the original authority; your church is THE Christian church; your church this, your church that. Man, can't you see that this would indicate you people depend on your church, that your church rules your mind and governs your affections; your church is the chief object of your delight? You worship your church as God himself.

Sonny: I resent that implication, Darrel. For us, the Church is a substitute for Christ.

Darrel: Yes, and you use the title "Holy Father" to refer to your pope; this title of course is what we call God so are you actually implying your pope is like God? I object to the use of the title "Holy Father" in reference to the Catholic pope. The word "holy" shouldn't be taken so lightly. Only God is holy and only he rates the use of the name "Holy Father." And only the Son, Jesus Christ, is head of his church, no one else. Please refer to Ephesians 1:22 and Colossians 1:18 for support of the Protestant position on this. Actually, calling anyone "Holy Father" is a clear violation of the First Commandment; you shall have no other gods before him. They violate the Second Commandment too with their icons of Christ on the cross.

Sonny: By definition, holy means to be "set apart," and in his unique position as Vicar of Christ, the pope is set apart to address matters of faith and morals. He is set apart to be infallible whenever he speaks *ex cathedra.* In all other matters, he can be fallible, but he is the substitute for Christ on earth; for all intents and purposes, he is Christ on earth to us. Our pope (and Magisterium as well) are thus guided by the Holy Spirit in matters of church doctrine. Secondly, it's possible for a person to be holy since the Bible says we are to be holy as your Father in heaven is holy.

Darrel: We Christians are to be set apart from the world; that's what holy means. Your reference to the "Holy Father" implies he's set apart from the rest of you, "holier than thou." You confirmed that when you said he was infallible. He's just as flawed as the rest of us.

Sonny: Recall when Christ was speaking to Paul on the road to Damascus and asked him why he was persecuting Him. Since He was in heaven, Christ was obviously referring to Paul persecuting His Church, not Him personally. The Church and Christ are therefore to be considered as one. In Matthew23:1-3, Jesus said "The scribes and the Pharisees have taken their seat on the chair of Moses. Therefore, do and observe all things whatsoever they tell you." Jesus recognized the authority of the Pharisees, the Old Testament Magisterium which now speaks for Jesus Christ Himself.

Darrel: There is absolutely no indication Christ is referring to some church authority other than the Pharisees that would succeed them in occupying the chair of Moses; and, even if you believe the Pharisees are to be considered as your church leaders in this passage, remember that, consistent with his low opinion of the Pharisees and their hypocrisy,

Christ goes on to say, "but do not follow their example. For they preach but they do not practice." I think it's ironic you should mention your church magisterium in the same sentence as the Pharisees. We Protestants certainly see the resemblance. And, in your reference to Paul's conversion, Christ of course was referring to his church, not the Roman Catholic Church. As usual, these biblical references are twisted to support yet another Catholic tradition that didn't even become dogma until 1870 when it was deemed necessary to establish credibility for the church in proclaiming whatever it wished to be understood as the actual word of God. This affirmation of infallibility is a sign of apostasy and the anti-Christ predicted by Paul in 2 Thessalonians 2:2-12 and John in Revelation 17:1-9, 13:5-8, 18. By the way, why does the Catholic Church insist your priests be called "Father?"

Sonny: We don't elevate any person to the level of our heavenly Father. The name refers to their position as head of the Church. We refer to our priests as Father because their duty is to communicate the nature of God to us just as biological fathers communicate their nature to their children through teaching and their example.

Darrel: By example, eh? Some example! I'm your father; I'm a pedophile. These sex scandals in the priesthood are tragic for Catholicism and Christianity. It doesn't seem as though God is happy with the Catholic Church at this point in time; maybe it's time for another Reformation.

Daniel: You say you don't consider your pope to be on the same level as God, but when you use this "Vicar of Christ" title for him, that's what you're really doing. As Darrel said before, "vicar" means "substitute" for Christ. In Matthew 24:4-5 Jesus warned that many will come in his name, saying, 'I am the Christ, and will deceive many."

Darrel: Luther recognized what this term "vicar" really meant and this is why he referred to the pope as the anti-Christ. We find the clearest teachings regarding the anti-Christ to be Paul's letter to the

Thessalonians. Luther was merely applying Paul's description to the Roman Catholic pope.

Sonny: We consider Martin Luther to be an apostate and a heretic. He not only renounced his religion, he changed our Christian doctrine.

Darrel: By the time we're finished with these sessions, Sonny, it will be obvious who the apostate church is and who's the heretic.

I should also mention that Jesus tells us in Matthew 23:9 that we are not to call anyone on earth our father. Pope actually means "papa" in Latin.

Sonny: Using this verse in Matthew is an example of "eisegesis," imposing one's views on a biblical passage.

Darrel: It's ironic you should accuse us of doing what I have known you Catholics to do to support the majority of your extra-biblical traditions we'll be discussing in these sessions. So tell us, my man, what do you think this verse means?

Sonny: Jesus was discouraging His followers from elevating the scribes and Pharisees to the titles of "fathers" and "rabbis" because they were hypocrites.

Darrel: Sure, like your popes believe they represent apostolic succession, the Pharisee's believed they were the successors of Abraham, and Jesus was warning them to never presume a connection where no connection exists; and, like your Catholic Church, the Pharisees elevated their own traditions above the authority of the Word of God. Like the Pharisees, the Catholic Church persecuted all who opposed them.

Bobby: But at least you both seem to agree on the authority of the Bible, right?

Darrel: That's the premise; but, with these Catholics, it's another "yeah, but."

John: If we cannot agree on this premise, we won't be able to focus our discussions on context, linguistic analysis and theological unity and development. Unity is critical. Our great need right now is for convicted Christians, both Catholics and Protestants, to be willing to stand together for the truth of the gospel. We both need to commit to being shaped by the Word of God, and we both need to able to distinguish those issues that have lasting significance in our pursuit of the truth.

We have more in common with Catholicism than you Catholics think we do. Christian apologist, C. S. Lewis, "found it ironic and fascinating that from his many books he constantly received letters from Roman Catholics, Orthodox Catholics, Anglicans and every Protestant denomination under the sun, thanking him for confirming their particular denomination as the true Christian faith and Biblical world view. What becomes apparent is that beneath all of the denominational differences and tug points there exists a unity among all of the diversity in Christendom because unity does not necessarily mean uniformity. Scripture is quite clear on who is a 'Christian.' One who confesses with their mouth and believes in their heart that Jesus Christ is Lord and that God has raised Him from the dead. That's it!

If I'm asked 'What does it take to be a follower of Christ?' my answer will be brief. If you ask 'What does it take to belong to a particular denomination?' it will have to be a much longer answer because of the distinctive's that denomination adds. Then you may ask 'What does it take to teach in a theological institution?' now you have to be even MORE protracted in the answer because theologically one has to be extremely precise. I've known so many people from all denominations who were true followers of Christ, though they differed on all of the peripheral accretions added over the centuries. I always have to keep in mind that there may be true followers of Christ who are very bad Catholics, and very good Protestants who are very bad followers of Christ AND, vice versa. I have also known some true followers of Jesus who stayed in some denomination so that they could make changes in it."

Sonny: I am familiar with the work of C. S. Lewis. In fact, he is the only non-Catholic author I have ever read whom I thought I could completely trust and understand. Did you know that he believed in purgatory, the real presence of Christ in the Eucharist? He was no Calvinist because he didn't believe in man's total depravity.

Darrel: I'm not familiar with Lewis' acceptance of the concept of purgatory, and I've read a lot of what he wrote, but he never admitted to be a theologian, and we're talking about theology here. Lewis didn't like to classify Christians into '*isms*, and that's what we're trying hard not to do in these discussions. Lewis was reformed in the sense that he accepted such concepts as our inherent sinful nature, and man's inability to make himself righteous before God. One of the strengths of the theology of the Reformation is that it has a solid biblical understanding of this particular concept, and Lewis was certainly well-versed in the tenets of the theology of the Reformation.

Personally, I like Lewis' description of many theological concepts of reformed Christianity; he takes an intuitive approach in his explanations, and *Mere Christianity* should be a must read for all Christians, regardless of denomination. I mentioned his quote to illustrate his focus on unity, but we should never pursue it to the extent the truth is compromised to attain it. With this concept of unity in mind, for purposes of our discussions, can you Sonny, accept the supremacy of the authority of the Bible? That has to be our premise, and I think you can understand why it has to be from what I just said.

Sonny: Yes, of course I can. I accept the Bible and our Church tradition as my authority.

Darrel: "And?" There is no "and." The Bible alone is God's authoritative Word on whatever knowledge of him he wishes to share with us. Its purpose is to command our lives in order that we might please God. That's the conviction of every believer, or at least it should be. God's Word is either sovereign over the life of every believer, or it's to be discarded as an ancient myth as non-Christians believe it is.

Sonny: God's limits His sovereignty to allow us to have free will.

John: The two concepts work together; their relationship is a paradox and it's difficult to explain. They exist together because the Bible tells us they do. We should understand that neither our free will nor God's sovereignty have been compromised. Theologian Arthur W. Pink dealt with this paradox in his classic *The Attributes of God.* "There is perfect harmony between the sovereignty of God and the responsibility of the creature...Human responsibility is based upon Divine sovereignty." Another theologian, John Feinberg, described the paradox of God's sovereign rule and our free will in his book *No One Like Him: The Doctrine of God*, by stating that God rules by "soft determinism," and we have "compatibilisitc free will." Luther told us that only God truly has free will, and, by its nature, our free will must be compatible with his will. Theologian Dr. R. C. Sproul said that God is the primary cause, we are the secondary cause. But just because God does not rule us with an iron hand doesn't mean his power is compromised. Just because our free will must always be compatible to his will doesn't mean it's been compromised either. Placing limits doesn't mean compromise. I know it feels that way, but that's because sinful man is a rebel (as I said before) and doesn't want to accept limits. Personally, I'm glad my Creator places limits on what I can do. I don't want to be totally responsible for every choice I make, particularly when it may affect my own salvation.

The hope is greater for those of us who rely totally on God's grace rather than on our good deeds. There's no guilt for those of us who know the slate has been wiped clean.

Sonny: Soft determinism is merely God placing a limit on Himself. I can agree with that concept.

John: God may place a limit on *the exercise* of His sovereignty in allowing for the expression of our free will, but He maintains veto power; that's not the same thing as you just said. I would challenge you Catholics to consider that defining the limits of God's sovereignty in terms of our understanding of our own esteem and identity is to look at the issue backwards. God created man for his own purposes, not the other way around. His purpose is mysterious and largely unknowable to us. To assume that it adds to human worth for man to have the freedom to deny God is to write history from a human rather than a divine perspective. Jonah used his "free will" to flee from a God who cannot be fled from. David said, "Even if I take the wings of the morning and dwell in the uttermost part of the sea, even there, your hand shall guide me!" Even in my sin God's perfect will for history plays out perfectly. Our sinful human inclination is to want to be God in the sense that we want to share some of His sovereignty. Augustine asked in *Confessions* "How could anything be more proud that to assert, as I did in my incredible folly, that I was by nature what you (God) are?" Augustine stressed giving the glory to God; he once said that "He who has ears to hear may glory, not in himself, but in the Lord." We also know from Scripture that God is glorified when we recognize His sovereignty, and the only thing he places above the importance of our free will is His sovereignty.

Sonny: God does give up some of His sovereignty. In Colossians 1:24, Paul says, "I now rejoice in my suffering for you, and fill up in my flesh what is lacking in the afflictions of Christ, for the sake of His body, which is the church, of which I became a minister according to the stewardship from God which was given to me for you, to fulfill the word of God." Paul equates the Church with Christ's body. He tells us that he rejoices in his sufferings for the sake of the Church, and implies there is something lacking in the afflictions of Christ; our justification must involve faith and works acting together.

John: That isn't what this verse is saying, Sonny. Let's utilize the best method of analyzing the meaning of Scripture and, presuming God doesn't contradict Himself, use the more clear verses to explain the less clear ones, okay? In all his letters, Paul, under God's guidance and influence, presents a consistent message. He certainly isn't implying that the Christian church is a continuing incarnation of Christ whose members add saving merit beyond what Christ achieved. This verse in Colossians is obviously an example of one of those less clear verses. In

Romans 3:21-26, and 2 Corinthians 5:17-21, we can clearly understand what Paul is saying to us: Christ's atoning sacrifice was sufficient. There is no need for us to cooperate in saving ourselves.

So then, assuming God doesn't say one thing through Paul in His epistles to the Romans and Corinthians and say something contradictory to the Colossians, here's what I think Colossians 1:24 means. In its context, ironically Paul is actually stressing the sufficiency of Christ (as I mentioned in referring to these other two verses). Paul therefore can't mean what you are implying, Sonny, that Christ's saving work on the cross is deficient in some respect because that would mean he is contradicting what he said to the Christians in Rome and in Corinth, and, as we assumed before as our premise, God is not a God of contradiction. Paul says that because the church is called to suffer for Christ (2 Corinthians 4:7-12; 1 Thessalonians 3:2-4), there is a divinely appointed requisite of suffering to be endured by Christians. Our suffering is meaningful, but not in our salvation. Paul may also have in view here the sufferings which will accompany the end times, a period ushered in by the death and resurrection of Christ. This also explains the reference to Paul's suffering for the sake of the church as he also addresses in Ephesians 3:13 and 2 Timothy 2:10. When we read these verses, we see that Paul is saying that, as a servant of the gospel, he rejoices in the opportunity to participate in the sufferings of God's people.

Ray: The Church is under the influence of the Holy Spirit, and I believe what my Church tells me, regardless of what you think Paul says. The Magisterium formulates dogma and is to be considered equal or greater than God's word. This is why we consider our sacred tradition to be God's Word, and it integrates with the Bible to provide us with God's truth. No individual Christian has the Spirit of Truth in them. We Catholics believe that the Spirit discourages us from independent interpretation, and we are to rely on the teaching authority of the Church. We have just the one authority for God's truth. Our centralization is critical. Yes, our Church interprets God's Word for us, but you Protestants have these men Calvin and Luther who do the same for you, right?

Darrel: History's respected theologians do not claim to have the authority your church has. The Holy Spirit is our only guide to what we are to believe. When man tried to claim sole authority to the truth, God intervened and destroyed the Tower of Babel; he did the same thing to man in inspiring men like Luther to cause the Reformation.

Bobby: Okay, it's that time again. See y'all next week.

Week Four

Bobby: Let's talk about what Catholics and Protestants have in common. What do each of you think it takes to be saved? That's what Christianity is really all about, right?

Sonny: Exactly. We Catholics believe we are saved by:

1. Believing in Christ (John 3:16, Acts 16:31)
2. Repentance (Acts 2:38, 2 Peter 3:9).
3. Baptism (John 3:5, 1 Peter 3:21, Titus 3:5).
4. Eating the flesh of Christ, drinking His blood (John 6).
5. The work of the Spirit (John 3:5, 2 Corinthians 3:6).
6. Declaring the gospel with our mouth (Luke 12:8, Romans 10:9).
7. Coming to knowledge of the truth (1 Timothy 2:4, Hebrews 10:26).
8. Our works (Romans 2:6-7, James 2:24).
9. God's grace (Acts 15:11, Ephesians 2:8).
10. Christ's blood (Romans 5:9, Hebrews 9:22).
11. Christ's righteousness (Romans 5:17, 2 Peter 1:1).
12. Keeping the commandments (Matthew 19:17)
13. Our words (Matthew 12:37).

John: These 13 points do describe the Christian doctrine and what we are to do to practice our faith, and we can agree with our Catholic brothers in Christ that this is exactly what every Christian should believe. You'll note that this summary included appropriate and relevant support from the Bible for each point listed. The authority is the key.

Sonny: Yes, as I said before, it all comes down to who your authority is. Protestants rely on John Calvin and the heretical reformers as their authority. I'm a Catholic because I believe in one authority, my Catholic Church as the only source of truth. Our Church tells us of God's plan of salvation. When you understand the purpose of the dogma and participate in the Eucharist, you will fall in love with Jesus and ask for wisdom from the Church Jesus gave to you to teach you the truth of God's Word.

Darrel: Yes, your entire theology comes from your corporate church. We don't relate to our church that way, nor do we relate to any theologian in that way. Calvin and Luther, Augustine, et al, don't tell us what to believe, and no Protestant church acts as an authority in telling us what to believe; we don't require a church to do that for us. We don't rely on any authority but what Scripture tells us; we refer to Christ's authoritative view of the Bible in his interactions with Jewish traditionalists. "It is written" carried a lot of weight with him even though he was God incarnate, the author of truth.

John: The beauty of our connection with Christ is that it is on an individual basis. A corollary to the doctrine of *sola Scriptura* is the doctrine of Christian liberty that I mentioned before. I remind you that *sola Scriptura* guards against the unlawful usurpation or abuse of authority by people or institutions over the consciences of God's people; I remind you that the doctrine of Christian liberty states that if Scripture (or truth legitimately deduced from it) does not address a particular doctrinal issue, the Christian is at liberty to decide what opinion to have on that issue. A Christian's conscience cannot, and should not, be bound by anyone or anything. Thus, the Christian is protected from the tyranny of institutions like the Catholic Church. So then, I'll just exercise my

God-given Christian liberty, trust in the guidance of the Holy Spirit and stay the course with the theology of Augustine and the reformers who patterned their theology after him.

Sonny: I really object to you including Augustine with your heretical reformers.

John: I have read Augustine's *City of God*, and when you put it side by side with Calvin's *Institutes of the Christian Religion*, you'll see how close the doctrines really are. It's ironic that this saint of Catholicism was ironically the father of reformed theology.

Calvin relied on Augustine's theology to develop reformed theology; Catholics rely on their masters of the magisterium, who in turn ironically claims to rely on church fathers like Augustine to formulate their dogma. It's unfortunate the Catholic Church didn't learn what Calvin learned from Augustine, eh? If that had happened, and they would have relied on Augustine's theology, the Reformation would not have had to occur. We'd all be on the same page today. There would be no Protestant churches, just the one holy catholic and apostolic church influenced by Augustine theology as a guide to the teachings of the apostles; but, alas, Satan would have none of that, and, the Catholic Church transitioned away from its moorings as it became what it is today, a Christian church corporate institution. The RCC couldn't resist the prideful temptation to add traditions to the original apostolic tradition that were not biblically supported, and we end up with a church that Augustine wouldn't have recognized. We Protestants rely on the Holy Spirit to guide us in our understanding of Christian theology using only God's Word because it only makes sense that God would be the best interpreter of what he says, right? It's always best to rely on the author to explain his book. Of course, we also consult different theological sources to assist us in understanding God's Word. I mentioned Augustine's two classic books and Aquinas *Summa Theologica,* but rely particularly on Calvin's, *Institutes of the Christian Religion*, the most complete description of Christian theology ever written.

Sonny: With so many so-called theologians telling you people what to believe, how can you tell what is false doctrine and what is truth? It's an advantage to just rely on one authority we trust to tell us what Scripture is saying to us. We are told not to rely on private opinions. St. Peter warns us about interpreting the Bible on our own in 2 Peter 1:20. "No prophecy of Scripture is of any private interpretation."

Darrel: I just told you the names of the primary theologians who best articulated reformed theology, one of them being Augustine. I am familiar enough with Augustine's theology that I could even just claim him as the one theologian I rely upon as a tool of the Holy Spirit who serves to guide me in understanding the Bible, our only source of knowledge. What would you say then?

Sonny: I would say again that you don't understand Augustine's theology. He didn't believe in your *sola Scriptura*.

Darrel: Augustine said that "knowledge of Scripture is knowing the truth." He believed the Bible offers the only test for the truth in Christianity. If it isn't biblically supported, it isn't truth. That sounds to me like a ringing endorsement of *sola Scriptura*, doesn't it?

He also advocated that the church should "go back to the fountain," the "apostolic tradition" to be more relevant to the times in which the apostles lived. He was clearly stating his concerns over the traditions of purgatory and praying for the saints not being biblically supported, and, in fact, as we shall see when we discuss these traditions in a later session to come, he didn't exactly give them a rounding endorsement.

Sonny: Here's his quote taken from "On Baptism, Against the Donatists 5:23": "there are many things which are observed by the whole Church, and therefore fairly held to have been enjoined by the apostles, which yet are not mentioned in their writings." And he stated in his "Letter to Januarius," "But in regard to those observances which we carefully attend and which the whole world keeps, and which derive not from Scripture but from Tradition, we are given to understand that they are recommended and ordained to be kept, either by the apostles themselves or by plenary (ecumenical) councils, the authority of which is quite vital in the Church." He is stating we should accept Church tradition.

Darrel: Augustine said many things to many people in his lifetime, but we have to be careful not to take quotes out of their context to support our presuppositions. You Catholics of course want to believe Augustine supported the addition of tradition developed by the ecumenical councils but, as I said before, he could only have been referring to the two traditions he mentioned in his writings, purgatory and praying for the saints which hadn't even been declared to be dogma at the time. We know he didn't generally favor traditions as we can see from what he said in *Confessions*, his autobiography which was written during his first years as a bishop of Hippo. He complained about being "weighed down by the burden of custom" and about "being hurdled into the hellish river of custom." He could only have been referring to what he was being subjected to as a bishop in the Catholic Church. Of course, he only had just a few of these church traditions to consider, and I can't help but think, based on his frustration with traditions in general and his statement about trusting only the Bible, he would have gone along with all those traditions to come from the Catholic Church after his time.

Sonny: Augustine did not support *sola fide*.

Darrel: I don't see how you can read Augustine or anything about him and not clearly see how devoted he is to God's sovereignty. That means he supports all five *solas*. Here's another quote from City of God addressing *sola fide*: "The just lives by faith, for we do not as yet see our good, and must therefore live by faith; neither have we in ourselves power to live rightly, but can do so only if He who has given us faith to believe in His help do help us when we believe and pray." He also said that "no one is sufficient for himself, for the beginning or the completion of any good work whatever...our sufficiency is of God, so no one is sufficient for himself, either to begin or to perfect faith." It's ironic that you Catholics ignore what he's saying here and trust in your ability to do good works to earn your salvation but don't trust yourself to study God's Word on your own. Of course, as you've said, your church really doesn't give you that option, does it? You don't need to answer that.

The Catholic Church has to reject or redefine most of the *solas* to suit its need to be the sole authority. I've said that before. The church ignores *sola Scriptura* because it knows its traditions aren't supported in the Bible. If it can't convince people that the Bible has been interpreted or translated incorrectly, it resorts to claiming the additional traditions are oral and weren't recorded in the Bible. Its "grace plus works" tradition is the tradition I abhor because it represents bad theology. The concept is fuzzy math. We Protestants believe what the Bible says that grace equals salvation which in turn equals works. That's what Augustine is saying in the quote I gave when he states in *City of God*, "neither have we in ourselves power to live rightly." The confusion over what Augustine believed about *sola fide* results from differing definitions of what the phrase means. It must be correctly understood to mean that our justification comes only from God's grace through faith, not by any merit of works. Good works are necessary evidence of our saving faith. You could say that we are justified by faith alone but not by a faith that is alone. This is the reformed position and also the Augustinian position. You people ignore your own saint, man!

As you can see, *sola fide* is related to *sola gratia* because our faith comes from God's grace. Do you recall when you told us that Catholics have a different understanding of *sola gratia*, God's grace alone? You're ignoring what Augustine said about that too. He never implied what you imply that God's grace is insufficient to save us without our cooperation. In citing Romans 11:5, 6, Augustine is admitting that good works belong to the grace of God. He also cites John 15:5, Ephesians 2:8, 9, and 10, and Matthew 16:17. Theologians call this heretical Catholic concept of cooperating in our salvation "synergism" which means "working together." When applied to salvation, it means that we work together with God for eternal life, and indeed Catholics believe that good works are a necessary component to our salvation. That's Pelagian, Augustine's rival.

Look, man, when Christ said "It is finished," he meant that his sacrifice was sufficient for our salvation; nothing more was necessary. If we believe we must use our free will to do something to complete the process, we are not taking God at his word. We're also compromising his sovereignty and thus diminishing his glory. The only thing more important to God than our free will is his glory. It's the worst of the "yeah, buts." *Yeah*, I'm saved by God's grace, *but* I need to do good too for salvation to take effect. This is contradictory to what the Bible says; it's another one of your traditions.

Ray: Oh, yeah, where does it say that God's glory is so important?

Darrel: Scripture is full of references to the importance God places on his glory, but, I particularly like what Jesus says to the Father in his prayer recorded in John 17:4. Jesus prays, "I glorified you here on earth, having accomplished the work which you have given Me to do." Jesus had free will and could choose to not do this work, but he recognized that God the Father wished to be glorified and that took precedence over his human will to avoid being sacrificed for our sin. Remember in the Garden of Gethsemane when he pleaded with God not to require him to atone for us?

Before you come back with your comment about the Bible not being the only source of knowledge again, I'd just like to reiterate that we Protestants rely on the Bible as our sole authority because we trust that it is the Word of God, the source of all truth and author of our faith. That's our premise, and we surely don't accept your premise that the Catholic Church not only is your trusted biblical interpreter, but has added its own sacred tradition to God's Word, and that's where you come up with this "yeah, but" approach of grace plus works. This misunderstanding of the way grace works in God's plan of salvation is an example of how some, if not all, of these sacred traditions of your church actually contradict what the Bible says. Paul tells us in Romans 3:28, 4:3, 4:5, 5:1 and Ephesians 2:8 that we are justified solely on the basis of our faith, and that works are not required for salvation for it is by grace alone we are saved.

Bobby: I'm obviously not an expert on Christianity, but that only means if I can see the obvious, everyone should be able to see it; and it would seem to me that this *sola fide* is a key point of difference between not only Catholics and Protestants but between biblical Christianity and all other world religions. After all, we've had discussions with Muslims, Jews, and secular humanists in previous years down here under this cabana and I think that's a conclusion anyone would be able to draw. Every other religion believes good deeds earn the believer salvation. So then, in light of that statement, do Catholics really believe that good works are necessary to supplement God's grace?

Sonny: Yes and no. Our Catechism states that grace is the help God gives us to respond to our vocation of becoming his adopted sons. It introduces us into the intimacy of the Trinitarian life (CCC 2021); and Canon 14 of the Council of Trent states: "If any one saith, that man is truly absolved from his sins and justified, because he assuredly believed himself absolved and justified; or, that no one is truly justified by he who believes himself justified; and that, by this faith alone, absolution and justification are effected; let him be an anathema." Canon 12 states "If any one shall say that justifying faith is nothing else than confidence in the divine mercy pardoning sins for Christ's sake, or that it is that confidence alone by which we are justified, let him be accursed."

Darrel: Your church is not only teaching heresy, in cursing people who believe in what Paul said, your church is speaking for Satan. By the way, since you can only quote from your catechism instead of a Bible verse, you're proving that this grace plus works concept is not found in the Bible.

Sonny: Yes, it is. I'll list the verses. Nehemiah 13:14; Psalm 11:7, 28:4; Isaiah 3:10, 59:18; Jeremiah 25:14, 50:29; Ezekiel 9:10, 11:21, 36:19; Hosea 4:9, 9:15, 12:2; Matthew 16:27, 25:40; Mark 10:21. These verses all relate to us being rewarded for our good works.

Darrel: I've read all of them, and, yes, they do refer to our reward for doing good works. But, with the exception of Hosea 9:15, where God is referring to "driving the wicked out of his House" none of them are connecting salvation with being our good works. They will be rewarded in their earthly lives by doing good deeds and punished for doing evil.

Ray: I'll make it easy for you, Darrel. We believe that the first step in our salvation is being justified in our baptism; that is the instrumental cause. We believe that grace is poured into the soul of the person baptized. But, for this infusion to take effect and for us to continue on in a state of grace, we have to cooperate and give our assent. This state of justification continues until we commit a mortal sin which destroys it. Thus we have a need for purgatory and last rites.

Sonny: I don't think we're as far apart as you might believe, Darrel. I think any reasoned consideration will show that Protestants are <u>almost exactly correct</u> on this issue. I think Catholics have gotten muddled in our message and overcorrected by trying to over-emphasize the role of our own works in our salvation. We should emphasize love, "without which we can do nothing." But love isn't enough so we say we are saved by God's grace which is channeled through the Church, and that's where the good works comes into the picture.

The Catholic Church certainly does not teach that we receive initial justification by good works. We do not have to perform good works in order to come to God and be justified, The Council of Trent states in its Decree on Justification 8, "And we are said to be justified by grace, it is no longer by works; otherwise, as the apostle says, 'grace is no more grace' (Romans 11:6)."

I know this sounds like our council is contradicting itself, but please allow me to explain. When we talk about justification, we are talking about two types, initial justification and the ultimate justification accompanied by good works. God initially justifies us by His grace alone, but our works are a necessary accompaniment to complete the process; and when we refer to good works, we're talking about two types of works. In these verses you listed, Paul is defining works to be works of law, and we are referring to the good works we do out of obedience to

God; it is these works that are required to accompany God's grace for us to be saved.

Darrel: The credibility and believability of our opinion necessarily depends on whose authority we use to support that opinion. Well, our authority is the Bible, of course. As we've seen in these discussions, Catholics regard only their church as their authority.

Ray: Our Magisterium represents the word of the Holy Spirit; God's our authority.

Darrel: Men who want to act like God are your sole authority, can't you see that? These men have misled you in understanding what Scripture tells us about God's salvation plan, and no other Christian accepts their authority but you people. If you can't at least acknowledge that this co-dependent connection with your church institution restricts you from keeping an open mind when discussing points of our faith, I really don't see any need for this discussion to go on any further. You people ignore what the Bible says whenever it doesn't support what your church tells you is true; you say your tradition trumps Scripture anyway, right? You consider us heretics because we don't accept your Catholic Church as an authority on Christianity, and we consider you heretics because you ignore what the Bible has to say about Christianity.

Ray: You have your authorities; these theologians you mention, this Sproul guy and others.

Darrel: I remind you that the apostles stressed we should all be theologians; that means we are to examine what we believe and why we believe it; we are to practice an intelligent faith. Our theologians, who, by the way, include some theologians you people recognize like Augustine and Aquinas, are our advisors, not our authority. They don't tell us what to believe or be subject to excommunication, cursing and damnation. We trust the Holy Spirit is working through them in guiding us to the truth.

Ray: How do you know the Holy Spirit is working through these men?

Darrel: How do you know the Holy Spirit is working exclusively through your church? The Apostles Peter and Paul told us that we recognize Spirit-filled advice when it is in compliance with what we know the Bible is telling us. Are you including Augustine in this group of men you refer to? Was Augustine not spirit-led in his belief?

Sonny: Of course he was. My point is how can Protestants know what the Bible is really saying to us without the authority of the Church?

Let's take an example to make my point. Let's take Romans 11:6 and see what Paul is really saying. "And if by grace, then it is no longer of works; otherwise grace is no longer grace. But if it is of works it is no longer grace; otherwise work is no longer work." Paul's contrasting grace and works, but we need to understand what he really means by grace and works. We believe the grace Paul is referring to is infused into us through our Church's sacraments; and, as I said before, the works are the works of law, not what we refer to as "good works." Paul did this in several other verses in his letter to the Romans. Protestants can't know what Paul is saying without a guide. When we read the verse in its entire context and understood the verse the way our Church understands it, Paul is supporting our position of grace plus works equals salvation.

Darrel: That's your Catholic Church's interpretation. That's the error Luther was talking about. Two steps in justification, initial and absolute, and two types of works? It's your church that unnecessarily makes the Bible more complicated!

Sonny: This is our Church's interpretation of the way the Bible explains God's plan of salvation.

Darrel: Let's first consider your distinction as to what constitutes a good work. How does a good work differ from a work of law? Isn't obedience to God considered to be a good work?

Sonny: Sure, but our Church tells us that we perform good works when we follow the Church's sacred tradition.

Darrel: Okay, let me see if I understand what you've said. You Catholics believe that God's grace must be accompanied by good works to be saved; and your church tells you that you can perform these good works by obedience to church rules and traditions. Are you people not able to at least suspect church's self-serving interest here? This conclusion is consistent with my statement that your Roman Catholic doctrine is similar to the legalistic beliefs of the Judaizers and Daniel's statement that Catholicism is more legalistic than Protestantism. Of course, legalism plays to man's desire to have order and presuming works must accompany grace in our salvation also serves to give man what he wants to believe, that his good works count for something important, and what's more important than salvation? The minute you introduce works as a requirement for salvation, you're subscribing to Arminianism which states that grace is conditioned on our works.

Ray: You Protestants are wrong when you claim that the merits of Christ applied to us will remove all sin past, present, and future abdicating all responsibility for sin after justification. This is an unreasonable belief because Christ's death on the cross only makes us worthy before God the Father. We cannot stand before Him on our own merits. This is why we need Jesus Christ. Yet, we also have a personal responsibility in our justification before the Lord.

Darrel: First we see a "yeah, but" as in, *yeah*, you believe you need Christ to be saved, *but* then again you also have a personal responsibility in your own salvation. Then we see another "yeah, but" as in, *yeah*, you believe in God's grace, *but* then weaken that concept and God's sovereignty by claiming that somehow this grace is channeled through the Catholic Church." Now you guys are saying, *yeah*, God justifies, *but* He requires good works (which are defined as observance of Catholic Church tradition, not obedience to God's law) to complete the justification process. There are a number of these "yeah, buts" to come as we shall see when we delve into what all your traditions and rituals involve.

Daniel: Yes, when we discuss the tradition of the seven sacraments of the Catholic Church, we'll see how it always seems to make room for itself in its insistence that confession, forgiveness and penance for sin can only be effective if done through a priest, and, to be considered a good Catholic (and presumably worthy of salvation), one must perform a good work through obedience to these man-made traditions.

Darrel: The ultimate "yeah, but" is "*Yeah*, that's true according to the Bible, *but* the Catholic Church says... blah, blah, blah, fill in the blank.

I'm curious, Sonny, do you consider your faith a good work?

Sonny: Our faith is a gift from God which is administered through the Church as we follow our sacred tradition.

Darrel: There you go again! I hear you saying that "*yeah*, we consider faith to be a gift from God, *but*, it has to be administered through the Catholic Church as you folks follow the church's "sacred tradition." Even your faith in God depends on your faith in your church.

John: From what Sonny has been saying, we can see why Christian theologians believe that the Catholic Church teaches a weakened concept of grace. Donald McKim, in his *Westminster Dictionary of Theological Terms*, defines the Catholic concept as "cooperating grace." In Catholic theology, "the Holy Spirit's action enables humans to respond to God's initial action in establishing a divine-human relationship with a person." The Catholic Church teaches that God needs our cooperation, He needs us to do something for a gift he's bestowed on us. McKim defines the Protestant concept of grace as "unmerited favor" which is bestowed unconditionally in saving the elect. Catholics believe that for God's grace to be effective, they must accept God's grace and do good works as a condition to merit favor. The Catholic concept weakens the act of grace on God's part by requiring our cooperation. Pelagius first introduced this concept in opposition to Augustine's belief in the *unmerited favor* definition. This definition also gives all the glory to God, our chief purpose in life. I recall Sonny's quote issued by the Council of Trent which pronounced that "nothing that precedes justification, whether faith or works, merits the grace of justification." That statement would seem to demonstrate that Catholics seem to have the same understanding of grace that we Protestants have. So, I'm confused as to what they really believe about God's grace.

Bobby: I am too. I just happened to have a copy of it. Item 2027 of the Catholic Catechism states that "No one can merit the initial grace which is at the origin of conversion. Moved by the Holy Spirit, we can merit for ourselves and for others all the graces needed to attain eternal life, as well as necessary temporal goods." That mention of the word "merit" sure sounds like the Catholic Church teaches grace is insufficient, right?

Sonny: We believe grace is unmerited favor, but the definition isn't as simple as that. Grace is actually a participation in God's life (partakers of the divine nature referred to in 2 Peter 1:1-4. Grace is what makes it possible for one to do things that he was not able to do before. Grace enables one to have a right to go to heaven which we are not born with. Grace enables one to be Holy which we cannot do through our human nature. Grace enables us to do good works which we cannot do without grace. If one has grace, he can merit more grace. John 1:16. One without grace cannot merit anything more. Recall the parable of the tenants when those who have the most are given more. We do not merit the capability to have faith nor do we merit the capability of being able to do good works.

Aquinas distinguished between two kinds of grace: Initial or "operative grace" and "cooperative grace." Operative grace is the grace that operates "in regard to an effect which the will of God brings about in us." Cooperative grace is in regard to an effect that God's will does not produce alone, but with the cooperation of the agent. It can be said then, that operative grace is such that the human will is moved by God to provide the inclination to do good, without any discursive deliberation on our part. But, in cooperative grace, there is a deliberation involved by which we freely choose to cooperate with God's grace. There, in cooperative grace, we are, in a sense, accepting the gift that God extends to us as our loving Father.

Darrel: Two kinds of grace? This sounds like yet another "yeah, but." Yeah, we believe in God's grace, but there is a cooperative aspect to it. This belief of course is consistent with Catholic theology which is centered on man as well as on God. The cooperative requirement hints of Pelagianism, Augustine's arch rival. So does your belief that we aren't born with grace. Pelagian didn't believe in predestination, but guess who did? Yes, Saint Augustine did. So here we have a theology that is actually opposed to the theology of one of its most revered saints.

By the way, Bobby, you're right. In the one statement the Catholic Church affirms that works or faith cannot merit the grace of justification, and, on the other hand, it's saying that Catholics can "merit for themselves all the graces needed to attain eternal life. What are these "graces needed to attain eternal life?" I assume they are the means of grace administered through all seven of the Catholic sacraments which are designed to promote a dependency on the Catholic Church organization; the grace is merited when the good works are performed by following the Catholic traditions and rituals. It always comes back to the Catholic Church; the Catholic doctrine is designed to do that. The Catholic Church promotes itself as the means of grace over the Bible as a means of grace.

Sonny: We perform our good works out of faith; a good work is grace in action. A good work is prompted and completed by the work of the Holy Spirit. It's all grace; it's not works based. That's why we say that we are saved by faith and works because it is all grace, which is connects us with the God; it also connects us with His love in our hearts and entitles us to His help. Of course, we know that we must have love; we must love God and love our neighbor. So then, we demonstrate the authenticity of our faith by performing good works for God and for man out of love.

Look, I'm still wondering why you people think we have a weak understanding of God's grace. We believe that grace is how God has chosen to save us so our justification comes from the grace of God. Grace is favor, the free and undeserved help that God gives us to respond to His call to become His children. Grace is a participation in the life of God. Grace is not God choosing to save us; it is not God's mercy or His compassion. Grace is our participation in the Divine Nature (2 Peter 1:4); it is the love of God that has been poured into our heart (Romans 5:5). Grace is God's Divine help (2 Corinthians 6:1-2). When you understand what the Bible is saying to you, you will understand how we can say that works play a role in our salvation, and, at the same time, say we are saved by grace alone. They don't contradict one another. God's grace is in synergy with our works as we work together with Him by letting Him work in our lives through the Holy Spirit. Of course, even our desire to work with God is prompted by the Holy Spirit, so it is all God's grace. There is no contradiction between our works and His grace.

Darrel: There's no biblical support for this synergistic concept. In 2 Corinthians 6:1-2, Paul is warning believers not to live for themselves, a repeat of his warning in 5:15. We need to always interpret a verse in its context.

What you call synergy is simply another example of what I said before about this being yet another of Catholicism's "yeah-buts." You say, yes, God's grace saves us, but we must cooperate and participate in the process of our own salvation. Regardless of how you try to rationalize your belief, what you're really saying is that God's grace alone is insufficient to save those he has chosen for salvation. Again, we believe sanctification is the only step in the biblical Order of Salvation that involves our cooperation. God calls us to cooperate with him in working towards the same purpose, our holiness. That's what Peter is referring to in 2 Peter 6:1-2. The process increases throughout our life but is never completed until our death.

Ray: What's this Order of Salvation?

John: The Order of Salvation is what Paul is presenting in Romans 8:30. The steps in our salvation are:

Election. God chooses His people for salvation before they are born. He decrees their redemption from their fallen status.

Effectual or Effective Calling. The Holy Spirit calls God's chosen to righteousness.

Regeneration. The secret act of God causing a spiritual rebirth to occur and a new life enters the inner person.

Conversion. God sends His Word and powerfully enlightens the mind of the regenerated believer. The spirit is restored, and the believer willingly responds to the gospel through faith and repentance and trusts in Christ for salvation. The believer commits to a new lifestyle, spiritual outlook and religious belief system. New virtuous qualities are instilled into the will which becomes free from its bondage to sin. The believer is thus moved and strengthened to enable them to perform good works.

Justification. This is the instantaneous, gracious and judicial act of God by which He grants the sinner full pardon of all guilt and release from the penalties of sin. Through Christ's atonement, His righteousness is imputed to the believer, and *is recognized through our faith.* We are declared righteous in His sight.

Adoption. God's acceptance of us as His child, His heir, a work of Grace.

Sanctification. The process of being made holy and acceptable to God through the efforts of the Holy Spirit. The justified are renewed in the spirit and bear fruit of good works. Sanctification relies on God's preserving Grace and the believer's perseverance in the faith. This is where we cooperate with God in working towards the same purpose, our holiness and it is therefore the only process in the Order which evokes and involves our participation. The process increases throughout our life but is never completed until our death.

Perseverance. God's gift for His elect where we are enabled to endure in our saving faith to the end of our lives in full obedience to the commands of the Lord.

Death. The end of our physical life on earth and the journey of our soul to go be with the Lord.

Glorification. The final stage which occurs after our death at the final resurrection whereby we assume perfect conformity to the image of Christ. We receive a resurrected body and are made completely holy.

Although Romans 8:30 would seem to indicate that our salvation occurs in such a stepwise manner, some of the processes and certain aspects involved in the processes are believed to occur at the same instant or close to the same instant (such as repentance and faith) and some are spread out over a period of time as is the case with our sanctification. Although we are not able to fully understand the nature of these steps in the Order and how they are applied in the life of the believer, Scripture clearly indicates that God's calling is effective and the elect always receive Christ because God has regenerated and converted them. We are brought to the place where we are able to receive something from God on the authority of Jesus Christ, namely, the remission of sins. We are made righteous and acceptable to God, and this guarantees our perseverance in the faith and our ultimate glorification after we pass on from this life to our eternal life with our Father.

As you may be able to discern from these steps in our salvation, each involves what God does for us, not what we must do for Him. And that means that none of our deeds, whether one considers them to be performed in obedience to God's moral law (Paul's reference to "works of law") or other works that are done out of the goodness of our hearts, are worthy of ultimate justification in the sight of God. Only the merit of Christ through God's judicial act by which He grants the sinner full pardon of all guilt and release from the penalties of sin. Through Christ's atonement, His righteousness is imputed to the believer, and is recognized through our faith. We are declared righteous in His sight. Only by trusting in Christ alone can we be made righteous in the sight of God. That's the true gospel message.

Catholicism distorts this message by requiring us to do something to earn our salvation in adding good works to the formula for salvation; in this respect, it's not much different than any other religion that believes works are required for salvation. The only way it differ is that none of these other works-based religions have anything to say about God's grace. They all believe our salvation is solely dependent on our works.

Sonny: We believe that God's grace enables the ongoing living of the Christian life; but we must cooperate and participate because we have free will and that's a choice we make. Of course, our free will is influenced by God's grace.

Darrel: It seems you're trying to combine sanctification with our justification. We don't cooperate with God in any other step except in our sanctification. He doesn't need our cooperation to justify us. He does that entirely by his grace. Catholic theology weakens God's sovereignty in its belief that God can't save us without our cooperation. This is intentional. God's glory is reflected in his grace, and there's no glory left for itself if the church gives all the glory to God. Theologian Charles Spurgeon once described this reality. "Christ did not redeem His church with His blood that the Pope might come in and steal away the glory! He never came from Heaven to earth and poured out His very heart that He might purchase His people so that a poor sinner, a mere man, should be set upon high to be admired by all nations and to call himself God's representative on earth."

Many Christians have trouble understanding God's unmerited favor; man instinctively believes he should merit God's favor by doing something for him to be pleased enough with him to save him. I've never understood why any Christian would ever believe that we could possibly do that much good to please a perfect, righteous, just God. God doesn't grade on the curve. Luther marveled at that misconception in *The Bondage of the Will.* Christian theology is clear on all of God's characteristics; we should know what his holiness, justness and righteousness really mean; we cannot please him.

John: It's only natural for fallen man to want to earn our pay, to work for what we receive. Mormons play on this concept by emphasizing good works to pay off a debt to God, but we Christians have the Bible, God's description of His character and purpose, and we should know Him better than that. One of the law's purposes is to demonstrate to us how far short we fall in obedience to it.

It's hard for Christians to accept the belief that we can't do enough to please God, no matter how hard we try; and we aren't required to do this anyway because Christ has done the good work required by God for us. That's the gospel message.

Furthermore, if we are truly saved, we want to please God by obeying His moral law. This is what Paul means when he says to work out our salvation in Philippians 2:12.

Catholics do not clearly understand the sole role grace plays in our salvation, and that is an essential difference between Protestants and Catholics. I personally know Dr. Peter Kreeft, a Boston College professor of theology who converted from Protestantism to Catholicism many years ago. He said that he converted because he believed he connected best with Christ through Catholicism; "All the weird little Catholic pieties are really the best way to get to know and be in relationship to Christ, then He will surely draw you in. Try it, what do you have to lose?" Kreeft graduated from Calvin College and he thoroughly understood and accepted Calvinism's concept of God's plan of salvation, and recognized the essentiality of the difference in the way the Catholic Church taught God's plan of salvation and the way the Protestants understand it; this is why he said he could not accept this Catholic belief in "grace plus works." He correctly recognized that it compromised God's sovereignty and that the Bible did not support the Catholic interpretation of the salvation process.

Ray: We're back to that discussion again?

John: Well, yes, we are; as you've said before, our concept of what God's grace really is defines our difference; it goes right to the heart of our respective theologies. Of all your Catholic extra-biblical doctrine, this "grace plus works" is the most offensive to me because it is so unbiblical and heretical, and I see it as a man-centered concept; it dilutes Christianity's unique place in being the only world religion that is not works-based like Islam and Judaism.

It's critical to understand the salvation process as it is defined in the Bible, not by how your church defines it; and it's important we know that this does represent an essential difference between us. The sad result of a weak understanding of grace is that Catholics are taught that justification before God is a process that is maintained by the effort and works of the Catholic. This is unfortunate teaching since it puts the unbearable burden of works' righteousness upon the shoulders of the sinner. By contrast, the Bible teaches that justification/salvation is by faith alone.

But, that said, I don't believe we are saved by our precise understanding of how this great salvation comes to us, and should not let that divide us. That's what Satan wants. We are on the same page in our recognition that we are lost and damned, hopeless and helpless, and that nothing can save us but the grace of God. This is an essential, and we must understand that because we share this essential belief, we should not break fellowship with our Catholics brothers and sisters in Christ.

Sonny: Our Church is essential to us, and it defined the relationship of faith and works in salvation at the Council of Trent following controversy over Martin Luther's heretical doctrine of justification by faith alone. The Council also reaffirmed other practices that offended the reformers such as indulgences, pilgrimages, the veneration of saints and relics, and the veneration of the Virgin Mary. This was the Counter-Reformation.

Catholics have always believed that faith justifies initially, but that works perfect and complete justification. The decision of the Church to reaffirm that belief that our good works are a necessary aspect in our salvation as an accompaniment to God's grace is primarily based on James 2:24. "You see that a man is justified by works, and not by faith only." You can't state it any more clearly than that. Nowhere does Scripture teach that man is saved by faith alone.

Ray: We quote Scripture, you Protestants blather on with silly riddles you learned from pastor Billie Bob in vacation Bible school 30 years ago.

Darrel: Really? Well, let's talk about what the Bible says, okay? Here's some Scripture for you: Romans 4:5: "But to the one who does not work, but believes in Him who justifies the ungodly, his faith is reckoned as righteousness." Romans 5:1: "Therefore, being justified by faith, we have peace with God through our Lord Jesus Christ." And, of course there is Ephesians 2:8 again, "For by grace we are saved through faith, and that not of yourselves: It is the gift of God." There is no other way to interpret Paul's meaning here.

Give me an example of how faith and works act together.

Sonny: Paul tells us in Galatians 5:6 that the faith that justifies us is "faith working through love," not faith alone.

Darrel: There is it again: *Yeah,* we're justified by faith, *but* love must accompany that faith.

John: Yes, Sonny, faith and love are connected, but not in the way you imply. Love, like all good works, is the result of a true, saving faith, not a necessary act we must perform to make our faith genuine. Catholics get their means and ends confused. If love doesn't accompany faith, that faith is demonstrated to not be a true, genuine, saving faith. The good work of loving is the result of our true faith; it accompanies our faith in that respect, but it is not a good work that is required to actually save us. Can't you people understand the difference?

Sonny: I only know that my Church is the authority I must turn to in an effort to know God's truth. When it tells me that faith cannot justify without works, I believe it to be true.

John: Yes, I understand what you're saying, but, if you could allow yourself to think on your own about this point, I'm sure you would see my point. And that point is that Christians need to understand that God, through His grace, does everything for us in His plan of salvation, and we are thus not required to do anything for Him to save ourselves. Works are not necessary to complete our justification because we can't justify ourselves; that's what Scripture tells us. God is to receive all the glory, don't you see? When we understand that His grace is all-sufficient in our salvation, we give Him all the glory. There are many verses in the Bible that clearly state this, but I like what Paul says in 1 Corinthians 4:7. "What do you have that you did not receive?" As Darrel said before, this was the verse Augustine credited for the reason he believed in predestination. Works do play a role of course, and, through the sanctification process, we do participate to some degree in working towards becoming more holy as God is holy. Even then, we have the help of the Holy Spirit to guide us in accomplishing this objective. God justifies us, and we are renewed in the spirit and bear fruit of good works. Sanctification relies on God's preserving Grace and the believer's perseverance in the faith. God calls us to cooperate with Him in working towards the same purpose, our holiness, and that is why I say it is the only step in God's salvation plan which evokes and involves our participation. The process increases throughout our life but is never completed until our death.

Sonny: Hebrews 11:6 tells us that faith is indeed the minimum requirement without which we cannot please God; and this gratuitous gift of faith from God also includes the grace of hope and love the moment the person is justified. But this is just the beginning of the process leading toward justification. Faith alone does not justify a person. Justification is only achieved by faith and works as Paul says in Ephesians 2:8-9. We believe we are to cooperate with God through our sanctification, just as you said, but we believe this process not only involves growing in faith but in showing our faith by performing good works; sanctification is necessary for us to be saved. It does not occur automatically after the first justification which occurs without our works but only involves our consent.

Darrel: So you are saying, *yeah*, faith is a requirement for being justified by God, *but* it must be accompanied by works. This is putting the cart before the horse. *The Westminster Confession* defines the role of sanctification in our salvation as "They, who are effectually called and regenerated, having a new heart, and a new spirit created in them, are further sanctified, really and personally, through the virtue of Christ's death and resurrection, by His word and spirit dwelling within us" In other words, our sanctification follows our election, adoption, regeneration and justification which are the result of God's grace bestowed on us. So you can see how this "yeah, but" confuses the steps in the Order of Salvation because it presents faith and sanctification as being necessary for our justification, when, in fact, faith is merely a recognition of our justification. The Order of Salvation is biblical, my friend. Romans 8:29-30.

Sonny: Okay, let's go back to what Paul is teaching in Ephesians 2:8-9. Paul states that faith is the root of justification, and that faith excludes "works of law." That means he is saying that a person cannot save themselves by simply obeying God's law. He's speaking to the Ephesian gentiles and warning them not to think like the unbelieving, legalistic Jews. He is not teaching that the good works we do for others is not a requirement. These good works are different than the works of law we do out of obedience to God, and they need to accompany God's grace for us to be saved. Faith of course comes first, and those who do good works outside of faith are in a system of debt, not of grace. Therefore, I repeat again what James said, "A man is justified by works, and not by faith alone."

God is not a God of contradiction, so the only way to reconcile what Paul and James are saying here is to assume there are two types of works, "works of law" and works of a good conscience.

Darrel: So, we come back to these two types of works again, eh? When Paul talks about being under the law, he is not saying that people were under a system of legalism trying to earn their salvation. He is speaking about the period from Moses to Christ where the law revealed sin but gave no power to obey. It gave knowledge of sin and announced the curse. Being "under grace" means being in a relationship with God through Christ where we are forgiven and empowered by the Holy Spirit to obey the Father.

John: I think Sonny has brought up an important distinction. In Ephesians 2:8-9, when Paul says "We are justified by faith apart from observing the law," he is referring to the deeds of the unsaved man whereby he vainly hopes to gain acceptance with God, while in other verses in his letters, he speaks of "good works," by which he means the fruit that the justified man must produce. Paul is using works in two different ways, he's not describing two types of works. Just as we concluded before that there aren't two types of sin, one that damns us to hell and one that doesn't, it's an incorrect stretch of Scripture to assume that one type of work earns us salvation and the other type doesn't. No sin, no matter how you define it, is exempt from God's curse just as no good work, no matter how you define it, can earn our salvation or play any role in earning our salvation.

Darrel: Only Catholics distinguish between good deeds performed in obedience to God's law and those deeds we perform for our neighbor as you have stated in an effort to justify your grace plus works heresy. Works are works, regardless of whether they're performed out of duty or whether they are Spirit motivated, and works do not save.

Sonny: James 2:24 is making our case.

Darrel: No, it isn't. That isn't what James is saying. You are taking James 2:24 totally out of its context to support a heretical doctrine. When we go back to 2:14, we see the discussion focuses on faith without works is dead. So then, we can correctly assume that James 2:24 is stating that if you claim to be a Christian, but have no works, you aren't really a

Christian. A Christian with a true, saving faith will exhibit good works. Period. That's all James is saying. Again, you're confusing means and ends.

John: For James, the word "deed" means the believer's works, the outward evidence of a saved life. Neither one of these apostles is saying anything that would support "grace plus works."

Here's another way to look at the Catholic distinction between works of law and good works to support their grace plus works belief. You, of course, know that Christ summarized God's moral law, the Ten Commandments, in saying that they were really just two commandments: Love your God and love your neighbor. You have said that loving your neighbor is an example of a deed that is not a work of law because it's an act of good conscience, but here Christ is relating it to God's moral law, right?

Sonny: I'm not sure I get what you're getting at, John.

John: The Ten Commandments say we are to honor and worship the one, true God, and Christ is saying we are to love Him; that is the work of law; but then He says we are to love our neighbor, that's not a work of law, that falls into your Catholic definition of a good work, right? But then, Christ ties them together by saying they both represent a summary of God's moral law, the Ten Commandments. He is making no distinction between the two types of works, and, of course, neither should we.

Sonny: Based on your opinion, right?

John: It's an opinion that is obvious to anyone with a logical mind; but indoctrination quashes logic. I have expressed an opinion based on how a person would normally and logically interpret what the Bible is or is not saying.

Darrel: In his classic tome, *Mere Christianity*, C. S. Lewis said that 99% of what we know is based on some authority. The challenge is to select the right authority that guides you to knowing the truth; that's our goal here. So then, your authority is obviously your Catholic Church; ours is the God Himself through the guidance of the Holy Spirit residing within us. The same Spirit who called us to believe is the same Spirit who guides us in our belief. Utilizing that Spirit as our guide, I say that James 2:24 tells us that a person is not shown to be just by the mere profession of faith or by having a faith that remains alone. A person is only shown to be just by what he or she does. We know from reading many verses addressing this subject in Scripture that none of our deeds, including our faith, is worthy of ultimate justification in the sight of God.

Ray: Faith is not a work Darrel.

Darrel: It is in the way you use it, Ray. You imply that our faith, like our works, justifies us. You believe we must exercise our faith to justify ourselves. Faith is a noun, not a verb.

Sonny: I'm not sure what you people are trying to say. All I know is that there are a number of verses in the New and Old Testament that differentiate between works of law and good works. Here are a number from the O.T. Nehemiah 13:14, Psalm 11:7, 28:4, Isaiah 3:10, 59:18, Jeremiah 25:15, 50:29, Ezekiel 9:10, 11:21, 36:19, Joshua 4:9, 9:15 and 12:2.

Darrel: If you would trouble yourself to read every one of your church's spoon-fed references from an objective viewpoint, it would become obvious to you that none of them have anything to do with being saved by works or even with works contributing in any way towards salvation regardless of how you want to define what category of works is being referenced. In fact, all of them except Isaiah 3:10 refer to judging those without faith based on the evidence of their deeds. That person has rejected the forgiveness of Jesus to rely on works. Isaiah 3:10 is not talking about works saving anyone either. Rather, Isaiah is comforting those who have, by faith, remained faithful to God by saying that in this life, even though Jerusalem would be destroyed, it would be well with them. He is not talking about being saved in any way at all. Instead,

Scripture is very clear that righteousness is by faith apart from works. To support this statement, I refer you to Romans Chapters 3-5.

Look, man, I'd be willing to bet that you understand exactly what we've been saying to you; you just don't want to think about it. When we get you off your script, you get confused; we're just trying to clear up that confusion. John's comment is requiring you to think on your own, without being able to rely on one of your cue card answers provided by your church organization which purports to be the only authority on the meaning of Scripture. That routine may sell to the folks in the cheap seats, but it won't fly with us Protestants who practice an intelligent faith. We rely on our own research into the truth and rely on the Holy Spirit to guide us in correctly interpreting God's Word. We can also learn about God and his Word in discussions like the one we're having, and I hope you are learning as well.

Sonny: Personal opinions, no matter how they are formed, are unreliable. We can only know the meaning of Scripture through the authority of our Church.

John: First of all, as C. S. Lewis once said, most of what we know is based on other's opinions; very little is based on our own personal observation. We Protestants pay heed to the opinions of those theologians we respect to guide us in understanding the Word; you rely on the personal opinions of your appointed saints, early Christian writers and your magisterium, right? Well, they voice their collective opinion but it's still related to their individual, personal opinions. Case in point, Catholics refer to James 2:8-11 to make their case that there are two different kinds of works, works of law and good works; that conclusion is based on the personal opinion of their magisterium. Well, that isn't the way we understand what James is saying. When he tells us how faith and works go together in dealing with other people, he is referring to Mosaic Law. If you say you have faith, but no works, you are no good to anyone else. Faith and works, however, justifies you (in a non-salvitic sense) before your fellow man because your witness is consistent with your stated belief; they can see your works and know the genuineness of your faith.

As I said before, both sides need to understand we should examine Scripture as it would be taken normally. That means we, notwithstanding various linguistic styles used in the Bible, should assume that what the verse is saying is really what it's saying; no hidden nuances, no complex code. Scripture should never be stretched to accommodate a preconceived notion or bias. And I remind you of one of our rules of exegesis is to use Scripture to interpret Scripture. When in doubt, whether you are someone in authority in your church or as an individual, as Darrel said before, you should always use a more clear verse to explain the meaning of the more difficult verse. We each need to take a good look at what these verses mean when we look at them objectively and not from the view that we are trying to make them say something they're clearly not saying.

Sonny: How about these verses from the New Testament: Romans 3:20:28, Galatians 2:16:21, 3:2, 5, 10. Many Protestants error in their understanding of what Paul means by "works of law" in his teaching on justification.

Darrel: Is this "déjà vu" all over again? Didn't we dispense of this point of yours about two types of works? Come on, man, turn the page. Okay, here we go, one more time.

Abraham was saved by faith without any works of any kind. The "good work" of Abraham that was relevant to the Jews would have referred to his obedience to God's will that he be circumcised. Paul's point was that Abraham was justified by faith before he had done anything. As for James, when he's talking about faith and works, he is addressing a specific problem. When taken in its context (as we should always interpret Scripture), we see that some people were saying that because they were saved by faith, they didn't need works. James' point was, in effect, "that's not how a Christian acts." Faith does not contribute to salvation, but is visible proof to those around you that you are saved. Works flow from faith, so without works, faith is dead. Your assertion that the works Paul and James are talking about are different is just ridiculous. The moral law of Moses is the standard God give to determine what is good or not. If you are talking civil and ceremonial law, Colossians shows that those were fulfilled by Christ and therefore nullified. The moral law is still the Law of Moses. Trying to be saved by works would be guided by the moral law because God has given no other standard on which to judge works. Romans 3:20, the verse you used as support, doesn't prove the point you assume it does. Rather the verse says that you will never be saved by your works because your works prove that you are a sinner who can't be saved by works.

Now then, can we put this discussion to bed and move on?

Sonny: All I can say in conclusion is that you Protestants are incorrect in ignoring good works in our salvation. This promotes antinomianism. This means you support faith equals justification minus works.

Darrel: We don't ignore good works, Sonny! Please, pay attention to what we've said about that.

Bobby: What is antinomianism?

John: According to McKim, antinomianism is the view that there is no need for the law in the Christian life. It first raised its ugly head with the first century Gnostics who were misinterpreting what Paul was saying in Romans. That of course isn't what Paul meant at all, and every Christian should know that God takes His law very seriously and expects us to follow it as best we can; we of course all disobey His law, but He extends His favor to us while we were still violating His law to guaranty us our salvation.

Daniel: Antinomianism is associated with the concept of "cheap grace," the assumption that God wipes the slate clean if you just appease Him by saying you believe in Him, and this leaves you free to sin again. It's what James was talking about when he recognized that some people were saying that because they were saved by faith, they didn't need works. Just because God's grace is not earned, this doesn't mean it's cheap.

Daniel: James is attacking all forms of antinomianism that seek to have Jesus as Savior without embracing Him as Lord. Just as Paul demonstrated that trusting in one's own works is deadly, so James teaches that resting on as empty or dead faith is deadly.

John: This discussion brings us back to our understanding of the role grace or faith plays in His plan of salvation. We know Protestants see it differently than Catholics do. Forgive me for repeating myself, but it's important to understand that the Catholic faith plus works is not what the Bible is telling us. It means that Catholics believe God's grace is not sufficient by itself for salvation; good works are necessary as well. Luther objected to this approach, particularly where it was exemplified in the Catholic practice of granting indulgences, pardons for money. He mentioned them 45 times in his 95 theses. In reading his Bible, he discovered the powers that be were distorting the gospel message that salvation is by grace alone, not by works, so that no man can boast. God's forgiveness is not for sale, nor can it be earned by doing good works.

Darrel: In 2 Corinthians 10:12-18, Paul states that no one, person or institution, should not boast about itself. Let it glory in the Lord, and not in itself.

Sonny: We give glory to God in doing good works. If we believe that works are not necessary and that our sin is forgiven by grace alone, we would not try and do good because we would think we were saved by grace no matter how we acted.

Darrel: Paul, of course, anticipated this response and concern and, in Romans 6:1, stated that those of us who understand that Christ died for our sins will not continue to sin. Of course, we understand that we are still sinful even though we have been justified but because we should walk in Athe newness of life," we at least should focus on obedience to the commandments of God. All justified sinners automatically pursue holiness. Paul explained that if our faith is genuine, it will automatically produce good works.

This is exactly why all Reformed Christian denominations believe that faith and works are one and the same. John clarified this before when he said that *faith equals works.* If we have a saving faith, it will be seen in our good works towards others.

Ray: We are justified by our faith.

Darrel: This is what the Bible tells us about the grounds for justification. In Galatians 2:16, Paul tells us that Christ's righteousness is the only ground for our justification. And, as we said before, faith is the *only* means by which we lay hold of the righteousness of Christ. This is how faith is connected with justification in the Order of Salvation. It's not about what you do through your church or even what your church can only do for you.

Sonny: In Colossians 1:24, Paul is saying that he rejoices in his sufferings and "fill up in my flesh what is lacking in the afflictions of Christ, for the sake of His body, which is the Church, of which I became a minister according the stewardship from God which was given to me for you, to fulfill the word of God." I know you said before that Paul is not saying the Church saves, but, in the sense it enables us to believe, it does save.

Darrel: Why didn't you accept my explanation of what Paul is actually saying? He is clearly not saying that somehow the church (with a small "c" in every Bible but your Catholic version) is to continue to fulfill the work Christ has already performed for us in our salvation. I grant you that the verse is not as clear as those verses I quoted that are clearer in stating that Christ's death and resurrection are sufficient for our salvation.

Sonny: As I have been saying all along, I believe my Church's interpretation of that verse and every verse in the Bible over your opinion or any other person's opinion.

Darrel: But, as we have tried to point out before, your church is made up of persons who render their opinions in interpreting Scripture for you; and these people are not perfect, of course, and, when we take an objective look at their motive for expressing such opinions, we see it is self-serving and this should weaken or even destroy their credibility.

When we approach the meaning of these Bible verses with an open mind and not an indoctrinated mind, we can see that the Bible is saying we are saved by grace alone; and when we understand what Paul is saying in his various letters to the new churches he established, we see that this is completely consistent with our understanding that our purpose here on earth is to glorify God, not ourselves or some church. We glorify God in acknowledging his complete sovereignty in our lives and what happens to us after this life is over. When good works are added to the process of salvation, the Catholic Church is asserting man's sovereignty; it's saying that, *yeah*, God is merciful and bestows his grace on us, *but* we need to do something as well or he can't save us. Your church teaches that we need to partner up with God to save ourselves. That's unbiblical, and it suggests that again your church is trying to meet our natural want to have our good works count for something. I know I've made this point before, but it's important enough to warrant repeating.

Peter: Religions are designed to give folks what they want. In that respect, Christianity is no different than any other religion, including my atheistic religion of secular humanism. You Protestants say that Catholics give people what they want in designing some of these traditions like purgatory which gives man a second chance, but you Protestants do the same thing. In your belief that salvation is only through faith in God, who then wipes your sinful plate clean, you are giving yourselves a "get out of jail free card." Isn't that what everyone who believes in the burden of sin and how it affects one's salvation wants to believe? You can dismiss this concept as cheap grace and call it invalid, but you "doth protest too much, I think."

John: God's grace isn't cheap for Him or for us. There was nothing cheap about a perfect man suffering and giving up his life for a crime he didn't commit. And there's nothing cheap in what a Christian has to bear in suffering in following Christ either. Just because our sins have been forgiven, the ones we've made, the ones we make today, and the ones we'll make tomorrow doesn't give us license to be cavalier about sin and go on sinning. Paul cautioned us about that. The elect have been converted to faith and we are motivated to be righteous and live by that faith. This is what the prophet Habakkuk told us. We do good because we have first been forgiven.

Darrel: Hey, Pete, you're right about secular humanism being a designed religion. With God out of the mix, everything is permissible, right? Morals and behavior can change with the times, nothing is absolute, no moral governor looking over your shoulder, no ultimate judge to condemn you, just live and let live and try to do some good for your fellow man, or not. Heckuva deal! Christianity is not the religion man would design because it negates every single thing I just mentioned your belief system allows.

Peter: You're right; all religions are designed by man, and, from what I know about Catholicism so far, its expressed beliefs more resembles a designed belief system than Protestantism does. Catholicism has man's fingerprints all over its dogma.

Sonny: Our religion is "designed" by God! Christianity addresses man's need for salvation, and the Catholic Church has sole responsibility and authority to preach and teach the gospel.

Peter: Regardless of denomination, salvation is the basic need of Christians; it's not my need. You all want to be assured of heaven, I don't believe there is a heaven or a hell. But, from what I've heard so far, it seems that the Catholic dogma tacks onto addressing that basic need of salvation. Most men are followers, and desire to have a single strong leader in their spiritual lives to rely on to know the truth. The Catholic Church provides that one sole authority for them. It thereby enables itself to have influence and power over its followers to lead them wherever it sees fit to take them in addressing any want or need of their followers; and, of course, there's the suspicion of self-interest in attaining that objective as well.

Sonny: Of course there should be only one authority in our religion, Peter. If we can't depend on one authority to teach us God's truth, we are left adrift in the same deep waters you're trying to navigate relying on your meaningless atheistic beliefs based on your godless philosophies. People who do not belong to our Church are left only with their own opinions. You have your philosophers, Protestants rely on their theologians with their many different theologies which attempt to explain God's gospel truth to them. They have no one they can really trust; their opinions are just that, opinions. We know the Church has divinely given authority because the body of revealed truth in the sacred tradition of the Church says it does, and we trust the sacred tradition because the Church with its divinely given authority says it's inspired.

Darrel: Okay, so you're saying your Church has established a sacred tradition that assigns to your church inspired, divine authority. This means that your church stakes its claim on authority it has assigned to itself. Your church issues authoritative dogma that gives them the authority to issue authoritative dogma. This is circular logic, by definition. You're admitting to us your claim to authority is based on the weakest form of logic.

Please recall John 14:26, Sonny. Our opinions are guided by the Holy Spirit, the only authority God has provided for us on an individual basis. When your church, or any church, claims to speak for the Holy Spirit on a corporate basis, we should be suspicious of its opinion, and its motive. You've told us your magisterium is like a prophet for Catholics in that it speaks for God, the Bible tells us we're done with prophets after Christ and he left us with the Holy Spirit to guide and direct us in our Christian walk.

In our discussions, we always come back again to the question of authority. On the one hand, we Protestant Christians rely solely on the authority of the Bible, a book all Christians, including Roman Catholics, believe is the Word of God; and, yes, I'll say it again, we rely on the Holy Spirit God gave us who also inspired our Bible-believing theologians who have earned their credibility to guide us in interpreting God's Word.

On the other hand, you are told to believe that the pope is in the direct line of succession from the original apostles who were privy to hearing God's Word from God himself, and that you have these Catholic Church councils and this magisterium which tell you they're the ultimate authority in all matters relating to the Christian religion.. You should be skeptical about a church organization pulling this off because it seems to be so self-serving.

Look, man, for centuries you Catholic Christians have been severely restricted from expressing your personal interpretations on Scripture for a variety of reasons. First of all, the common man didn't even have access to the written Word of God until after Gutenberg's discovery; and, up until the past several centuries, the illiteracy rate was high anyway. But now, of course, we live in a different age, and now it seems personal interpretations are allowed but discouraged. This of course is because the Catholic Church is very reluctant to share any of its own authority. Regardless, in these discussions we put our theories to the test, and we Protestants know how to do that. We rely on our own opinions because God holds us individually responsible for our own actions. Can't you just see a Catholic on Judgment Day attempting to explain why it wasn't his fault he misunderstood God's Word, it was his darn Catholic Church's fault. That would go over with God about the same as Eve pointing to the snake and Adam pointing to Eve, right? You Catholics should consider assuming responsibility for what you believe.

Ray: It is not possible to personally and privately read Scripture and discover new Divine Revelation never known before.

Darrel: We don't read the Bible to discover new revelation, Ray; we read it to discover new meaning.

Ray: In 2 Peter 1:20, the Apostle is discouraging private interpretation of the Bible.

Darrel: I recall we discussed the meaning of this verse last week. Were you there? Man, I think the sun must be getting to you.

Ray: I took your point then, Darrel, I just wasn't satisfied with your explanation. In this verse Peter is clearly saying that no prophecy of Scripture is of any private interpretation, "for prophecy never came by the will of man, but holy men of God spoke as they were moved by the Holy Spirit." Doesn't that sound like Peter is discouraging Christians to utilize private interpretation?

Darrel: You answer him this time, John. I tire of repeating myself with this guy.

John: Peter of course is referring to prophecy, not interpreting Scripture. He is expressing his concern for false prophets as he continues to address in the next chapter. His concern is not over the reliability of the people who interpret the Bible, but over the reliability of Scripture itself. He is saying that the prophetic testimony in Scripture comes only from God which includes not only visions but also words used to describe and interpret them. See Daniel 8:15-19 and Zechariah 1:9). He is making our point when he concludes the verse by mentioning the role of the Holy Spirit in our understanding of Scripture.

Ray: That's your opinion, guys. Peter also warns in 2 Peter 3:16 about unstable and untaught people mistakenly interpreting Scripture to their own destruction.

John: The interpretation of such men is always to be tested by stable men led by the Spirit who are taught in the correct interpretation of the Scripture. Paul tells us that God gave the gift to some individuals to be teachers of the Word. Why would God do that if He intended for only some church to assume this authority? God has the power to make sure we understand His Word without designating one particular authoritative church organization to do His work for Him. Those whom He has chosen, will hear His voice and do not need a self-promoting authority to become their shepherd. We have Christ and the Holy Spirit for that.

Ray: You make it sound like we don't even consider the Holy Spirit at all in our understanding of Christianity. That's just not true at all.

Our Church leaders defined and correctly interpreted Scripture to declare doctrines and dogmas on faith and morals with the guidance of the Holy Spirit who has been given to the Church to protect it from error on these matters. This is the purpose of our Magisterium. Christ sent the Holy Spirit to be the Advocate of the Magisterium to not teach error when speaking an infallible dogma. Christians would not have the dogma today if it weren't for the Magisterium who proclaimed it always in submission to the Holy Spirit in these matters and to the glory of God. Actually the first dogma proclaimed by Peter, according to the Catholic apologists, was when Jesus asked, "Who do you say I am?" and Peter said, "You are the Christ, the Son of the living God." And Jesus said, "No man revealed this to you but My Father." God revealed the truth to the first apostolic leader of the Magisterium.

Darrel: This is exactly where your church takes liberty with Scripture. I say again that the gospel accounts do not refer to a group of men you call the "magisterium," nor does it refer to Peter as its first apostolic leader. While Peter certainly played an important role in the history of the Christian church, and we know a lot about him as recorded in the book of Acts, he was just one of twelve disciples who were all pledged to continue on with Christ's teachings. In the sense that we are also Disciples of Christ, we are also recipients of Christ's teachings through the writings of the apostles. Even though, unlike them, we were not eye witnesses, we believe their testimony by our God-given faith obtained by the righteousness of God and our savior Jesus Christ. That's a direct gift of God; it defines his grace.

Regardless, I should point out to you that you claim the Spirit guided your leaders, we claim the Spirit guides us as individuals in our understanding of the Bible; but we too have our leaders who are influenced by the Spirit to guide and teach us to correctly understand Scripture. The difference of course between us is that Catholics rely totally on their church's guidance, assuming the influence of the Spirit to get Scripture right; we rightly accept the responsibility of dealing directly with God, whether through prayer or in understanding his Word. There is no "middle man" in Protestantism. And we believe that's a good thing.

Ray: And, of course, that's just your opinion, Darrel.

Darrel: Of course it is, and I have done enough Bible study to trust my opinion to be true, Ray. Don't you trust your own opinion? Must you people always look to your "magisterium" to find out what you're supposed to believe? That's a rhetorical question, man.

Look, as I said before, we are here to express our personal opinions, and we'd like to hear yours. We don't want to hear you just repeat some script written by your church leaders; we want to hear what you believe, objectively and with an open mind. If a person can't even offer an opinion of what they think about whatever subject we're discussing, they are acting like indoctrinated members of some cult, not people who lead an examined life who are open to discussing issues with people who may not agree with what you believe. At this stage of our lives, we should all be living the examined life, my friend. Are you up to that challenge? Why do you feel you need a church to connect you with our Savior?

Ray: I've examined my belief and am content with knowing it's the truth, the only truth. I could not trust myself to know this truth without relying on my Church to assist me.

Darrel: Your church is really just us human beings; who do you trust more, God or man? We trust in God, through the Holy Spirit to guide us to the truth.

By the way, I'll believe you've examined what you believe when you at least concede that there appears to be a self-serving interest in your Catholic Church's insistence on its own authority. We've provided evidence that should at least make you curious. And, regarding this comment of yours about how content you are, I can address that by telling you a little story about a good Catholic friend of mine who knew he was dying of bladder cancer. I asked him if he was afraid to die, and he told me he wasn't sure he had been good enough to go to heaven. Does that sound like contentment to you, man! It doesn't to me.

John: How did you answer your friend, Darrel?

Darrel: I asked him if he believed Jesus Christ was his savior. He said, "Yes, I do." I said, well you should be content you're saved because that is all that is required. He said "yeah, but, I'm not sure I've led a good enough life to merit salvation." It was another "yeah, but" in Catholicism. Even though my good friend was one of the most virtuous, devoutly religious men I have ever known, I told him that he could never be good enough to be sure he was saved, but that his confession of belief in Christ as his savior was enough. I know it made him feel good to hear it, but I think it made me feel even better to say it.

Sonny: Our Church advises us not to worry about our final destiny. We are always to make sure we are in a state of grace each day. Salvation is today, neither in the past nor in the future. To keep in this state, we are to frequently participate in the sacraments, and pray every day. We are to pray as though everything depends on God, and work as though everything depends on us.

Darrel: You made my point, Sonny. No wonder my friend was concerned; how can anyone be sure they are frequenting the sacraments enough in the right way and praying enough in the right way in assuming everything depends on God, and how on earth are we to know whether our work has been sufficient to maintain this state of grace you talk about?

Sonny: We know when we are right with our Church, Darrel.

Darrel: Ah, yes, check in with the priest at confession, state your sins, do your assigned number of "hail Mary's" and call it good; you'll remain in that state of grace. Talk about encouraging antinomianism!

Okay, let's change the subject. I'd like to talk a little about this "unfolding revelation" Catholics refer to. You spoke earlier of the part that is not written down and that this part is your larger tradition that records the community's experience of God or more specifically of Jesus Christ. You said it's unfolding; and, as I recall, you said it was your magisterium's job to communicate this unfolding or unraveling revelation.

Daniel: This "unfolding revelation" sounds a lot like what cults include in their false doctrine. Joseph Smith kept coming up with new revelation. The Qur'an actually includes a provision for this concept in Islam as well. They call it "abrogation."

Sonny: Look, guys, this isn't more revelation, it's just more elucidation on God's revelation as our Magisterium sees the Catholic community's need for more explanation. Jesus had many things to say, but the apostles couldn't bear them at that point. This demonstrates that the Church's infallible doctrine develops over time. All public revelation was completed at the death of the last apostle, but the doctrine of God's Revelation develops as our minds and hearts are able to welcome and understand it.

Darrel: You mean the additional revealed dogma that your vaunted church has determined to free you people over the centuries to suit its own purpose in some way, right?

If only this "unfolding revelation" would be the same as what we've been saying about the process of sanctification, then it would be a good thing because it would be adding to our knowledge, contributing to our spiritual growth. But, in calling it revelation and making it seem as though God is speaking through your church, that's not the same thing, and it's not a good thing because it isn't really God's revealed Word. It's what your church wants to communicate to you under its presumed authority. As I said before, unraveling, or unfolding revelation gives your church a license to be very creative with Christian doctrine.

Again you people seem confused about God's plan of salvation. You don't really know what this process of sanctification refers to. You guys do seem to just stop learning about our wonderful faith the day you graduate from your catechism classes.

Sanctification seems to apply more to your church than to you as an individual believer. Hey, it's not about your vaunted church being sanctified and then relaying that information to the believers; it's about each individual believer being sanctified over his or her lifetime; it is each believer who is becoming more holy as we undertake to read the Word study the Word, hear the Word, and practice the Word. Separate yourself from your church just for a moment, if you can, and understand that it is each individual Christian person who continues to learn throughout their entire life to become more holy. We learn, not from unfolding revelation from God through your church, but from God himself through the person of the Holy Spirit which allows us to continually grow in the faith and in our knowledge of God's revealed Word.

Sonny: But there is in some sense continued revelation. Visions of Jesus and Mary have been instrumental in certain doctrines and practices of our Church. The vision must be judged by the Magisterium, however, and is evaluated for its consistency with the Traditions and Canons of the Catechism.

Darrel: Whether you call it "unraveling," "unfolding," or "continued" revelation, my point should be well taken. It's adding to God's Word. False religions like Islam allow for continued revelation and so do cults like Mormonism. You're not in good company with this concept, my friend.

Sonny: With all due respect, Darrel, you don't really know what you're talking about, okay? I just know we have to manage revelation; and to do this, Christianity developed a two-fold approach. First, it distinguishes between "public" and "private" revelations. We teach that public or "divine" revelation ended with the death of the last living disciple. However, private revelations continue. We accept apparitions, visionary experiences, and "interior locutions (inner voices) as long as they do not claim to "surpass correct, improve or complete public revelation."

Second, the Church manages revelation by setting authorities like the Magisterium over it. This group of bishops gathered in council to refute heresy and set boundaries of Christian truth. Their collective wisdom, understood to be guided by the Holy Spirit, crystallized into creedal formulations. We consider the papacy to provide us with infallible interpretation of the meaning of divine revelation.

Darrel: Manage revelation? What does that mean? Again, we see how your vaunted church forces itself into the middle between its believers and God, who seemingly has a problem communicating with his chosen believers without relying on the Catholic Church to help him attain his objective. You people attempt to take the hard edge off this assertion by claiming that your church receives guidance from the Holy Spirit. That should cover it, right? You guys accused us of relying only on the Holy Spirit to know what the Bible says, but how can you be sure it's the Spirit guiding your magisterium, eh?

Again I say that interpretation of Scripture is not the sole prerogative of any man or organization; the meaning of Scripture is made clear by the Holy Spirit to those who have been enlightened of Christ and approach God's Word in a spirit of humility and teachableness. Can we move on, please?

Ray: We can be sure because we trust in the authority of the Magisterium.

Peter: Why is such an authority necessary with Catholics? Protestants apparently are confident they don't need such an authority. That's the way an unbeliever sees it.

Sonny: As from the beginning, God speaks to his Church through the Bible and through sacred tradition. To insure that we understand Him, God guides the Church's teaching authority, the Magisterium, so it always interprets and defends the Bible and Tradition accurately. This is the gift of infallibility. Infallibility means without error, and is not to be confused with impeccability which means leading a perfect life. Only Christ accomplished that.

Peter: But are you actually saying that your pope speaks without error?

Sonny: Yes, in his position of the Vicar of Christ's visible church on earth, he is infallible. Whenever he speaks *ex cathedra,* from the chair of Peter, he claims to speak without error. This is biblically supported. This infallibility also extends to the body of bishops as a whole when they are in doctrinal unity with the pope. In John 11:51-52, God allows Caiaphas to prophesize infallibly as you may know.

Darrel: Yes, in this instance, it suited God's purpose to use Caiaphas to speak the truth, and God does use all of us sinners to accomplish his purpose. After all, we believe each of the writers in the Bible are speaking infallibly because we consider the Word to be infallible in and of itself; but the prophets are a tool through whom God speaks; they are speaking *for* God not speaking *as* God. When you call your pope the substitute for Christ, that's what you're implying. And to also presume this infallibility extends to everyone who's supposed to be on the same page as the pope is opening up a can of worms. <u>Abuse is encouraged</u>. By the way, as an aside, I assume the pope got out of his chair to bend down and kiss the Qur'an several years ago, right? What a crock! It goes to credibility.

Sonny: I don't know why Pope John Paul II did that, Darrel. As I said, just because he can speak infallibly doesn't mean he's sinless. Nonetheless, we must assume our leaders all solemnly teach the truth. Our belief is like a three-legged stool; we have the Bible, Tradition (including oral) and the teaching Magisterium. Each leg is necessary for the stability of the Church and to guarantee sound doctrine. This three-legged stool is firmly implanted on the solid rock of the Catholic Church. See Matthew 16:18, John 1:42, Ephesians 2:20, 1 Peter 2:4-8. If any of the legs is removed, the stool collapses.

Darrel: Our Christian three-legged stool is the Father, the Son and the Holy Spirit. I prefer the bicycle analogy over your stool analogy. We

Protestants ride a unicycle; we sit on the seat of the five *solas.* Christ alone, faith alone, Scripture alone, grace alone, and God's glory alone. Catholics ride a bike with training wheels. You can't ride the bike alone or it tips over so you need the church to prop you up. In regards to the Bible verses you threw out there, it's ironic that you use the Bible as an authority on those seldom occasions when you think actual Scripture supports some Catholic dogma. Regardless, let's take a closer look at several of these verses you mentioned.

The first two references you mentioned are typically used to support Catholicism's belief that Christ appointed Peter to be its first pope as the first in line of apostolic succession, and we've already denied that presumption. Regarding these other verses, both Ephesians 2:20 and 1 Peter 2:4-8 refer to setting up the Christian church. Taken normally, they don't point to a specific church but describe what the church is to be and what its purpose is to be. We've always understood these verses to be succinctly stating the essence of the true church. The Catholics hijacked these verses in an effort to support their claim to be the only group of people who composed the original church.

Look, we know that Christ requires his church to fulfill his mission. That means his church is to do the will of God; to serve the flock; to preach the Word and call out sinners to repent. It's the gospel, and that's the function and purpose of the apostolic church. Of course, it's obvious, and will become even more obvious as we proceed in these discussions, that, with Catholicism, it's really mostly about the Catholic Church. It, and it alone, is the authority, to be respected and served as it preaches a heretical doctrine.

Bobby: The north wind is beginning to pick up, so let's adjourn for today. See y'all next week.

Week Five

Bobby: Okay, do any of you have anything you want to get off your chest before we continue on with our discussion of Catholic traditions and which ones are supported by the Bible?

Darrel: The vaunted church magisterium creates Catholic traditions; none of them are biblically supported. It feeds responses to the indoctrinated followers, and the followers dutifully memorize or cut and paste its statements as though they seemingly are hearing from God himself. That's been my experience in debating with their ilk. They may delude themselves into believing they're in commune with Christ by deferring to the opinion of their church, but this connection they have with their church verges on idolatry, and those artifacts, the little statues of Mary, etc. evidences a hint of pagan idol worship; and, based on Old Testament history, we know what happened to the Israelites who violated the first several commandments stated in Exodus 20, right? History's a good teacher.

As the church grew as the state religion of the Roman Empire, it began to become more and more associated with the world and less connected with its purpose. It compromised God's word with worldly teachings and traditions. Catholicism paid no heed to Christ's warning to the church of Pergamum in Revelation 2:14-15. Over the centuries, as the church embraced pagan beliefs and disconnected from "enduring sound doctrine" to "accumulate for itself teachers in accordance to their own desires," the church became more and more apostate until in the early 1500's, people like Martin Luther had finally had enough of it.

Sonny: Ultimately, all attempts to prove Catholicism is pagan fail. Catholic doctrines are neither borrowed from the mystery religions nor introduced from pagans after the conversion of Constantine. To make a charge of paganism stick, one must be able to show more than a similarity between something in the Church and something in the non-Christian world. One must be able to demonstrate a legitimate connection between the two, showing clearly that one is a result of the other, and that there is something wrong with the non-Christian item.

Nobody has been able to prove these things regarding any tenet of the Catholic faith. The charge of paganism just doesn't work.

Before we move on, I'd just like to say one more thing about these priest sex scandals, if I may. No one is denying there has been corruption of ecclesial leaders from time to time in the Church's history, okay? Scandals occurred in the Old Covenant Church and have happened in the New Covenant Church. Human nature is always tempted and weak and corruptible.

Darrel: But the sex scandals in the priesthood are reaching epidemic proportions, and once the damage is done, the cat is out of the bag. I would assume that it would be difficult, if not impossible, for any Catholic to really trust a priest again, or trust a church that covers it up; at least that's the way I'd feel about it. The trust that was violated by the few affects the many. I object most when a man who represents himself to be a special, saintly man of God, a teacher of the truth falls from grace. The Bible tells us that God holds such men particularly accountable.

Bobby: Okay, let's move on. The real bone of contention between Catholics and Protestants seems to be over these sacred traditions in Catholicism. Let's talk some more about that.

John: None of these traditions are in the Bible; that's why we refer to them as being "extra biblical." Of course the Catholic Church knows this and this is exactly why it demeans the authority of the Bible, adding two more legs to their stool, the vaunted church and its traditions. Their position is that they know it's not in the Bible, but that doesn't matter because it's the Catholic Church which has the sole authority in all things spiritual. This is what Luther recognized had happened to his church. He understood how over the centuries it had become attached to its power and influence; he understood that neither the pronouncements of the pope nor the word of any man could or should be elevated above the authority of Scripture. God's Word is above the church. Luther insisted that preachers must prove their claims with the Bible. He objected to the Catholic Church relegating the authority of Scripture to a secondary position to the authority of the fathers and the pope and councils. He responded by stating that "our answer is those things have no claim on us, we demand the word."

Bobby: I have to say this Luther had balls; to go against the power of the Catholic Church took a man of conviction. What was it he said in response to the demand to recant?

John: "I cannot and I will not recant anything, for to go against conscience is neither right nor safe. God help me. Amen."

Yes, Luther was such a man. Like Moses, he had God's backing though. He was a very passionate man with a great deal of courage of his convictions. Imagine what it would be like to go up against a power connected with the Holy Roman Empire? He held his ground and was even at one time scheduled for execution. He had to remain in hiding for several years, during which time he translated the New Testament into German.

Luther also said that "Unless I am convinced by Scripture and plain reason, I do not accept the authority of popes and councils, for they have often contradicted each other; my conscience is captive to the Word of God."

Sonny: We don't presume to elevate the Church over God's word. We know that the Catholic Church, the one, true Church, must have authority in interpretation of God's Word.

Darrel: Which of course is tantamount to stating that the authority of the church is superior to the authority of the Bible; the church can interpret the Bible to suit its own self-interest.

Sonny: Can any of you tell me which traditions are not supported in the Bible?

Darrel: From our outline, I see we are scheduled to talk about each of these in detail in the weeks to come, but, for starters, here's a list of the traditions you people claim as being sacred that are not supported anywhere in the Bible: Praying for dead people; the existence of purgatory and prayers and Masses for people to be released from purgatory; indulgences or offering works or penance or suffering to release people from their sins or from purgatory; receiving an indulgence for release from purgatory; the categorizing of sin into venial and mortal sin; the categorizing of two types of good works, requiring sins to be forgiven through confession to a priest, a man you actually call "father;" praying or sacrificing as penance to release yourself or others from sin after your confession; baptizing babies to release them from original sin; using a special "holy water' for any reason; praying to saints and Mary; possessing statues and idols of Mary and saints; honoring Mary as infallible, co-redeemer and mediator alongside Christ himself and on and on and on. I can see why the church feels it necessary to include them in an effort to provide all the answers, but this veneration of Mary has me particularly confused. What's this one all about?

Sonny: We refer to Mary as being the "Queen over all things." Sometimes we call her the "Queen of Heaven." We are required to believe the four Marian dogmas: 1. Divine Motherhood. 2. Perpetual Virginity. 3. Immaculate Conception. 4. The Assumption. The Catechism (CCC 966) states that Mary "conceived the living God and, by your prayers, will deliver our souls from death." The Vatican Council II, page 42, states that "Mary has by grace been exalted above all angels and men to a place second only to her Son." In our Fundamentals of Catholic Dogmas, page 213, "Mary, by her spiritual entering into the sacrifice of her divine son for men, made atonement for the sins of man and merited the application of the redemptive grace of Christ. In this manner she cooperates in the subjective redemption of mankind."

Darrel: Wow, you Catholics sure seem to think a lot of this lady; but you should know that the title you chose to bestow on her, "Queen of Heaven," is a pagan goddess that God hates, just as he hates all who honor her. This name for Mary supports my contention of Catholicism's pagan influence. And I can't believe you really presume she played such a role as your church assigns her in the actual redemption of mankind. That's not only a ludicrous presumption, it's not biblically supported, and it's blasphemy!

Sonny: That's your opinion, Darrel; but we have it on the authority of our Church that this tradition and all our other traditions are valid, and this authority is equal to the authority of the Bible. You Protestants make such a big deal out of the Bible. Nowhere in the Bible does it say that the Bible is the foundation of truth! The Bible tells us that the Church is the strong foundation of truth. That's what Paul is saying to Timothy in 1 Timothy 3:15.

Darrel: Paul is saying to Timothy the same thing he said to the Thessalonians in 2 Thessalonians 2:15. "So then, our friends, stand firm and hold on to those Truth which we taught you, both in our preaching and in our letter." He is referring to the teachings of the apostles, not to your church or any church. You Catholics substitute the Catholic Church for apostolic teaching, and that's not good hermeneutics because it isn't what the Bible is saying. Of course, your church knows that and this is why it then responds by claiming its pronouncements, opinions, and dogma are superior to God's Word. Man's word trumps God's Word.

Peter: Yes, I see what you mean, Darrel. From my perspective as an unbeliever, it seems that the Catholic Church uses these extra-biblical traditions to add anything it wants to add to your Bible. It's a license to lie, but to serve what purpose?

Darrel: To serve itself, of course.

Sonny: Our tradition is derived from Jesus' teachings through the apostles, of course. As I've said before, not all of them were written down by the apostles, but it's still their tradition.

Darrel: Peter's right; we just have your word that this oral tradition is what God wanted to say but, for some reason, wasn't recorded in the Bible. Are you really saying that your sacred tradition is actually that apostolic tradition they each recorded in Scripture?

Sonny: Yes. Our sacred tradition also includes the word of mouth teachings of Christ and the holy Apostles which have been handed on from generation to generation, and, as I said, are not included in the Bible. These traditions and oral teaching include everything which contributes towards the sanctity of life and increase in faith of God's people.

Darrel: "Yeah," they weren't written down "but" they're God's Word anyway. Let me see if I understand you correctly, Sonny. You've told us that your church's "sacred traditions" and these undocumented, oral teachings of Christ are not included in the Bible. You have also said that they originated through revelation from God to your church magisterium through the Holy Spirit. Okay, but how can you be so sure they are to be considered God's truth? Do they contribute any knowledge to our Christian religion other than the glorification of your church? I question their purpose because they seem to be so self-serving, and you should question that too.

Sonny: As inspired by the Holy Spirit, our Magisterium has revealed these traditions and oral teachings to us. I will give you Bible support verses for each of these traditions as we take them up individually later on in these discussions.

Darrel: It sounds like we're back to our discussion about "unraveling revelation." Are you really telling us that God has continued to reveal his Word to the Catholic Church even after the Bible says that in the past the Word was revealed through the prophets but now it is revealed through Christ and what Jesus said in the gospel accounts represents God's final Word; and, didn't we determine the canon your church claims responsibility for was complete? It's just as I said before, Catholics believe in continuing revelation. This is what these traditions that have been added to our doctrine over the centuries really indicate. Islam included additional traditions and beliefs; the Qur'an is supplemented with the *hadith*, just as the Catholic Church supplements the Bible with its sacred tradition. I think it's ironic that any Christian denomination, which of course is to preach and teach God's absolute truth, actually would include a way of modifying or amending that truth, depending on circumstances. That methodology is apparent to us when we see how the Catholic Church has set itself up as the supreme authority of God's Word and can add to it or amend it whenever it sees fit to convene one of its divine Councils. This doesn't lead to relativism, of course, (no absolutes exist) but it sure provides us with a clear picture of a relativistic aspect to Catholicism. Even a hint of relativism is heresy.

Ray: That's ridiculous to compare Catholicism to Islam.

Darrel: If the shoe fits, Ray. Just give some thought to what I said, okay?

Ray: Jesus had the keys of the kingdom. Isaiah 22:22. Christ said "And I will give you (Peter) the keys of the kingdom of heaven; and whatever you bind on earth will be bound in heaven, and whatever you loose on earth will be loosed in heaven."

Darrel: Notice Christ said he would give the keys "of" the kingdom; he did not say the keys "to" the kingdom; there is a difference. Peter was to be an announcer not an authority.

John: Right; neither Peter, nor any other apostle, was given the authority to write their own doctrine for the Christian religion. The apostles were told to preach and teach the doctrine they had learned from Jesus Christ to the world. The phrase "loose on earth" is a metaphor which refers to opening the kingdom to those who share Peter's confession and "binding" (which means to exclude) those who will not receive the apostles' testimony to Christ. Christ is only referring to what has been and what will be revealed in Scripture through His testimony to the apostles and the apostles' testimony about Him as revealed in their eye witness accounts which constitute our gospel. This is why I consistently caution Catholics about how we must always be on guard against "traditionalism." Through traditionalism, the Catholic Church has attempted to bind the consciences of Christians in areas that the Bible does not address. This is exactly why we Protestants believe in *sola Scriptura*. If the tradition isn't mentioned in the Bible, how can we be sure whether it's true or something the Catholic Church made up? And, as I mentioned before, we should question everyone's credibility but Christ's. We are protected from false teaching by simply limiting what we know about God to just His Word in the Holy Bible.

Darrel: If we just use common sense instead of applying the Catholic bias to what the church wants the Bible to say, every Christian should understand that binding and loosing didn't mean that the Word of God was to be loosened up to add sacred tradition to and believers were not to be bound up by some church organization that wanted to control their conscience and their souls.

Peter: You Catholics do seem to be bound up by your "sacred tradition," Sonny.

Sonny: Our sacred tradition is important to us. Not everything about our religion is in the Bible. Many of our traditions relate to the way we worship and have very little to do with theology. It's the same with the Protestants. For example, this is the exact way the Lutheran liturgy is conducted.

John: You're right; the Bible doesn't provide us with details like that; it's adiaphora. But we have no Lutheran traditions relating to our theology that aren't biblically supported; Catholicism does. "Grace plus works," purgatory, veneration of Mary, transubstantiation in the Eucharist, and infallibility of the pope are examples of traditions not supported in Scripture; and declaring these traditions to be equal in authority to the Bible is certainly not supported in the Bible.

Sonny: We have it on our Church's authority that there are traditions taught by the apostles orally that aren't in Scripture. The Church gave us the canon of the Bible on inspiration from the Holy Spirit, so we must assume it knew which oral traditions handed down to us from a variety of sources were inspired. No new teachings could suddenly appear when it comes to what the apostles taught because they've been passed down intact through the centuries. Oral tradition has to be faithful to the original writings. And even if they appear to contradict what Scripture says, because our Church authority is superior to the Word of God in the sense that it interprets the meaning of the Word of God. Why is that so difficult to understand?

Darrel: Oh, I understand exactly what you're saying only too well. Your church, your pope, your councils and bishops determine what you are to believe about Jesus Christ and the Christian doctrine. You Catholics are to trust what your church tells you to believe without questioning its authority. I have always been amazed how it was able to convince you all of its authority. Why is that so difficult for you people to understand?

Sonny: We believe we are the one, true Christian Church and consider this reality to be our strength. We believe our Church is divinely inspired by the Holy Spirit, and we can therefore trust its ultimate authority in telling us the truth of Christianity.

Darrel: But you've also said you believe the Holy Spirit inspired the writers of the books of the Bible, and when one of your traditions is contradicted by the Word of God, you've said that "our Church authority is superior to the Word of God in the sense that it interprets the meaning of the Word of God." That statement doesn't make sense to me. How can the Holy Spirit guide the apostles to teach one thing and, according to your church, inspire it to say another that directly contradicts apostolic teaching? God is not a God of contradiction or confusion. That has to be our premise among Christians.

Sonny: Yes, of course. But I don't agree with you that any of our traditions do contradict what the Bible says or are clearly prohibited in the Bible. Some of them may appear to contradict Scripture, but, as I've said before, we rely on the Church to interpret the meaning of Scripture accurately. If you think some of them are inconsistent with Scripture, that's your opinion, and these contradictions are the result of a Protestant misunderstanding. We have the authority of the one true Church to guide us, and you have nothing but other people's opinions to guide you. This is exactly why there are so many Protestant denominations.

Look, Protestant people, the Church, in her teaching, life and worship (the Creeds, the Sacraments, the Magisterium, and the Holy Sacrifice of the Mass), perpetuates and hands on to all generations all that she herself is, all that she believes. The Bible must be interpreted within the context of sacred tradition and within the community of the Church.

Darrel: Ah, yes, nothing can be known from Scripture unless filtered through the Catholic Church and its traditions and worldly community.

I say again that all of us Protestant believers trust in God through the Spirit to know God's Word. We believe that is our strength because we cannot be misled by some church organization that has its own self-serving interests in the mix. Protestants are typically more of an independent group of believers than Catholics; most people are followers, and the Catholic Church gives them the leadership they apparently require to be connected and remain connected to Christ. Freud said that we all desire to worship something whether that be God, some Emperor or some church. Is the Catholic Church worthy of worship? Certainly not! No church is; no magisterium no group of churchy men. In Acts 14:8-18, Luke tells the story of Paul and Barnabas's visit to Lystra and how the citizens there believed that they were "gods in human form" and worthy of worship. The people even wanted to offer sacrifices to them. Paul responded by stating, "Men, why are you doing this? We too are only men, human like you." Nonetheless, "they had difficulty keeping the crowd from sacrificing to them." And, based on your comments in this discussion, both of you Catholics indicate your difficulty in understanding this worshipful relationship you have with the Catholic Church, which after all consists of "only men, human like you," and how wrong the Bible says this is. It seems to be a classic co-dependency: Your church wants to control believers, it needs to control believers to maintain the co-dependent relationship it enjoys with its dutiful followers who seek to be controlled by one, distinct authority you believe you can trust, and some of you may even worship your vaunted church.

Ray: That's a ridiculous accusation, Darrel.

Darrel: Is it really? Well, I would like you and Sonny to think about what I just said about man's instincts and my opinion that you and your church depend on each other in an effort to discover why you believe what you believe. When you claim you alone know the truth because your church has told you the truth and you trust them, do you ever question where they come up with some of these sacred tradition that your reason tells us aren't clearly supported in Scripture and your church's insistence that that's not a problem because what they say goes anyway, regardless of what the Bible says?

Take this Catholic concept of purgatory. God is not the whimsical Allah of Islam. He is a serious God, and life is a serious business. In telling believers they have a second chance to please God with good works and earn their stripes before he opens the trap door to Hell, they are saying we have a "do-over" opportunity. This belief compromises Christ's redeeming sacrifice and tends to reduce the urgency of getting it right the first time, eh? Of course, we know we can't get it right enough to please our perfect, righteous, just God, no matter how many do-overs we are given; that means our good works can't possibly save us because they will never, ever be good enough. That motivates us to rely on God and, through his grace; he comes through for those of us who believe in Jesus Christ. That's the gospel message, man.

Peter: This concept of purgatory is like the Eastern religions' concept of reincarnation. Both concepts give man a second chance.

Sonny: You both misunderstand our concept of purgatory. Purgatory is not a second chance for conversion; we've already been converted and justified. But, if there is no intermediate state of purification, we would all be damned to Hell. No one would be saved. I refer you to 1 John 3:2-3 and Psalm 51:6. "We are children of God; and it has not been revealed what we shall be, but we know that when He is revealed, we shall see Him, for we shall see Him as He is. And everyone who has this hope in Him purifies himself, just as He is pure." And the psalmist says, "Behold, You desire truth in the inward parts, and in the hidden part. You will make me to know wisdom."

Darrel: As you say, we've already been converted and justified so you create purgatory to solve a non-existent problem. The Apostle John is referring to how our hope gives our lives a focused purity resembling God's and when He is revealed at the Second Coming "we shall be like Him." David is referring to the sanctification process that occurs in our lives here on earth. Neither verse supports the existence of some place in the afterlife where purification occurs and we grow in wisdom.

Sonny: The Church, under the direction of the Holy Spirit, has always taught that purgatory does exist. It is not a second chance to be saved but a place of cleansing for the already saved before entering into heaven. Only the saved go to purgatory.

Darrel: If we've been converted and justified, according to God's plan of salvation, we are saved; there's certainly no need for "an intermediate state of purification." To imply this need is to imply that Christ's sacrifice wasn't enough for our purification even though the gospel is quite clear on that subject. This is a good example of where your traditions contradict God's Word. Why do Catholics want to believe there's more need for a cleansing of sin? This sounds like a description of a second chance to me.

Sonny: People die with unexpiated sins or the attachment to sin on their souls and must go there to be cleansed in the purifying fire of purgatory for a period of time. Once they are purified, they go to heaven and enjoy the Beatific vision forever. In purgatory, these souls remember who prayed for them. It offends God greatly when people say that they will surely have to spend time in purgatory after death. Jesus would rather not send anybody there and He would prefer that one has total trust in Him now so that they would not have to spend one second in purgatory after their death; but, of course, we believe that very few people go straight to heaven, and that means that most believers will spend some time in purgatory. This belief dissuades us from the confusion of a "cheap grace" (God erases our sin no matter how many times we sin), and motivates us to focus more on our sinfulness than on the infinite mercy of God to forgive us. The more good we do, the less time we need for cleansing and hence the less time we shall spend in purgatory.

Bobby: I was told this in my catechism classes. Venial sin, if confessed properly and penance paid, (of course) would be somehow okay. Of course, mortal sins are a different story. Regardless of whether one confesses and repents or not, we go to purgatory; no exceptions. I was in a constant state of confusion though whether my sin was venial or mortal so I just assumed I'd go to purgatory along with most everyone else I knew. This didn't give me much more comfort than believing I'd go straight to hell though; the cleansing fire thing bothered me. Nonetheless, I was told that everything would be straightened out there once and for all. That's what our Church told us to believe.

Ray: What do you think will happen when you die, Bobby?

Bobby: I don't really know. Of course no one knows for sure, right? But I have to tell you I'm no more certain with unbelief than I was when I was a Catholic. I would hope there's a heaven and I'll be eligible. I think I'm a good person. I guess I believe in what John once called "salvation by death;" every good person who dies goes to heaven. How about you, John? Do you think you're going to heaven?

John: Yes, I do. I'm as certain as anyone can be about their ultimate destination because I have God's Word on it. I believe by faith. As a believer in Christ as my Savior, I believe I'll spend an eternity at His feet. I can't of course say this with the same degree of certainty that I can say that I'm sitting in this chair looking out at the Gulf of Mexico, but it's close...very, very close. This belief brings me contentment.

Look, we know we can't atone for our sin, only Christ can do that; and He did that for us. No need for further cleansing action. A good Catholic friend of mine told me he wasn't sure he had not committed a mortal sin; he wasn't sure he had properly repented of his venial sins, and, even though purgatory seemed a relief because he'd get a second chance, he wasn't sure about its existence either. This created discontent.

Sonny: Purgatory is a biblical concept. See 2 Maccabees 12:42-45 which supports this.

Darrel: As we mentioned before, this is exactly why Catholics want Maccabees to be considered as Scripture; regardless, this verse is a stretch. Doesn't the fact that the Apocrypha wasn't officially added until the 16th century at the Council of Trent raise a suspicion that it was added to support the concept of purgatory the Catholic Church needed to create a need for indulgences? Or have you been that indoctrinated?

Look, over this next month of discussion sessions, I'm going to prove to you that these various man-made, extra-biblical traditions of your church are not Christianity. For now, it's enough to know that we of the Reformed faith do not believe in purgatory because we believe God's grace is sufficient to cleanse us of our sin and no further cleansing is required in some other place in the afterlife. We understand from reading and studying the Bible more about God's grace and its efficacy in our salvation than you Catholics understand. That means we are more certain of going to heaven than you people can be, and that brings us contentment. Catholics don't have that blessed assurance because they not only believe that works must accompany God's grace while we live out this life, but works play a role in the next life as well. <u>Any belief in works compromises or even destroys the contentment we should have as Christians</u>.

Sonny: Nonsense! We understand God's grace.

Darrel: In a very weak way, yes, you do; but, in claiming it's not sufficient, you prove it's an ineffective and incomplete understanding.

John: I once read book authored by the late Lutheran theologian, Dr. Siegbert W. Becker entitled, *The Foolishness of God.* Becker talks about our differences with our Catholic brothers and sisters in Christ. Becker says that Catholics characterize all certainty of salvation as a proud assumption on the part of man. While they believe that some men may have a special revelation from God, and only they can be thus certain of their salvation, all the rest of us have no such assurance. Catholics therefore live in confusion and fear of damnation all their lives. Catholic contentment is an oxymoron.

Sonny: In Catholic thought, it is the Sin of Presumption to believe we are saved when we are neglecting the conditions for Salvation that Christ haws specified. We cannot therefore have certainty of our salvation now like your Protestants have with your "cheap grace."

John: Presumably the Catholic Church can offer assurance of salvation now, but only if the followers are assured they are following the conditions Christ has specified, conditions which your church interprets for you, and added a few of their own as well. But, you see, we don't believe God imposes conditions on our salvation; His grace is offered unconditionally. We'll get into that when we officially present our reformed doctrine. Catholics are supposed to focus more on the sin than on their sin being wiped clean through God's grace. This practice serves to keep the believers more in line so they don't assume they can go on sinning just because they know God forgives them anyway regardless. Apparently, the Catholic Church doesn't believe Paul adequately warned of that possibility when he warned people not to wrongly interpret what he was saying about how God's grace alone saves. They came up with their own way of dealing with the threat of cheap grace by officially recognizing the heresy of purgatory to cover this base.

This mindset illustrates the difference between the pure grace-based belief Protestants of the reformed faith share and the Catholic compromised version of God's plan of salvation. I think Catholicism's weak understanding of God's grace in our salvation could possibly represent an essential difference in our respective doctrines because it may serve to interfere with our connection with Christ.

I might also add that the Catholic Church's emphasis on certainty of salvation now by following its dogma emboldens its purpose of serving its constituents as sole authority in their spiritual lives even to the degree of it being necessary for their very salvation.

Sonny: We do not have your Protestant Absolute Assurance of our salvation; we don't believe in that; but we do have a Moral Assurance of our salvation if we have faith in the Holy Trinity, attend Holy Mass on Sundays and Holy Days and receive the Sacraments regularly, obey the Ten Commandments and perform corporal and spiritual works of mercy.

Darrel: You just made John's point. According to the Catholic Church's interpretation of what Christ has specified, and adding a just a few of your own like regularly attending mass, properly and consistently taking communion and confession and performing these corporal and spiritual works of mercy are understood to meet the requirement of salvation according to your church and thus give you some "moral assurance" you've been saved.

Sonny: We are not what you have called a "works-based" religion, Darrel, like Judaism or Islam. A simple subjective certainty of our salvation is insufficient. Christ said if we love Him, we are to keep His commandments. The keeping of the commandments is a presupposition, without which the claim to love Him becomes meaningless.

We acknowledge works are critical in the salvation process, but we differ from all other works-based religions in that we place the emphasis more on God's grace than on man's works. These other religions don't even address God's grace at all. We recognize works are important because we must pay heed to these warnings of God to obey His law and avoid falling into temptation. If men are not kept in fear of eternal damnation, they will be tempted to follow the ways of the world and fall away from the faith.

Darrel: But you know you can't possibly perform these works perfectly to satisfy our holy, just and righteous Creator, right? Whether you are even close to following Christ's specified laws is subjective, right?

Sonny: The laws are defined in our Catechism.

Darrel: Yes, legalism serves the objective of the Catholic Church. It has an ulterior motive in focusing on works (one of which of course is to obey its catechism rules) and in reminding people of eternal damnation for not performing them; in creating fear of damnation in its followers who disobey its rule, it maintains its membership. Fear of going to hell, is one of the main reasons people don't leave the Catholic Church.

Ray: In a beautiful dialogue between Christ and Saint Catherine of Siena, Christ said, "Catherine, do you not realize that if you performed the most extreme penances for your entire lifetime, the merit would not be enough to atone for even one venial sin? It is when you attach your works to My Passion that they participate in its infinite Merit. Then I look at the love with which you have offered your penances, and apply the Merits of My Passion to them. It is in this way that you atone for sins."

Darrel: What are you talking about, Ray? Are you actually claiming that Christ actually engaged in a conversation with some saint of yours? This is either a delusion of this Saint Catherine's or your church has made this up to teach heresy. The Bible of course does not support Christ's need to have us somehow attach our good works to him in any way, shape or form. Christ attaches his good works to us through infusion.

John: What Ray just said is an example of unfolding revelation. It is just one of the many unbiblical made-up tales, traditions, icons, rites, sacraments and rituals of the Catholic Church which serve to dramatize our connection with Christ to emphasize the relationship we should acknowledge we have with our triune God. Man relates better to the visual, and this exaggeration of Christianity has served as an effective tool in attracting people to the faith, particularly those uneducated, primitive people living in third world countries. The historic approach of the Roman Catholic missionaries has been to motivate people to believe out of fear of damnation, to stress good works to motivate them to act properly, and offer more of a visible representation of Christianity with its icons, rituals and dramatization of the sacrament of Holy Communion. Unfortunately, in believing the ends justified the means, the Catholic Church took some liberty with biblical doctrine, and heresy reared its ugly head.

I grant you that God's grace and His plan of salvation is a difficult issue to teach to anyone, and there is the concern of course that it might be received as some kind of "get-out-of-jail-free card" which might encourage people to continue to sin. The Catholic Church recognized that punishment and reward, the carrot and the stick, are powerful tools to use to get your message across. Fear of damnation and emphasis on doing good to avoid it have proven to be effective techniques for acquiring converts throughout the church's history, and is still effective; but, more intuitive and educated Catholics should question the relevancy of the church's use of means to achieve that end, and examine the history and doctrine of their church with a less than indoctrinated eye. That's why we're meeting together. Our objective is to be objective in our pursuit of the truth, and we Protestants do not believe the ends (the truth) justify the means (adapting Scripture to achieve peace, attract converts and keep followers in line). It's time for intelligent Catholics to read what their "first pope, Peter" has to say about what we believe they have become and think about what they believe and why they believe it.

Darrel: Catholics believe the ends are power for the church, and this justifies any means to achieve that objective. Peter said that if anyone teaches other than <u>the words of Christ</u> and instead teaches the doctrines of men, false teachers who are defined by their contentiousness, "useless wranglings of corrupt minds and destitute of the truth, who suppose that godliness is a <u>means of gain</u>. From such withdraw yourself."

Sonny: Catholicism's objective is to know the truth and the truth will set us free. Of course, to achieve this objective, the Catholic Church did borrow from other religions prevalent at the time that operated in a similar fashion. I suppose the people of Rome had certain expectations for a religion, and they needed to meet them in order to spread the gospel. I know that Protestants reject the pomp and circumstances of Catholicism, but not all of them do. The Anglican Church of England engages in a certain amount of this sort of thing too. I assume they do this for the same reason we do, to draw people into the Church who wish to best experience their relationship with their Savior.

John: Sure, it's reasonable to assume that it's easier to relate to what we experience with our five senses than to connect with what is invisible. Christ's disciples were faced with that challenge when Christ ascended to heaven. (John 14:27). They of course adjusted to that reality by understanding that Christ is present with us every moment of our lives. His invisibility does not keep His presence or His power away from us. Wherever two or three gather together in His name, He is there among them. (Matthew 18:20). But it seems that some people need to rely upon some authoritative church organization to act as their visual representation of God's presence in their lives to better connect with Him, and there's nothing wrong with that as long as that church doesn't go too far as we believe the Catholic Church has in promoting itself to be a substitute for our triune God.

Darrel: There's a psychology behind this. Some people are like the Apostle Thomas who had to touch Christ's wounds to believe; they need something visual; others don't need to do that; they're more able to use their imagination to envision a concept. Some people prefer to be told what to believe while others are more independent and prefer to arrive at their own conclusion after examining the evidence from a variety of sources of knowledge. Evidently these folks disregard what Paul said about walking for faith and not by sight.

Ray: <u>You don't see what we see;</u> we see the Holy Spirit, not the Church. Our eyes are on the Saints, the law, the beautiful theology, the history and the Church's awe inspiring place in it, but, most importantly, we experience Christ, His Body, His Blood, His Soul and Divinity in the Eucharist. We don't expect a Protestant to understand this. Any Catholic who knows what the Eucharist truly is can never be led away. Why do we need physical things? Ask Jesus why He took on a physical body when God could have just flipped a switch to save us? Why was He born of a woman when He could have sewn together the body Himself? Why did He use spit and dirt for the man's eyes? Why did the woman have to touch His cloak" He knew she was there. Why did God choose to use all these physical, visual things when, according to you people, He just works through the Spirit?

Daniel: You have a good point, Ray. The physical and the visible do help us in knowing spiritual things, and the Catholic rituals, the artifacts, the traditions and pomp along with a strong church authority do indeed serve to make Christianity more real to people. We're just saying that some people need more of this than others, particularly when the physical, visual things can serve to misdirect us in our theology by changing the focus to the church and not to Christ. For this reason, we see the limitation of pledging allegiance to a strong, visible church authority and the downside of the rituals which, for us Protestants, act more as a distraction than a necessary aid to relate to Christ. We also believe that focusing on the extra-biblical traditions motivates people to focus on the works they think they're supposed to be doing for the Catholic Church and for God, thus downplaying God's favor; we want to focus on what God has done for all of us in bestowing on us His grace.

Darrel: Good point, Dan. We're actually addressing two issues in Catholicism: The rituals and the traditions. Catholics need both; we do not. As you say, the rituals are a distraction for us, and the traditions are heretical. For these reasons, I believe the Catholic Church went too far in taking creative license with the Christian doctrine to accomplish its objective of becoming an institution. The rituals and traditions served to draw unbelievers into the fold, particularly in undeveloped countries among primitive people. The Catholic Church not only created some images and artifacts and traditions to showcase Christianity, it also attempted to fill in the gaps it believed God left in his Word with made-up doctrine like purgatory, veneration of Mary, etc. People want answers and the Catholic Church gives them answers. This was (for lack of another word) a good marketing tool to sell Christianity to the masses because the traditions appeal to people who want answers to certain questions about their faith that are not presented in the Bible. But in coming up with answers to questions not answered in Scripture, Catholicism is forced to make them up to convince itching ears of its sole authority to provide adequate and seemingly authentic answers to the questions we all have about the meaning of Scripture, eschatology, what happens after we die, etc. Truth is compromised, not revealed.

Here's an example of what I'm talking about. Instead of trying to explain the difficult concept of God's grace, and, as Sonny has said, risk people misinterpreting the concept as an encouragement to keep on sinning, the Catholic Church arbitrarily added good works to God's plan of salvation. I don't believe this was just a misunderstanding of what Paul said and how his concept actually does correspond with what James said; no, I believe the concept of adding works to grace appealed to our natural instinct to want our good deeds to count for something. I know we've said this before, but it's relevant.

Sonny: Augustine and Aquinas both believed in the importance of good works.

Darrel: Sure, but Augustine, in particular, didn't believe in combining works with salvation the way Catholic theology does in its grace plus works concept.

Look, the Catholic Church gave its followers traditions to follow because our traditions play an important role in every aspect of our lives. Dan mentioned this before, but it's obvious that the Catholic Church gave its followers parents, a mother and a father; the church is the mother and the pope was the Holy Father, the royal King. Mary, of course was the royal Queen. The pomp was patterned after royalty. The Church created an important role and purpose for itself by persuading folks that they were the only authority in Christianity, and the magisterium had more authority than the Bible. Whatever the Church said was the only truth they needed to hear. As I said before, over the centuries, by trial and error, the Catholic Church devised a version of Christianity that it believed to be most effective way to market to the masses; under the guise of promoting Christianity, its thrust was more about promoting itself to gain in wealth, power and influence.

Daniel: I suggest that this is also the reason the Catholic Church is against birth control. More babies mean more Catholics. Muslims follow their example.

Ray: That's a ridiculous, speculative conclusion, Daniel. It was not so long ago when the majority of your Protestants churches opposed birth control too.

Darrel: Maybe so, but I know of no Protestant church which opposes birth control now.

Why can't you Catholics understand what we've been saying about the purpose of your traditions? It just makes sense for an intelligent, well-educated people, folks who claim to lead an examined life, to wonder why your church authorities came up with all these traditions which they tell you are either not in the Bible at all or the Bible is wrong and the Church is right? If you really led an examined life, you would prioritize examining why your church tells you to believe what you think you should believe. Why do you arbitrarily dismiss the writings and teachings of other Christian leaders like Martin Luther and John Calvin as being heretical when you've never read anything they've ever written and thus given some thought as to what they had to say about Christianity?

Ray: I'm not interested in what heretics have to say about Christianity, Darrel.

Darrel: You shouldn't arbitrarily dismiss the reformers as being heretics until you read what they had to say and judge for yourself whether they are heretics or not. Oops, I forgot, you don't do anything without your vaunted church's permission. You're still stuck in the dark ages when no one was permitted to read the Bible, much less think about what God is telling us in his Word. I just want you to use your good brain and think. That's what we're supposed to be doing here; act like a man who leads an examined life. We should all want to know why we believe what we believe. Are you up to that challenge? This is our third year of our initial group meeting together, and we've all accepted the challenge of being more enlightened, to think outside the box. It's not an easy task to examine one's life and his beliefs the way we do in these discussions. But, personally speaking, you will come out the better for it. You will derive a clearer understanding of the truth.

Peter: I can second what Darrel just said from my own experience in this discussion group. I knew I wasn't going to be talking trivia with a bunch of lightweights. I can grab any "Winter Texan" to talk to for that experience, but I bore easily when all they talk about is fishing.

I have a question for Sonny about these traditions of his church he keeps referring to. You say these traditions came from the apostles and oral teachings and that your church tells you what they are. Darrel has a point in asking you to think about why your church should be the only authority to literally convey God's word to you.

Sonny: The Church is our sole authority; it is the mother of all believers and the Fathers of the Church are invaluable guides in teaching us the faith. No one can have God as Father who does not have the Church as Mother.

Peter: Yes, in Catholicism, it certainly seems to be a family affair. I see that now. The problem in having this mindset it that you are the children who never grow up. It's like living in the world of *Peter Pan*.

Sonny: Christ honored children because they were so simple; our faith is simple. The Holy Spirit works in our lives through the Church. The developers and conservators of our tradition adequately convey what the Holy Spirit reveals to them. We leave our pride at the door and rely on the wisdom of the Church to correctly understand the Scriptures and convey the sacred oral tradition so we will not be confused as Paul warns in Ephesians 4:14.

Peter: "Developers" of the tradition? Does this mean they made up this tradition?

Sonny: They developed the tradition under the guidance of the Holy Spirit.

Darrel: Or not. In John 7:18, Jesus tells us we should be so familiar with the doctrine of Christianity we should recognize when some self-appointed authority is speaking for itself and not representing our doctrine. He said that when some entity or person does this, they are promoting their own glory. This sounds like what has happened to the Catholic Church over the centuries, doesn't it?

John: I think we need to understand that it's possible our Catholic brothers and sisters in Christ have not been able to mature spiritually as they should. Even though Christ singled out the little children as playing an important role, He certainly wasn't advocating we remain stagnant in our belief; we talked about how important the growth process is in our religion when we discussed the process of our sanctification.

William R. Newell (author of *Romans Verse by Verse*) clarifies immature believers in stating that they are devout believers who have been "spiritually influenced under John the Baptist's ministry of repentance but have not matured spiritually to really be more than a quickened but undelivered soul in struggle under a sense of 'duty,' not a sense of full acceptance in Christ and sealing by the Holy Spirit." I thought of Catholics when I read this description because Catholics believe deeds play a role in our justification for salvation (a sense of duty) and it intentionally does come between its followers and our triune God in prayer (requiring Mary as an intermediary), repentance and forgiveness (requiring a priest for confession) and interpretation of God's Word (requiring the magisterium for explanation of doctrine) so it would be consistent to assume that the Catholic Church would also assume the position of being a conduit for the Holy Spirit as well. In its presumed role as a parent for its children, it serves to come between the believer and the object of our belief, our triune God and thus discourages the spiritual development of its members. Instead our church should encourage our spiritual growth.

Darrel: That makes complete sense to me. Of course, not being an indoctrinated Catholic, I can see things from a more objective perspective.

I object mostly to the Catholic Church magisterium's role. Since the real key here is to know our Christian doctrine well enough to know when someone or something is not representing it correctly, we can only trust the Holy Spirit, God himself, to make sure this doesn't happen. It's a life-long pursuit to understand God's Word through consistent study, and the Catholic Church has discouraged its followers from doing this for centuries and only recently has backed off on this to some extent; but old habits die hard, eh?

Ray: Look, what do you want from us? Do you expect us to renounce our beliefs and join one of your 30 or 40,000 Protestant churches on the basis of your arguments? All I know is that if I stick with what the Church teaches I'll be fine.

Darrel: Status quo may work best for those who don't lead examined lives, but, if you lead an examined life, you are motivated to take a good look at what you believe and why you believe it, and then get back to me, okay?

Do you really feel you need some authority to tell you what to believe? We have this holy book and it's an easy read. Why not just take it up and read what it has to say on your very own recognizance? Protestant denominations who subscribe to the doctrine of the Reformation teach that the Bible alone as a sufficient basis for all Christian teaching; we don't need to rely on any church to add any traditions or tell us what the Bible is saying to us. Our only authority is Christ, and we believe we can connect directly with him, God the Father, and the Holy Spirit.

Ray: I mentioned before that the Church IS the body of Christ. Our sacred tradition and Christ and the Holy Spirit are one and the same. Sheen said that "The Church is Christ!"

Sonny: Functionally, the church is the Holy Spirit in the sense that it speaks for the Holy Spirit. This is why we believe the Church is our only authority.

Darrel: As with all authority on earth, that authority can be abused of course by your bishops. When your pope makes some pronouncement from his bloody pulpit, he is "pontificating," and what he says through some continuing revelation will depend on whatever subject he believes needs to be addressed at the time. He is in charge of maintaining but also in establishing the sacred tradition on an ongoing basis, right?

Sonny: Yes, that's correct. I don't mind admitting that our tradition is much more like a living organism than a mathematically precise body of doctrines.

Darrel: That exact statement was uttered from the mouth of our Muslim guest last year. It also relates back to what we talked about before about "unraveling revelation."

Ray: Here you go again with the comparison to Islam. What I just said doesn't mean that it's impossible for any Catholic to know the doctrines of our belief; that's what the Catechism is for, to teach us that doctrinal content.

Darrel: Okay, so let me see if I have understood what you've just said. You claim that your tradition is Christ and the teachings of the apostles, but then go on to say that it is a living tradition in the sense that it reflects everything that contributes to the sanctity of life and increase of faith of believers, right? I want to be clear on this because it surely sounds like what the Muslims have told us when they say that all their additional writings like the *hadith* are to be considered as additional revelation equal in authority to the Qur'an. Since, as you claim, Catholicism came before Islam, it would seem Muhammad borrowed this concept from you people.

Ray: I don't know or care to know how this looks to an unbeliever, Darrel. Our sacred tradition is understood as the fullness of divine truth proclaimed in the Scriptures, preserved by the apostolic bishops and expressed in the life of the Church through such things as the Divine Liturgy and the Holy Mysteries (Eucharist, baptism, marriage, etc.), the Creed and other doctrinal definitions of the Seven Ecumenical Councils, canonical Christian iconography, and the sanctified lives of godly men and women. As I said before, some of this tradition is written down, and that's what we refer to as sacred tradition, and some of it is not. The part that is not written down is our larger tradition, and that records the community's experience of God or more specifically of Jesus Christ. It's unfolding.

Darrel: "Unfolding, eh? This is just another reference to "unraveling revelation." By the way, Ray-boy, did you just called me an unbeliever? Did I hear you correctly? You don't call a fellow Christian an unbeliever, buddy! Please give me the same regard as you did when you referred to C. S. Lewis as a "non- Catholic." Do you assume that I'm not only headed for hell because I don't believe in Catholicism, you can't even concede that I'm at least a Christian? Sonny has never revealed he thinks of us in this way.

Ray: I obviously don't know you, Darrel, and only God can know what's in a person's heart so I don't know whether you possess a true, saving faith in Christ or not; I was referring to a person who doesn't believe in the Catholic Church; we consider all Protestants to be rebels and heretics.

Darrel: And we consider you to be misguided children of the faith; we think of you people as also being heretics in the sense that you left the original, apostolic church.

Bobby: And so never the twain shall meet? Do you all think we should just call it quits to these discussions this season and go fishing?

Darrel: We are to be fishers of men, and that means I'll keep going in my attempt to open this guy's mind to at least consider Christianity from our point of view.

John: The direction of this conversation reminds me of a comment one of the Catholics made in response to something I'd posted. He totally ignored the substance of the post and instead asked me a Bible trivia question. He asked me where was Jesus when John the Baptist was filled with the Holy Spirit? I thought he was referring to the time John baptized Jesus and the spirit fell on Christ. The Catholic told me I was a fool because any kindergartner could tell me both Jesus and John were in the womb of their respective mothers when the spirit filled John's mother, Elizabeth. Do you see what I mean, Sonny, when I said most of my discussions with you folks haven't been very productive?

Sonny: Exactly. He shouldn't have baited you with a trick question like that.

John: Right. Not content with embarrassing me in my Bible knowledge, he went on to conclude that I was not a believer; and he wasn't talking about a believer in Catholicism; he was talking about being a Christian. Well, this really set me off, so I took a deep breath, went to refill my coffee cup and composed myself enough so I wouldn't just jump down his throat. I responded to him by saying "Now you Catholics think you're God who sees what's in my heart?" I asked him if claiming his church was Christ gave all Catholics the ability and authority to judge whether an unbeliever is damned, much less another Christian? I said that since he knew where Jesus was when the spirit filled John the Baptist in the womb, shouldn't he know that only God can know what's in a person's heart?

Sonny: What did he have to say to that response?

John: Nothing. He "unfriended" me.

Peter: He didn't have an answer for you because he had to admit that what you said was true. The Catholic Church does have a God complex. In claiming it's in reality one and the same with Christ and the Holy Spirit and even calling the pope "HOLY" for Pete's sake, well that covers all the bases of the triune God, right?

Sonny: It may sound that way, but that's not what we mean.

Peter: If it walks like a duck and quacks, it's a duck.

I've got another question for Sonny about this sacred tradition of his church. You said before that some of your tradition has not been written down. Why not?

Sonny: Ray addressed this subject several sessions ago. All I can add is that some of our sacred tradition can't be written down since it consists, not so much of just words as of a particular way of seeing the world. We call this the sacramental/liturgical way. If you're looking for the authentic summary of the Church's tradition, look for it in the ordinary places, namely the Mass. The Catechism, because it is the new, authoritative exposition of the one and perennial apostolic faith, serves as a valid and legitimate instrument for ecclesial communion and as a sure norm for teaching the faith (according to Pope John Paul II). The way we worship is the way we believe. I'm just saying that this way of seeing is not so much learned as inferred; it is a way of seeing the world that is not communicated simply by the written word. It is communicated by gesture (especially the gestures of the liturgy, and by the assumption that the world is a giant sacramental by which God communicates His grace not merely through word, but through creation and especially through the sacraments.

Darrel: Okay, let me see if I have this straight; you have these traditions, some of which you say are gleaned from the Bible, some from the Apocrypha, some from oral traditions that weren't written down, and now some from just some kind of emotion you feel when you attend Mass, and of course, there is that "unraveling revelation" your magisterium receives now and then. Wow, that's a lot of extra-biblical stuff to believe in, guys. Aren't you curious though that, as we've been saying, about most of them seeming to embolden the Catholic Church? That's a rhetorical question; indoctrinated people aren't curious.

Well, I think once we wade through all this rhetoric, the bottom line is that your sacred tradition came from your Church, by one of several different ways; some of it is consistent with the Bible and some may not be. That's what we're here to find out. The apostolic tradition is derived directly from Scripture. Where your sacred tradition deviates from the apostolic tradition; your claim to be the original, apostolic is exposed.

Sonny: Catholicism holds that the faith once delivered by the apostles continues to deepen and mature over time through the action of the Holy Spirit in the history of the Church and its understanding of that faith.

Darrel: Sure, that's the "unraveling revelation." Are you actually saying that the teachings of the apostles' changes over time based on your church's understanding of those teachings? This is a relativistic view, isn't it? That's what secular unbelievers believe about our changing moral code, right, Peter? You're the expert on relativism, right?

Peter: Exactly. There is no absolute moral code; it changes with the times and the wants and needs of society. That's straight from our "Humanist Manifesto."

Darrel: Again, you Catholics find yourselves in bad company, Sonny. First we find you too close to the pagans; then you sounded like a Muslim when you were talking about how works are necessary for salvation and this concept of additional revelation which Muslims call abrogation.

Now Catholicism seems to have relativism in common with the atheistic secular humanists. We assume there's some Christianity somewhere in that hodgepodge, or we wouldn't consider you our brothers and sisters in Christ, but it's not as obvious as it certainly should be. There should be absolutely no confusion as to what the gospel message is, and it should certainly not even have a hint of these other belief systems. Obviously Jesus would have nothing to do with any of these other religions I just mentioned. Christians know we are to remain apart from the world. Paganism, Islam (and Judaism), and secular humanism are all very cozy with the material world.

Sonny: The Church is expected to change, but it doesn't change in doctrine; the changes are those little traditions that have either been changed or modified. The Church is a living expression to meet the needs of the people of its day.

Darrel: Yes, but once the door is opened to change, it's not such a stretch to change doctrine too. It's a license to get creative with the Christian doctrine and that's just what the Catholic Church has done over the centuries and continues to do so with your liberal pope.

Sonny: If history teaches us anything, one of its clearest lessons is that great institutions like the Catholic Church of Rome are not easily changed. That's a good thing.

Darrel: It's a bad thing when change is required as it was in the Reformation. Your church resisted change when its power and influence are threatened. Because of our sinful nature, we abuse power, and what started out in the first century to be the universal (catholic) Christian church degenerated from something divine to something very human. The Roman Catholic Church has indeed changed with the time, but not in a good way. The direction of its move has not been towards the simplicity of the early churches, but towards the complexity inherent in any organization that has established its own set of rules and regulations based on the church's requirements, not on God's.

Sonny: Look, I don't deny we've had our rough times as a Church. At times, our history has been like the history of the Jews, our leaders fail in their appointed duties, but we trust that God will purify His Church, and it will continue on. It will never end until the end. The core belief in Christ as our common foundation will always remain with us, and what the Church proclaims is the source of our truth. Protestants will never understand the ultimate graces available to us through the sacraments and the sacred tradition until they divest themselves of the Reformation/Protestant view of the Scriptures which clearly state there is an apostolic institution which interprets Scripture and Tradition on matters of faith and morals that is infallible. There is no such binding authority in those Protestant churches that have separated from the one, true Church.

In conclusion, I am certainly not advocating a relativistic approach to morality. Although it may seem to be a relativistic point of view, it is not the same thing. Our Church's understanding of the apostolic teachings changes with continuing revelation, but our doctrine nonetheless remains identical in essence and substance. Thus, the doctrines of the Trinity, the two natures of Christ, the divine motherhood, the Immaculate Conception, and the Assumption of Mary, along with our other dogmas were always part of the orthodoxy of the Church, but were not precisely defined for many years, according to the need for clarification. Moreover, the understanding of these doctrines may continue to grow and be enriched in the future, not only through mystical experience, but through the practice of sciences, philosophy and theology as guided by the Holy Spirit. A common metaphor used to explain such a process is that of a seed: the acorn itself has neither branches nor leaves; yet once planted in fertile soil, it gradually grows into a tall oak; throughout its lifetime, however, it ever continues to be the same tree that was planted.

Darrel: The progress of the Catholic Church in history is compared more to a weed than a seed, Sonny. Weeds choke out good plants. Your "doctrines" (which originate from your traditions) were made official over the centuries when your church leaders recognized how they would serve to further embolden the Catholic Church in accomplishing its objective of preserving its wealth, power and influence.

John: Sure, that may be, Darrel, but I understand what Sonny is saying and agree with him on some of the points he makes. I don't agree with him that Christians need a "binding authority" in their lives though. I believe God knows how to reveal His truth through His Word and sacraments, and we can be assured we have the correct understanding by leaving us the Holy Spirit at Pentecost to guide us. That's what Protestants believe.

Darrel: I want to talk more about the historical timeline when these various traditions were added over the centuries later on, Sonny, but you mentioned some "mystical experience," and I'd like to comment on that. This reference to mysticism creates yet another opportunity for the Catholic Church to communicate heresy. We are on the outside looking in because we don't want to go on your "magical mystery tour" with you people. Your tour is led by a magisterium which creates dogma to suit its purpose and accommodate to the times.

John: Mysticism is really just a philosophical concept which describes man's struggle to be more attuned with the divine and maybe even aspire to be God himself. That's how cults operate, right? Do Catholics really want to admit to being compared to them? More bad company?

Sonny: That's a ridiculous presumption, but I will admit there can be some confusion in trying to understand this process. That's the downside of mysticism.

Darrel: Mysticism can be used as a tool to open the door to creative Christianity.

Ray: We trust our Church Magisterium to correctly interpret God's Word and will.

Darrel: Yeah, well your magisterium hasn't done so well with performing its job lately. Several of your researchers into your doctrine like Bernard

Hoose and Mark Jordan, to name a few you might recognize, have found that these claims your church makes to offer a continuous, consistent teaching on matters of sexuality, life and death and crime and punishment are "simply not true." They objected to the "inconsistency, contradiction and even incoherence" in the Catholic Church's doctrines and they concluded that "the tradition itself is not the truth guarantor of any particular teaching."

Sonny: I might add that others disagree and argue differently.

Daniel: I have to admit, Sonny, that, after listening to this educational discussion, I agree with what Darrel is implying about the relevance and role of your sacred tradition in conveying your doctrine to folks. When you said that the sacred tradition was defined by the Seven Ecumenical Councils, the sanctified lives of godly men (whoever they may be), and described as a living tradition expressed in the life of the church, it occurred to me how self-serving this approach really is. The inclusion of the sacred tradition in the education and even the salvation of believers provides a great deal of latitude in determining what it wants its members to believe.

Darrel: Yes, of course, as we shall see as we later uncover some more of these other differences between Protestantism and Catholicism, the inclusion of this sacred tradition in the mix is strictly by design to serve the objective of the Catholic Church, which is to preserve and maintain its power and influence over people's lives. From an objective viewpoint, it's not hard to see that in Catholicism, it's all about the church; and when it's all about one thing, something else has to give, and that's the gospel. Luther talked about that.

Daniel: I think Catholics are so focused on their church they forget there are other denominations, and unity among us is critical. They miss the big picture: the preservation of Christianity. Satan conquers through division. It's like when Robert E. Lee chose to be more loyal to his state of Virginia than join the effort to maintain the United States of America.

Given his brilliance as a military leader, it goes without saying that if he had chosen the support unity, thousands of lives would have been saved.

Sonny: My Church is my church and your church is your church. From my perspective, it's the Church that has served me well in enabling me to most thoroughly understand the gospel.

Bobby: Different strokes for different folks? What's wrong with seeing it that way?

Daniel: Nothing, as long as the strokes chosen reveal the truth of the gospel.

Darrel: Catholics won't accept they are just a different denomination though; in believing they alone represent the true Christian church, they believe all the rest of us are heretics, lost sheep who must come to their church for the truth and even for our salvation. In believing that their church is sole authority for the truth, they delegate thought to their church. The Church is supposed to do the thinking for you people.

Ray: Christ intends for the Magisterium to accept that responsibility, Daniel. We're supposed to delegate trust to them. It is the Church that believes first, and so bears, nourishes and sustains our faith. (CCC 168).

Darrel: Christians have Christ as their mediator, we don't need a church.

Daniel: Catholics of course are the only Christians who believe in the sole authority of some magisterium and your pope. Protestants recognize that the pope is merely the leader of your church organization. You revere him as a prophet, priest and even a King of the Catholic Kingdom and that's a role no man on earth is to play because we Christians are to recognize that only Christ is our prophet, priest and King.

Ray: Christ is King, and reigns over the Kingdom our Church has been entrusted to rule.

Daniel: Yes, your pope rules over his earthly kingdom of believers in issuing his papal decrees which become dogma to be obeyed. His pope's infallible pronouncements ("ex cathedra") are to be considered the words of God, right? Well, that's what prophets do. Your pope serves as your spiritual leader, and your priests replicate Christ's atoning sacrifice in your Eucharist, right? As your sole authority, your pope rules over his church as a king would rule over his kingdom, and the church councils he heads make up the rules as they go along, depending on whatever the spiritual issue is that needs to be addressed. In declaring various rites as sacraments, the Catholic Church has done what Christ did in designating baptism and Holy Communion as sacraments. So there you are, all three roles of Christ are played out by a church which claims to be Christ. I can see why your Bishop Sheen claimed the church is Christ.

In effect, the Catholic Church has gone where no Christian church should go in having established itself as a separate authority to God's Word, the Holy Bible. I agree with what Darrel has said before; in Catholicism, it's primarily about the church and it has been that way for a very, very long time.

Ray: You're a liar, Daniel!

Bobby: Hey, Ray, take a chill pill; we don't talk to each other like that in these sessions.

Daniel: I must have hit a nerve. Such a term is derogatory and untrue. If you think I'm mistaken, say that, don't' call people liars when you yourself aren't sure of what's true.

Ray: I'm sorry, but the Catholic Church is true; everything else is a lie.

Sonny: Personally, I think we could understand that this need not be an either-or situation; it can be, and is, both: The Church and the gospel. They go together in a symbiotic relationship.

Darrel: It's more like a parasitic relationship between your church and the gospel, Sonny. Your church uses the gospel to give it credibility to pursue its own materialistic self-interests.

Daniel: I agree with you Darrel when you say that the church lays claim on its followers and forces them to focus on its dogma, rituals and traditions which require the time and effort a believer could, and should, better spend in reading and studying the Bible. We have to avoid focusing more on dogma than on Christ.

Sonny: The dogma connects us to Christ. For us Catholics, rituals are the foreplay of worship. Does not music enhance the spiritual experience?

John: Of course it does. Luther considered music to be almost as important as theology. In fact, the Catholic Church has recognized Luther's musical talent in writing hymns and backed off on labeling him a heretic because they use some of his hymns in its Mass.

Sonny: Really? I wasn't aware of that. I merely wanted to emphasize how important music and rituals like candles and incense are to our connection with Christ. These rituals were all observed in the Old Covenant when celebrating in worship ceremonies throughout church history. And they are not limited to just religious expressions; ritual is fundamental to engage the psychological and emotional stimuli that generally inspire a person in many activities. I'm sure you have watched precision military rifle parades or the baseball player who adds drama by exercising his body language of swinging the bat and tapping his shoes before he steps up to the plate. If there was no ritual in any sports, religious, romantic military, political or social event, it would be the most boring experience.

Daniel: So we should be Catholics because the Catholic Church and its various rituals practiced in the great cathedrals to enable us to experience the true connection with God?

Such rituals of course can serve as foreplay to worship and certainly no one who's ever been in a Catholic cathedral or in an old European Protestant church, would deny that this experience doesn't serve to put us in the right mood to worship our God. If the Catholic Church had remained loyal to its roots as the original church in the tradition of the apostles, this would have been ideal for all Christians; we would in that sense all be Catholics, right? Alas, it strayed from its roots in pursuing its worldly objective as it transitioned from its focus on the City of God to the City of Man over its centuries of existence. Augustine is rolling over in his grave at the sight of what has become of his church. As the church added members and grew in influence, power and wealth, it transitioned into what we now have today in the Catholic Church, a corporate institution, a continuation in the spirit of the old Holy Roman Empire portraying itself as sole authority as its co-dependency with its followers serves to minimize its ability to serve its original function: To convey the gospel truth to the world.

The Reformation, in restoring the original church in the apostolic tradition, provided an alternative for those Catholics who were aware of what I just said had happened to their church; the emphasis on the five *solas* enabled Christians to focus solely on the apostolic tradition because there was no longer some powerful, influential church inserting itself between them and their relationship to God. *Sola Catholic Church* was replaced by *sola Scriptura* as believers were enabled to cast off the extra-biblical, man-made tradition and dogma of the Catholic Church which it had added to the apostolic teachings of the Bible over its centuries of existence. With the birth of Protestantism, our focus on Christ and God's Word alone was restored. Focus of course is critical, and it's important we get it right. We should focus on reading our Bible because it's critical that believers understand the Word as God is directly speaking to us, and not rely on some self-appointed organization to act as our intermediary. Believers were able to approach Scripture with an open mind, a mind that craves more and more and more knowledge about God and our relationship with Him as we pray for guidance from the Holy Spirit for understanding, and thus be able to worship in truth and in spirit. We began in the Spirit (Galatians 3:3) and cannot be made perfect in the flesh. Yes, the earthly rituals, the pomp, the architecture are important but not important enough to neutralize the reasons I just listed for being a Protestant.

Darrel: Indoctrination is the antithesis of awareness, and Catholics are indoctrinated. With apologies to *Pink Floyd*, "We don't need no indoctrination. We don't need no thought-control. Bishops! Leave those kids alone!"

John: It's of course critical for every believer to know what their religion is based upon, and most important to know why they are members of a particular church. Only through the Bible can we hear the truth directly from the apostles themselves; they speak plainly, in common language, and we don't need some authority to tell us what they said or what the authority thinks they meant or what they left out that should have been included in their teachings but somehow omitted. Christ of course meant for His church to be based solely on the teachings of the apostles.

When, in pursuit of its own interest, a church, any church, forces itself into this intended connection between the believer and the Word, the truth can be compromised, and indeed it has been by the Catholic Church with its heretical traditions that have no basis in Scripture. The only way we can know God's truth is to read and understand His Word. For this reason, every Christian should become as familiar as they can with their Bible. God relies on his Word to accomplish his will. He spoke our world into existence. His Word is in fact all we have to go on for our knowledge of God and how He relates to us and how we are supposed to relate to Him. We are to glorify Him, and we compromise that necessary obligation by following the dictates of a church like the Catholic Church which seeks to glorify itself.

Christians should never forget that the *final* authority must rest in God's Word. His Word is the only inerrant and infallible guide for life that God gave us all. So, if any of the church's traditions conflict with scripture, they must not be followed.

Ray: We don't believe the Bible is the only authority. Christ left us the Church not the Bible. Christ gave our Church the keys to the kingdom and the authority to govern the kingdom. We recognize that the Bible is an important source of knowledge, but there is also the sacred tradition of the Church. You may recall my reference to the three-legged stool.

Darrel: Christ left us with the apostles who subsequently committed his Word to writing; Christ's church is to represent those teachings and do nothing else.

Look, man, as I said before, Christ did not intend for any one church organization to claim sole responsibility for proclaiming the gospel. Michael Grant, secular author of *Saint Peter, a biography*, observed that "there is no evidence that Jesus meant for there to be a visible, concentrated, personalized center of the Church." He referred to the invisible church when he said that "the Church is universal, evoking the idea of the people of God as a temple, and embodying the divine Jewish people, the people, now of Jesus, the new Israel, the eschatological kingdom that has succeeded to the old Israel, which has failed to live up to its calling." Here's an unbeliever telling it like it is.

The church visible is supposed to govern believers, and we are all subject to church authority and discipline, and we rely on our church to preach, teach, and practice the gospel. The visible church was not to have temporal power though. When the Catholic Church went down that road, it lost its primary focus: To represent the apostolic teachings. The Catholic Church wants to be the invisible and the only visible church and rule over Christ's kingdom; it claims that it has been given this mandate by Christ. This, of course, is what the reformers objected to. From the day it named itself *The Catholic Church*, it has determined a course that gives it the power and influence it pursues. Such power corrupts, and indeed the Catholic Church has abused its authority over the years in persecuting everyone who stands in its way of achieving its objective to rule over its subjects like some damn ruling monarch. Can't you see it from our perspective, Sonny? Surely you are familiar enough with church history to see how your Catholic Church has become a self-appointed ruler over its subjects over the centuries.

Ray: That's a ridiculous accusation. People worship kings; we do not worship our Church.

Darrel: You may deny it, but all the signs of worship are there. Daniel referred to your church usurping all of Christ's roles, prophet, priest and king, and I can see what he means.

You Catholics always defer to your church for its official opinion on every aspect of the Christian doctrine; you not only genuflect to the altar in your Mass, you bow down to Mary at her separate altar, and you worship your pope by referring to him as Christ's substitute on earth. Though you may not be conscious of worshiping the Catholic Church as you do Christ, you've admitted that your church is Christ and the Holy Spirit; you've said your pope ("Holy Father") is infallible as God is infallible. This behavior and mindset is evidence of a form of worship. The real problem isn't so much with your incorrect orthodox Mariology as it is with the way it's applied in practice. Can't you see how the praise and adoration you exhibit towards Mary and even your church could be construed as a worship experience? Loyalty is one thing, worship is another. It's like the loyalty Marines are to show for their Corp except that they put God first before country.

John: William R. Newell, in his commentary on Romans, talked about this subject. He stated that "The witness of the Spirit is to the fact of our relationship (with Christ). How foolish it would be, and how sad, if a child should fall into the delusion that it must have a certain 'feeling' if it is to believe itself a child of its parents. The unconscious certainty of the relationship is the beauty of it." The conscious feeling Catholics have for their church trumps the unconscious certainty of our relationship with our triune God. They miss the beauty of that connection by focusing on something else.

Ray: Scripture tells us to respect and obey our parents. It's one of the Ten Commandments. Take a breath, Protestant people! Your assumptions are ridiculous. I hope you'll all see the light by the time we finish up with these discussions.

Darrel: Your church isn't the object of the reference to parents in Scriptures, and you know it. The reference is to our actual mother and father not to some church that wants to fulfill that role. How can the blind see the light? Your church has blocked your vision which should be solely focused on Christ. We focus on Christ through the sacraments and the Word. We commune with God through his Word; this is one of the most distinguishing marks of a Christian. Catholics' hearing is impaired as well as their vision because their church does not encourage them to read Scripture to hear God's voice. The Bible is the only place we'll hear the voice of God. God doesn't speak through prophets anymore and he certainly doesn't speak through your pope.

Peter: Catholics are indoctrinated into their belief, but isn't this the case with most religions? Members have all been indoctrinated into their beliefs to some extent?

Daniel: Yes. By definition, indoctrination is the process of instilling an ideology in a person. Indoctrination implies that a person has been spoon-fed a doctrine to believe in. We can avoid such indoctrination by following what John Calvin said about a true faith being an intelligent faith; that means we not only know what we believe but why we believe it. If we can only admit that we believe something because that's the way we were raised or that's what the church tells us to believe, that's not a true faith; it's a blind faith. John briefly touched on this subject before. Philosopher William James called a belief acquired in such a way a "second-hand religion" because it was handed down from generation to generation. Such a belief is a habit. Habits, particular those that are based on superstition, discourage thinking, and we should never discount the importance of learning more and more about our great religion as we go through this life.

In my opinion, it seems that the Catholic Church provides a secure, spiritual home for those who don't seem to care about leading an examined life; these are people who are indoctrinated into their belief and blindly follow it as best they can without giving it a second thought. Actually, as Peter surmised, that's the case with most people in the world, isn't it? My experience with Catholics leads me to believe that, while their depth of commitment to a belief in Christ as their Lord is there, the depth of their understanding of the Christian doctrine is relatively shallow. They're content with just following along with the traditions and the dogma of their church with no awareness of the importance of having an intelligent faith Calvin referred to. The mechanical repetition of saying grace and confession of sin, and mechanically praying to God on the beads demonstrate what I'm saying. They just appear to be going through the motions. Muslims do this too, but, hey, at least Catholics are praying to THE God and not some false God like Allah. Of course, this rogue pope of yours seems to think Allah is the same God as we worship.

John: Luther had this to say about prayer in general. "The babbling and droning in church that used to be taken for prayer was of course no real praying...To pray is to call upon God in every trouble. It is this that He requires of us, and He does not leave it up to our own choice...By calling on God in prayer, we honor His name and use it purposefully." Mechanically may be purposefully, but it isn't honoring God.

Peter: People who lead an examined life aren't mechanical in their thoughts or actions. I believe that leading the examined life is critical to any believer no matter what your belief is. Aristotle and Plato both said that to lead a full life, it must be an examined life; and that means we should not only know exactly what we believe, but, more importantly, why we believe it. People who have been indoctrinated with a belief from birth are religious merely out of habit. Muslims and cult believers are indoctrinated like this.

Darrel: Right; they believe a lie until they die, and then their blind faith becomes sight. While this is the case with atheists like you, Pete, it is not necessarily the case with Catholics, our fellow Christians. They are our brothers and sisters in Christ so your fate will not be theirs, but, since our objective is to know the truth (also according to Aristotle), no one should merely rely upon what some magisterium or any self-appointed authority tells us what is true.

Sonny: You certainly give Aristotle credibility.

Darrel: So should you. He's recognized as the father of philosophy, and he was the philosopher your St. Thomas Aquinas referred to in his classic *Summa Theologica*.

John: Aquinas demonstrated that we must keep an open mind and try to be objective in testing every hypothesis or opinion or authoritative statement to find the truth. Indoctrination is meant to control what is perceived as the truth. The result of indoctrination into a belief is that you don't think about what you believe; you just believe it because you were told to believe it.

Darrel: Were you raised a Catholic, Sonny?

Sonny: Yes, both of my parents were Catholics. My father's side of the family is Irish; we've been Catholics for generations. But I renounced Catholicism as an adult and have only recently returned to my religion because I believe it to be the truth. Of course, I know I'm no exception. Many of the people who were raised as Catholics and have left the church do come back to the fold; and even some of you Protestants see the light and join up with the true Christian church.

Darrel: A reaffirmed Catholic is even more determined to represent his belief as the only truth than a person who has never questioned it so that explains your enthusiasm in these discussions. However, I should tell you that you are actually in the minority; surveys indicate that the majority of Catholics who leave Catholicism don't ever intend to come back to Catholicism. Some of them I've spoken with say they've left the church because they didn't want to adhere to its dogma and tradition. They claim Romanism was too "religious" for them. By this I assume they meant it was too legalistic for them. Too many laws, too much stress to be virtuous or suffer the consequences. This can also be the case with people who were raised as Pentecostals and other more fundamentalist Christian denominations that have strict traditions to follow like foot washing, prohibition of drinking and dancing, and so on, and emphasize damnation for all those who don't strictly adhere to their doctrine. Unfortunately, a rejection of these denominations is like throwing the baby out with the bath water. In rejecting Catholicism, ex-Catholics believe they are rejecting Christianity, because their church has indoctrinated them to believe there are no other Christian denominations; that's a tragedy that could be avoided if Catholics just understood that their church left them. See Jude 19.

Darrel: A 2015 Pew Poll indicates that, of all the Christian denominations, Catholicism has experienced the greatest net losses due to religious switching. I will just read it to you: Nearly a third of all U.S. adults were raised Catholic like you were, and like Bobby says he was, but one of three of these folks no longer identifies as a Catholic. That's significant. In fact, now nearly 13% of all Americans are former Catholics like Bobby here. This exodus results in a net loss because the number of those converting to Catholicism is much less than the number leaving. I should point out that the polls also tell us there are far fewer converts to Catholicism than those switching to Protestant denominations. In fact, there are more than six former Catholics for every convert to Catholicism. In comparison, there are approximately 1.7 people who have left mainline Protestantism for every person who has joined a mainline denomination. So we can see that no other religious group analyzed in the survey has experienced anything close to this ratio of losses to gains for Catholicism. In general, the various polls indicate many more Catholics are leaving Catholicism than are joining the church. The exit polls indicate that those leaving your denomination have a list of objections, and we can discuss those in detail, but they are also leaving because they are fed up with the legalism in Catholicism and question the legitimacy of the papacy to guide them in knowing the truth of Christianity. This is the reason some of them have joined Protestant denominations.

Sonny: Membership in all Christian churches is in decline; we are now living in post-Christianity America.

Darrel: Yes, we are in the West, but Christianity has made great gains East in Africa and China, in particular. The lampstand's moving East; we should know that the membership in the invisible church remains the same since the beginning of time because it consists of only the elect of God.

The polls I've seen confirm that Catholicism's retention rate has slipped since 2007. At that time 68% of respondents who were raised Catholic continued to identify as such as adults. Today, 59% of those raised Catholic still identify with Catholicism as adults, while 41% do not. Of course, with the exposure of more of these sex scandals in the priesthood, we can assume this number will probably increase. Other polls indicate that most Catholics are Catholics because they were raised as Catholics. These polls show that very few people actually convert to Catholicism in comparison to people converting to Protestantism. Polls indicate that out of a sample of 4,000 Protestants, just 32 became Catholics. On the other hand, of the people raised as Catholics who have left the church, 10% now identify with Evangelical Protestants denominations, the fastest growing Protestant domination. We can infer that some of the other 90% are among those who list "none of the above" for their religion in the latest polls. As Darrel said, it's tragic when folks throw the baby out with the bath water in renouncing Christianity because they disagree with some denomination's preaching and teaching of God's Word.

Bobby: Okay, it's time to adjourn. See y'all next week.

Week Six

Bobby: Doesn't God want everyone to be saved? Doesn't the Bible say that?

Sonny: Yes, Paul states this in 1Timothy 2:3-4 and Peter states it in 2 Peter 3:9. But, obviously not all men are saved so there must certainly be more to salvation; and there is.

Recall what I said before about the two types of grace Aquinas defined: Initial and cooperating grace. We Catholics believe that God offers salvation to all, but offers grace through the Church to us. We need His grace to be saved, but we can't receive it unless we concede to it. It's only after we accept His initial grace that we contribute to our salvation by choosing to follow God and not reject Him.

Darrel: We agree that God is loving and wishes he could save all men; but we understand that he doesn't do this because he is also a just, righteous and holy God, and though he loves us and wants the best for us, he will not save us because our sin has destroyed our relationship with him. The penalty for sin must be paid for mans' injustice; his justice is satisfied through the sacrificial atonement of Jesus Christ on the cross. We disagree on our role in salvation; we believe God saves us without us doing anything to help him out.

Sonny: God has established our Church as a means by which all people can come to Him.

Darrel: Yes, yes, I know the drill; you Catholics believe in a corporate salvation, God gives grace to people through the Catholic Church. Everything goes through the vaunted church.

Bobby: But it doesn't seem fair that some are saved because God wants to save them, and all the others are damned through no choice of their own. They just weren't chosen. I know we've talked about this predestination before, but it just doesn't seem right or fair.

Darrel: Well, predestination is a hard concept to understand and accept; Luther had trouble with it, but because it was clearly stated in the Bible, he acquiesced. I told you before, Sonny, that Augustine believed in it too.

Bobby: What happens to the unsaved? When the pope says atheists can go to heaven, what is he saying? Is he implying that they can only be saved if they are connected to Christ in some mystical, unseen way? Do I hear him actually claiming that there are exceptions to the requirement a person express a belief in Christ as savior to be saved? This is a good question to begin today's session, eh?

Darrel: Yeah, it is It's another "yeah, but" in Catholic theology" *Yeah*, we believe salvation is only through Christ, *but* people can be united to Christ without expressing that belief.

Sonny: God will judge people according to their knowledge. If they live in a way which accords with their best knowledge of God, we trust that He will be merciful to them. But, that said, we simply cannot know how many people who don't have knowledge of Christ may still be united to Him in a way known only to God. There are also people united to Christ who are not aware of their connection. We don't know what God will do for those outside the Church, so it's best not to presume to judge. We can only hope and pray that God will have mercy on them. The usual and expected means of salvation is being united with Christ, but we also know from the Bible that "The Lord is merciful and gracious, slow to anger and abounding in steadfast love (Psalm 103, vs. 8). We hope that those who, through no fault of their own, never know the gospel in a conscious way may be united to Christ in a way known only to our sovereign and loving God.

Darrel: You of course know there's nothing in the Bible to support your hope, right? Sure, it only seems right and fair from our perspective that God somehow in some way takes unbelief due to lack of knowledge of Christ into consideration in his plan of salvation, but the Bible simply doesn't provide us with an answer and neither should your church.

Bobby: How does a person know they're saved?

Darrel: That's a toughie, Bobby; I can only say I know I'm saved. None of us should assume for others or judge them.

Sonny: I believe that those inside the Church are saved, but, based on what I said last session about how God, in His mercy, wants to save everyone, inside and outside the Church, and mentioned there may be other avenues of salvation open to people who have never heard the gospel or haven't recognized their knowledge of the gospel, I have to admit that it's possible a Protestant who professes Christ as their Savior is saved. I will say though that a Catholic has a better chance of getting to heaven than a non-Catholic because the Catholic has recourse to the sacraments, which strengthen the Catholic in his Christian journey and God's normative means of bestowing supernatural grace. CCC 1129 of our Catechism states that the sacraments of the New Covenant are necessary for salvation. "Sacramental grace" is the grace of the Holy Spirit, given by Christ and proper to each sacrament.

Darrel: Luther believed the sacraments were one of the two means of grace, the other being God's Word, the Holy Bible. We have access to both. Catholicism's heavy on the sacraments, but light on the Word. The emphasis on the one minimizes the other.

Sonny: If you want assurance of salvation, you must be grafted back into full communion with the Church.

Darrel: Is that moral assurance or absolute assurance? When works are added to any doctrine, assurance is compromised because one never knows if they've done enough good.

In Catholicism's confusion over how our free will works with God's will, it stresses the insufficient of God's providence; with its belief in "grace plus works," it stresses the insufficiency of God's grace; in its insistence that its Catholic tradition is necessary to supplement the Bible, it indicates the insufficiency of God's holy Word. It would seem that your church alone is sufficient to cover all your spiritual needs, right? So then, if I joined the Roman Catholic Church, would that be sufficient for my salvation?

Sonny: Yes, but you must also have a valid baptism. Our Church offers recourse to all of the sacraments, the normative means of receiving justification and persevering in the Christian journey to salvation. We place the most emphasis on baptism because without it, none of the other sacraments count. We place emphasis on the Eucharist because it connects us with the body and blood of Christ.

Darrel: You turn the sacrament of the Eucharist into a special membership ritual promoting your exclusivity. Protestants believe the sacraments of baptism and Holy Communion are one of God's means of grace, but, are you really saying my baptism in a Protestant church doesn't count? Do I have to be baptized in a Catholic Church? Are you really saying that, in addition to all the other insufficiencies I mentioned before, we need to add one more; a baptism that must be valid according to the Catholic Church for it to be sufficient?

Sonny: You don't necessarily have to be baptized in our Church. If a person has been baptized in any church by triple immersion (by the Father, Son, and Holy Spirit), this is an acceptable baptism for membership in our Church.

Darrel: Whew, that's a relief; at least my baptism seems sufficient for your requirements because I was not sprinkled, I was baptized by immersion. But of course, as you must know, the Bible really doesn't make this distinction. It only states that we are only to be baptized once, and that is sufficient.

Sonny: Look, all I know is that the correct observance of the sacraments was required by Jesus and is therefore required of all Christians to be saved. So, if the shoe fits.....

John: But we Protestants don't place the other five ordinances you Catholics label as sacraments in that same category; this is why Luther and the other reformers considered only these two to be sacraments.

Luther included a reference to their importance when he comprised the steps in God's plan of salvation:

1. God has truly reconciled us into Himself through Christ.

2. God offers and distributes to us the grace purchased by Christ through the means of Grace (Baptism, Communion, the Word)

3. The Holy Ghost works faith through His offer of grace in the means of Grace.

4. God justifies through this faith.

5. God sanctifies those justified.

6. God will not forsake them in their great weakness and in all manner of temptation.

7. God will, however, strengthen, increase, and support the good work to the end.

8. Until finally He will eternally save and glorify in life eternal those whom He has elected, called and justified.

Sonny: We believe in all these steps. In regards to number four though, we understand that God justifies us through His grace, and we accept that gift through our good works. As I've said before, faith justifies initially, but works perfect and complete our justification.

And, in regards to number five, I would add that we believe we are sanctified through the seven sacraments of the Church; we can't contribute to our sanctification because we can't administer the sacraments to ourselves. In this way, the New Testament is consistent with the Old Testament where the Jesus priesthood was responsible for administering the sacraments.

John: But, to us, sanctification refers to our spiritual growth. How do the sacraments contribute to that?

Sonny: Catholicism teaches that the other five sacraments (besides baptism and the Eucharist) lead to our spiritual growth by requiring the performance of good works (offering confession, being confirmed, performing penance, etc.).

John: So, good works refers to works for the church.

Sonny: Yes, but not limited to just doing for the Church; we are to be charitable to all.

John: We have what we call rites that contribute to our spiritual growth, but we don't consider them to be ordained by God so we don't elevate them to the level of sacraments. If you make too many rites sacraments, the importance of a sacrament is cheapened, and that is exactly what we believe the Catholic Church has done by adding five more sacraments to the two that are stated in the Bible: Baptism and Holy Communion.

Okay then, this is the way we see it. As you may recall, sanctification is the only step in the Order of Salvation that we can truly participate in as we work daily towards making ourselves more holy. We grow through our dedication to reading the Bible, studying the Bible, hearing the preaching and teaching of the Word and worshiping in truth and spirit. The sacraments are relevant for us too, but are not directly connected to our spiritual growth as you believe your extra five apply. Baptism contributes to our sanctification in the sense that it makes it possible for us to complete this step in the Order by opening up the window to salvation through infusion of God's grace. The sacrament of Holy Communion contributes to our sanctification in maintaining and emboldening the process by which we are becoming more holy by that same infusion of grace.

According to Calvin, the sacraments are one of the two means of grace; the other is God's Word, the Holy Bible, and sanctification is connected to that means of grace as well because we are being made more holy as we read and interpret God's Word.

Catholics designate these various ordinances as sacraments, and we don't accept that since they weren't ordained by Christ. They certainly aren't considered to be necessary to motivate us to be more holy. We understand that we do gain in holiness as we perform those good works which please God as a result of our faith. These are the ways we contribute to our sanctification.

Sonny: The Church is God's only means of grace in the sense that grace has to flow through the Church. Thus grace is infused by the administration of all the seven sacraments. During the spiritual growth of a Christian he or she must adhere to the Liturgy of the Word, Liturgy of the Bread of Life and receive Holy Communion with God and in these instances receive the grace for sanctification and guided towards holiness. Holiness is the separation from the seven capital sins and submission unto God. Only through the Church which Jesus Christ built (upon Himself) can grace be conferred for sanctification and holiness.

Daniel: This "through the Church," that "through the Church," and on and on it goes. Instead of the truth that Jesus taught us, that we can do nothing apart from Him, the Catholic Church teaches you can do nothing apart from it. Can't you see how your church inserts itself into the life of its followers in any way it can? It misses no opportunity in its quest to be an indispensable part of your lives. Your church doesn't seem to believe you can do anything on your own when it comes to connecting with Christ; you need it to be there for every step you take in your walk in faith. Every time you turn around to face Christ, you bump into it. Can't you people see that's what your church is doing?

Ray: Yes, and we prefer it this way. Our church is Christ, and we need our Church for our salvation. Pope Leo XII pronounced there's no salvation outside the Catholic Church.

Darrel: There's no salvation outside of Jesus Christ. In John 14:6, Jesus says "he (not some church) is the way, the truth and the life; no one comes to the Father but through me."

Ray: As I said, the Catholic Church is the substitute for Jesus Christ on earth.

Darrel: Don't you know that we live each day in *coram Deo*, in the face of God? Aren't you folks the least bit concerned about making such an outrageous and false claim in front of him? Wouldn't that outrageous presumption of yours that you are Christ's substitute sound to him like you're asserting authority that is his alone? Our trine God's position is already taken by him (thank God), and, as history has proven, the Catholic Church isn't any good at playing God anyway. The Masters of the Magisterium are just men.

We Protestants are confident that we understand the true meaning of God's grace and how Christ's sacrifice wiped our slate clean; we are confident we glorify him by honoring the unmerited favor he has bestowed on us. Catholicism complicates this simple understanding with a "yeah, but," adding good works to the plan of salvation like every other world religion does. We believe our salvation is totally up to God, and it has nothing to do with random chance or our good deeds; it has to do with God's grace and his election of believers. In sum, it's obvious that we Protestants understand the power and significance of God's grace in our salvation, and you Catholics don't or won't. Again, this church institution of yours must make room for itself in every aspect of your beliefs, particularly relating to your own salvation. You guys seem to think we heretics are going to hell, but you also aren't even sure whether you're saved because you're not sure your works have pleased God; and, since Catholics believe that all must submit themselves to the authority of the pope to be saved, you're never sure whether your pope is pleased with you either. No contentment there.

Sonny: We believe you need to be in the body of Christ, which is the Church, to be saved. That doesn't mean though that you have to be a member in full communion, in good standing; although you lack the ability to receive the graces offered by the Church through the sacraments, and that's very important. Of these sacraments, it's particularly important you be baptized in the Church to be saved.

Bobby: My catechism states that "Those who die for the faith, those who are catechumens, and all those who, without knowing of the Church but acting under the inspiration of grace, seek God sincerely and strive to fulfill his will, are saved even if they have not been baptized."

Darrel: Hey, here is an example of a "yeah, but." *Yeah*, we believe you can't be saved except by a special type of baptism administered in the Catholic Church, *but* those who don't know the Catholic Church have a special dispensation.

Sonny: Do you Protestants have a better answer as to the final destination of people who have never been introduced to the gospel and don't know Christ?

Darrel: Yes. The answer is "I don't know." This sort of question falls under God's mysterious will. Not all questions we have are answered in God's Word. We don't need a church that makes up answers to fill in the blanks. <u>I'd rather not know the answer than be fed the wrong one.</u> We trust God has given us all we need to know for now and are content to wait for the answers to these questions when our faith becomes sight. Our churches don't assume an "I don't know" answer is wrong. When you put yourself out there as the only church in town, I guess you have a self-proclaimed reputation to live up to, eh?

Ray: Why can't you people understand that we are Christ's church, His only church?

Darrel: Since we Christians believe that salvation can only come through Christ and is not connected with any particular denomination, the Catholic assertion to be the only Christian church is false. We're getting tired of hearing you spout your default position. It's a premise no one but a member of your church accepts. So then, if we don't accept this premise, and we don't, where do we go from here? How can we move on in what is supposed to be an intramural discussion, a discussion among fellow Christians, if you don't recognize we are Christians? Can't you both try and open your minds to make any appropriate contribution to a discussion about Christianity and Jesus Christ. That's what we should be talking about.

Look, guys, I don't mean to offend, but you really should know by now that you're not preaching to the choir here, and I hope you know by now that we are all educated, well-informed students of theology and religion. Repeating mantra your catechism classes have taught you isn't going to cut it in these discussions. We are here to learn as much as you can teach us about what Catholics believe, and I hope you are here to learn what Protestants believe.

Ray: I seem to have hit a nerve with you people, and I'm sorry for that. It's just that it's hard for me to talk to people I believe have been so misled by heretics like Luther and Calvin that they have been separated from the truth.

Bobby: But why do you believe what you just said is the truth, Ray? I know why I believed the Church was the only authority for the truth; I grew up in a Catholic family and was educated in Catholic schools all the way through high school. My belief was a tradition I inherited from my parents and culture; it was a habit. We ate fish on Fridays and so on.

Darrel: Bobby's got a point. There is an actual Catholic culture. By that I mean, you have your traditions and you know tradition is the weakest source of knowledge. Tradition encourages habitual behavior and can therefore stifle thought. Maybe this is why I have only on rare occasions debated with a Catholic who seemed to understand why they are a Catholic and not a Protestant and can participate in a discussion with an open mind. So far, you guys don't seem to be any exception to what seems to be the rule. You seem to be missing the point of what we're supposed to be doing here. We all got into this by understanding we were to keep an open mind or we wouldn't get much out of meeting together to discuss religion and theology. Leading such an examined life establishes our intellectual credibility. If you people just continue repeating what your church has indoctrinated you to believe, neither you nor any of us will get anything out of this endeavor. We learn best through such discussions. You're here because we want to learn about Catholicism so please return the act by showing some interest in what Protestantism is really all about. I know that Catholics believe we are just heretics and don't have anything to add to their theology, but I would hope that by now you've formed an opinion of us that would enable you to trust what we have to say about what we believe and why we believe it. You might even learn more Catholicism as well; a different perspective can do that.

I think that Catholics are generally leaving the Catholic Church because they have recognized they have been indoctrinated and have examined what they believe and the nature of their relationship with their church and found it wanting. Did you people know that now one out of every ten Americans is an ex-Catholic? If ex-Catholics were a religion in itself, it would be the third largest denomination in the U.S. after Catholics and Baptists. That is a significant statistic.

Bobby: What is the Catholic Church doing about this exodus?

Darrel: As I said before, this new, liberal pope seems to believe that becoming more worldly will bring members to the church. When he is soft on atheists and gays, he's sounding desperate in trying to fill some of those empty pew seats; of course we know that if the church preaches the Bible, they won't stay long. And the Catholic Church is certainly not doing much about this pedophile scandal with some of their priests. The Apostle Paul urged the new Christian churches to invoke church discipline on errant members who commit unrepentant sin. The papacy seems to be ignoring this mandate. Since the first of these scandals began to appear during the reign of Pope John Paul, instead of ridding itself of these bad priests, the church has been covering up for them, reassigning them to different churches. In speaking with my Catholic friends, and from what I've been reading, the American bishops have never devoted any time at their national meetings to discussing this exodus. Nor have they spent a dime trying to find out why it is happening. They may ignore these scandals, but more and more of them keep showing up.

Sonny: We aren't losing members because some people are questioning their beliefs in light of these sex scandals. According to an article called "The Hidden Exodus: Catholics becoming Protestants" in the *National Catholic Reporter*, some are leaving because they disagreed with Catholic teaching on abortion and homosexuality, divorce, celibacy of priests, birth control, the way the church treats women, and were not satisfied with the church's teachings on poverty, war, the foreign bishops' interference in American politics and the death penalty.

Darrel: Yes, I've read articles that come to the same conclusion. Almost half who left to join Protestant churches said they found the catechism teaching unacceptable. In general, people are leaving the Catholic Church because they believe it has failed to provide them with what they consider to be the fundamental products of religion: Spiritual sustenance and a good worship service. As I said before, they may be leaving because they have recognized they have been indoctrinated by their church to minimize Scripture and are thus ignorant of the Bible and Christian theology. Those who have joined a reformed Protestant church clearly do so because they have recognized the differences between Protestant and Catholic doctrines, and want to be a part of a church that most represents that original apostolic church the Catholics have always claimed to be.

Sonny: I think they are leaving because they have succumbed to the liberal influence on the Christianity in general. The reason for people's dissatisfaction with Catholicism is no different than the reason people are dissatisfied with the Protestant churches. It has to do more with people's unreal expectations than with any failing of the church.

Darrel: You are correct, Sonny, but the dissatisfaction with your church deals with spiritual needs which can no longer be met through the indoctrination process. They're dissatisfied with the quality of what they're getting out of their worship service too. Protestant churches are losing members over doctrinal issues, and, as you say, the liberal influence has taken its toll as well.. I will say though that there are a number of surveys that indicate many Catholics stay in spite of their disagreement with specific church teachings based on doctrine.

Bobby: Why do they stay?

Darrel: Stats indicate that the ones who stay are less knowledgeable about the Bible and the gospel than those who are leaving because they do understand the difference in doctrine between Romanism and Protestantism. The article concludes that this means Catholicism "is losing the best, not the worst." This is evidence of my point about indoctrination. The indoctrinated ones are the ones who are staying because they don't know any better.

Ray: We believe you Protestants are indoctrinated.

Darrel: Yes, we are indoctrinated in the Word of God. Look, we all have to rely on a trusted authority for our knowledge of what God's Word is saying to us, but I wouldn't call that indoctrination because we are free to think about what that trusted authority is telling us and not just blindly accept it as the truth without question. There is of course no one Protestant Church we rely upon, as you Catholics relate to your church, and we consider that to be an advantage to Protestantism.

I don't mean to insult your intelligence, Ray, or Sonny's either. From what we've talked about so far, it seems you are both very well informed about the dogma of the Catholic Church. But, your responses also indicate a high degree of indoctrination because you often repeat the same mantra in response to a variety of questions or comments we make. And, when you refuse to at least examine your beliefs from our perspective and constantly defend the authority of your church over all other opinion as though it must be speaking for God like some kind of prophet, this indicates the presence of a closed mind, and that's what indoctrination does to a person.

Have you ever at any time questioned what the authority is telling you? Have you ever studied the Reformation or read anything about the reformers to analyze why they opposed your church? Why would you arbitrarily assume the reformers had absolutely no point to make at all? Have you thought about why you need to have some influential, powerful authority in your spiritual life to tell you what you are to believe about Christ and Christianity? You are such educated, articulate, intellectual people who should be certainly able to read the Bible yourselves instead of just having it read to you in your Mass? Why would you automatically just accept what your church dishes out without giving it a second thought? That's what we mean by indoctrination. After we're finished with these discussions, I hope you'll both at least give these questions some thought. If a person can't successfully defend to themselves what they claim to believe, that should be a sign they should consider modifying what they believe or discarding it entirely. It's one of the tests of truth theologians came up with. We are here to do that, man. As I said before, a true faith is an intelligent faith; that means a true faith is an examined faith.

Sonny: So, we are indoctrinated; what are you Protestants? Enlightened?

Darrel: In the sense that we do not consider ourselves to be under the burden of obedience to anyone but God and are thus free to study the Bible and the Christian doctrine independent of some authority telling us what to believe, yes, I suppose you could say we are enlightened compared to indoctrinated Catholics. Indoctrination results in a belief set in concrete. Enlightenment is a growing experience.

God gave us free will to exercise liberty, a brain to make good decisions, and a conscience guided by the Holy Spirit to strive for enlightenment in our pursuit of the truth. But I realize we humans are all subject to some form of indoctrination in our spiritual lives. We've all been influenced by the way we were raised, our society, our education, etc., and we have different needs to address, but I'm saying it's critical that we each recognize our presuppositions, climb out of that rut we're in and examine what we believe to determine if it's true or if we believe it because someone influenced us to believe it's true. That's what we're here to do, man. Think back to your student years. Who was the better teacher, the guy who lectured to you, and expected you to regurgitate what he told you from your notes on his lecture, or the guy who encouraged you to engage in the thought process and was himself open to learning from his students? Who did you learn more from?

I say again, we're here to converse with one another, learn from one another, test what we believe and discard it if it doesn't make any sense to continue to believe it. That's why we all need to be good listeners, free and open thinkers, not argumentative, bull-headed defenders of some indoctrinated belief. We need to understand how to get around our prejudice and bias, particularly if that bias is based on some indoctrination we've received. We need to understand how indoctrination works and why it can be a barrier to the truth. We know we can't reason with people who have been indoctrinated into what they believe.

Ray: I believe what I believe because I know it's the truth; you guys have it all wrong.

Daniel: That kind of response just isn't good enough for this group, Ray. That's what Darrel has been trying to tell you. As I said before, we need to resist presuming the other guy is always wrong and we are always right. We must avoid drawing a line in the sand and closing our minds to any opinion that doesn't match with our preconceived opinions. We must examine those preconceptions and ignore them if they don't make any sense.

Ray: Examine all you want, but don't expect me to play this game.

Sonny: Well, I personally believe I've been doing that all along. I've always thought of myself as a free thinker and a good listener. I don't believe I've been indoctrinated.

Darrel: Well, you came to believe what you believe in some way, and that's what we've been trying to get out of you in these discussions.

Sonny: What you've "gotten out of me" is the truth. You sound like a shrink! I didn't come to discuss me; I came to discuss my religion.

Darrel: Right. That's what we're all here to do, but our psychology of belief is connected with our theology. That's what I've been saying. .

Sonny: I'm sorry, I thought you wanted us to present our beliefs to your group.

Darrel: Sure, but, we need to keep our eye on the big picture here. We need to be discussing Christianity, not just Catholicism.

Sonny: When you dialogue with us, you are discussing Christianity.

Darrel: Ah, if that were only true, we could just talk about the gospel and call it good, but, from our discussions with you two so far, neither of you has convinced me you're experts on the Christian doctrine or that you can keep an open mind. Please try to be objective in examining the Scriptural evidence we have presented and will present soon and understand that the Holy Spirit is intended to be our guide in knowing God's Word. Try to see it from our perspective and consider what we've been saying about the ulterior motive of your church to assert authority and provide you with traditions that reveal man's fingerprints, okay?

Sonny: Give me an example of what you're saying, Darrel.

Darrel: I have said this before, but it bears repeating for effect: I believe the primary motive of your church is to feather its own nest, to further its objective to remain an institution; to remain and maintain the largest and most wealthy and influential visible church on earth. In keeping with that objective, the Catholic Church must maintain credibility and authenticity, and that is why they claim to be the one and only, original Christian Church. Catholic with a capital "C." Can't you at least try and see it the way we see it, that your denomination makes this assertion for the reason I just stated? <u>Couldn't that at least be a possibility</u>, given the fact that your church is made up of fallen men, just like you and me? Isn't that most obvious with these sex scandals and the cover-up?

Couldn't you at least try and entertain the opinion that your church has been slowly and deliberately separating itself from the original teachings of the apostles from its very beginning in assuming authority, developing traditions that are not supported by the Bible and, as a fail-safe, have even established the opinion that these traditions trump Scripture? Are you so indoctrinated, you are blind to looking at your church organization and your doctrine objectively?

Ray: Are you so blind, Darrel, you can't understand what the Bible is telling you? Are you even familiar with the Bible?

Darrel: Of course I am; we all are. In fact, it's very likely I've forgotten more about God's Word than the majority of Catholics I've communicated with even know, or may ever know. While you were being indoctrinated in Catholicism, I was studying Christianity.

Ray: We are Christianity, Darrel! We don't recognize you Protestant heretics or your so-called "invisible church;" we believe the church is visible and almost 2,000 years old. What you call the Roman Catholic Church today is the same church as the original church of the first century. Peter was appointed by Christ to be the visible leader after the ascension. We believe this gift of God's spirit was subsequently granted uniquely to the bishops of Rome, and Peter was our first pope. You are wrong to assume otherwise, Darrel.

Darrel: Okay, I tire of this robotic rhetoric from you, Ray! I brought my kite with me today, and the wind's right so I think I'll leave this discussion and go fly it.

Ray: Yeah, go fly a kite, Darrel! I'm sorry you're offended, but I keep having to repeat this because you people just don't seem to understand that Christ said it was so. I mentioned Matthew 16:18 before. Here Christ tells Peter, "On this rock I will build my Church (not churches)." He gives Peter the keys to the kingdom of heaven. There is only one Church built upon one rock with one teaching authority, not many different denominations, built upon various pastoral opinions and suggestions.

Daniel: We keep cycling back to the claim game your church plays. I'll say this again, Christ is not saying that the Catholic Church will be built on Peter and that this particular church will represent that one teaching authority. The word "rock" is mentioned many times in the Bible (just look at your Concordance) and it never refers to a leader of a church. You do recall John 14:26, where Christ tells us that one teaching authority is the Holy Spirit; he doesn't refer to a church.

John: Good point, Darrel. If it were not for the abuse of Matthew 16:18 by Roman Catholic Church to serve its purpose, it is unlikely that there would be any confusion in its interpretation at all. There would be absolutely no doubt that the reference here was only to Peter, and that arbitrarily appointing one of the apostles as the first of many to follow in the establishment of your church governing hierarchy is a false claim.

Ray: In Ephesians 4:11-13, Paul refers to the hierarchy to be set up in the Church.

John: Paul is referring to all the people, with different talents, who are equipped by Christ's ministry. Effective teachers help each believer to find their own way of benefitting the rest of the church.

Ray: You call these teachers "elders;" Christ warns against using that title in Matthew 23:8.

Daniel: Jesus is referring to the use of any pretentious forms of address. To us, teacher is not a pretentious title, it's a job description. Calling your priests "Father" with a capitol "F" is bestowing a religious title and that is very different.

Sonny: The priesthood and fatherhood have always been identified together. See Judges 17:10, 18:19. I can give you at least 15 other biblical verses that describe a fatherly relationship between Paul and Timothy and Onesimus and his churches in Corinth and Thessalonica. John calls the elders of the church "fathers" and members of the church "children."

Daniel: It's all about elevating the Catholic Church and the papacy. In Ephesians 4:11-13, Paul is not talking about setting up the institution of the Roman Catholic Church. Dr. Leonardo De Chirico, a pastor of Breccia di Roma in Rome and author of *A Christian's Pocket Guide to the Papacy*, said that the "opening and closing of doors with keys was the subordinate role of the steward on behalf of his king. It was not a self-referential, absolute power in and of itself. It was not something a steward could do as if he were the king. So, by receiving the keys of the kingdom, Peter would be a servant of God, the King, who would use him as a steward of the church that Jesus would build." De Chirico concludes by stating that "Matthew 16 can be seen as the biblical basis for the papacy only if the doctrine of the papacy has already been established apart from Scripture and then subsequently and retrospectively read into it." Of course, this is exactly what the Catholic Church has done.

The origin of the pope and the apostolic succession through this arbitrarily assigned leader mimics the Jewish Pharisee hierarchy with a little pagan monarchy thrown into the mix. In arbitrarily setting up a succession of leaders of the church, the Catholic Church revived this concept of being ruled by a special group of churchy leaders with special religious functions to perform. Christ challenged the authority of the Jewish hierarchy by associating with sinners, aliens and gentiles. And Paul warned us about this sort of thing happening in Ephesians 6:12. "For we do not wrestle against flesh and blood, but against principalities, against powers, against the rulers of the darkness of this age, against spiritual hosts of wickedness in the heavenly places."

Sonny: Paul is referring to false religions and cults, not the Catholic Church.

Daniel: It's not such a stretch to imagine the present day Catholic Church as a principality, a power, a spiritual host in the heavenly places we should wrestle against not idolize the Catholic Church as the sole authority in ruling over our spiritual lives. In *City of God*, Augustine warned that man was not to rule over man as your church does.

Ray: Peter accepted the keys Christ offered to him, and, as they say, the rest is history.

Daniel: On the contrary, Ray, Peter accepted the keys on behalf of all the apostles who were pledged to teach and preach the gospel. When we examine other passages in the Bible which deal with this subject, which of course is the best way to interpret Scripture, we see that Peter himself tells us that our interpretation is the correct one. In 1 Peter 5:3, Peter said that he wanted to be considered, not as a lord over the flock but as its representative, its example. In 1 Peter 2:4-8, he says that *all believers* have become *living stones* by virtue of their association with Christ along with the apostles as the foundation.

Ray: Okay, so then why did Paul go to Rome to meet Peter if not to acknowledge that Peter had been given the keys to the kingdom and was the rock on which the church would be built?

Daniel: The Bible tells us Paul went to meet Peter to get acquainted with a fellow apostle. You must be careful not to infer things that haven't been presented in the Bible, Ray.

Ray: Peter is the rock; the other apostles are the stones.

Daniel: The rock is the same as the stones, Ray. In Ephesians 2:20, Paul confirms what Peter said by repeating what Christ referred to Himself as being in Matthew 21:42, the rock, the cornerstone of the church. These verses specify that while Christ is the cornerstone, Peter and the rest of the apostles were to have pivotal roles in the church. They were the stones, the building blocks placed on the foundation of Christ.

John: Let's talk about the significance of Peter's role in the new church. As Darrel said before, Peter did have a special significance, but not as the leader of the church. Jesus didn't mean to establish a perpetual office for his "successor," as Catholics want to believe, but Peter did have a key role to play in the church Christ established.

Let's discuss this apostle. Peter of course is well known for his prominence among the Apostles and from being the first of the original disciples to recognize that Christ is the Messiah; but, many people don't know that he is regarded as the "Apostle of Hope.' Peter deserves this title because of what he said in 1 Peter 1:3. "Blessed be the God and Father of our Lord Jesus Christ! According to his great mercy, he has caused us to be born again to a living hope through the resurrection of Jesus Christ from the dead." Peter emphasizes the great mercy of God in causing us to be born again to a living hope. He refers to the sovereign regenerating power of God and the resurrection of our Savior and the hope that God always fulfills His promises to us. Dr. R. C. Sproul tells us that this is what the word "hope" means in Scripture.

When Peter tells us that our hope is a "living hope," he is communicating the certainty of our hope to us. The hope of salvation is not dead but alive and active. It has a sustaining power that manifests itself in faith, since "faith is the assurance of things hoped for, the conviction of things not seen (Hebrews 11:1). Dr. Sproul says that "Our faith is the manifestation in the present of what we will enjoy in our glorified state." One of Peter's most important roles in the church, therefore, is to emphasize to us that "the reality of our future hope serves to generate and sustain faith in our hearts. We believe because what God has revealed is true."

Bobby: That sounds like a pretty important role. And Peter, along with all the other disciples, was also given the power to forgive sins, right?

Daniel: Yes, in John 20:23 Jesus tells his disciples to receive the Holy Spirit. If you forgive the sins of any, they are forgiven them. If you retain the sins of any, they are retained. Since all true believers have received the Holy Spirit, Jesus is saying all true believers have the power to forgive.

John: But when we talk about forgiveness of our sins, Psalm 103:1-3 tells us that God alone forgives us our sins. And Matthew 9:1-8 tells us Christ alone forgives the sins of the paralytic.

Daniel: ABut that you may know that the Son of Man has power on earth to forgive sins." To me, this verse says that, while true believers can forgive specific sins, only Christ has the power to forgive sin in general. There are no references in the Bible to Christ transferring this power to anyone. Since the Jews understood that only God has that power, they knew Jesus was saying He was God. And God also knows nothing deters sin like the forgiveness of sin because it not only removes guilt, it also multiplies love for God, the One who forgives.

John: Exactly. John Calvin has interpreted John 20:23 to indicate that Jesus is enjoining His disciples, in His name, to proclaim the forgiveness of sins. Christ is saying that through their representation He is operating through them to reconcile them to God. In our Lutheran liturgy, our Pastor forgives us of our sins in the name of the Father, the Son and the Holy Spirit.

Daniel: So, Christ is not actually transferring the right that is His alone to forgive sins to His disciples. He is merely giving these church leaders the same authority He gives any true believer: the ability to discern whether a professing believer is in a state of salvation or not.

Sonny: You derive all of your knowledge of Christianity from the Bible. We do not.

Daniel: Yes, you Catholics believe in "*sola magisterium.*"

Sonny: I said it before and I'll say it again, there is no *sola Scriptura*. That's your Protestant hang-up. God's truth is conveyed to us through the Bible and our sacred tradition.

Daniel: It's not our hang-up, Sonny, it's what our belief is hung on. We don't accept your church's man-made sacred tradition; we confine our knowledge to only what is God-made, His Word presented in the

Bible. This is not to say we don't believe that the stories and teachings of Jesus and the apostles weren't communicated orally during the early Christian era, and we don't deny that truth doesn't exist outside the Bible; we just believe that the Bible is the only inspired source of our knowledge of God. This means that other traditions which have not been committed to Scripture cannot be proven true or false, one way or the other, and there is no way to verify which parts of the Catholic tradition are authentic and which are not. Based on your church's history, however, we are skeptical and inclined to believe that these traditions represent a self-serving interest.

Ray: Who are you to come to this conclusion?

Daniel: I'm just an un-indoctrinated person who can objectively and logically draw this conclusion. You should step back, get out of your box, and try to be objective. That said, I will clarify my statement to say that not all traditions of the Catholic Church are clearly self-serving. Some, like the traditions that serve to place the church in authority are of course obviously self-promotional; others like arbitrarily designating some rites like confession, confirmation, and last rites into sacraments draws more attention to the value of these rites, and that's a good thing.

Whenever someone starts talking about sacred tradition, I'm reminded of what we talked about last year when we were discussing Islam with a Muslim and Judaism with a Jew. They each told us how their religions have these sacred traditions which are considered to be as holy as the Qur'an and the Hebrew Bible respectively. God's Word, His revelation, has been effectively supplemented with these add-on, non-biblical, sacred traditions. This not only compromises God's sovereignty, it confuses the believers as well. This is particularly true in Islam where the sacred tradition often contradicts the Qur'an. Add-on, extra-biblical, sacred tradition from our Catholic brothers and sisters in Christ is not acceptable to us.

John: Right and this is because the Reformed, biblical Christian doctrine, which we all subscribe to, is based purely on the revelation of God, not on any man-made tradition conjured up by some church organization. The Bible warns us of supplementing the Word with traditions of men. When we recognize any religion which purports to be a religion of the book is supplementing that book, we should be aware that its doctrine is being influenced by man and is no longer purely based on what they believe is the revelation of God.

Bobby: But, as Christians claim, we should not always believe some revelation is from God. How can we know this? What's the best way to judge the authenticity of God's revelation?

John: Good question, Bobby. If it isn't in the Bible, we should question whether the revelation is from God because the Bible is God's Word, His only Word so we believe it is our only guide to God's revelation. We are to accept no supplements or substitutes. So we should understand we are to always look to the Bible and only the Bible for answers to doctrinal questions. Every other source of knowledge should be suspect. That's what Peter tells us to watch out for.

Bobby: We talked before about what constitutes a true believer. How can it be known whether a person is a true believer?

John: A good indication of true belief is when a person who professes to be a Christian actually shows he hates sin, loves God and loves his fellow man. And, as theologian Simon J. Kistemaker used to say, one of the first indications of a lack of love toward God and neighbor is for a Christian to stay away from worship services. I would say the fact that a person is regularly attending church in the first place would be a good indication they are a true believer.

Daniel: Yes, if a professing believer proclaims a credible profession of faith in Christ and evidence of their true saving faith is observed by the fruits of the spirit in their actions in their lives, the church leaders can confirm that the person has been forgiven by God.

Much of what Jesus said was only meant for true believers.

John: I should note again that Jesus said a lot more than was recorded in the Bible. Actually the Bible tells us that if every word Jesus uttered was recorded, the book would be so much larger than it is that it would not be possible to read it all. So, we must take what Jesus said on faith, understand that God cannot be inconsistent and interpret those verses which seem to need further interpretation by referring to other verses in Scripture which more clearly express what God wants to say to us.

Sonny: Our Catholic dogma is our formally revealed truths promulgated by the Church and revealed in Scripture and tradition either explicitly (as the Incarnation) or implicitly (as the Assumption). Moreover, their acceptance by the faithful must be proposed; they may be taught by the Church in a solemn manner, as with definitions of the Immaculate Conception, or in an ordinary way, as with the constant teaching on the malice of taking innocent human life.

Darrel: This is one of your catechism statements, right? I think your CCC stands for Catholic Claims Crutch. You Catholics make your claims relying on the support of your masters of the magisterium to back you up.

Ray: You're back! What's the matter, not enough wind to fly your kite?

Darrel: You two Catholics are producing enough wind for me. Look, the five *solas* were all taken directly from Scripture and are all interconnected, particularly *sola fide* and *sola gratia*. We cannot really understand one without the other; God's grace is the anchor for our faith. As Sonny said before, Catholics have a different understanding than we do of *sola gratia* and *sola fide*.

Catholic sacred tradition was derived from whatever pope or group of bishops wanted to add to Scripture. All I can say is that, if a Christian denomination doesn't accept them, this would certainly represent an essential difference in belief with what reformed Protestants believe.

Daniel: Yes, because Catholics have told us they don't accept all of the five *solas*, that does represent an essential difference between us and them. We've seen why they reject *sola Scriptura*, the Catholic Church needs to make room for itself and its dogma. It wants to establish its own sovereignty, man's sovereignty, particularly in the process of salvation. As Swiss theologian Roger Nicole once opined, fallen man by our nature emphasizes his own sovereignty. That's why man has a natural bias against reformed theology. Pelagius was the first theologian of note to introduce a man-centered theology in the 4th century.

Darrel: Pelagius was Augustine's antagonist because he focused on man's sovereignty over God's, the opposite of what Augustine believed. Pelagianism was declared a heresy by the Catholic Church, but a belief theologians call semi-Pelagianism still survives and raises its ugly, heretical head in many of our denominations, particularly in the Catholic Church as Daniel just said in stating that the Catholic Church theology is man-centered. A man named Jacob Arminius, a 16th century theology professor, followed up on Pelagian theology with a doctrine which was similar to semi-Pelagianism. Arminianism challenging the validity of the Reformed Christian doctrine just as the Catholic Church rejected all of the tenets of that doctrine at the Council of Trent in the Counter-Reformation. Protestants rejected Arminianism at the Synod of Dort.

Sonny: Arminius was not a disciple of Pelagius. He once referred to Pelagianism as "the grand falsehood" and stated that he "must confess that I detest, from my heart, the consequences of that theology."

Darrel: Nonetheless, like Pelagianism and Semi-Pelagianism, Arminianism is a man-centered doctrine, and, based on what we've heard so far from you, in focusing on its all-powerful church, Catholic theology is more centered on man than on God. The irony here is that Augustine's theology was clearly God-centered as we have seen, and it seems the Catholic Church was more influenced by Pelagius than by Augustine in determining the relevance of God's grace in his plan of salvation with their "grace plus works" view. Your church should have made Pelagius the saint instead of Augustine.

Ray: We are not a works-based religion, Darrel. Were you absent when we discussed this before? Our good works don't earn us our salvation; it's more like we have to supplement God's grace in our salvation through performing good works.

Darrel: Supplement, eh? Works are in the mix, even if just a little. Works-based religions imply that God exists for man's convenience rather than man existing for God's glory.

Sonny: I agree with you. As I said before, we believe that all other religions except Christianity emphasize what man can do for himself to be saved. We are on the same page.

Of course, as I've said before, works do figure into the equation. In John 5:29. Jesus calls people to Acome forth, *those who have done good*, to the resurrection of life, and those who have done evil, to the resurrection of condemnation."

John: Yes, this one particular verse does seem to support your position, but, since it contradicts all the other verses in the New Testament that refer to God's grace as the <u>only</u> requirement for salvation, it really can't be saying that good works save because God doesn't say one thing in one verse and contradict Himself in another.

So then, what exactly is Jesus really telling us? R. C. Sproul tells us Christ is merely pointing out those people who are condemned. This is the most probable interpretation of this verse because it's consistent with all the many verses that deny works are important in our salvation. Christ certainly can't be referring to people's faith because that is not a visible characteristic in and of itself. So then, He must be pointing out people's good actions, which are visible. He's reminding us of what He's told us before that He's pleased when we serve Him by exhibiting good works in serving and loving others. He's also indicating that faith is not just another good work. Faith can only be a gift from God.

I think the easiest way to understand what I am saying is to know that *God acts first.* He acts first so that we can be enabled to be justified through our faith. He doesn't need our cooperation or supplementation in saving us. He has already predetermined our reaction to Him. We know this is how it works because we have God's Word on it. The Bible is very clear on how God's grace works and on the significance of our good works in His plan of salvation.

Daniel: There is also the issue of the Catholics believing that faith is the ultimate good work.

John: There's a difference in believing the act of faith is in itself a good work and believing it's evidence of our true belief and the presence of God's grace in our lives. Our faith is the ultimate good work, but it's not our good work, it's God's because He gave us our faith. Christianity is a works-based religion in the sense that our salvation is based on the work of Christ, and man takes no part in it. Do you see the big difference in the role faith plays in the Roman Catholic doctrine and the Protestant doctrine?

Ray: Well, the original Christians certainly understood the importance of the act of faith in their new religion.

Daniel: Sure, under the teachings of the apostles, they correctly understood that God gave them their faith; it was not something they could come up with on their own.

Ray: So you are saying we have no part in our faith? We just have it by the grace of God?

Daniel: Why is that so hard to accept? We've seen how Catholics believe they have to earn God's grace by doing good works, and that's not the way it works according to what the Bible says. Grace means an undeserved favor. We don't deserve it, and we can do nothing to earn it. When Catholics say they believe their good works are part of the process of salvation, they are really saying that God's grace is not sufficient for our salvation.

So then, we can see that *sola gratia* is yet another one of those *solas* you reject, right?

Ray: If you say so.

Darrel: No, Ray, actually it's you guys who say so. You've told us what you think of the five *solas*; your church rejects or compromises the majority of the five *solas* because it needs you to believe in only one: *Sola Catholic Church.*

Let's review what you both have been saying to us all along in these discussions, okay? In telling us good works needs to accompany God's grace, you are saying his grace is insufficient; in believing in purgatory, you're telling us that Christ's sacrifice is insufficient. You're a religion based on the need to overcome God's insufficiencies. I referred to this issue before, but I'll just go ahead and ask the direct question; are you saying that only your church is sufficient for salvation?

Ray: In the functional sense that our Church is Christ, yes, I guess I am saying that.

Darrel: Unbelievable! No wonder a Reformation was necessary. When God saw that your vaunted church had become an institution in asserting its own god-like authority, he worked through Luther, et al, to put an end to this nonsense. There are several other examples in Scripture where God took us all down a peg like he did with the Jews when he supported their enemies in defeating them, and when he dealt with King David and Solomon when they got too big for their britches.

John: As we have seen, Reformed Christians are at odds with Catholicism over the five *solas* and this is primarily due to the fact that Catholic theology is more works-based and man-centered in its focus on the church alone. Sonny has said before that Catholics believe in Christ alone and giving all the glory to God, but their focus on their church as a necessary means of salvation compromises the concept of *solus Christus* and their obvious intent to share in God's glory weakens the concept of *soli Deo Gloria*. Their rejection of each of the five *solas* represents an essential difference between us and them.

Daniel: What do Catholics really think about the efficacy of Christ's atonement, Sonny? Do your really believe it was insufficient for our salvation?

Sonny: The effect of the crucifixion of Jesus Christ was not given to anyone outright but was reserved for His Church so that people must worship God through His Church. The model for this process was illustrated in the Old Testament where God instructed the Israelites on how to worship Him as a precursor to the way He wanted all people to worship Him through the New Covenant. God created the priesthood and prophets in the OT and created priests and discipleships in the NT to channel His grace for salvation.

Darrel: There it comes up again, Sonny. *Yeah*, Christ's death saves those sinners who believe in him, *but* only if they demonstrate their belief through membership in the Catholic Church. The 'Holy Father" wants you all to "Make room for Daddy," right? It seems like a belief in the Catholic Church is as important to our salvation as a belief in Christ as our savior is. This attempt to partner up the Catholic Church with Christ on the cross is as essential a difference between us and them as their works-based plan of salvation.

Bobby: As I recall from our discussion last year with a Muslim, Islam is a works-based religion, right? What else does Islam have in common with Catholicism?

Darrel: Islam borrowed Catholicism's concept of honoring Mary as a special person. Like the Catholics, Muslims call her "Our Lady" and venerate her as a pure and holy saint. I've read the Qur'an and I can tell you that Mary is mentioned more times in their holy book than in ours. Like Catholics, Muslims make it clear that Mary is coming for all her children including them even though they don't accept Christ; they're saved because they've done good. Catholicism and Islam are both anti-Semitic. History records that the Vatican stood by while Hitler almost wiped out the Jewish culture, and the pope issued over 100 anti-Semitic pronouncements and taught that Jews should be cursed because they killed Christ.

Muslims don't know anything about Jesus except to acknowledge he was a person "without error." Catholics claim to know about Christ, but they don't understand his purpose and don't believe they need to be saved by his crucifixion.

John: Yes, Jesus' work on the cross is at the heart of biblical Christianity, for we could not be saved without the atonement. Yet, in one way, Christ's death in itself is insufficient to save us. It's all about His resurrection. Paul tells us in 1 Corinthians 15:17 that if Christ has not been raised, our faith is futile and we are still in our sins. If Jesus had not been resurrected, it would have been an obvious indication that God did not accept His atonement, and we would still be under the Lord's curse. But, He did accept the atonement Christ offered as evidenced by the eyewitness account of the empty tomb and the various appearances Christ made after dying.

Darrel: Good point, John. I was referring though to the Catholic's lack of understanding of the power of God to save us solely through his will, an act of grace. That's the way they see it. All other religions believe God cannot save us without our performance of good works, and while I'm not implying Catholics are like these work-based religions, like Islam, for example, they are certainly in bad company with their grace PLUS works. The implication is that somehow God's grace is insufficient to save us. I have said this before, but it bears repeating, the RCC is all about asserting its sole sufficiency for believers.

Ray: I take offense at your comparison of Catholicism with Islam.

Darrel: We know the objective of Islam is world domination, and the destruction of anyone or any nation that opposes them in attaining this Satanic goal. I've mentioned before that the objective of the Catholic

Church is to rule over its subjects and persecute heretics. That's been their history. It's a natural tendency for fallen man to want to control his life and the lives of others; it relates to the sin of pride.

John: Persecution by the Catholic Church served to strengthen Protestantism, as it often does. The early Christian church grew as it was threatened with extinction. But there was a downside to that growth. As it grew, the visible Christian church become more and more concerned about its growth, and gradually became less focused on the invisible church of Christ which was established by the Holy Spirit after Christ's ascension. Over time, the Christian church became more and more about itself than its purpose. This of course is how Satan, the father of lies, works to destroy the truth of Christianity. Paul saw this happening and addressed several letters to warn the churches he had established of the challenge to remain apostolic and not be tempted by apostasy. Read 2 Corinthians 11:3, for example. When the Roman Emperor Constantine put a halt to further persecution by making Christianity the official religion of the Roman Empire in the fourth century, this seemed like good news for Christianity, but, in its bolstering of the church, the power of the bishop of Rome (the pope) grew to the point that he exercised considerable political clout as well as religious influence. Power corrupts, and to keep and increase their power, the Catholic Church began to make more and more blasphemous claims about its importance requiring followers to submit to the pope in temporal and spiritual matters in order to be saved. This merging of the church and state resulted in a continuing downward spiral of Christian church into apostasy. We've talked about this before. Some historians believe this period of time was the genesis of the Roman Catholic Church.

Daniel: Good point, John. We know this often is what happens when a church makes civil government its business. It not only had a negative impact on the church, but on how others perceived the church. When some people rightfully objected to their church abusing its power, the Catholic Church persecuted them as heretics. The Spanish Inquisition was a dramatic example of this persecution.

After the Council of Trent, at the end of the sixteenth century, under the Counter Reformation, the Catholic Church was organized for an aggressive onslaught on Protestantism; and under the brilliant and brutal leaders of the Jesuits, regained lost territory and crushed the Reformation by all but exterminating the French Huguenots. This action was followed by a century of religious war. According to biblical expert, Henry H. Halley (*Halley's Bible Handbook*), every one of these various wars was started by Roman Catholic Kings, urged on by the Pope of the time and Jesuits for the express purpose of crushing out Protestantism. There was persecution by popes too. In fact, the number of martyrs created under papal persecutions far outnumbered the persecution by Rome of the early Christians. Such persecution is of course, in the spirit of the devil, not in the name of Christ who never, ever advocated that heretics be executed.

John: Yes, the general perception people had of Christianity was negatively impacted as the Catholic Church gained a reputation for dealing very harshly with people they believe to be heretics. The papacy maintained its power through the Inquisitions, a terrible time in the history of Christianity. I also have an ancestor, George Wishart, teacher of John Knox, who was burned at the stake by the pope for heresy so I have a personal issue with how the Catholic Church treated those they considered to be heretics.

Sonny: For centuries before the Reformation, the Catholic Church was persecuted. The world rejected the Church because it claims to be infallible, as Pilate rejected Christ because He called Himself the Truth.

Darrel: As I said before, I personally reject any church that makes the claims your church does. Okay, I still have some more comparisons to make between Islam and Catholicism. Muslims, of course, deny the authority of the Bible. As we have seen in these discussions, so do Catholics, at least insofar as their tradition conflicts with the apostolic teachings presented in the Bible. Did you know that Muslims use prayer beads too? Catholics pray the beads to remit punishment for sin; Muslims use the beads to pray as an act of obedience to escape the punishment imposed on those who do not pray. Like Catholics, Muslims take pilgrimages to obtain favor from God. Catholics take pilgrimages for religious purification and the promise of indulgences. Muslims do it as a religious duty that must be carried out at least once in their lifetime. Both Catholic and Muslim believe in having human mediators; Catholics rely on the priesthood to intercede with God on their behalf. Muslims rely on the intercession of Muhammad on Judgment Day. And, last but not least, the most important belief they share is their salvation is based at least partially on works. Granted Muslims don't believe in God's grace and believe totally in salvation by good works, but Catholics head down that slippery slope when they add works to grace as a requirement to be saved.

Ray: What is your point, Darrel? This information only indicates that Muslims have a hint of truth in their beliefs. We of course preceded them, and they borrowed from us.

Darrel: Sure, but the fact Muhammad used any part of your doctrine to design his own false religion indicates there's something wrong with the Catholic doctrine. If it were true, a false prophet like Muhammad wouldn't want any part of it.

Sonny: Or you could say that Muhammad got some of his false doctrine right. That's the part he stole from us.

Darrel: When any religion deviates from the apostolic teachings, they have it wrong, so we could say you both have it wrong. Neither Islam nor Catholicism has the biblical understanding of God's grace; you don't rely on the Bible as your sole source of knowledge of the truth, but, like the Muslims, have invented all these traditions which serve to supplement Scripture and mislead your followers as they take their eye off of Christ and look at you for their very salvation. Karl Barth once opined that religions can often serve to distract or even disable followers from connecting with Christ. I believe yours does.

Sonny: Why do you keep comparing Catholicism with Islam?

Darrel: I mentioned this comparison between Catholicism and Islam for two reasons: First of all, in stating all these beliefs and traditions Islam has in common with Catholicism, whether Islam borrowed from you over the centuries since its existence or you borrowed some of these false concepts from Islam, you are indeed in bad company. Second of all, this is a list of all those beliefs that are clearly not biblically supported nor are they in the apostolic tradition. These are essential differences between us Protestants and you Catholics, and there are so many of them, it looks like you folks are Christian in name only; but then your church seems to be very adept at attaching itself to such things as the first church claim, the first pope claim, the only church claim, the sole authority claim, the savior claim, and your claim to be the only Christian church when, in fact, you differ so essentially from the biblical Christian doctrine, the teaching of the apostles, this claim and your claim that you are Christian is false.

Bobby: What are some examples of non-essential differences between Protestants and Catholics?

John: As we go further along in these discussions about Catholicism, we may find some example of how we Protestants differ from Catholics in the non-essentials.

Bobby: Okay, but how about non-essential differences in Protestantism?

John: As I said before, all Protestant denominations that follow the Bible-based doctrine of the Reformation (which is summarized in the five *solas*) are unified on the essentials, but we do differ on some non-essentials such as whether Holy Communion represents Christ's actual physical presence or is merely symbolic in nature in representing the spirit; whether adults should be baptized again after their infant baptism; how we should observe the Sabbath; whether a person is a pre-millennialist, an amillennialist, or a postmillennialist; how one interprets some of the nutritional concepts presented in Scripture or whether alcohol is prohibited or some activities like dancing are prohibited or whether certain religious days on some church calendar were to be honored and such issues like that. None of these differences interfere with our union with Christ and so are considered to be, by definition, non-essentials. We shouldn't allow them to divide us.

Daniel: A friend of mine gave me a very large chart produced by The Church of Christ in 1891 which graphically illustrates the history of the Christian Church since its inception after Pentecost. I brought it with me and will lay it out on our table here. As you can see, the chart shows two major splits in the church's history and all of the little branches coming off the main branches created by these two major splits. It also lists reasons why the splits occurred, and we can see the majority of the reasons for these splits do not meet our standard of what is considered to be an essential difference. They are not pertaining to our basic Christian doctrine.

The two major splits in our history, however, did occur over what was considered to be an essential doctrinal difference. The first split occurred in the ninth century when enough people objected to the church in Rome adding man-made tradition to orthodox, biblical doctrine over several centuries to split off and form the Greek Orthodox Church. The remaining church wasn't officially called the Roman Catholic Church though for another 200 years when it was organized with the first actual pope actually being installed.

The second separation, which we call the Reformation, occurred in the sixteenth century. Martin Luther and John Calvin are the names most often associated with the beginning of the Reformation with Luther nailing his 95 Theses on the door of the Castle Church in Wittenberg, Germany; but previous to them, people like John Hus and John Wycliff protested against corruptions such as bribery to attain a church office, and the sale of indulgences, payments to the church to obtain forgiveness of sins. The church branded these men as heretics. These giants of the faith stood up for their belief that the Bible alone is the sole source of knowledge of truth. They all believed the Roman Catholic Church had added man-made traditions which were not biblically based to the orthodox, biblical doctrine of the original Christian church. Luther particularly objected to the tradition of buying indulgences. The papacy denounced Luther to protect its own self-interests, and the resulting split formed the Protestant Church.

Darrel: Such extra-biblical traditions should send up a red flag and, indeed, that's exactly what eventually happened. Both major splits of the church in Rome occurred over opposition to what the Romanists had been doing in adding to God's Word. In the Reformation, the Protestants wanted to split away from a church they believed had gone too far in adding on tradition to the orthodox doctrine of the original church. The papacy had successfully established a power base for its organization and its authority even to the point where it usurped the authority of the Bible itself; this accomplishment served to denigrate the very position of Jesus Christ as the foundation of the church. As we've said before, the Protestants simply wanted the church to turn to its strictly biblical roots and its primary focus on Jesus Christ as the foundation of the church.

Sonny: We acknowledge Jesus Christ as the foundation of the Church; yet, in Ephesians 2:20, the apostles are called the foundation of the Church. Similarly, in 1 Peter 2:25, Jesus is called the Shepherd of the flock, but in Acts 20:28, the apostles are called the shepherds of the flock. I think these verses demonstrate the Bible uses multiple metaphors for the Church, and that words used by the inspired writers of Scripture can have various meanings. Catholics agree that God is the rock of the Church, but this does not mean He cannot confer this distinction upon Peter as well in order to facilitate His desires for the Church.

Darrel: Of course, as was said before, various metaphors are used in Scripture, but in these verses you mention, it's obvious that Christ is THE Shepherd (with a capital "S") and the apostles are his appointed shepherds (with a small "s"). I think the best way to understand this relationship Christ has with his church is to view him as the cornerstone and the apostles as those building a foundation on that cornerstone. The Bible never refers to the apostles as the cornerstone of the church.

John: In keeping with my intention of responding to any Catholic whenever they make the claim that the Catholic Church is the only authority that God intended to represent the teachings of the apostles here on earth, I would like to dispute that claim and use the verse Sonny used, Ephesians 2:20, to do it.

In this passage Paul is talking about the church as being built on the foundation of apostolic teaching with Christ as the cornerstone, but he goes on to describe the church as becoming this whole building which is to become the temple of the Lord, a dwelling place of God in the Spirit. He's talking about the church being very closely connected to the Holy Spirit and indeed that is what Jesus told the apostles when He said He would leave them with a "helper," which of course was the Holy Spirit. The Spirit alone is to guide us in remaining true to the apostolic teachings. It seems to me that the Catholic Church's objective is to either downplay the role of the Holy Spirit or actually substitute for the Holy Spirit in establishing itself as the sole authority of apostolic teaching.

Darrel: Catholicism is all about substituting a church for God, but they dispute that reality, of course, but we should know that it's not any visible church organization that is supposed to be the authority on the teachings of the apostles, it's the Holy Spirit working through the church who is God's authority on earth. The church's purpose is to function as the dwelling place of God, not become an entity unto itself as the Catholic Church has become over the centuries.

Ray: Yes, we are the dwelling place of the Holy Spirit.

Darrel: Every Bible-believing Christian church is the dwelling place of the Holy Spirit.

Ray: There's only one Christian church, Darrel, and it is the Catholic Church. You people have consistently implied that the Catholic Church exists only for itself, to be a glutton for wealth and power. That is the ideology of dictators and tyrants. The Catholic Church is the most charitable organization on earth and has been for many centuries in our history. We exist only to serve the Body of Believers.

Bobby: But didn't Sonny refer to politics and power as a reason for the splitting of the church into the Roman Catholic Church and the Greek Orthodox Church? Didn't that indicate a self-serving interest?

Darrel: Good point, Bobby. This has been my point all along. In Catholicism, it's always been about the power of the church as an institution.

Sonny: The church is a man-made institution, and that's a good thing. Sure, it has its faults; we are constantly under Satan's attack and tempted by the world and heretics who would bring us down, but the Catholic Church still stands, as strong as ever.

Darrel: You mean as wealthy and powerful as ever, don't you, Sonny.

Sonny: The Bible does not deny God's church the acquisition of power and influence.

Darrel: John has already quoted Scripture, actually referring to the same verse you used, Sonny, to define exactly what the Bible has to say about the purpose of the church, to house the Holy Spirit, and not to create a church organization to accumulate wealth and acquire more power and influence. That's what the world values, and Christians know we are to remain apart from the world.

Ray: And you heretics, you're supposed to be the church that houses the Spirit?

Darrel: If you hadn't been so blinded with your indoctrination, Ray, you would have at least considered how far your church has strayed from its purpose.

John: Regardless of how we differ from our brothers and sisters in Christ or who split from whom, we know that Satan works by dividing and conquering. I'm no expert in church history, but, with the exception of the two major splits, as we see from the chart, the majority of these other splits occurred over non-essential differences. As the saying goes, "the devil's in the details." Ignoring these little non-essentials and maintaining unity is still a major challenge for the Christian church today. The visible church is divided, yet, invisibly, we're already one. We should be aware of that reality. But the presence of sin and error keeps us from realizing our invisible unity in Christ. We are challenged to remind ourselves of that invisible unity as we patiently wait for God to finally consummate His objective of establishing a new world of believers in Christ. We should remember we're all brought to eternal life in this same way. In fact, you could say our Christian unity is a consequence of our salvation. As in the Trinity, there is diversity, but there should be no divisions among true Christians. God's Word tells us we're being drawn more and more together as one people until that time when we will be one in belief, one in worship and one in love for our Creator.

Bobby: Yes, as go along here with our discussion, I'd like to ask you all to try and focus on what your respective Protestant denominations have in common with Catholicism rather than on how much they differ. Look at the glass as being half full, okay? The claim game that these guys have exhibited in these discussions bothers me, and I know that every denomination is tempted to claim that their church has it right, and the rest of the denominations don't, but I would hope you each keep in mind our discussion about what constitutes essential and non-essential differences. This focus should be considered one of our special rules of engagement for this intramural discussion.

Daniel: Good point. I also need to reiterate that just because there are many different Protestant denominations, this doesn't mean the Protestant church is divided into different ideologies, different versions of the truth. There is only one truth and, as John said before, that truth is expressed in the tenets of the invisible church as expressed solely through the apostles. To the extent Catholicism shares this reality with us, we are united with them. Unfortunately in their denial of the existence of an invisible church in their objective to emphasize their visible church over all, we differ. Their focus on their church in lieu of the invisible church ideology is what the reformers opposed. Even though this chart isn't presented this way, it is the Roman Catholic Church which has actually split off from the main line of the original church, corrupting the gospel with its man-made, unbiblical tradition. All of the various Protestant denominations that were formed soon after the Reformation in the early part of the sixteenth century, with the exception of the Anabaptists, were all unified under the doctrine of the reformers and understood themselves as a continuing branch of the *catholic church* with a small Ac".

Darrel: Spot on, Dan, the man! The reason there are more Protestant denominations than the Catholic Church is divided into is that, with us, it isn't about the establishment of a church organization; it is about focusing on the invisible church and how best we can connect with its precepts. There are naturally going to be more views on how that purpose is accomplished than in mandating there be just one church, whether it's connected to the invisible church or not.

Ray: There is only one church and it is visible. Our leader is the pope and he is visible.

Darrel: Enough with the canned comment, Ray. You really need to stop saying that! Please. You're beginning to bore me, and I get even more aggressive when I'm bored.

Sonny: What would it take to convince you people that our church is the original apostolic church?

Peter: Why is that important for you to do this, Sonny? Who cares which church is affiliated with these apostles? Why not just focus on unity. After all, you now have a pope who stresses unity to the extent where he's coddling up to Muslims and even atheists.

Sonny: There's nothing quite like the original to establish credibility; and that's us.

John: I like Sonny's method of using rhetorical questions to elicit responses. Socrates used this method, and, in my communication with Dr. Kreeft about my books, he recommended I use this approach in writing my books because he used it effectively in his book *Between Heaven and Hell.* He likes the dialogue format of course and advised me to use the Socratic method more in the dialogue in my books. He said that there should be more leading questions asked which were designed to make a point, but I told him that many intelligent, intuitive folks are on to this method and are insulted by someone who seemed to be talking down to them by asking obviously leading questions to elicit responses they intend to rebut.

Darrel: Yes, the Socratic Method is condescending. People like us veteran discussion participants in this group surely don't need to be led into some thought you want to present; just say what you want to state and trust we'll pick it up, okay?

Sonny: I'm familiar with Dr. Kreeft. I'm somewhat impressed you know him personally, John. I've read several of his books. You know of course that he converted from Presbyterianism to Catholicism forty years ago and has never looked back, right?

John: Yes, I do. I am particularly interested in why such an educated Protestant would decide to become a Catholic. I say this because the majority of Catholics are Catholic because they were raised as Catholics. It's that way with all religions. Most people are followers, tradition is their main source of knowledge, and most people do not lead an examined life so they just connect with the religion of their forefathers and call it good for the rest of their lives. I'm not singling out just Catholics; many Lutherans, for instance, are Lutherans because they were raised by Lutherans, attended Lutheran schools and have never been to any other church but a Lutheran church. In my opinion, this is not a good thing because it suggests that the person believes simply out of habit without thought, and, as a Calvinist, I believe we should know what we believe and be able to defend it. We need to think about why we believe what we believe. To that end, I've always been curious about the specific reasons a person like Peter Kreeft would convert to Catholicism. He wrote a book listing 40 reasons for his conversion. We can discuss that later, if you like.

Darrel: Like every religion or denomination, the Catholic Church needs to establish and maintain its credibility. The irony is that in making this assertion that you are the one, true church, etc. is that you run somewhat of a risk in possibly motivating non-members, who may not know much about what they believe or the church's history, to really take a good look at what the original apostolic church stands for and compare its tenets to what the Roman Catholic Church represents today. When we finish accomplishing this task in these discussions, we will see how false this forced identification with the original church really is. My only hope is that you and every Catholic with the ability to lead an examined life would take a good, objective look at how his church today differs in the essentials with what the original apostolic church stood for.

Sonny: I have done that, Darrel. As I told you before, although I was raised in a Catholic home and attended Catholic schools, I left the church for a time and then came back.

John: We want to know your reason for doing this, Sonny.

Sonny: My main reason for coming back to the Church is my recognition that it is the only true Christian Church.

John: Yes, that was a reason Kreeft listed too. It seem that this false assertion has been an effective tool in recruiting new members. I recall asking a Winter Texan in the county park here on the Island why he joined the Roman Catholic Church at the ripe old age of 70, and he told me it was because it was the oldest Christian church. I told him that this was a false assumption, and went into the same explanation we've been discussing in these sessions to prove my point. I concluded by asking him to demand evidence of the Catholic Church claim. The burden of proof is on each of us to clearly demonstrate we teach what the apostles taught and nothing more.

Ray: And your proof of course is the Bible. Even if you can prove to me that the Bible doesn't support one of our sacred traditions, I say that, if the Church teaches something and the Bible is silent or ambiguous, that does not mean the teaching is any less truly a part of the original deposit of faith given to the apostles. We need to stop thinking of what is just biblical and think about what is true. The first is always contained in the second, but all of the second is not necessarily contained in the first.

Darrel: Let me see if I understand what you just said. Both you Catholics keep saying that the Bible is an authority, but so is your sacred tradition; that means if we object to some tradition of yours, like purgatory, for example, because it's clearly not supported in the Bible, then you point to 2 Maccabees, and when we successfully question the credibility of these books in the Apocrypha, you finally end up referring to your sacred tradition and rest on that as some kind of evidence. The problem there, of course, is that this isn't acceptable evidence to anyone but a Catholic.

Ray: As Sonny said before, we consider our sacred tradition to be equal to, or greater than, the authority to the Bible.

Darrel: As I have said before, the Catholic Church split itself off from the teachings of the apostles which were only recorded in the Bible. Any other claim about what your church thinks they said orally or was left out of Scripture cannot be supported.

Ray: I believe the Church is the super-system; the Bible is our brainchild and therefore considered to be a sub-system. It is the Protestants who have divorced what God has joined together; the Church and the Bible.

Darrel: God joined his elect, his invisible church to his Word; every visible Christian church should join to the invisible church and that means we're joined to the Bible and only the Bible, not some church organization.

Ray: We need the organization an institution provides. Christians need an authority to interpret the Bible. Would God create an infallible book in the year 397 through an all Catholic authority, and not create an infallible authority to interpret its meaning? Makes no sense.

Darrel: God did leave us with an infallible authority, himself in the person of the Holy Spirit. As I said before, it makes more sense for the author of a book to be its best source of knowledge in explaining what he wrote; and I can assure you God's up to that task.

The Catholic Church isn't content to be the sole authority in explaining the meaning of the Bible; it also claims authority in adding to God's Word with its traditions as though God had left something out of his Word he meant to say or said but it wasn't recorded. Such arrogance! The Christian church is under attack from the left and Catholicism emboldens their cause to discredit Scripture when it claims the Bible isn't the only source of knowledge in Christianity. These liberal folks who want to design their own version of Christianity to reflect more of God's love or whatever, are encouraged to do so by the example set by the Catholic Church.

Sonny: People have been interpreting, changing, reassessing and remaking the Christian church since it began. Isn't that what Daniel said before. The Church exists to strengthen and maintain the biblical Christian doctrine and focus on obedience to God's moral law and on Christ's love for us all. We know we must strongly resist those who would deconstruct our religion.

Bobby: It's time to adjourn. See y'all next week.

Week Seven

Bobby: We'll begin today's session with a question for Sonny. Why do Catholics believe their tradition is to be considered the Word of God?

Sonny: Can't you see that our sacred tradition is indeed Christian doctrine? Don't forget what I said before about some of these traditions being been passed on orally from the apostles and other godly men to follow, and that's why they don't appear in the Bible.

Darrel: Man, you guys have an answer for everything. Most indoctrinated people think they do. First you say that these traditions are biblically supported; but then you say, if we somehow disprove that, they are sacred anyway and equal in authority to what's in the Bible because your church, which is the ultimate authority, has declared they are. And then, if we still don't buy into this weak explanation, you say that many of these traditions don't appear in the Bible because they are oral traditions. It's as though Paul left something he wanted to say out of his letters to the churches he planted. Nonsense.

You seem to have all the bases covered except one: What if we find clear biblical support which contradicts one of your traditions? As you know, our premise is that God isn't a God of confusion or contradiction, so then we have a choice to make: Is the Bible the truth or is the sacred tradition the truth?

Sonny: I would just say the sacred tradition is more accurate. I said before that we have to stop thinking about what is just biblical and think about what is true.

Darrel: For us, the Bible and the truth are one and the same. I want to reiterate the importance of using the Bible, and only the Bible as our source of knowledge in these discussions. No one but Catholics accepts what their church says is true unless it is biblically supported. This is particularly the case when whatever they're proclaiming contradicts

Scripture. For us, it really doesn't matter if church traditions are passed on orally or through some mandate of one of their popes or in some other way their church comes up with, my point is that we will only consider biblical support for purposes of these discussions. That's our premise and it's one every Christian in this group must accept or we won't be able to get anything out of these discussions.

Bobby: What about that, Catholics? Are you each able to use just the Bible to support what you say your church believes?

Sonny: I told you before, the Bible doesn't contain all the truth; the sacred oral tradition is equal in authority to Scripture. It is Scripture.

Darrel: Yes, you need to defend those traditions that are not in the Bible. So you have to focus on denigrating the importance of the written word, the "book," as Ray has referred to it. You use biblical buckshot to try and support these traditions of yours, and when that fails, you have no other alternative but to diminish the Bible's authority. Unbelievers try to do that.

I think we're done here. It's such a nice day, we ought to be doing something besides sitting around this table talking to each other. Why don't you Catholics just throw in the towel and join up with us, and we can all call it a day and go get our fishing poles?

Ray: I'm a fisher of men.

Darrel: Yeah, your church has hooked a lot of people who potentially could be taught the truth, but the hook's in too deep for most of them to spit it out and swim in deeper waters.

Look, man, based on our discussions up to this point, it's become obvious that the majority of what both of you opine is based on what your church has told you to say. I want to hear your own, independent opinion. As I said before, I would rather hear from the consumer, like you Catholics, than from a salesman for the product. That said though

I've yet to meet a Catholic who has a mind of his or her own. That's the resultant tragedy of indoctrination.

I'm not suggesting you people just categorically discard your Catholic beliefs without considering the evidence we have been presenting and will present in the sessions to come. You should though try to keep an open mind. The sign of a true Christian is his or her humility and willingness to learn from others. We've talked about that before.

Ray: Why would I consider joining a Protestant church? Christ established the Catholic Church as His Church. As you said before when you quoted John 16:13 where the apostle refers to Jesus saying that "when the Spirit of truth has come, He will guide you into all truth; for He will not speak on His own authority, but whatever He hears He will speak; and He will tell you things to come." Christ is referring to the Bible which His Church produced.

Darrel: Am I missing something here, man? I don't understand how this verse established the Catholic Church. It seems as though whenever the N.T. refers to the Christian church, you want everyone to believe that's your Roman Catholic Church. Nonsense!

Bobby: It's obvious that throughout these discussions Catholics would like us all to accept their church as THE Christian Church, the only Christian church. So, let's discuss more about how they believe they can support that claim. Let's get back to the claim that Peter was the first pope in a succession of popes to follow. We of course have our rules of verification so then, Sonny and Ray, have you been able to come up with any verses that support your church's assertion that Peter was your first pope?

Ray: We refer to the one verse, Matthew 16:18; it clearly states that Christ gave the keys to Peter, period, end of discussion. It is obvious in the gospel accounts that Peter was the leader of the disciples. We can reference a number of pronouncements of our Magisterium to support our belief.

Darrel: I remind you Ray that, in our discussions, we express our opinion on what we think the Bible is saying, not on what some church thinks it's saying. Since we are all Christians and believe the Bible is the Word of God, we should be able to use the Bible as our source of knowledge to support what we believe; and that is what we must do.

So then, with that in mind, let's take a look at Matthew 16:18, the one, standard verse you always refer to, and see what it really means, okay?

When we look at it in its context, we see that the text cannot bear the weight that Rome has placed on it. When we look at the context of the passage, we see that the "rock" Jesus is referring to must be Peter's confession; that's the context of Matthew 16 beginning at verse 13. This means that the church is built on Peter's confession of Jesus as the Messiah and Son of God. We know that the reference is not to apply to just Peter. After all Christ referred to the "keys," not "key" to the Kingdom. We believe that the "rock" that Jesus refers the church being built on Peter's confession of Jesus as the Messiah and Son of God. Of course we know that Christ did have a special relationship with Peter, and Peter did play a key role in the church as a representative of all the disciples on a number of occasions in the gospel accounts. Peter was the first apostle to confess the faith and the first apostle to preach the gospel to the gentiles; he also of course wrote two letters that became part of the canon and his teaching was the basis for Mark's gospel, but it's a stretch to assume that this give us evidence that Jesus singled just Peter out to be THE leader. The commission was not limited to Peter but extended to all the apostles.

You Catholics may not be able to come up with any more verses to explain your position, but I can come up with verses that support mine. In 1 Peter 5:1-4; Peter explains that the commission was given to all the elders throughout the church age. Author Michael Grant explains that Peter "did not lead the Roman church at all, but only went to Rome as a missionary and was, as he implies in his first epistle, one elder among others." So then, the only conclusion we can objectively draw from these biblical passages is that Peter was acting as representative for all the disciples, all of whom were called to promote the church.

Ray: I don't agree with you. It's obvious Christ is addressing just Peter.

Darrel: This is a tradition you want to believe is true, Ray, and, as I said before, it's ironic that the man you Catholics want us to believe was the first pope is the very same apostle who warned us against adding all these invented traditions of men to the Word. We also know that Peter didn't want to be the leader anyway because that's what he's telling us in 1 Peter 5:1-4. And I might add that Paul was also considered to be a leader in the church because it was he who took the gospel to the gentiles and founded so many churches throughout the area. These two men are the solid rock Christ built his church on. Both men were responsible for initiating the transformation of the pagan Roman Empire into the Christian church with the mission to spread the good news of the gospel throughout the known world. Both were martyred, and both should be considered as patron saints of Rome; they do share a feast day which goes back to the early centuries of the church.

Man, I have to say that of all the heretical traditions your church has added to the doctrine of Christianity in its endeavor to appoint itself sole authority of the Christian religion, this blatant assertion that the Roman Catholic Church is in fact the original Christian church with Peter assigned the title of its first pope to legitimize the papacy is the most offensive to me. Do you really seriously believe that when Jesus indicates that he is the church's one foundation, he wants us to believe that he means for Peter to now be that foundation and all the church leaders you've designated to be popes to follow his lead? How arrogant that must sound even to you people.

Ray: The truth can sometimes be offensive and sound arrogant, Darrel.

Darrel: The truth isn't what you or your church wants it to be; it's what really is, by definition. There can only be one truth and it isn't what your church preaches and teaches. God tells us his truth in his own Word, the Holy Bible; your traditions are not biblically supported and are not to be considered true. The tragedy of the Catholic Church is that, in its earliest beginnings, it recognized the Bible, and only the Bible, as God's true Word. Irenaeus stated in 180 AD called the Bible "the ground and pillar of our faith."

Ray: What would you say if I quoted verses from Scripture to support each and every assertion we make and every tradition you say we have established and see whether they are biblically supported?

Darrel: I would say you couldn't do it, but it would be nice if you could. So, give us the verses for support, and we'll discuss them and examine them objectively. Regarding Scriptural interpretation, by way of review, there are several basic rules to keep in mind: **1.** We must be careful that we do not choose verses out of their context in order to make them conform to a conclusion we have already drawn. The support verse must be consistent with all other verses in the Bible that refer to the same issue being presented in the Word. The theologian, J. Gresham Machen, once said Apicking and choosing which parts of scripture to believe is the first step toward a wholesale rejection of orthodoxy." **2.** A general rule in interpreting Scripture is to only use the Bible to interpret itself. Whenever any ambiguity occurs in Scripture, the more easily understood verses are utilized to explain the meaning of the less understood verses. Only in following these rules can we correctly arrive at what the Bible is telling us. We need to use our heads, cast off the presuppositions, and try to look at everything objectively. We aren't here to preserve our own bias; we are here to pursue what's true. And, as I mentioned before, we won't accept as evidence any statement by one of your church hierarchy about what they've told you to think about the meaning of Scripture. We don't consider your bishops, popes and priests to be authorities. You'll have to rely on your own resources and your own ability to think as an individual instead of relying on the thought control your church requires of you. To that end, I personally can tell you that, while I accept different interpretations of the same biblical verse, I do not accept what you say when you try and tell me the Bible is saying something it clearly is NOT saying.

Ray: But, in the end, it all comes down to just your opinion, right? Look, we can only know what the Bible tells us if it is based on the authority of the Church's interpretation.

Darrel: Your church's interpretation is a just another opinion, can't you see that? It's a collective opinion, but it's still an opinion.

Peter: Why does the Catholic Church insist that Peter is their first pope anyway? Let me guess. Would it be because the Catholic Church wants to support its objective of establishing a hierarchy for its religious organization?

Darrel: You got it, Pete! When we look at this passage again, we will see that Jesus is addressing all of his disciples. That's what verse 16:13 tells us. Remember also that Christ reprimanded his disciples when they speculated on who was the greatest in Luke 9:46.

John: Matthew 16:18 is obviously an important verse for Catholics in support of their claim so let's take a good look at it to see if we can understand what Jesus is really saying to us.

The New Testament was originally written in Greek and so it's sometimes helpful to look at what the Greek translation is to help us understand what a particular verse is saying to us. The Greek word *petra* is used when Christ addresses Peter by name in this verse. This word means Astone" or Asmall rock" in Greek, and it was of course Christ's name for this disciple. Jesus then used the word *petrus* for the rock He would build his church on. *Petrus* is the plural of *petra* and means a bunch of rocks or a foundation. So, Christ is telling Peter He will build His church on a foundation of His disciples, only one of which is Peter.

Darrel: And it's imperative we consider the biblical context of a verse we are trying to interpret. As I said before, several verses preceding this verse present Peter's confession that Jesus is the Christ in 16:16, and this statement indicates Christ is the real rock upon which the church will be built. The confession establishes who Jesus is, and the purpose of his appearance on earth. By this confession, Peter merely is acting as the representative apostle for the formation of the new church which has been established with Christ as its cornerstone.

John: Good point, Darrel. And we also need to take a look at verse 23 where Christ actually refers to Peter as Satan. Is this any way to speak to a man He wanted to appoint the first pope of His church? Of course not! But, when He went on to say that Peter did not have in mind the things of God, but the things of men," that does sound like what happened within the Catholic Church over the centuries through the influence of Rome as it became more and more centered on itself, on man. I will say that, in that regard, Peter seemed to fit the job description of the first pope.

Bobby: Some of the popes I've read about in history were pretty satanic, right?

John: All the more reason to believe Christ did not set up a church hierarchy with a succession of popes beginning with Peter.

Daniel: In its blatant attempt to rewrite history and subvert Christianity, the Roman Catholic Church published a book of biographies of the popes beginning with Peter to the mid-fifteenth century. They called the book the *Liber Pontificalis.* This book is an important historical source, but its naming of Peter as the first pope is assigning a title that is not fact. There was no papacy in the first century.

Bobby: In my Catechism class, I was taught that by virtue of its divinely-appointed authority from Christ by him giving Peter the keys to his kingdom, the Catholic Church determined the canon of Scripture at the end of the 4th century. As Catholics, we were therefore to believe in the Scriptures on the authority of the Catholic Church. We were taught that the Church is the ultimate interpreter of Scripture. The Bible and Church Tradition that makes up part of the Catholic doctrine were equally and independently authoritative.

Sonny: Correct. There is nothing in Scripture that tells us what Scriptures are inspired, what books belong in the Bible, or that Scripture is the final authority on questions concerning the Christian faith. Instead, the Bible says that the Church, not the Scriptures, is the pinnacle and foundation of the truth. Our Church cites 1 Timothy 3:15 for support. The Church also cites Matthew 18:17 to support that it is the final arbiter on questions of the Christian faith. It is through the teaching authority and Apostolic Tradition (2 Thessalonians 2:15, 3:6, 1 Cor. 11:2) of this Church, who is guided by the Holy Spirit (John 14:16, 26, 16:13, that we know of the divine inspiration of the Scriptures, and the manifold wisdom of God.

Daniel: One of your church fathers, Irenaeus, advised your people to "revert to the scriptural proof furnished by those apostles who did also write the gospels." This sounds like he's supporting *sola Scritpura.*

I also have a question about what you said about the Catholic Church being guided by the Holy Spirit. The Holy Spirit also guided the church in what books were to be included in the canon of the Bible, right? Give the credit where credit is due.

Darrel: I'm sure if we looked at every single one of these verses Sonny listed here, we would agree with him when he concludes that Christ's church on earth is supposed to represent God's truth, the invisible church of Christ; we just don't accept your church's assertion that it is that one church.

John: Let's take a look at a couple of these verses right now. The verse in 1 Timothy does say that the truth of the gospel is found in and sustained by God's church. As I said before, the purpose of the visible church is to sustain the solid foundation of God, the invisible church of God's elect. See 2 Timothy2:19. And, by the way, since the Christian church was not established until after Christ's death, it's obvious that in

Matthew 18:17, Jesus is referring to Israel when he speaks of referring to the "church." This is a good example of how Catholicism incorrectly utilizes Scripture to support its position. The other verses mentioned do support the teaching authority of the church, guided by the Holy Spirit, but it is only the Catholics who want to believe that church is actually the Catholic Church.

Ray: Our church is the original Church because Peter, our first pope, was given the keys to the Kingdom. Jesus said "And I will give you (Peter) the keys of the kingdom of heaven; and whatever you bind on earth will be bound in heaven, and whatever you loose on earth will be loosed in heaven."

Darrel: There you go again with that mechanical, default response, Ray; that style of yours just doesn't cut it in discussions like this, my friend. We're supposed to be aiming higher than that as we delve into what each of us really believes about Jesus Christ. Your "biblical buckshot" and these mechanical, repetitive responses serve absolutely no purpose but to reinforce my belief that Catholics I've spoken with just don't seem to be the sharpest tacks in the box.

Sonny: And there you go again with your personal insults, Darrel.

Darrel: Sorry about that. There are just times in our discussion with you guys when I get frustrated about your general dogmatic attitude. I just don't get the impression you want to indulge us in our objective to pursue the truth with an open mind. You have never indicated you have even attempted to see your theology except through your own narrow field of vision; you have maintained an indoctrinated mindset from the very beginning of our discussion sessions. Catholic theology is all you know or all you want to know.

Sonny: Why should we study heretical theology, Darrel? I am a member of the Christian Church, which has the keys of the kingdom of heaven; and when Christ told Peter that whatever he would bind on earth will be bound in heaven, and whatever you loose on earth will be loosed in heaven," He laid the foundation of the Catholic Church, my Church, not yours.

John: Actually, at the risk of repeating myself, Christ is referring to the church He founded on the apostolic teachings which were to be recorded in the Bible. The apostolic foundation of the church is laid in the written Word of God; the Scriptures, not your extra-biblical traditions, are now the keys of Christ's authority in the church (Ephesians 2:20, 3:5) through the power of the Spirit (18:18).

Darrel: Sonny, it's sad and ironic that this Catholic Church of yours doesn't do what Christ willed for his church to do with those keys of the kingdom. The apostolic foundation of the church is indeed laid in God's written Word, the Bible, not in any of those man-made extra-biblical traditions your church added to the Christian doctrine as it assumed Christ's authority.

Ray: That's your opinion, Darrel. You reveal your obvious bias against the Church.

Darrel: It's not a bias, Ray, it's a natural reaction to a false doctrine. In case you hadn't noticed, you're speaking with Christians who are very well educated in the doctrine of Christianity and well versed in the history of the Christian church. We'd like to discuss Christian theology and Christology with you guys, but, because we Protestants aren't even recognized as being Christians, you two will have none of it. Sure, we're coming from a different point of view and have a different opinion of the Christian church's role in our lives, but that doesn't mean we can't discuss Christianity with each other. It's extremely difficult though to talk to people who consider their Christian denomination to be the only Christian church by virtue of its assumption of that role as it rolled forward through history, establishing itself as a damn institution. When we naturally question that this is not what any one Christian denomination is supposed to assume, we are treated as heretics. You guys certainly could polish up on your evangelistic technique.

Ray: We tell it like it is, Darrel. Peter was given the keys, period, end of discussion!

Darrel: Okay, let's look at this claim of yours from another angle. We've talked about how you Catholics believe your church began in Rome, right?

Ray: Yes; as Sonny has said before, the history of the Catholic Church begins with Jesus Christ and His teachings, and our Church is the continuation of the early Christian community established by Jesus. The Church considers its bishops to be the successors to Jesus'apostles and considers the Church's leader, the Bishop of Rome (aka the Pope) to be the sole successor to Saint Peter, who ministered in Rome in the first century AD, after his appointment by Jesus as head of the Church.

Darrel: Although Peter was the first apostle to preach to the gentiles, his ministry was to the Jews; and, as we've said before, the Bible doesn't provide us with any proof Peter was ever in Rome; However, author Michael Grant does state that while "very little is known about this phase" of Peter's life, the general consensus among church historians is that he did go to Rome; historians just can't be certain of the dates and neither can your church be certain. I should also mention that the times you people were told Peter was in Rome, the Bible clearly shows he wasn't.

You just said that Peter ministered in Rome in the first century, right? In fact, you should know that Catholics actually claim that Peter was Bishop of Rome from 43 AD until he was martyred in 68 AD. Well, in 45 AD, we find Peter being cast into prison at Jerusalem (Acts 12:3-4). In 51 AD, on Paul's first visit to Jerusalem, he found Peter there, not in Rome where Catholics say he should have been. That same year Peter was chastised by Paul in Antioch for refusing to sit or eat with the Gentiles. Isn't that strange that your first "Pope" was not at the head of his church in Rome, and that he would actually not want to have anything to do with the people he's supposed to lead? Peter stayed on in Antioch until about 56 AD, but, as Grant stated, "the tradition of the Fathers that he became the first bishop of Antioch is anachronistic." In other words, it has no basis in history. In 66 AD, we find Peter in Babylon, not in Rome.

Sonny: Come on, Darrel, you must know that Peter didn't have to live in Rome to be pope.

Darrel: Why not? Didn't we discuss before how the first Christian church was established in Rome? Doesn't it make sense that we should expect the leader of the first church to have actually resided in Rome?

Even if Peter was in Rome, there is absolutely no evidence that he actually served the Church of Rome as its first bishop or pope. Although Grant did state he didn't want to get into this controversy, he did say that "Peter was not the founder of the Roman church, since otherwise Paul would have mentioned his name when he wrote of that foundation."

Sonny: Our Church has no human founder, and what we believe is based on what we received from those who were before us and the duty of those who are alive is to pass on the same to the future generations, and this leaves no room for anyone to invent new things on the spot which means what was believed 2,000 years ago is true today.

Darrel: Sure, we both agree Christ actually founded his church; but that fact is compromised by your belief that Peter was the first of many popes who possessed infallibility like Christ. Do you really believe your human leaders are on an equal level with our founder? And it just goes on and on. The list of popes who you say succeeded Peter is presented in Richard P. McBrien's book, *Lives of the Popes, The Pontiffs from St. Peter to Benedict XVI*. But the *Catholic Encyclopedia* admits that Catholicism "possesses no precise information regarding the details of Peter's Roman sojourn." In other words, we can't be sure Peter ever assumed the duties and responsibilities of the office he had been allegedly appointed to hold.

Ray: What about the *Donation of Constantine*? This was Emperor Constantine's grant to Pope Sylvester I (who served from 314 to 335) and to all the popes to follow him of spiritual supremacy over the other major patriarchates and temporal dominion over the entire western world. That's history.

Darrel: This so-called *Donation of Constantine* was fake history, Ray. Grant said that "the Donation was a forgery, composed either at Rome or, more probably, in the Frankish empire during the second half of the eighth century. It was based on the conviction that Sylvester I, and all subsequent popes, were direct successors of Peter as bishops of Rome. Indeed, its contents included a fictitious account of Constantine placing the document upon the body of Peter himself, as a gift to him."

Ray: You sure seem to think a lot of this Michael Grant fellow, Darrel. What makes some secular guy the expert on one of our apostles?

Darrel: First of all, the mere fact he is secular gives him objectivity in the sense he isn't Catholic or Protestant so he has no hidden agenda. Second of all, he has good credentials to write about this subject. Michael Grant was a Fellow of Trinity College, Cambridge, and Professor of Humanity at Edinburgh University. He is acknowledged to be one of our great chroniclers of ancient culture.

Bobby: I'm curious, Darrel, if Grant doesn't conclude who was the first leader of the Christian church wasn't Peter, who did he think was?

Darrel: Grant states that if there was anyone who could be thought of as the first leader of the church, it would be James, "the man who will henceforth take the lead among the Jewish Christians of Jerusalem."

Look, man, the bottom line here is that there isn't any proof from a credible source like the Bible that there even was a Catholic Church in 100 AD. From church history, we know there were many of your bishops, but no organized religion with some pope at the head of it. It seems that it's only important to Catholics whether there was an original leader and then a succession of leaders over the church or not because they want to point to a foundation for the establishment of their papacy. This is precisely why Catholics make more of this than there is in insisting Peter was the first leader of the church. The point is that the

Bible does not designate a leader of the first Christian church; it does support the fact that Christ established his church in the tradition and teachings of the apostles, and every church that supports these teachings and traditions is Christ's church.

Sonny: Okay, so whether you disagree with me on the identity of the first pope or not, historians identify Saint Ignatius, along with his friend Polycarp, to be disciples of John the Apostle, and we know that later in his life, Ignatius was chosen to serve as the third Bishop of Antioch.

Darrel: So we jump from the alleged first pope to the alleged third pope, eh? Regardless, it's a moot point, man, no papacy or succession of popes was ever mentioned in Scripture.

Sonny: Jesus Christ taught divinely revealed truth to the Apostle John who handed it on to Saint Ignatius, so there's your connection to Christ. Ignatius said this in 107 AD: "See that ye all follow the bishop, even as Christ Jesus does the Father, and the presbytery as ye would the apostles. Do ye also reverence the deacons, as those that carry out the appointment of God? Let no man do anything connected with the Church without the bishop. Let that be deemed a proper Eucharist, which is administered either by the bishop, or by one to whom he has entrusted it. Wherever the bishop shall appear, there let the multitude also be; by the bishop, or by one to whom he has entrusted it. Wherever the bishop shall appear, there let the multitude also be; even as wherever Jesus Christ is, there is the Catholic Church."

Darrel: But, you see, none of these early church leaders like Ignatius were addressing what you believe is <u>your</u> Catholic Church.

Sonny: They were all Catholics, Darrel! Ignatius referred to bishops, priests, deacons, and used the term "Eucharist" and the formal name of the church. It's obvious he's talking about the Catholic Church, right?

Darrel: Yes, he's addressing the Christian church which was called the Catholic Church, but my point is that the original church organization isn't the same as it is today. Over the many centuries since Ignatius wrote this, many changes have taken place in your church beliefs and tradition, and it is the heretical nature of these changes that reached such a level of intolerance, the first split created the Orthodox Church and the Reformation created the Protestant church.

Sonny: It is you Protestants who left the Church to form your heretical versions of the original church. You heretics had no keys to the kingdom, no connection to Christ.

John: The splits, as we've been saying, were the result of the heresy the Catholic Church had become. The church split itself.

Ray: We kept the keys.

John: In regards to this repetitive comment about the keys to the kingdom, Daniel mentioned this before, but let's take another look at what Christ's reference to the keys of the kingdom is. The Bible is full of metaphors; could it be that Christ was using a metaphor which specified how the apostles were foundational to the church; they have been given binding and loosing powers, or "key," which lock and unlock doors? That's certainly a possible way to understand this verse, is it not?

Ray: That isn't the way our Magisterium tells us to interpret that verse. We are to take it literally. The keys signify the responsibility to assume leadership of Christ's church.

John: The "keys" are given to Peter as the federal head of the apostles to open the kingdom to those who share Peter's confession and exclude those who will not receive their testimony to Christ. Through them, Jesus reveals his own word of kingdom authority. The apostolic foundation of the church is laid in the written Word of God, the Bible which is not the keys of Christ's author in the church through the power of the Spirit. This is what Paul is saying in Ephesians 2:20 and 3:5 and 18:18.

Daniel: Dr. De Chirico stated that "'binding and loosing' is another expression that Jesus used to define what Peter would be called to do. It is a Jewish saying that implies the exercise of discernment (forbidding and permitting) that leads to decision. In fact, Peter would be part of various decision-making processes in the church's development that would affect the life of the community of Jesus."

Darrel: Here's another way to look at this binding and loosing. When Christ gave Peter the authority to bind, he certainly did not expect him to establish a church that would bind the conscience of its followers the way the Catholic Church does. The Christian church is supposed to reveal the teachings of the apostles, that's what I refer to as the loosing part, and the Catholic Church's binding restricts that loosening from occurring.

My point is that the Catholic Church didn't use these keys responsibly. In Matthew 23:13, Christ says "Woe to you, scribes and Pharisees, hypocrites! For you shut up the kingdom of heaven against men; for you neither go in yourselves, nor do you allow those who are entering to go in." That sounds exactly what the Roman Catholic Church has been doing since its formation.

Ray: You don't know what you're talking about, Darrel! Anyway, it's just your opinion.

Darrel: But I actually quoted Christ, did I not? Should not we assume that Christ knew exactly what he was talking about?

Bobby: So, if not Peter, who do you think was the first pope in the Catholic Church, Darrel?

Darrel: I referred to this subject before when I gave a reason why we call the Catholic Church the Roman Catholic Church, but, in answer to your question, history is not definitive in giving us an answer, Bobby. As I said before, Leo I was the first Bishop of Rome to have himself proclaimed to be the head of all the bishops and then lord of the whole church and this is why some historians believe that he should be called the first pope in church history. Some other historians consider Gregory II, who was installed in 728, to be the first pope. But Gregory I, The

Great, who was elected pope in 590 AD, is generally regarded by most historians as being the first actual Pope of the church in Rome. I suppose they say this because Gregory actually established complete control over all the churches of Italy, Spain, France and England. By the way, just for the record, unlike many corrupt popes to follow him, Gregory was a good man.

Darrel: But these references are unofficial. In his *Ryrie Study Bible*, Dr. Charles Ryrie tells us that officially, the Lateran Council of 1059 permitted the College of Cardinals to elect the pope for the first time.

Ray: Protestants have their version of history, and we have ours.

Darrel: There are no versions of the truth, Ray. Our version, as you call it, is the same as yours except that we don't agree with your conclusion that the Catholic Church of today has been with us from the very beginning. The Christian church is not the Petrine church or the Roman Catholic Church; it is the church of Jesus which was founded by Christ as our Messiah. As we get more into the details in comparing our two denominations, we shall see that the Roman Catholic Church, which Ryrie says was officially established in the eleventh century after the split, bears little resemblance to the original Christian church, which was established in the first century.

John: The time frame is very important; it's important to know that the church we Protestants call the Roman Catholic Church wasn't officially established until the papacy was officially established, and, as we've already discussed, we're not exactly sure who the first pope of the church was, but whether we assume it was Leo in the fifth century or whether we side with what Ryrie tells us about the College of Cardinals official election of the pope in the eleventh century, the point here is that the Catholic Church of today was formed centuries after the first Christian church was established in the Book of Acts, and it soon began to drift into apostasy and gradually evolved into a church that has little resemblance to the beliefs of the original church. This is history, and we may keep referring back to it in sessions to follow. For this reason, the Catholic Church cannot, and should not, be considered the original church. The papacy is not to be confused with the Christian church. It is a political organization which attached itself to the apostolic church as a means to an end. In establishing its power structure, it successfully inserted itself between God and His people.

Darrel: Here's a little more history to digest. Throughout the Middle Ages, support for the primacy of the pope (spiritually and temporally) and his ability to speak authoritatively on matters of Christian doctrine grew significantly. Two popes, Innocent III (1198-1216) and Boniface VIII (1294-1303), were especially influential in advancing the power of the papacy. Innocent asserted that the pope's power was a right bestowed by God, and developed the idea of the pope not only as a teacher and spiritual leader but also a secular ruler. Boniface, in the papal bull, asserted that the spiritual world, headed on earth by the pope, has authority over the temporal world, and that all must submit themselves to the authority of the pope to be saved. In the medieval period, statements of this papal power were common in the works of theologians as well. In the late Middle Ages, Domingo Banez said that the pope had the "definitive power to declare the truths of the faith." Thomas Cajetan, in keeping with the distinction made by Thomas Aquinas, distinguished between the personal faith manifested in theologians and the authoritative faith presented as a matter of judgment by the pope.

I provide you with this history to prove that the papacy is a man-made creation, and, anyone can determine, by objectively analyzing how it established its power and influence, that the Catholic Church institution of today is not a God-thing, but a very, very man-thing. Through the development and growth of the papacy and papal authority, as I said before, the Catholic Church is a diversion; it diverted the purpose of the original Christian church to serve their own purpose, the establishment of a religious industry. Over the centuries, it became like a very large corporation with its members as shareholders who have limited power to make decisions and must relate to Christ only through them. In this sense, the Catholic Church acts like a mediator between man and Christ, and we believe Christ is our only mediator between us and God. Catholics then have two mediators to go through, their church and Christ. If we can't accomplish anything else in these discussion sessions, hopefully we can at least motivate you both to step back and take an objective look at your church as I've just described it to be.

Daniel: Catholics of course still remain the largest Christian denomination. I've found that when some people criticize the "Christian religion," for its religiosity and how the Christian church has become a big business over the centuries and what it really represents today, they're really criticizing the organization epitomized by the Roman Catholic Church. They have a good point. The ultimate in power is expressed in control, and the papacy is all about power, authority and control. History records that the Roman Catholic Church achieved its power through the prestige of Rome, the name of Christ, and by shrewd political alliances, by deception, and even armed force when necessary, the Roman Catholic Church established and maintained itself as a world power. It seems inconceivable that men could use Christianity to develop a domineering political machine whose aim is more about world power than a witness for the gospel, doesn't it? Nonetheless that's what has happened. Isn't it ironic that the apostle they have arbitrarily appointed as their first pope, Peter, actually warned us about the church empowering itself over the centuries?

Bobby: Do you even consider Catholics to be Christians, Daniel?

Daniel: Yes, I do.

Darrel: The jury's still out for me. You may recall what I said before about the differences between us being so essential, I'm not sure I can call them Christians, and, from what these guys have been saying to us, neither one of them seems to consider us as Christians either. Heck, from what they've been saying, I'm not sure they even consider themselves to be Christians. I remind you of what I said before about my friend proudly stating, "I'm not a Christian, I'm a Catholic." Catholics would seem to be so proud to be Catholic, they've lost track of their church's presumed connection with Christianity.

John: In addressing Catholics in discussions on social media, I have consistently referred to them as being my brothers and sisters in Christ. While I agree with much of what Darrel has said that seems to indicate this is not necessarily the case, I still consider them in that way because we both worship our triune God. I believe it is unfortunate that they have been so indoctrinated in their beliefs that they cannot know what they believe with any certainty outside their church and certainly don't seem to know or care why they believe what they believe. When challenged with the question, they come back with the default response of being the original and only Christian Church.

Darrel: Let me tell you all what I think about this church of yours, Sonny. I think that through the establishment of its extra-biblical traditions assigning authority to them which is equal to Scripture, the Catholic Church has successfully hijacked our Christian religion for its own purpose, and I resent that this has happened. I don't appreciate the reality that many unbelievers don't see a difference in Catholics and Protestants and assume Catholicism represents and speaks for Christianity; particularly when your damn priests commit these horrendous crimes against these children and your pope goes around spouting liberal nonsense. People who renounce Christianity should really be renouncing Catholicism.

Christ meant for his church to be the group of people who trust in him, not the ecclesiastical organization with its popes, bishops and clergy. These church leaders, who have been specially elevated to a lofty perch through the sacrament of ordination, have no such authority to define Christian truth and compel obedience to their decrees. These church offices were, in fact, of human origin. Peter had no special place among the apostles, and clerical distinctions were foreign to the Word of God.

Daniel: Catholicism's legalistic traditions successfully compete with the reading of Scripture and the study of the Bible. They insert themselves in between Christ and His followers; every moment spent dutifully adhering to one of their traditions is a moment that could be spent reading the Bible. The traditions have served their purpose well; they endear the church to its followers (as tradition often does); but they have also unfortunately diverted the focus on Christ to a focus on it and the church organization that spawned them. Indeed, through the implementation of its sacred tradition and papal pronouncements, the Catholic Church has successfully managed to insert itself in between its followers and Christ and even into the very process of salvation. Under its usurped authority, the papacy sells a heretical version of Christianity, and that is particularly unfortunate for those who accept it as the truth.

Sonny: Are we going into summaries here? I assume we have several more sessions left which will allow me the time to reveal what Catholicism really represents to me, as a member, to all who believe in Christ as their Savior and to the world. I truly hope and pray, you people, that, by the time we finish up with these discussions, you'll all have a better understanding of Catholicism and recognize it as the only true version of the Christian religion. Whoever said they weren't a Christian but a Catholic is not a Catholic either.

Bobby: Do any of you know who has the authority in Protestant churches?

Daniel: We have no authority to act as the Catholic Church functions in determining our theology as it binds our conscience. Churches are made up of men, fallen men, and an church that claims sole authority to God's truth and that we must come to them to understand what God's Word is saying to us has discredited itself to anyone who cares about maintaining any intellectual integrity at all. Christ is the invisible church, the foundation of our church; He and He alone is our authority over this one true church that bears His name only and is united by the Holy Spirit and transcends all denominations. There is therefore no need for an infallible pope who holds office through some process of usurped apostolic succession. We Protestants are much more autonomous than Catholics.

Main denominations like Lutherans, Baptists, Methodists, Anglicans and Presbyterians are each represented by their own central church council. Southern Baptists, for example, are supported by their Southern Baptist Convention. Methodists have their General Conference, Presbyterians have their Presbytery, Lutherans have their Synods and so on. These church councils are representative of a group of churches and do not govern the individual churches. Each individual church is typically governed by a church council consisting of members designated as elders or deacons. This is all biblically based.

In general, you could say we're definitely not an "organized religion" in the same sense as the Roman Catholic Church. The Roman Catholic Church fully intends to remain a church organized around itself and indeed has made a business out of religion; today it is probably one of the richest land owners in the world. That's clearly not what the Christian church was originally supposed to be all about.

Darrel: Protestants have no such organization which rules over us. We also differ from the Romanists in that we surely don't recognize our church governments to be equal or superior to God's Word. Our churches serve a very different purpose in our lives; they are our guide, not our monarch.

Ray: Yes, your Protestant churches are not organized. Your different denominations all present a different gospel.

Darrel: Not true, Ray. As I said before, those Protestant churches that teach and preach the doctrine of reformed theology are all on the same page.

Peter: As we talked about before, Catholics must have their pope, their supreme leader, their ultimate, infallible authority in church doctrine and tradition. It's all about the psychology of belief. Could it be that Catholics are people who need a monarch as you suggested before, Darrel? I have always wondered why the British Commonwealth has stuck by their ridiculous monarchy for centuries. This monarchy mentality or mindset is Britain's tradition, and, just as Ken Follett said, the monarch mentality is also the tradition and history of the Catholic Church.

Darrel: Yes, in calling Mary the Queen of Heaven, it sure seems like they need a reigning monarch in their lives.

Peter: Nothing unifies quite like a monarchy. "For God and Queen," eh?

Ray: Christ promoted unity, and it is best to have unity in any religion; otherwise there is the chaos and confusion. We have one Church; there are over 47,000 Protestant denominations.

Darrel: I'll say this again. Regardless of how many there are or when they were established these various denominations of Protestant churches and non-denominational churches are all unified under the banner of the enlightened in the fear of the Lord and the comfort of the Holy Spirit as Luke described in Acts 9:31. These are the churches that all practice, teach and preach the apostolic teachings. Had it not been for the Reformation, we'd still be stuck with the Catholic heresy.

We understand this reality and know that God supports our effort because he did not intend for there just to be one denomination, but did intend for all Christian churches to represent the apostolic teachings. We have no need to do what God didn't want done and arbitrarily set up one religious monarchy as you Catholics have done.

Christ emphasized unity under the apostolic teachings, and that is what we believe Protestantism is all about. Any differences in those Bible-believing apostolic churches are considered to be non-essential differences in how the church is to practice Christianity.

Daniel: Does the fact that we don't need a Christian monarchy make us heretics, Ray? Most of our differences within Protestantism are non-essential; we have more in common than we differ doctrinally. So far, all I've heard from you is a monologue of mantra about how your church is the oldest Christian church, blah, blah, blah, and somehow this means the Catholic Church is Christianity and the rest of us are heretics because that's what your Catholic Church tells you. I don't know whether you truly believe this hype or not, but you should at least consider its relevance to our discussion.

Sonny: I find our association with antiquity very relevant, Daniel, and find it difficult to understand why you all wouldn't want to be a part of the church that was founded by Christ through the apostles almost 2,000 years ago. The Catholic Church even preceded the Bible, and, as I mentioned before, actually gave Christianity the Bible. Why wouldn't you want to affiliate with the church that did this for Christianity?

Darrel: We would of course join your church if it really stayed the course and represented what it claims to be, Sonny; but it is clearly not that church; I think we've proved that.

Even though history tells us that Catholic Church was the only Christian church existing at the time (and this is why we can agree that the Christian church was established before the Bible was produced), that shouldn't motivate a person to become a Catholic. We discussed before how age, in itself, shouldn't be a determining factor, particularly since we continue to prove that your Catholic Church is clearly NOT that original church it claims to be. I will say though, I agree with Luther when he said that the Catholic Church does deserve credit where credit is due in organizing the canon of the Bible for us; but your church shouldn't make more of this feat than it deserves. As with the original writing of the books, the organization of the canon was inspired by God. The church was merely the tool used to do his will. Your claim game goes on.

Sonny: Doesn't it follow that the very same church that received the Scriptures and organized them into the canon of the New Testament would be the authority to interpret those Scriptures?

Darrel: Logically, there's some sense to that, but there are two aspects to consider. First of all, organization and interpretation, although related to a degree, should actually be seen as being two very different functions. Just because the Catholic Church was the only Christian church at the time that the biblical canon was organized doesn't necessarily give it sole authority to tell us what God's Word means. Second of all, as we've maintained throughout these discussions, the Catholic Church of today is clearly not the same Christian church that gave us the canon, and, because of its transition into heresy, it should not be utilized to interpret God's Word.

In trying to connect these two functions, your church is laying the groundwork to attain its true objective of claiming to be sole authority in interpreting God's Word. In this position, it can take its followers anywhere its leadership desires to take them. Can't you at least suspect that this is the true objective of your church? Can't you begin to see man's fingerprints all over your Catholic doctrine?

Sonny: No, I don't see it that way at all, Darrel. The leaders of the Church had access to the Scriptures and literacy rate was very low in the Middle Ages. The only way Christians could know anything about the Bible is what the Church was pledged to reveal to them.

Darrel: Sure, that's the reality; but the Catholic Church abused this privilege and continued to hold itself up as the only authority on the meaning of the Bible even after Gutenberg in 1439 made the Bible available to anyone who could read. This changed the way people were to learn about the Christian religion, and the church didn't like its power being compromised. Your church should have quit while it was ahead and taken Luther up on his offer and discarded the traditions it had installed over the centuries to make it more marketable to the masses. They ignored him, of course, for reasons we've already discussed and the rest was history. One of the great accomplishments of the Reformation was to put the Bible into the hands of the masses and enable them to learn God's Word.

Sonny: How can we learn the truth of God's Word if there is no authority to interpret it for us? Regardless of changing times, people will always need the Church to interpret Scripture.

Darrel: And to add to it when deemed necessary? I think not. Authority is only appropriate and useful when it actually conveys the truth. When the Catholic Church got off that track, Luther was into damage control and the Reformation he initiated brought the Christian church back to its original roots.

Sonny: The Church is indispensable, and Luther tried to destroy it.

Darrel: All Bible-believing Christian churches are indispensable, but, not in the same way you mean it. We need our churches to provide us with a means to worship our God in truth and in spirit, to hear the gospel truth preached and taught and to fellowship with one another. Your Catholic Church wants to do so much more than that. Are you so indoctrinated in Catholicism, you can't see that you belong to a church organization whose sole purpose has become simply to continue to remain a church organization? It's like what has become of our politicians; they are mainly focused on being re-elected.

Daniel: This is why the Catholic Church rejected Luther's offer to discuss his 95 theses with them. He was rejected just as Catholics reject discussing Catholicism with Protestants. The Catholic Church of course considers Luther to be a threat to their set up as a business of religion, and may have been concerned too because it recognized the times were changing as the Bible was being made available to more and more people, and it feared it would lose its authority as sole interpreter of Scripture.

Darrel: I'll say this again, and then maybe we can put this matter to bed. God inspired the church to identify and organize the inspired books into one Bible. That was to be their only function. There is nothing in Scripture which delegates the sole responsibility of interpreting the Word to the church nor is there anything in Scripture that would even suggest that the authority of the church is equal to God's Word.

However, the Bible does encourage believers to interpret God's Word on their own as assisted by the Holy Spirit. In other words, God assists us in finding out what he's saying to us. Doesn't that follow? Wouldn't God himself be the best interpreted of the meaning of his book? Makes sense to me. And, speaking of making sense, I should remind you that the motto of our group is to "Just Make Sense!" It's the only way to interpret the true meaning of Scripture.

Sonny: I'll come back to this discussion of interpretive authority later on with you when I present what we Catholics call the transfer of authority by the sacrament of ordination.

Darrel: Ah, yes, a sacrament for every occasion the church sees an opportunity to promote itself and assert its influence. When it wants to really stress something important, it just makes a rite into a sacrament to place even more importance on itself and its papacy and what it wants to accomplish with its followers. My one hope, Sonny, is that when we've finished up these discussions, while you may still dutifully cling to Catholicism, hopefully you will have understood what it means to lead an examined life.

Sonny: And my only hope for you, Darrel, is that you will see the truth. We believe the Church is the pillar and bulwark of truth. This is what First Timothy 3:15 is telling us. Maybe you Protestants are not open to what God wants to tell you through His Church about His greater mysteries.

Darrel: And I'll bet your church, as the "bulwark of truth," has plenty to tell us about those mysteries through your invented traditions. No thanks; I'll just stick with Luther's advice and stay with God's written Word and trust in him through the Holy Spirit to reveal whatever he wants to tell me, and leave it for later for him to reveal what he has not revealed in his Word.

Sonny: You Protestants have your traditions too. Lutherans, in particular, right?

John: There are some traditions affiliated with the Lutheran Protestant denomination, but it's not like it is with the Roman Catholic Church tradition. We probably emphasize some traditions more than other Protestant denominations because Martin Luther founded our church, and, since he used to be a monk, our service, as I said before, is liturgical, and we also follow a church calendar. The Lutheran *Book of Concord* states that "Falsely are our churches accused of abolishing the Mass; for the Mass is retained among us, and celebrated with the highest reverence. We do not abolish the Mass but religiously keep and defend it...we keep the traditional liturgical form...In our churches Mass is celebrated every Sunday and on other holy days, when the sacrament is offered to those who wish for it after they have been examined an absolved."

The Mass historically represented Christian worship becoming more elaborate and more unified. But Romanism introduced errors into Christian worship which were not biblically supported and so reformed Christians rejected them. Luther rejected parts of the Roman Rite Catholic Mass, specifically the Canon of the Mass, which, as he argued, did not conform with Hebrews 7:27, the verse that contrasts the Old Testament priest, who needed to make a sacrifice for sins on a regular basis, with the single priest, Christ, who offers his body only once as a sacrifice. This point is also addressed in Hebrews 9:26, 28, and 10:10. We've already discussed how the Catholic Church teaches that Christ is sacrificed every time Holy Communion is celebrated, and that the bread and wine are turned into the body and blood of Christ when the priest consecrates them. Fear of spilling the wine/blood of Christ led to the withholding of the cup from the communicants. In fact, active participation in the Mass worship was limited to the clergy and the choirs. There is no biblical foundation for these concepts at all. In fact, Christ told his disciples they were all to participate in the sacrament. And in First Peter 2:9, we're told that we are all "a chosen people, a royal priesthood, a holy nation, a people belonging to God, that we may declare the praises of him who called you out of darkness into his wonderful light."

Darrel: I know that Catholics emphasize the Eucharist in their Mass, and I see from our outline, we'll take up this discussion of Holy Communion in a couple of weeks. Anyway, back to what I was saying. My point is that the reformers were not denying the original creeds like the Nicene Creed which the Catholic Church had instituted; they merely wanted to talk about the extra-biblical traditions that had been added to the Christian doctrine by the Catholic Church. As theologian Dr. R. C. Sproul said, "The goal of the reformers was to restore the current Roman Catholic Church doctrine to the original, orthodox doctrine of Augustine and Aquinas." The formation of the Protestant Church was the successful result of their effort. The Reformation imposed a Reformation theology which "left unchanged the soundest biblical reflection from the 1,500 years of church history that preceded them. Where the church had gotten things right biblically, they left things alone."

Ray: So then, are you really saying Sproul claims Augustine and Aquinas were Protestants?

John: Let's just say that those of us who understand the theology of these two great theologians believe it is much closer to our Protestant theology than it certainly is to current Catholic theology. The reformers must have thought so too because both Calvin and Luther gave both Augustine and Aquinas credit for influencing reformed theology. Augustine's beliefs were particularly valuable to the reformers. Protestants discredited the Catholic Church's illegitimate use of Augustine's philosophy of history and recovered his true teaching. The Christian church was once again seen as more than a visible institution, and the germ of the idea of the invisible church Augustine had presented in *City of God* was developed.

Darrel: Yes, the Catholic Church should have stuck with the theology of Augustine and Aquinas, but, as it grew in power and influence and wealth, it left the beliefs of these guys far behind. You recall that Lord Acton said that power corrupts, and absolute power corrupts absolutely. Luther threatened to break up the Catholic Church's power structure, his protest caught fire and the Reformation was born. The Christian

Church divided into Protestants and Roman Catholic Churches. Both sides maintained their belief in Jesus Christ as our savior, but the doctrines of the two factions are markedly different as I hope we are all beginning to see from what we've been discussing so far.

John: The question we have before us now is whether these differences are considered to be essential differences. Luther and other reformers who protested against the Roman Catholic Church traditions believed the differences were essential enough to risk their lives over.

Bobby: What are examples of essential differences between Catholicism and Protestantism?

John: Any difference of opinion in interpretation of the meaning of the various doctrines associated with Reformed theology (The Doctrine of Scripture, The Sovereignty of God, the Doctrines of Grace and the Cultural Mandate) could indicate the possibility of an essential difference. I'd like to examine each one of these doctrines in an effort to determine whether we should consider Catholic Church as an apostate church or an apostolic church as they claim to be. Once we've completed this task, then we can each weigh in on the position of the present day Catholic Church's in our Christian religion.

Peter: It's apparent to me that these Catholics can only refer to their church to their truth claim, and you Protestants stubbornly refuse that authority, and express opinions Catholics don't recognize. I didn't come here to learn about your denominations; I came here to discuss your common religion.

Darrel: Good point, Pete. This discussion has turned into Catholic apologetics. We Christians, Catholic and Protestant alike, should at least spend some time talking about Christ and not attack each other. It has become a dialogue of the deaf.

Ray: We wouldn't have to spend time defending ourselves if you Protestants would stop attacking us.

Darrel: No one's attacking you. Whenever anyone questions what you have to say or disputes your claim to be the only Christian church, you see that as an attack on Catholicism.

Believing that the Catholic Church is THE Christian does not only serve to retain its members, this false claim attracts people to join up for this reason. The Catholic Church needs to represent itself as being the original church to give itself credibility. That's the need of your church organization, but what do we Christians need? We need to know the truth of the gospel, and we believe our Protestant churches which subscribe to the theology of the Reformation reveal that truth for us.

John: I think it's a good time to summarize what we Protestants have to say about this subject.

Until the Reformation, the Catholic claim was uncontested. The courageous reformers stood up for God's intent to reverse what the church had become over the centuries and bring it back to its roots, the apostolic teachings stripped of all those man-made, extra-biblical traditions, the trappings imposed by the church institution on the religion of Christianity. Whatever the church was initially described as in the book of Acts is clearly not what the Catholic Church is now and its hollow claim to be the original church should be recognized as a false claim. I think we've offered concrete evidence to support that conclusion in these discussions. So then, what's important to know now is which Christian denomination most closely represents the teachings of the apostles today. It is our contention that the Catholic Church has strayed from the teachings of the apostles in adding their extra-biblical tradition to the Christian doctrine. The reformers, of course, believed the same thing, and that's what the Reformation was all about. During the course of these discussions, we have been offering evidence of how these traditions are not biblically supported, and, in some cases, even contradicted by Scripture; I hope to offer more when we discuss each one of these traditions separately.

Daniel: Christ intended for His church to be formed to enable the spread of the gospel. Jesus did not mention that one particular, visible church would be selected to represent His teaching; His mandate applied to any church which consisted of believers who accepted these apostolic teachings. He didn't intend for the church to transition into "when two or three are gathered in my name" to become what the Catholic Church organization has become over the centuries.

Peter: But since you guys don't obviously accept the Catholic premise the church is the only Christian church, what difference does it make whether his church traditions have any merit or not? His church's credibility has been sacrificed, right?

John: Theoretically speaking, yes, you are correct; but, since we share the same basic belief in Christ as our Savior and believe the Bible to be the Word of God, it is imperative we continue to challenge our brothers and sisters in Christ to understand God's truth.

Ray: We don't need you heretics to tell us what to believe. We are the 2,000 year old Christian Church. The truth is in the word, the sacraments and our sacred tradition.

Darrel: There he goes again! Each of us in this discussion believe we have the truth to tell.

It's time to discuss Christian doctrine; it's time to examine your traditions of yours and determine whether they are what the apostles taught or not.

Sonny: Our traditions and the Bible comprise our sacred tradition which of course is the truth.

Dr. Kreeft believes it's these traditions that serve to strengthen his faith in Christ.

John: As I mentioned before, I know Dr. Kreeft personally; he is one of my mentors, and we communicated about my first book in *The Cabana Chronicles* series. I am also quite familiar with why he converted from

Protestantism to Catholicism. He said that he identified more with Christ in knowing He was physically present in Holy Communion. He believed we should come to where Christ is. Dr. Kreeft also said that the Catholic Church is the church Christ founded, and that it was temporally, literally, and historically connected to Him in body and blood. He admitted his love for the architecture of the old Catholic Churches in Europe and "the little rituals" and is attracted to a denomination that provides him with what he believes he needs: a more visible, tangible connection to Christ through the church. Luther would disagree with Kreeft's reasons, of course. He called these rituals "trifles rather than issues."

Kreeft was previously a Calvinist and admitted Catholicism had a weak understanding of grace, and he surely didn't accept the "grace plus works equals salvation" belief of the Catholic Church, but he did say that our good works serve to connect us with Christ, the object of our faith as an "extension of the incarnation." He also seemed to recognize a man-centered aspect in Catholicism with its man-made traditions added onto our Christian doctrine over the centuries. Nonetheless, these concerns weren't obviously enough to trump his belief that he was best connected with Christ through membership in the Catholic Church regardless of whether he believed this was the same church as the original Christian church or not.

I think Dr. Kreeft is expressing the desire every Christian should have in wanting to prioritize our connection with Jesus Christ. If we are truly honest with ourselves, none of us would admit we are completely satisfied with the strength of our faith or our relationship to our Savior. There's always room for improvement, and I pray for more commitment to my connection with Christ every day of my life; but I guess I'm more of an intuitive guy than a visual guy and firmly believe that Protestant theology of the Reformation is the right theology and that my church is my best guide in building on that relationship with Christ. While I can appreciate the positive effect the incense, the candles, the idols, the traditions, habits and rituals and the magnificent architecture of the church has on Catholics, I don't require this experience to relate to Christ. Do you recall when we talked about the psychology of religion? I think the psychology in Catholicism is apparent in the Catholics obvious need to experience Christianity the way they do. It helps us all conceptualize the grandeur of God and our relationship to Him. I am impressed by the otherworldliness of the impression the Catholic Church creates. It's like a massive metaphysical rush, a sugar high feeling of the sense of the sacred that lasts a little while but then wears off and we go into a slump until it's repeated. It's like the marathon runner who loads up on carbohydrates for quick energy, but it's the fat that provides the most efficient energy and the protein that builds the muscles necessary to run the distance. We need to focus on the theology and our relationship with Christ, not on some church. Our relationship with Christ is paramount; it's the steak; the visual experience is the sizzle that should only serve to whet our appetite to eat the steak.

We must always keep in mind that the world hates Jesus Christ so we are constantly tempted to ignore our relationship with Him or to be distracted from our focus solely on Him; but we must remain diligent to our cause, to glorify God and enjoy Him forever and so we are motivated throughout our lives to continue to work on improving that connection with Christ. The Catholic experience through its traditions, rituals, idols, vestments, Gregorian chants and architecture serves to point us to Christ, to strengthen our connection with Him and to our faith; this, of course, is a good thing. But when it becomes more about the visual experience than about conceptualizing the right theology which is only presented in God's Word, the focus on Christ is replaced or weakened by the focus on the church and the pomp of Catholicism serves more as a distraction than an attraction to Christ.

There's also the psychology of our need for authority which we talked briefly about before. When Moses left the Israelites at the foot of Mount Sinai to relate to God, they fashioned a golden café to take his place. I believe the Catholic Church serves as that authority for its followers. But the pope isn't just an authoritative father to his flock, Catholics believe he is actually a substitute for Christ on earth and at times is even infallible. In going beyond the role of a parent, he becomes that golden calf; it's bad theology. Protestants don't require a man to be our infallible guide; we have a perfect guide in the Holy Spirit.

Bobby: Different strokes for different folks?

John: Yes, as long as nothing we do serves to inhibit our understanding of correct theology and negatively affects our relationship with Christ. That's the essential difference between Protestants and Catholics. Everything else is non-essential.

Sonny: No, it isn't just a matter of us differing on some non-essentials; you Protestants completely miss the true meaning of the Eucharist which is the body and soul and Divinity of Christ. Like Erasmus, you go too far in wanting to simplify Christianity. This represents an essential difference between us and you Protestants.

Darrel: Erasmus was a great humanist and peer of Luther's, and the two often disagreed. Erasmus wanted to remove all the fat of Catholic traditions and rituals and return to an apostolic life and doctrine; and that's what Luther wanted too, but, unlike Luther, for Erasmus, Christianity was essentially just morality. In slimming Christianity down, he ignored our belief that the life that pleases God comes only from trusting Christ for our salvation. He went too far in his attempt to oversimplify and missed the core concept of our religion.

John: I'd like to respond to Sonny's comment about how Catholics connect through the Eucharist and his implication that we don't do that when we observe Holy Communion. Just because we Protestants don't believe the bread and wine have been physically changed into Christ's body and blood in observing Holy Communion doesn't mean we are not properly connecting with Christ or God's means of grace. That's an assumption that has no basis in Scripture.

Darrel: Personally, I agree with what John said. I don't require the paraphernalia, pomp, rituals, traditions and the drama that Catholicism brings to Christianity. Yes, the architecture is aesthetically pleasing, the history is interesting, particularly the history of the personalities and character, or lack of, in their popes, but they cross the line when they create traditions, some of which are intentionally designed to be self-promotional or enhance the credibility and authenticity of the Catholic Church. The church crosses the line when it actually calls their traditions sacred as the Bible is sacred; this heresy only serves to distract, not connect. The focus always needs to be on Christ, of course, and, though Kreeft and others may say the traditions serve to better connect them to Christ, the other side of that coin is these entrapments can also obstruct that connection.

Sonny: Give me some examples of what you're saying.

Darrel: As we've seen from these discussions, Catholicism is more about the Catholic Church and its authority to speak for God through added oral traditions and unraveling revelation than it is about theology and God's plan of salvation. We share the same creeds, yet we've barely touched on their substance. Sure, Romanists claim that their church's objective is to clarify God's Word and enhance the believers' worship of Christ, but their unbiblical dogma seems to mainly serve to promote the usefulness and importance of the Catholic Church.

The Bible tells us we must confess our sins; your church tells you this must be done formally through a priest in a box. That act enhances your experience and emboldens the church by requiring one of its officials to certify the confession. Scripture tells us that Mary is the mother of Jesus; your church tells you Mary is the Queen of Heaven and is your mediator to God. This belief provides the Catholic with the other parent (the pope is the "Holy Father"). Scripture tells us that our works display our salvation; your church tells you your works are a necessary part of the salvation process, and one of those works is to obey all the requirement of church dogma. The "grace plus works" concept also addresses man's wish to have his good works count for something important. Scripture tells us we are all saints; your church tells you that saints are a special, select group of super-Christians. Scripture gives us a doctrine which defines our belief; your church gives you rules and more rules to more clearly define that doctrine for you, and provide a purpose for itself. I've only met a few Catholics who can step back away from their own indoctrination and recognize this reality.

John: It all comes down to our human desires. All Christians desire to be connected to our Savior. This is our end objective. The Catholic Church addresses that desire in providing its followers with extra-biblical tradition designed to enhance the experience of belief (as it does for Dr. Kreeft) and a visible church authority to maintain belief in its traditions. But, in focusing on the means, the Catholic Church loses sight of the end. In its focus on tradition over the Bible and on itself as the sole authority of Scripture, the Catholic Church distorts the proportionality of the desire-end relationship. Followers are encouraged to have a strong desire for the means to the end, the mediocre or trivial, and this creates a weak desire for the end, the clear understanding of the gospel, God's grace and His sovereignty. The Catholic Church presumes to be a substitute for Christ on earth; it attempts to partially inhabit that place God occupies within every Christian. Thankfully though, as Catholics cling to their tradition, God is working within those He has elected to renew their hearts and minds regardless. It is a mystery that He persists in our lives, and we should rejoice that He is ever faithful to His promises.

Darrel: The majority of human beings have difficulty identifying with the conceptual; what they can't see, feel or touch, the invisible, the supernatural. A visible presence which points to an ethereal, supernatural concept like our connection with Jesus gives us something to grab ahold of. I have to admit that I sometimes go to a little Benedictine monastery near me to just listen to the Gregorian chants to experience my faith. I admit that this experience is beneficial to me in relating to Christ. I need that spoonful of sugar that makes the reality of this harsh world go down easier. I don't require this experience, but I admit it's helpful every now and then. But I sure don't require for that experience to get out of hand as it attempts to bind my conscience as it claims to be Christ to me. In going beyond embellishing the image of Christ to becoming Christ for its followers, the Catholic Church has committed heresy in embellishing itself.

Daniel: I agree with you guys. I personally don't need the drama, but it's helpful. I surely don't need the authoritative legalism of Catholicism though. The added structure the Catholic Church enforces on its followers is for those who need such structure, I suppose. Some folks just need to talk to a churchy man in a box in a church, and use beads to pray through Mary and other such rituals to relate to our triune God; I do not.

Bobby: Each to his own, eh?

Sonny: There is that, of course, but that isn't the way we look at it. We believe there is only the one way to commune with Jesus Christ and that is through His Church and only His Church. Imagination, intuitiveness, and creativity play a valuable role in our lives; they don't just attach to how we practice our belief. They are necessary accompaniments.

Darrel: Only a person leading an examined life can really hope to understand what he believes and why he believes it. Intuitiveness is a gift from God; our sensitivity to those things that are spiritual and supernatural is how the Holy Spirit most effectively communicates with us, and that guidance insures we won't get carried away with our imagination or creativity in understanding God's Word. We must trust in that.

On the other hand, over the centuries, the historical leaders of the Catholic Church have certainly used their own imagination, creativity and intuitiveness in coming up with their various extra-biblical traditions to meet the wants of itself and of its followers in maintaining the co-dependency that exists between the church and its followers. Since many of these traditions are not only not mentioned in Scripture, but some actually contradict what the Bible does say, it would appear as though your church's talent of imagination, creativity and intuitiveness was not guided by the Holy Spirit to reveal God's truth. God cannot contradict himself; your traditions must not contradict what he says in his Word.

Sonny: None of our traditions contradict what the Bible tells us.

Darrel: That remains to be seen, my friend; and I intend to prove you wrong. I'd like to address the major ones we've already mentioned and, keeping in mind the Catholic Church's intention to promote itself, go over each of them and see whether the Bible contradicts them.

Sonny: We focus on learning the richness of our sacred tradition, and, if and when the written word doesn't support them, we presume the oral tradition does.

Daniel: Are you saying there are two types of traditions.

Sonny: Yes, those traditions written in the Bible and the oral traditions which are not included in Scripture.

Darrel: Yes, there is the apostolic tradition in the Bible, and then there are those extra-biblical traditions which are just made up by your church. They fall into two different categories: Those traditions like the observance of Holy Communion and traditional rites like confession, and marriage that have been modified to suit your church's purpose, and then there are also those oral traditions that have been flat out just invented by the Catholic Church to appeal to man's wants (grace plus works), purgatory, etc.

Sonny: Our traditions have only one purpose: To connect us with our Savior.

Darrel: More than likely they serve the purpose to connect you to the Catholic Church and thus lead you astray from connecting directly to Christ. The challenge for you Catholics is to recognize which traditions are apostolic and which have been clearly designed by humans to meet the needs of your church. It's obvious to us which is which because we haven't been indoctrinated into believing your church can do no wrong.

Sonny: We trust the teaching authority of the Magisterium.

Bobby: Okay, so let's finally get around to discussing each of the major Catholic traditions, one at a time. Which one should we begin with?

Darrel: I'd like to start out by discussing the two traditions that particularly offended Luther: The Roman Catholic belief in purgatory, penance and the practice of paying for indulgences. They are inter-related. Purgatory, the belief that there exists some intermediary, holding area where people have a second chance to repent of their sin, is borrowed from paganism. Penance is payment for sin. Indulgences is the concept that a person can pay to help get some dead relative out of purgatory, is the worldly attempt to financially take advantage of a person's belief in purgatory. Luther objected to how worldly his church had become. He also objected to the bad theology of "grace plus works." He once said, "If any man doth ascribe of salvation, even the very least, to the free will of man, he knoweth nothing of grace, and he hath not learnt Jesus Christ aright."

Sonny: Some of the Catholic churches were accepting payment for indulgences at that time, but it's important you know that the Catholic Church never supported paying for indulgences, and indeed this practice was deemed illegal in 1567 at the Council of Trent.

John: I object to this belief in purgatory because its only purpose was to set up the practice of indulgences. It was, as Darrel said before, a pagan concept. Homer referred to it in the Aeneid in the first century B.C.; but it didn't actually become part of the sacred tradition of the Catholic Church until Gregory the Great established it in 593, and wasn't officially proclaimed a dogma of faith until 1439 by the Council of Florence. There is absolutely no biblical support for it. The blood of Jesus Christ cleanses us from all our sins. (1 John 1:7-9, 2:1-2; John 5:24 and Romans 8:1).

Darrel: The concept of purgatory is only a reality in the minds of those indoctrinated people like our friend here, who will spend his entire life on this earth in intellectual purgatory waiting to be released from his own prejudice for his eyes to be opened to the truth.

Sonny: Augustine accepted the concept; so did Aquinas.

Darrel: As I've said before, the concept of purgatory has been around for a long, long time, and both Augustine and Aquinas were certainly familiar with it even though it wasn't declared part of the sacred tradition until after Augustine's death, and declared part of the official dogma of faith until centuries after Aquinas died.

For your information, Augustine admitted he was an agnostic on the concept of purgatory, and didn't believe we could glean enough from Scripture to believe in it.

John: Augustine didn't presume to know whether these verses were speaking of a literal purgatory or not; he believed the passage probably pertains to experiencing a loss of worldly attachments, not to purgatory. Here's his actual quote: "It is not impossible that something of the same kind may take place even after this life. It is a matter that may be inquired into, and either ascertained or left doubtful, whether some believers shall pass through a kind of purgatorial fire, and in proportion as they have loved with more or less devotion the goods that perish, be less or more quickly delivered from it. This cannot, however, be the case of any of those of whom it is said, that they shall not inherit the kingdom of God unless after suitable repentance their sins be forgiven them. When I say 'suitable,' I mean that they are not to be unfruitful in almsgiving; for Holy Scripture lays so much stress on this virtue, that our Lord tells us beforehand, that He will ascribe no merit to those on His right hand but that they abound in it, and no defect to those on His left hand but their want of it, when He shall say to the former, 'Come, ye blessed of my Father, inherit the kingdom,' and to the latter, Depart from me, ye cursed, into everlasting fire.'"

Bobby: What exactly do you think Augustine is saying?

John: Let's allow him to speak for himself. Augustine put it another way when he said that "It is a matter that may be inquired into, and either ascertained or left doubtful, whether some believers shall pass through a kind of purgatorial fire, and in proportion as they have loved with more or less devotion the goods that perish, be less or more quickly delivered from it. This cannot, however, be the case of any of those of whom it is said that they shall not inherit the kingdom of God, unless after suitable repentance their sins be forgiven them."

The bottom line is that Augustine felt that the concept, or any theological concept, should be argued from Scripture if it was to be supported. That's what Protestants believe. Catholics believe in purgatory strictly on the authority of their church.

Sonny: What about Aquinas? You Protestants obviously consider him to be a credible theologian, do you not? Well, he believed in purgatory. He said so in *Summa Theologica*. He said that "if the debt of punishment is not paid in full after the stain of sin has been washed away by contrition, it follows that one who after contrition for his fault and after being absolved, dies before making due satisfaction, is punished after this life...This we preach, holding to the teaching of truth, and this is our belief; this the universal Church holds, by praying for the dead that they may be loosed from sins." This cannot be understood in any other way but as a reference to those souls existing in Purgatory, "and whosoever resists, the authority of the Church, incurs the note of heresy."

Darrel: In other words, if you don't believe me, you're a heretic. That sounds like something a Catholic would say.

Sonny: You need to understand what Aquinas is saying in this verse, Darrel. We understand that Christians are in a state of grace when we die, but that any outstanding temporal punishment we did not endure on earth we will go through in a state called purgatory before we can enter heaven. Using the biblical image of a purifying fire, after we have died, our earthly works are tested. Our good works will survive the fire, purified as precious metals and stones, whereas any bad works will be consumed like flammable straw, and though we will suffer loss we will be saved, but only through fire.

Darrel: The gospel tells us our sins, all our sins, are wiped clean; these are no outstanding sins left to be punished by your church enforcers.

John: In comparing the two views of Augustine and Aquinas on this subject of purgatory, we can see how the Catholic Church has grown in its power and influence over the seven centuries from Augustine to Aquinas in imposing its dogma on its followers. So let's see if we can find out what Aquinas meant when he claimed that praying for souls in purgatory is justified because they need assistance to "loose" them of their sins.

As I understand it, Aquinas is referring to some church tradition procedure whereby the sinner confesses the sin which incurs a debt of punishment and, if that person dies before he or she completes the assigned "hail Mary's," or whatever, the debt is still due and owing and the sinner will continue to be punished in purgatory until prayers from the living serve to release him from bondage. Is this a correct understanding of what he's saying here?

Sonny: Yes. We know that temporal punishment accrues to every sin, even venial sin. Mortal sin without repentance is a one-way ticket to Hell. Repented mortal sin is a sure ticket to purgatory, no exceptions. Although venial sin doesn't lead to Hell, like all sin, it does incur a consequence and, even with contrition, requires penance. It's a fact of life, however, that we rarely do enough penance to satisfy the debt we owe; we don't get the punishment we deserve. Hence, the need for further temporal punishment in purgatory.

John: I'm certainly no expert on Aquinas, but his statement indicates a weak understanding of God's grace and the value of Christ's sacrifice. The Bible tells us that Christ's atonement satisfied God's justice and our sins are wiped clean in His eyes through our faith in Christ. No further cleansing is required, particularly from us. What you say Catholics believe, and apparently what Aquinas also believed, is not biblical, it's heresy; but that doesn't mean his overall theology was more Catholic than Protestant.

Bobby: What about that, Sonny? Is there any biblical support for purgatory?

Sonny: Here are some verses in the Bible that support purgatory: Matthew 5:26, 48, 18:34, Luke 12:47-48, 58-59; 16:19-31, 23:43, 1 Corinthians 3:13, 15, 17, 15:29-30, Philippians 2:10, 2 Timothy 1:16-18, Hebrews 12:14, 22-23, 1 Peter 1:6-7, 3:19, 4:6, Jude 1:23, Genesis 50:10, Numbers 20:29, Deuteronomy 34:8, Isaiah 35:8, 52:1, Zechariah 9:11, 13:1-2, 8-9, Malachi 3:2-3, Revelation 3:18-19, 21:4, 27, Daniel 12:10, and Job 14:13-17.

Darrel: More biblical buckshot! We don't have the time or the inclination to discuss the meaning of each one of these verses. Can you just focus on the ones that are most clear to you?

Sonny: Each of these verses supports purgatory in a different way. Some verses refer to another supernatural state other than heaven or hell, and some of them refer to God's purification of the righteous at their death as in Zechariah 13:8-9 where the prophet refers to 2/3 shall perish, and 1/3 shall be left alive, put into the fire, and refined like silver and tested like gold. Those being refined are in purgatory. In Matthew 5:48 Jesus himself supports it in saying, "Be perfect, even as your heavenly Father is perfect." We are only made perfect through the purification process that takes place in purgatory.

Darrel: In the first example, Zechariah is referring the refinement of Israel, not individuals who will go to purgatory to be refined. See Isaiah 48:10 where God is saying "Behold, I have refined you (Israel), but not as silver; I have tested you in the furnace of affliction." It's always best to use Scripture to interpret Scripture.

And, in your second example, Jesus is not referring to some process that occurs after we die. He's simply saying our objective is to be perfect while we are here on earth.

John: Of course we know that perfection is not attainable in this life; nonetheless, the goal of every saved person in Christ is to grow spiritually in our faith, a process called sanctification, as we come closer and closer to that perfection. We are all saints and yet we must become saints in aspiring to imitate the righteousness of Christ. Our behavior must exceed that of the Pharisees which consists of both our external acts of obedience to God's law and an internal disposition of love for God and neighbor (Matthew 5:20, 22:34-40). Since we have been saved through God's grace, our sins are wiped clean; there is no need for further purification in some transitory, supernatural state of existence.

Sonny: In 1 Corinthians 3:11-15, Paul describes purgatory when he talks about anyone "building on the foundation of Christ with gold, silver, precious stones, wood, hay, straw, each one's work will become clear; for the Day will declare it, because it will be revealed by fire, and the fire will test each one's work, of what sort it is. If anyone's work which he has built on it endures, he will receive a reward. If anyone's work is burned, he will suffer loss; but he himself will be saved, yet so as through fire."

Daniel: We need to keep in mind that Paul is addressing the Corinthians here. When you read the passage, you will conclude that the works of some of the church builders in Corinth will be tested by fire; he is not saying that all believers are purged by fire after death. Other references like Psalm 66:10-12, Zechariah 13:9 and Malachi 3:2-3 likewise do not refer to the concept of purgatory. They tell us how believers are disciplined by trials in life.

John: According to Dr. R. C. Sproul in notes from his study Bible, "these verses address the evaluation of Christian ministry. Some who were seeking to build God's building in Corinth, but who depend on human wisdom, were using perishable materials ("wood, hay, straw") that will not survive the judgment of God's fire, while the builder themselves will barely escape destruction. Paul warns the church that they, like Solomon's temple (1 Chronicles 22:14-16), should be built up with what is lasting" We take them in their context, and Catholics don't because these verses don't support purgatory.

Sonny: In Matthew 5:26 and Luke 12:59, Christ is condemning sin and speaks of liberation only after expiation. "Amen, I say to you, you will not be released until you have paid the last penny." Now we know that no last penny needs to be paid in Heaven and from Hell there is no liberation at all, so the reference must apply to a third place; that's purgatory.

Darrel: If we take this verse literally, and we should, Christ is merely saying that we should agree with our adversary quickly lest he deliver us to the judge and the judge will hand us over to the officer and we will be thrown into prison. We won't get out of prison until we've paid the last penny. He's referring to an actual incarceration, not some supernatural place in the afterlife. That's clearly Christ's point here, not your church's interpretation.

Can you see a pattern here? Each of these biblical references Sonny gave us provides us with a clear example of how Catholics stretch passages in the Bible to support their man-made traditions. When Jesus says "Be perfect," Sonny says that can't happen in this life, so Christ must be referring to some transitional supernatural place where it will happen even though he mentions no such place; Peter refers to "spirits in prison," Sonny says prison is purgatory. You can make the Bible say anything you want it to say if you want to try and stretch it far enough and take verses out of context.

Bobby: Okay, it's time to adjourn. See y'all next week.

Week Eight

John: I've actually taken the time since last week to read every single one of the verses Sonny listed in support of purgatory last week. Even though the word "purgatory" is never mentioned in the Bible, which seems odd if it really existed, I can see how some of the verses that weren't obviously referring to something else could be construed as support for the concept of purgatory; so I can understand why Augustine took the fifth on this subject, and poor Aquinas was stuck with it because he took a vow to support his church.

Sonny: Even though the Apocrypha had not been officially declared as part of the Bible, Augustine was certainly aware of 2 Maccabee 12:43-45 which directly refers to prayers for the dead, and this concept supports purgatory. Baruch 3:4 relates how Baruch asks the Lord to hear the prayers of the dead of Israel. Prayers of the dead are unnecessary in heaven and unnecessary in hell; therefore these dead are in purgatory.

Darrel: Ah, so you have to resort to the Apocrypha, eh? You said you haven't even read it, but you presume Augustine was familiar with it? Augustine may have been confused about the purpose for these prayers to the dead, if he believed that's what they may have been. Were they supposed to lessen the idolatrous soul's time in purgatory or would they perhaps sway God's judgment away from condemning them in hell instead of heaven?

Peter: You Christians have a real thing about sin, don't you? Catholics even go one step further in trying to categorize sin into two types. As an unbeliever, I can be objective; I know there's something very wrong with this world and this idea of sin seems to best describe the problem; but, for me, sin is merely a wrong choice.

Darrel: The big difference between us believers and you, Pete, is evidenced by what you just said: the way we view the importance of sin in our lives. You claim it's just a bad choice which may or may not be that big a deal; it may or may not have dire consequences. We say that sin is an offence against God, by our definition. We don't rationalize our sin as you people tend to do, we ask for God's forgiveness and repent; repent means to change our behavior, to not continue to sin.

Daniel: Do you believe in a Judgment Day, Peter?

Peter: Of course not. I told you guys that before. For us atheists, sin is just a bad choice for which we suffer earthly consequences. And there is no day of judgment.

Sonny: We Catholics believe in a Particular Judgment and the General Judgment at the end of time. When Christ comes again, we will all be judged; this is the General Judgment. Those who die before Christ's second coming will be judged at their death. This is known as the Particular Judgment. There are three possible outcomes to the Particular Judgment. Those whose love for God has been perfected in this life are taken straight to heaven; those who die in God's love but still love Him imperfectly must be purified in the intermediate state of purgatory. We've already discussed this subject. Finally, those who reject God's love by committing a mortal sin and die without repenting are condemned to the everlasting torments of Hell. The General Judgment at the end of time simply solemnly confirms the Particular Judgment of each person.

Darrel: The Bible only refers to "The Great White Throne Judgment" as described in Revelation 20:11-15 and the "Bema Seat Judgment" described by Paul in 1 Corinthians 3:10-15. Only the unsaved appear at the Great White Throne Judgment; these people are unbelievers who are judged by their works and receive the punishment we all deserve for our sin, eternal damnation. The Bema Seat is the Judgment Seat of Christ, and only the saved appear before our Lord; we are awarded heaven at the Bema Seat; our works don't count towards our award because that happens solely through God's grace, but we are rewarded in heaven for our works. Of course, purgatory is not mentioned in either of these verses or anywhere else in Scripture.

Sonny: I've never heard of this distinction before; I stand on what I just told you about the Particular and the General Judgment.

Bobby: Okay, are we finished with this discussion about purgatory now? We've got a lot of ground to cover and need to move on to the next tradition to discuss.

Darrel: The point of our discussions is to try and resolve our differences; that doesn't mean we don't quit until the other guy gives in, it means we each present our cases for belief and offer our evidence to support that belief in an effort to determine the truth. That's what we're all here to do.

Sonny: Look, we believe we are one family in Christ in heaven and on earth, and we are to continue to pray for those souls who have passed on as we are to pray for those souls living among us on earth. In Ephesians 3:14-15, Paul refers to "the whole family <u>in heaven and earth."</u>

Darrel: Paul means our family of believers here on earth is also our family of believers who are now in heaven. They don't need our prayers to save them, they've already been saved. . Paul was of course a very learned Jew, and Jews, in their intertestamental and rabbinic literature, often referred to families of angels; that's a reference to their families in heaven. Luke 15:7, 10 refers to the angels and saints experiencing joy in heaven over our repentance, then they are still connected to us and are aware of our behavior."

Sonny: There are many verses that refer to this unity and support praying for the dead. When saints were mentioned in this verse, this title corresponds to the saints on earth. The same Hebrew word for "holy one" is applied to both humans and angels in heaven. Hence, there are angel saints in heaven and human saints in heaven and on earth. Loving beings, whether angels or saints, are concerned for other beings, and prayer is the spiritual way of expressing that love.

Darrel: Actually there are many Bible verses that refer to our Christian unity with those living and those who have passed on who shared our belief. But, there is no reference in the Bible we are supposed to pray for the dead. The Catholic Church instituted this requirement in 310 AD, one of the first of their many add-on traditions.

Sonny: The living and the dead are still united because Romans 8:35-39 says we are. Jesus converses with Moses and Elijah. The angels and saints experience joy in heaven over our repentance; the good branches are alive in heaven, etc., etc.

Darrel: Sure, we are all one family for eternity; but that doesn't mean we are required to pray for the dead. Why would you think we even need to pray for those in heaven? Oh, I get it, you're referring to praying for those poor folks residing in purgatory, right?

Sonny: Correct. Revelation 21:27 supports the concept of purgatory in saying that nothing unclean will enter heaven. That means that no one who has committed what we call a mortal sin will be forgiven and will not enter heaven when they die. They will go to purgatory. Those who committed moral sin are residing there and need our prayers for support. The Church actually devotes the entire month of November on our liturgical calendar each year to praying for souls in purgatory to attain heaven more quickly.

Darrel: It is true that nothing unclean will enter heaven because true believers have been cleansed in the blood of Christ and unbelievers don't go to heaven; and, regarding these two types of sin you bring up once again, I said then and I'll say again, the gospel tells us that all the sins of believers are forgiven; ALL SINS. Another "yeah, but." You say, *yeah*, our sins are forgiven through Christ's atoning sacrifice, *but*, mortal sins are not forgiven until washed away in purgatory. By the way, I assume the Catholic Church has defined which are mortal sins and which are venial sins, right? More dogma to remember?

Sonny: Yes. As I said before, generally speaking, mortal sin involves a radial rejection of Christ and His atonement for our sin and ruptures our relationship with God. Venial sin is an act that is not so serious as to ruin our relationship with God and take us out of a state of grace.

Darrel: Then you're all guilty of a mortal sin because your theology rejects the value of Christ's atonement for your sin. And determining which category a particular sin belongs in is of course a very subjective judgment call. This determination obviously gives the Catholic Church yet another necessary purpose for it to fulfill, right? As John said before, Scripture does not refer to mortal and venial categories, but it does allude to the concept that there is the outward manifestation of sin, and the secret sins we hold in our hearts like envy, covetousness, as I said before.

When we were discussing the meaning of 1 John 5:17 before, we talked about John referring to the sin that leads to death, the unpardonable sin of blasphemy of the Holy Spirit (Mark 3:29). What makes the unpardonable sin different from others is its relation to the Holy Spirit. It is the Holy Spirit's work to enlighten the mind of sinners and teach the gospel, persuading souls to repent and believe the truth. We've talked about this role of the Spirit before when we discussed the subject of authority in interpreting the Bible. When the influence of the Holy Spirit is deliberately and knowingly refused, then the irreversible sin can be committed as a voluntary, informed act of malice towards God. When Luther said that impenitence is the unpardonable sin, that's what he meant to say. The unpardonable sin then is basically unbelief. In response, there is a hardening of the heart from God that rules out repentance and faith. God actually permits the decision of the human will to be permanent in this case. God doesn't not do this lightly or without cause, but in response to an offense against his love. No one who has been regenerated in the Spirit though will commit this sin. Jesus said that "all sins" and "whatever blasphemies" will be forgiven, except this one sin against the Spirit.

Daniel: Supportive verses for what Darrel just said include Ephesians 1:17, 18, John 14:26, 2 Corinthians 3:16, 17, Hebrews 6:4-6, and 10:25-29. These more clear verses help us understand what 1 John 1:9 is saying to us. When we pray directly to God, the veil is taken away. There is no need for a mediator between us and our God. Halleluja!

Darrel: Regardless of whether you Catholics believe a sin is mortal or venial, the Bible tells us that sin is sin; it is missing the mark, a disobedience of God's law; it separates us from being able to relate to our creator. I know that Jesus' suffering and death was the perfect sacrifice for all our sins, and he is the only one whose sacrifice could open the gates of Heaven for repentant sinners. Without his sacrifice, heaven would be closed to us. His sacrifice is sufficient for us; again I say, no further cleansing is required.

Sonny: The sacrifice of Jesus does not make us perfect; that's obvious, isn't it? Scripture is full of examples of imperfect humans, including the apostles.

Darrel: The sacrifice of Christ makes believers perfect in God's eyes. He doesn't see our sin.

Sonny: It is up to God's children to cooperate with His grace to become as perfect as possible. We must make reparation for our sins either here on earth or in purgatory. God is perfect in love and mercy, but also in justice. Jesus opened heaven's gates, but we must repent and make reparation before we can enter. We must pay our debts before God.

Darrel: You Catholics have a weak understanding of God's grace which clouds your vision to see this from God's perspective. Catholics express the human perspective, and <u>from our perspective,</u> we are inclined to believe we must always do something for what we receive, and this even includes playing a role in saving ourselves. We talked about his before, and this belief is very unbiblical. Your church has directed you away from Scripture again. No wonder the Catholic Church downplays the importance of the Bible.

<u>From Gods' perspective</u> (which we know from reading his Word), Christ's sacrifice made God blind to our imperfection. The slate has been wiped clean. We know we still screw up, but, thanks to Christ's atonement, God doesn't see our sin. It doesn't seem as though you Catholics can really grasp this concept. Your only perspective is the

perspective of the Catholic Church, and that belief is designed by men to cater to our human perspective. It accomplishes this feat through its traditions. Catholics have a weak understanding of God's sovereignty and his power because you can't understand that it is not for believers to limit Christ's atonement by claiming that this act of grace wasn't enough to save us and that good works are necessary as well to ensure our salvation. It is God who has limited the atonement to apply only to believers; that's the way the Bible tells us the plan of salvation works. It seems you're saying that it's fortunate that God can rely on the Catholic Church to help him save sinners.

This mindset is evidence of a weak understanding of God's role and our role in our salvation. It's obvious that your Catholic Church's objective is to center on itself and man in general. The Catholic Church is made stronger in inferring the weakness of God's grace, power and sovereignty. The false belief in purgatory is evidence of this because it compromises the necessity and effect of God's grace.

Sonny: I disagree, Darrel. None of our doctrine contradicts the historic Christian truths regarding grace, or the impossibility of earning salvation through works. Enjoying the benefits of the ultimate sacrifice our Lord made for us on the cross does not exclude our suffering temporal punishment and so gaining indulgences does not compete with God's perfect, salvific act. Purgatory is not about salvation: we must be saved in order to go through it.

Darrel: Salvation means we're bound for heaven, not bound for someplace else. The Bible tells us that when we're saved, we're saved; that means we go to heaven, not some made-up, in between place where we're further cleansed of our sin. This is heresy.

The Catholic Church gets away with this heretical teaching because it discourages its followers from pursuing the truth outside the auspices of itself. This is why Catholics do not understand what the Bible says about the nature and purpose of God's grace. The Catholic Church accomplishes its objective by declaring itself the sole authority in interpreting God's Word and establishing its extra-biblical tradition and rituals. Christians need our Bible; we need to know God's Word. Dr. Johnson said that "Each biblical text is a road, taking its readers from their present situation toward a fuller understanding of God's grace." Catholics miss out on achieving this fuller understanding by not focusing on reading and understanding the Bible.

Daniel: Catholicism reminds me of another religion, Mormonism. When Sonny mentioned paying our debts before God, he seemed to `be saying what the Mormons tell us. They believe good works need to be performed because we owe God for saving us.

Darrel: Mormons also believe in becoming perfect so they can be a God of another world; they also go one better on Catholics in specifying various degrees of heaven, not just purgatory. Catholicism of course preceded Mormonism, but, I would feel a little squeamish if some cult borrowed anything from my beliefs to use in its false doctrine. That could be an indication that something is wrong in your doctrine.

Sonny: We have nothing in common with cults like Mormonism, Darrel. They borrowed the concept of purgatory from us because they recognized it made perfect sense. It is another way God shows us His love and mercy. If only the perfect can enter heaven, who could go there? Purgatory purifies our souls if needed so we can enter heaven. Do you think a murderer who converts on his deathbed will fly into heaven without delay and as quickly as God's most faithful servant? Does God's justice not allow for purification of our souls that have been stained by a lifetime of sins and if there has been little attempt to make reparation to God? I pray that God will open your heart and mind to the truth about purgatory.

Darrel: You've actually brought up several points so I'll try to take them in order.

To your first point that purgatory makes perfect sense, yes it does make sense, but only from our human perspective. Remember when I contrasted our perspective with God's? From God's perspective, he's done his job through the blood of Christ; he is blind to our sin, so every believer goes to heaven. Period. From our human perspective though we see how the concept of purgatory caters to fallen man's desire to wants a do-over; he fears the finality of death, particularly since no Catholic can know whether they'll go to heaven or to purgatory. As with other heretical belief systems, the Catholic Church has always historically been very intuitive; it knows what to give man to meet our wants, and a wish for a second chance is one of these wants. As evidenced by all your extra-biblical traditions, the Catholic Church organization is very good at addressing many more of our "wants," but it skews God's Word to accomplish its worldly objective and, in so doing, misleads its followers from understanding what God tells us in his Word we need. We don't need a do-over; we don't need yet another futile attempt to try and earn our salvation; we need God to save us; and we Protestants understand that he does save us; he meets our need for salvation. Again, I repeat, when we die as saved sinners, our slate is wiped clean by Christ. That's what God's grace is all about, and, as I've said before you folks have a weak understanding God's grace and what it means.

Look, Sonny, if we truly understand what the Bible is telling us, we are all sinners and our sin separates us from God; we have a "need" for salvation and, through his only son's atoning sacrifice, God demonstrates his love and mercy for us by enabling us to be reconnected with him. His concept of justice is appeased by the atoning sacrifice of his son. Only through the death of Christ can the souls of true believers be purified. Once saved, always saved. We don't need to be purified after we die; Christ has already done that for us. This is the essence of the gospel, man. Time doesn't permit us to discuss each and every one of the many biblical verses supporting our understanding of God's plan of salvation.

Sonny: I know my Bible, Darrel. You don't need to tell me what it says.

Darrel: No, of course not. You have your church do that for you. Trust me, I'm your masters of the magisterium!

In summation, man wants a do-over purgatory; we need God to save us through his grace. So you see, it all comes down to our understanding of the big difference between "needs" and "wants."

To your second point, Sonny, I'm sure you are familiar enough with your Bible to recall what Christ said to the thief on the cross when the convicted criminal expressed his faith in him. He said that this man would this very day join him in heaven. So then, it's patently obvious that indeed even a very bad man who confesses a true belief in Christ as his savior with his last breath will go to heaven without delay. That's exactly what Jesus is saying in his parable of the Workers in the Vineyard. You say you know your Bible so you should recall that the last workers to be called by the owner of the vineyard to work were paid the same for their labor as the ones who worked all day, right?

Sonny: Yes.

Darrel: When the workers complained about this unfairness, Christ reminded them that they were paid fairly for their work and that if the vineyard owner, who represented God, chose to pay the workers who did less work the same wage that was his business. "Is it not lawful for me to do what I wish with my own things?" As I said before when we were distinguishing between the two judgments, it's God's will to *award* sinners heaven through his grace; by definition, none of us earned God's favor. We need to distinguish between being awarded heaven and being rewarded in heaven. The Bible tells us we will be rewarded in heaven for the good we have done. Mark 10:21 explains this concept. Christ said, "give to the poor and you will have treasure in heaven." This distinction between *award* and *reward* explains why the thief on the cross goes to heaven but, because of his bad behavior, gets a seat in the balcony in the throne room while people who have done more good over their lives get to sit in the front row seats. It all comes down to an understanding of the difference between "award" and "reward."

Sonny: But Mark 10:21 says that a person must sell his stuff and give to the poor to go to heaven.

Darrel: No, that isn't what the verse is saying. Jesus doesn't tell the man to sell his stuff and give to the poor so that he may go to heaven; he says that, if he does this, he will be rewarded in heaven. There's a big difference between award and reward.

Bobby: What about indulgences? Let's talk about that.

Sonny: The Bible teaches us that sin has two components, the guilt of the sin and the temporal punishment for the sin. When the Church remits temporal punishment, this is called an indulgence, a remission. In her wisdom, the Church makes this remission conditional on the performance of pious actions, through what are known as "concessions." These exist to help the Body of Christ grow in holiness and virtue. Some of these concessions are plenary, which remit all temporal punishment, but most are "partial" and remit some punishment according to devotion of the individual believer. These need not be gained for the person doing the pious action, but may be heroically offered up in loving solidarity for others, such as those holy souls in purgatory who by their condition have no ability to gain any indulgence for themselves.

Darrel: Whew! I think I get the gist of what you just said, but it's complicated. I assume any Catholic would have to totally rely on the Catholic Church to make sure I understood and obeyed its traditions, rituals and sacraments. But then I assume that's the real motive for the Catholic Church to make this all so complicated, eh? As I've said before, it's obvious that <u>the objective of the Catholic Church is to make itself necessary</u>.

Ray: It is necessary! Without our Church, we would be just like you Protestants with your 30,000 different denominations! Who do I go to instead? Martin Luther? John Calvin? King Henry VIII? The street corner preacher?

Darrel: First of all, we don't believe that any of these people you mentioned are to function as your church functions for you in acting as our sole authority for understanding God's Word, so, if you need to have an authority like that, I would advise you to stay put and remain a Catholic. You don't need to leave the Catholic Church to replace it with another authoritative idol. We learn from Luther and Calvin and others whom the Spirit guides us to learn from. We only worship our triune God, not some church.

I'm only suggesting that, if you didn't have your Catholic Church, you would be free to choose a Bible-believing church that taught and preached to gospel truth, and enlighten you on what Christianity is really all about. *Hint:* it isn't about your church or any church; it's about our relationship with Christ, our DIRECT relationship with Christ. Most importantly, you would be free of the concern for your salvation because you would thoroughly understand God's grace and Christology.

Ray: I will never leave the Catholic Church because I will never leave Christ. The Catholic Church is Christ. Fulton Sheen said it, and I believe what he said.

Darrel: Wow, such a blasphemous claim and it came out of the mouth of one of your most respected bishops! Of course, in our sessions, both you Catholics have hinted that this is what you really believe your church to be for you. First you referred to your church as the one, true church, the church of the apostles, our Christian heritage functioning as the body of Christ and the Holy Spirit, the only authority, and now you come right out and say it IS actually Christ himself! Your church is God and worthy of worship? Do you really believe that to be true? In worshiping your church, you do of course realize that you are worshiping a man-made idol. It's a violation of the Second Commandment; it's heresy. Calvin once said man is an idol-worshipping machine so it's only natural for you.

Sonny: I don't think Ray meant to imply that our Church is Christ.

Ray: Yes, I did!

Bobby: Okay, can we get back to our discussion on indulgences? Sonny, can you provide us with an example of how this somewhat convoluted process of indulgences works?

Sonny: The best example of how indulgences work in Scripture is in 2 Samuel 12:13-14 when Nathan told King David that God had forgiven his sin of killing Uriah and stealing his wife Bathsheba, but that his punishment would be the death of his son by Bathsheba. Adam and Eve were also forgiven for their sin, but they had to endure the temporal punishment of toiling in the sun and the pain of childbirth. Of the two components, guilt is the most important. If the guilt isn't forgiven by going to confession, then the punishment could be permanent, the eternal damnation of Hell, not purgatory.

Now, you may ask, what does this have to do with indulgences? Well, here's another scriptural reference to consider. When Jesus awarded the thief on the cross by giving him complete remission of his sins for his belief, that same power of binding and loosing sins and punishment was given to the Church by Jesus. In Matthew 18:18, Christ said, "Truly, I say to you, whatever you bind on earth shall be bound in heaven, and whatever you loose on earth shall be loosed in heaven." "Whatever" means anything and everything, including punishment for sin.

Darrel: So, you now seem to now understand the message of Christ's parable of the Workers in the Vineyard in reference to Jesus power to instantly pardon a repentant sinner, but also believe God gave your church that same power? We Protestants of course believe in church discipline, but are you saying that Christ gave the church the authority to punish or pardon sinners?

Sonny: Yes. I am saying that; through the power given to it by Christ in John 20:21-23, the Church has the power to punish sinners, pray for those souls in purgatory and pardon those sinners for the debt that remains even after they have repented and been forgiven of guilt. This practice is called indulgences. The practice preceded its official recognition as Church tradition in 1190; but before then, beginning in the 11th century, the practice of indulgences was misconstrued by the Church. It was based less and less on penitential acts and more and more on contributions made to a Church or monastery.

Darrel: Given human nature, that was a predictable outcome. The Catholic Church saw a good way to raise money to feather its own nest and increase its wealth and power. How does that work? If you are faithful and make special indulgences and tithe to the church, the church will pray for someone in purgatory to be released sooner, right?

Sonny: Right; but the practice was redefined by the Second Vatican Council. The number of indulgences which are supposed to remit the entire punishment was reduced, and the Council did away with the former distinction between personal, real, and local indulgences. The purpose of indulgences under the new definition is to induce a total conversion of the heart from all sin through fervent contrition and charity. The bottom line is that our Church does not believe in collecting money to pay for indulgences.

Darrel: This just seems to me to be such an unnecessary ordinance. What is it supposed to do for a Catholic? It seems to do more for the Catholic Church, doesn't it? Is this why this practice got so completely out of hand and became the last straw for Luther? But we know that Luther not only objected to the church's greed, he also objected to its usurping the power of God to forgive, pardon and punish sinners. Even if no money was collected, the practice of indulgences is a corruption of what Christ taught about the consequences of sin and God's uniquely sovereign role in our sinful lives. As usual with you folks, it's always been about the Catholic Church. The concept of indulgences morphing into the practice of indulgences which, of course, involved money changing hands is a good example of how the Catholic Church became more and more worldly and less and less what Christ's church is supposed to be.

Ray: Have you not been paying attention, Darrel? That's typical of you Protestants! Sonny has already told you that the Church outlawed payment for indulgences in the sixteenth century.

Darrel: Was this another unraveling revelation? Had the Holy Spirit finally had enough of the graft and the greed and revealed to your church leaders that this particular sacred tradition could no longer stand? Well, it didn't work because the spirit of this heretical concept is still alive and well in your church. As I understand from my Catholic buddies, you can gain an indulgence by giving to some charity. Hmmm, I wonder what non-profit institution would first come to mind? The Roman Catholic Church perchance?

Daniel: How does one gain an indulgence, Sonny?

Sonny: Okay, here's how it works. To gain any indulgence, you must:

1. Be a Catholic already. No one assigns a penance to a non-Catholic to begin with. You have to have a penance to get an indulgence from one.
2. You have to have gone to confession (where the priest would assign the penance).
3. You must have no desire to commit any sin.
4. You must receive the Eucharist while believing it is the body and blood of Christ.
5. You should then pray for the Pope's intentions. That is, for whatever good thing he is praying for, you add your prayer to his.

Then, and only then, will any prayer or act of yours receive an indulgence. If you do not complete these five things, the indulgence is only partial; it will only make up a part of the original assigned penance, but you can get more than one partial one at a time.

Darrel: Don't take this personally, Sonny, but you've got to be kidding, right?

Sonny: I don't kid about my religion, Darrel.

Darrel: What I mean is that this process just seems so naive; so ridiculous. It's no wonder Luther brought it up in so many of the 95 theses he posted on the door of the church.

Sonny: It's the opposite of naïve, Darrel. As you have seen, our Church is very descriptive about our doctrine. That's maturity, not naïveté.

Darrel: A better word to describe all your church's "descriptive" rules, regulations, traditions and rituals from a follower's perspective, would be "unnecessary." From your church's perspective of course all of this stuff is very, very necessary for its survival as a necessary institution. You've admitted to this yourself when we first began these discussions.

Sonny: Catholicism requires a certain formality in connecting its members to Christ that Protestants oppose. You people oppose it because you are independent, rebellious heretics who would complete what the reformers began and destroy the Christian Church. It's these very rules, regulations, ordinances, traditions and rituals that man needs to best connect him with and direct him to Jesus Christ.

Darrel: Well, it is these very rebels who most thoroughly understand God's grace and his sovereignty and how he wishes to be glorified over some self-serving church organization. You can have your ordinances, your church authority and your habitual, perfunctory relationship with God, we'll pass on all that *schtick* and seek the truth and knowledge of our God. God is not glorified through ritualistic formality, through your mumbling rote prayers over your little beads and other such behavior. He is glorified by our recognition of his expression of his means of grace through his Word and the sacraments.

Bobby: But penance is a sacrament, right? Is it therefore a means of grace?

John: Not for us, Bobby; we don't believe penance is a sacrament because Christ did not mandate it be performed. Luther objected to portraying God as dispensing His means of grace indiscriminately. Luther believed

God expresses His means of grace through the two sacraments of baptism and Holy Communion and through His Word.

Penance provides us with a good example of how the Catholic Church creates a purpose for itself by forcing its way in between a believer and the object of his true belief, Jesus Christ. By definition, penance is a punishment or atonement which is supposed to eradicate a sin; but our sin is an offense against God, not man or a group of men who compose some church, and thus it is God who will deal with us when we sin, not some church. God, and God alone, has the power to punish sinners. Apparently, the Catholic Church believes God should share this power with it. The church wants the power to punish sinners, and does so through this ordination of penance. Catholics are expected to confess their sins to a priest at least once a year (but it's best to do this regularly) and perform this sacrament as a good work to put them right with God to warrant their salvation. Confession (to a priest) is supposed to be good for the soul. The believer's confession to the priest is then accompanied by an assigned punishment of repeating a number of "Hail Mary's." Indulgences, of course, can reduce this punishment.

Darrel: Penance is yet another practice the Catholic Church has come up with to make a use for itself. A church representative, the priest, is required, of course; he is to act as an intermediary between God and man. He has sacramental power to be a conduit of divine grace and to forgive sin.

Sonny: I cite John 20:23 to support the practice of reconciliation or penance. "If you forgive the sins of any, they are forgiven them, if you withhold forgiveness from any, it is withheld."

Darrel: Again, when we look at this verse more closely, the text does not justify your conclusion. As you have said before, your Catholic Church teaches that the authority to forgive sins is conveyed uniquely to the apostles and then to their successors, your priests and bishops, who have a special sacramental authority through their ordination, another one of your sacraments, right?

Sonny: This is correct.

Darrel: Except that we find absolutely no indication that Jesus gave perpetual, sacramental authority to those who come after the apostles. We've talked about this before, of course. R. C. Sproul tells us that the Apostolic office is distinct in function and authority from the offices of elder and shepherd (see Ephesians 4:11). Regardless, Jesus did give authority to forgive sins to select individuals, but he also gave authority to the entire church as we see in reading Matthew 18:15-20.

Sonny: Correct. The Catholic Church, the only Christian church existing at that time, and the only Christian church in existence today, is the Church Christ gave authority to forgive sins.

John: But we don't recognize that premise to be true, Sonny. Christ gave authority to His church, the invisible church of the elect, and only to those visible churches that represent that invisible church. We do not believe your church represents the invisible church. In fact, on several occasions, each of you has even denied the existence of Christ's invisible church of believers.

Ray: Our visible Church is the same as the invisible church.

John: So you keep saying, but I'm only saying that the Catholic Church certainly doesn't have the right to do something that is exclusively God's prerogative, and yet, as we have seen, it does; but, then again, at least this assertion is consistent with your belief your church actually is Christ.

As Christians, of course, we are to recognize how important it is for us to confess our sins and ask for forgiveness. Even the scribes and Pharisees recognized that necessity and understood from Scripture that only God can forgive sins even though they failed to recognize that Jesus had that right because He is God. What we mean in saying that the church has the authority to forgive sin is to believe the church has an obligation to declare that God has forgiven the sins of those who repent and trust in Christ. In this regard, John 20:23 may be translated more literally as "If you forgive the sins of any, they have already been forgiven by God."

Jesus commissioned the disciples, and the wider church, to evangelize the world. God promises to forgive all those who turn from their sin and believe in Jesus, so we can tell people that God has in fact forgiven them when they trust in Christ alone. Paul tells us this in Romans 5:1.

Ray: You said you recognize that Christians are to know we are to confess our sin, ask for forgiveness and repent. Well, only our Church truly emphasizes the importance of repentance by labeling penance as a sacrament.

Daniel: By definition, a sacrament is labeled by Jesus Christ, not by some church.

Darrel: Look, Ray, of course we know that we're to repent of our sins and ask for God's forgiveness; but we understand we are to do this before God, not be required to go through yet another of your intermediaries, some priest ordained through another of your faux sacraments to possess some special, mystical, sacramental power to forgive us. We don't need to falsely claim penance as a sacrament to emphasize what every true Christian should be aware of. We know we can confess our sins directly to God in prayer and I do. We can also offer a public confession of our sin in our worship service every Sunday. And James 5:16 exhorts us to confess our sins to one another as well. This is not required, but there is a benefit in such confession. We ask God, through his grace, for his forgiveness based on the atonement of Jesus Christ; we don't need to go through some kind of penance performance to atone for our sin.

The reformers understood that forgiveness is centered on God and his grace, and you Romanists believe forgiveness is a process that must involve a priest and view this as performing yet another good work as credit towards salvation. Catholics have thus directed our focus away from praying to God for repentance to regularly confessing our sins to the priest and performing the act of penance. Repentance is biblically supported, penance is not. To God be the glory.

To me, the Catholic Church epitomizes what Jesus was talking about in Mark 7:6-8 in saying, "These people honor me with their lips, but their hearts are far from me. They worship me in vain, their teachings are but rules taught by men. You have let go of the commands of God and are holding onto the traditions of men."

Ray: That's a lot of crap, Darrel! We are not discouraged from confession our sins to God in our prayers.

Darrel: Maybe so, but you still need to confess to a priest or it doesn't count, right?

Ray: For our confession to be effective, we must list our sins to the priest, who represents Christ. Only in this way can we demonstrate we take our sin as seriously as God does.

Darrel: God knows our hearts, Ray, and it's not necessary to confess only to a priest or to list our sins, one by one; I know of no passage in the Bible that demands the actual listing of our specific sins as a condition for receiving forgiveness; such a demand would be impossible to fulfill anyway. Our sins are so many we don't even recognize them all. Luther recognized this impossibility as he agonized over trying to repent of all his sins he could recall that he committed on a daily basis. It frustrated him until he realized the reality of God's forgiveness through his grace. His realization planted the seed of his dispute with his Catholic Church. And, as we know, he didn't appreciate the practice of paying indulgences. We know what Christ thought of the money changers setting up shop in the courtyard of the Jewish Temple, right?

John: The Bible does not require us to go through a human intermediary to confess our sins. We don't do this in remembrance of Christ. We're to recognize, confess, and repent of our sins directly to our gracious God who mercifully encourages and allows us to come to Him directly. He accepts our humble plea that lays before Him all our sins. He also allows us to come to Him directly to confess specific sins that we regret and troubles our conscience. God, be merciful to me, a sinner.

Sonny: It's also important that penance be a part of this confession process. Without consequence, without punishment, we are inclined to take our sins for granted. I know it's hard for Protestants to understand penance because in your Bibles, the word penance has been replaced by the word "repentance." Luther did this because he wanted to support his "sola fide" position by asserting that good works were not necessary for salvation and that penance was considered to be just another good work. We believe that until penance is performed by a priest, the injury remains in the heart and soul and must be satisfied or healed through good works, although the good works are actually accomplished through the strength of Jesus Christ so that no one can boast.

John: I can't confirm what you say about the replacement of the word "penance" with the word "repentance," in Luther's translation of the Bible into German, but I can tell you that I believe it's appropriate if Luther did do this because "penance," as you've described it, relates to an act man performs for man whereas repentance, of course, distinctly relates to our connection with God. The Bible says we sin against God, not man (although men suffer the consequence of our sin); and it is therefore God whom we owe an apology to and a commitment to sin no more. Yet again your church barges in where it clearly doesn't belong, inserting itself right in the middle of God relating to man.

Sonny: Look, we need to understand the importance of our sin, and the best way to understand that is to accept the consequence a penance represents. We know we've been forgiven.

John: The theology is incorrect. Penance is an act, and we don't do deeds to absolve our sin nor save ourselves. And we also know there are times when our conscience won't let us rest even though we know we are forgiven. Perhaps we can't bring ourselves to admit a sin or make amends to someone whom a sin has hurt. Or maybe life situations tempt us to wonder if God is punishing us or if this sin is too great to be forgiven. King David had this problem as you may recall. He realized he had been forgiven, but he also realized that sins have consequences as he experienced continual strife within his own family. At the end of his life, he didn't feel forgiven; he felt overwhelmed. See Psalm 38:4. As Darrel indicated, Luther was like David in that he had a sensitive conscience. He urged Christians to publically confess specific sins to trusted fellow believers and to seek a spoken absolution so, in this sense, it's helpful to talk to a priest, but it need not be a priest. As I say, it could just be a trusted fellow Christian.

Sonny: All I can say in response is that motivating a non-Catholic to the point where he at least accepts that a sacrament is useful is the first step towards accepting that it is necessary; and that is just one step away from the acceptance that they are not just man-made, practical religious devices, but divinely instituted initiatives that incorporate the soul into the mystical body of Christ.

John: I understand that labeling penance a sacrament can motivate believers to receive absolution and such absolution can bring a degree of contentment in bringing some relief to anguished sinners; and I also concede that pastors and priests are uniquely qualified to provide personal comfort. But this doesn't mean I support your church's objective to empower its own position by formalizing the process of absolution and by calling it a sacrament as though Christ had instituted the procedure. We Protestants don't believe that the ends justify the means. We believe that such absolution can, and should, be primarily a matter between the individual and God, and such public absolution involving a priest should not be required as representing just the performance yet another good work towards earning one's salvation. Private absolution is a special comfort for troubled sinners and is as valid and certain as if Christ dealt with us Himself.

Sonny: Christ gave the keys of the kingdom to the apostles to forgive sin, to decide between absolving or retaining guilt. This authority was passed on to the bishops of the Church, and from them to priests through the ordination process. If confession is not treated seriously as a sacrament should be treated, then we view this judgment as being arbitrary.

This sacrament of penance helps people understand how important it is to express our sorrow for our sins; Protestants just don't understand this because, for them, it's like a person just saying, "I'm sorry," and then just moving on; but, when we approach God formally in the Church, we acknowledge not only our sins, but our sorrows for them.

Darrel: You seem to infer that only Catholicism effectively communicates this concept of feeling sorry for our sins. That's arrogant, and incorrect. We've mentioned before how Catholics showcase Christianity through some of these rituals required by their church, and just because we don't make such a show of it by routinely talking to this little guy in a box going over our list of sins, doesn't mean we don't take sin seriously and express sorrow over our sin.

Sonny: We also confess our sin to God privately and also confess to one another. That's what James 5:16 is referring to; and, if we see this verse in its context of verses 14 and 15 which are referring to the elders administering healing, this means we are to confess our sins to a priest.

Darrel: That's an unsupported assumption, Sonny. Verse 16 stands alone in specifying we are to confess our sins to one another; there is no reference to a requirement a public confession must be given to an elder or a priest. Again, your church bends Scripture to suit itself.

Bobby: In Catechism, I was taught that there are different forms of penance. Is that true, Sonny?

Darrel: More dogmatic details to memorize to make the Catholic Church necessary?

Sonny: Yes, Bobby, CCC1434 in the Catechism states that the interior penance of the Christian can be expressed in many and various ways. Scripture and our tradition insist above all on three forms, fasting prayer and almsgiving, each of which stands for conversion in relation to us, to God, and to others. We obtain forgiveness of our sin through reconciliation with the wronged party, tears of repentance, concern for the salvation of one's neighbor, the intercession of the saints and the practice of charity which covers a multitude of sins.

Darrel: So many rules and regs; when do you people even have the time for reading and studying God's actual Word? You don't need to answer that; it was rhetorical.

Bobby: Okay, what tradition's next?

Darrel: Let's take up the celibacy next. The tradition of requiring celibacy for priests, of course, is not biblically supported. Jesus imposed no such rule, nor did any of the apostles. Nonetheless, the Catholic Church has clung to this ridiculous and harmful requirement ever since Pope Boniface VII, decided that celibacy should be a requirement for the priesthood in his decree in 1079. By the way, your church's "first pope," Peter, as you know, was a married man; isn't that ironic? There's no precedent for church leaders to be celibate. In 1 Timothy 3:2, 5, 12, Paul said that elders were to have a wife and children.

Bobby: Yes, it is a harmful requirement; in light of these sex scandals, I would think that celibacy may have something to do with the pedophilia of these bad priests.

Darrel: Yes, the requirement that priests remain celibate during their priesthood sets them up for the fall. Celibacy isn't normal, of course; the majority of men on the planet would not be willing to give up sex with a woman so it only stands to reason that people who want to be priests either have no interest in ever having sex with a woman or have an abnormal sex drive. Of course, that didn't stop some of the popes in church history, and, in these instances, the celibacy requirement resulted in some embarrassment to the church. As Luther once chided the pope in saying: "Do as we say, but don't do as we do!" When Emperor Louis of Bavaria deposed Pope John XXII for violating the celibacy requirement, the pope he appointed to replace him appeared one day with a wife. Over the centuries the Catholic Church has had nothing but problems enforcing this ridiculous requirement. The Bible does address the subject, but there is no verse in Scripture that makes celibacy a requirement for the priesthood.

Sonny: Hey, it's not as though Protestants haven't had any scandals!

Darrel: Two wrongs don't make a right. At least there's nothing in the Bible-believing Protestant doctrine that requires celibacy for ministers and sets church members up for such a fall.

Sonny: Scandals have always existed in the Catholic Church. We don't deny that. My point is that this should not cause us to lose hope in the Church, nor cause people to reject Christianity. God's mysterious plan requires the wheat and the weeds to exist side by side in the Church until the end of time. God's plan is that the Church is a net which catches fish of every kind, good and bad. God revealed this to us so that we will not get discouraged by the sinfulness of the Church's members. Chapter 13 of the book of Matthew supports this opinion.

John: But these people are your trusted, special, super-Christian leaders in your church institution; you believe their ordination is a sacrament just like baptism is.

Sonny: Eighty percent of pedophilia is linked to homosexuality. Most of the victims were male. Both are mental illnesses; we must show mercy as God shows mercy.

John: Extending mercy doesn't mean the church can cover it up, and that's what it has done; and God tells us that He will hold most accountable those people who are entrusted to teach the gospel truth. I pray that unbelievers won't judge the Christian religion by the bad acts of some who claim to be Christians but clearly are not; but that's a wishful hope.

Sonny: Let's get back to discussing the tradition, okay? Protestants are surprised to learn that even today celibacy is not the rule for all Catholic priests. In fact, for Eastern Rite Catholics, married priests are the norm, just as they are for Orthodox and Oriental Christians. That said, in the

Eastern churches, there have always been some restrictions on marriage and ordination. Although married men may become priests, unmarried priests may not marry and married priests, if widowed, may not remarry. Moreover, there is an ancient Eastern discipline of choosing bishops from the ranks of celibate monks, so their bishops are all unmarried. These variations and exceptions are permitted, and they prove that celibacy is not an unchangeable dogma but a disciplinary rule.

Darrel: When you say that bishops are chosen only from the ranks of celibate monks, that's the same as making celibacy a requirement for priesthood, right?

Bobby: What does the Bible have to say about celibacy?

Sonny: Of course we know that neither Paul nor Jesus had a wife. In Matthew 19:11-12, Jesus says that celibacy is a gift from God and whoever can bear it should bear it. He praises and recommends celibacy for full time ministers in the Church. Because celibacy is a gift from God, those who criticize the Church's practice of celibacy are actually criticizing God and this wonderful gift He bestows on His chosen ones. In Matthew 19:29, Jesus praises celibacy when it is practiced for the sake of His Kingdom. The Apostle Paul concurs as he states in 1 Corinthians 7:1, 27, 32-33 and 38.

Darrel: In advocating celibacy over marriage for his elders, Paul was voicing his own personal opinion. "I say this by way of concession, not of command. I wish that all were as I myself am. But each has his own special gift from God, one of one kind and one of another." Why do you suppose the Catholic Church made celibacy a disciplinary rule for its priests?

Sonny: Paul said that the unmarried man is free to focus more on God because he is not distracted by a wife and a family. That makes sense to me.

Darrel: What doesn't make sense is that a church that has been so intuitive in catering to man's natural instincts we talked about before, seemed to ignore one of the most important basic natural instincts we have, to engage in the sexual act with the opposite sex.

Sonny: But doesn't celibacy prove that we don't intentionally cater to man's basic instincts?

Darrel: Not when you cater to so many others. It only proves your church unintentionally missed this one instinct, that's all. It addressed the other instincts we talked about before, desiring our works to count, wanting a second chance, desiring order and authority and appealing to man's attraction to tradition, but it overlooked our natural hormonal sexual instinct and God's desire for us to populate the earth.

Sonny: As I say, celibacy is preferred by Christ and Paul for leaders in the Catholic Church. Celibacy is a gift; it is not unnatural or unbiblical; it is supported in Scripture, and is not something we came up with that unfortunately backfired on us.

John: Celibacy is not natural for any man; that is exactly why the requirement has created a position in the church that attracts people with very unnatural sexual desires.

History records incidences where priests who have violated their celibacy and either married or had illegitimate children (and many of them did over the centuries) were actually murdered by the Catholic Church. Of course, the practice of celibacy is not only violated by having sex with children, but the very act of pedophilia is of course an abhorrent, unconscionable sin. Yet, I will say that those priests who possess a true, saving faith in Christ, earnestly confess their sin and repent are forgiven.

Sonny: Yes. I might add that the Bible says that those who practice celibacy all their life and endure, like the eunuchs Isaiah refers to in Chapter 56:3-7, will have a special place in the kingdom of heaven.

I might also reiterate that the majority of our priests and bishops who practice celibacy are free to focus on the true teaching of God's Word.

Darrel: Sure, but, as usual, the few screw (pardon the pun) it up for the many. This is a damn mess and reflects very badly on Christianity, not just Catholicism. As trained representatives of the Catholic Church and the presumably the gospel, these priests who have received the gift of celibacy have a greater responsibility to teach the truth and to behave as Christians should behave than the rest of us do because they represent Christ. As John said before, the Bible states that they will suffer greatly for their indiscretions when they fail in their appointed task; and the Catholic Church's cover up reflects on the Church as a whole and portrays it as being dishonest; these leaders too will be held more accountable by God. They, of all people, should know this!

John: Good point, Darrel. I can understand how the sexual desire can trump reason, we see this happening all the time with politicians who destroy their entire career over some dalliance, but, for the life of me, I can't understand how the Catholic Church bishops don't understand the wrong of a cover up of this scandal. These people should know what the Bible says about this. In 1 Corinthians 5, Paul warns that immorality defiles the church and must be judged. "A little leaven leavens the whole lump." The church is to "put away from yourselves the evil person."

Peter: Right. That isn't the kind of behavior we would expect from someone who claims to be a Christian, much less from your Catholic Church leaders. It goes to credibility. A cover up serves as a very bad example to society.

John: Good point, Peter. There's a crisis in trust in our society in this day and age. My daughter opined that she just yearns for people in this day and age she can trust, whether it be a teacher, a coach, a parent, a babysitter, a boss, a step parent, a politician, a police office, a judge and yes, a priest. These pedophiles acted in a manner that betrayed that trust. This sinful act is bad enough in itself, but what is worse is the cover up. We expect those in authority over those who sin to accept accountability and responsibility for the actions of those who work for them. Slapping them on the wrist and sending them to another church just doesn't fit the crime. I thought Catholics were the experts on penance.

Darrel: I would only add that the Apostle Paul lectured the Corinthians on their attempt to ignore the apostasy in their church. Paul was a huge proponent of church discipline.

Bobby: Okay, so what's the next Catholic tradition you guys want to talk about?

Darrel: Let's talk about a related subject, the Catholic Church's position on contraception. As I understand it, the church has affirmed that the illicitness of contraception is an infallible doctrine, right?

Sonny: The Church has always taught the intrinsic evil of contraception because it is a martial act that is intentionally rendered unfruitful. Contraception is contrary to the good of the transmission of life, the procreative aspect of matrimony. It blocks the expression of true love that God intends for married partners to enjoy and denies the sovereign role of God in the transmission of human life.

Darrel: That mantra sounds like it came right out of your catechism, Sonny.

Sonny: It came from our *Vademecum for Confessors*. It was reaffirmed by Pope Paul VI in his "Humanae Vitae" pronouncement in 1968 in response to the development of the birth control pill.

Darrel: Of course you must know there is no biblical basis for this position, right?

Sonny: There's the story of Onan in Genesis 38 where God strikes him dead because he spilled his semen on the ground. That story demonstrates that God supports intercourse only to procreate and that's why we are against artificial birth control.

Darrel: The story can (and should) be interpreted literally as God's retribution for Onan being evil in disobeying a direct order from him in being unwilling to father a child by his widowed sister-in-law. Sexual intercourse between a man and a wife need not always be for the purpose of procreation either. God could have designed sex to suit just this one purpose, but he made it pleasurable. The bottom line is that there is no clear biblical reference that supports Catholic opposition to birth control.

Sonny: There doesn't need to be biblical support, Darrel. As I just said, the prohibition of contraception is a Church tradition which was instituted by the bishops. Apparently, some of your own respected Protestant leaders agree with our stand on this issue. Several of your Protestant denominations were opposed to it until 1930. Martin Luther himself called birth control "a most disgraceful sin, far more atrocious than incest and adultery." John Calvin was also opposed to birth control calling it an "unchastity, yes a sodomitic sin." He said that "The voluntary spilling of semen outside of intercourse between man and woman is a monstrous thing. Deliberately to withdraw from coitus in order that semen many fall to the ground is doubly monstrous. For tis is to extinguish the hope of the race and to kill before he is born the hoped-for offspring."

Darrel: You sure seem to respect Luther and Calvin when you can use their quotes to support your positon, Sonny; but neither Calvin nor Luther cited any biblical references either so it seems they bought into your tradition. And I might add that what you said before about your church's official reference to the "sovereign role of God" is used when you need to make your point even though you seem to downplay his absolute sovereignty in the role of salvation by coming up with this grace plus works doctrine of yours.

And, by the way, as Daniel mentioned before, many Catholics are leaving the church because of its unreasonable stand on this issue of birth control, and those that stay ignore the church's opposition. This opposition also has disastrous economic affects because people have unwanted children and spread sexual disease like AIDS.

Peter: Good point. Like celibacy, the Catholic Church's opposition to contraception just doesn't make any sense unless of course, you see the obvious benefit to church growth through birth of more folks who will become church members. When birth control is not used, obviously this results in a higher birth rate, and, like Mormon and Muslim families, Catholic families are larger. This opposition to birth control results in a geometric growth of little into big, tithing Catholics which of course emboldens the church organization through increasing membership; but, this isn't good for many Catholics who can't afford more children; birth control can reduce poverty.

It seems most Catholics have finally figured this out based on what Darrel just said. Both this ridiculous requirement of celibacy and this unreasonable opposition to birth control have caused unwanted consequences. In going against the grain of our natural instinct, celibacy has created an environment to attract some folks who have a sexual problem; opposition to birth control limits a Catholic to one option for preventing an unwanted child: abortion, a practice the Catholic Church also opposes of course. What a quandary the Catholic Church leaves its followers in: They're told that having no sex is a virtue; that birth control is a sin, so more pregnancies occur, but abortion is a sin. The choice is to either be celibate like your priests and have no children or get married and have an unlimited number of children you may or may not be able to afford. Ironically, the Catholic stand on artificial birth control actually promotes abortion as the only viable option left to avoid the birth of an unwanted child; and, of course, adoption is out because that might mean the kid wouldn't be raised a Catholic. What a frickin' dilemma, eh? No wonder Catholics are leaving in droves.

Darrel: Right; and I take your point regarding the Catholic Church's motive to oppose birth control to focus on its growth. After all, we know that tradition, what your parents believe, is the most influential source of what the child ends up believing. Muslims and Mormons are certainly aware of how this formula works. In the next 30 years, Islam will top Christianity in membership mostly because of their higher birth rate.

Bobby: Okay, so now what's the next Catholic Church tradition you want to discuss?

John: I know we've already talked about the Catholic sacrament of penance, but they recognize six others and I'd like to discuss all of them in more depth, one by one. As we know, the majority of Protestant denominations recognize only two sacraments, Baptism and the Last Supper or Holy Communion. Episcopalians, like the Roman Catholics, recognize seven of them: Baptism and Holy Communion, which they call the Eucharist, Confirmation, Reconciliation (their name for Penance), Anointing of the sick or Last Rites, Marriage, and Holy Orders which they also refer to as Ordination. I should note here that Episcopalians don't place as much emphasis on penance as Catholics do.

Bobby: So, what's wrong with recognizing these other five ceremonies as being sacraments?

John: You hit the nail on the head, Bobby, when you called them ceremonies, or, as Darrel called them before, rites. That's really what they are. They are not sacraments by the Bible's definition: A sacrament is an outward sign instituted by God to convey an inward or spiritual grace. It must be initiated by Christ, connect with an earthly element (water in Baptism, bread and wine in Holy Communion), and involve forgiveness. Only two meet these criteria: Baptism and Holy Communion. Lutherans and most other Christian denominations recognize them as being a means of God's grace in addition to His Word. So, the sacraments obviously have great significance in Christianity, and we take them very seriously, as we should.

There is no biblical support for these five additional "sacraments" the Catholic Church to be considered sacraments. Protestants don't believe in just arbitrarily labeling some church ceremony traditionally observed by Christians in order to give it a special power and emphasis with believers that the Bible does not intend for it to be given. The addition of five sacraments was another tradition that Luther objected to. He believed a sacrament must be instituted by Christ, not invented by the Church, and indeed the Bible only refers to baptism and the Last Supper or Holy Communion as being instituted by God. So these other five "sacraments," recognized by the Catholic Church in the late 13th century are indeed merely religious procedures promoted to the importance of an actual sacrament. As with the rest of the Roman Catholic tradition, there was no biblical support for adding these as sacraments.

Sonny: The Church has organized the seven sacraments into three categories.

Darrel: More Catholic categories, why am I not surprised?

Sonny: The first category, the sacraments of initiation, consists of baptism and the Eucharist. The second category, the sacraments of healing, consists of penance and healing of the sick. The last category, the sacraments of service, consists of marriage and ordination of clergy. We believe the sacraments are instituted by Christ as a way He could be present to His people even after His Ascension into Heaven. They are not only signs of His presence, they are celebrations of our continual journey and relationship with God's teachings through our Church to help us live out His Word and demonstrate our devotion to Him. We believe the sacraments point to and are channels of God's grace, which we define as God's free gift of His presence, His help, and His salvation.

Darrel: God's salvation? Do Catholics believe these sacraments are necessary for our salvation?

Sonny: You could say that the normative way we receive the gift of salvation is through the seven sacraments, beginning with baptism. Sacraments are sensible signs Christ instituted to confer grace. The sacraments are made possible, first of all, by God becoming man in Jesus, and their saving effectiveness is derived from Jesus'one paschal sacrifice, that is his passion, death, resurrection and ascension. Jesus established the Catholic Church as His instrument of salvation through which the faithful are able to receive the sacraments. You could say that the sacraments are entrusted to the Church. Christ gave the sacraments to the Church so that the Church could dispense them to the faithful. They dispense life. Those who receive the sacraments actually share in the divine life of God. His presence enters into their souls. He helps them to live the Christian life, and He saves them so they may reach eternal life.

Darrel: As I recall from what you said before, you said the sacraments sanctify, but are you saying now that they also justify? God makes you holy and saves you through the sacraments? God makes believers holy only through the Catholic Church? That's of course what you're implying.

Sonny: I'm not implying anything; I'm stating the truth. I'm say that the sacraments are instruments of salvation; they are a requirement for salvation.

Darrel: And, as you said, they can only be administered through your church, right?

Sonny: That is correct.

Ray: In order to be a real, true Christian, a person must be a baptized a Roman Catholic!

Darrel: So, as you said before, my baptism in a Protestant church doesn't count for salvation, right?

Sonny: Yes and no; it's complicated. It's up to God whether you are saved or not; for us, baptism represents more than our salvation. Our baptism relates to our profound union with the living Lord rather than simply being saved or justified by a personal belief in Christ.

Darrel: It really isn't that complicated, Sonny. I like your response. Our baptism does indeed relate to our union with Christ rather than just being considered a necessity for salvation.

John: Of all their sacraments, I would think that our Catholic brothers and sisters in Christ would at least rate baptism and Holy Communion as the most important because there is absolutely no doubt from Scripture that these were the sacraments Christ actually mandated in person, and I think all of us Christians can agree that baptism is a legitimate, biblically supported sacrament. So then, let's start by discussing baptism.

Sonny: Of course. The sacrament of baptism takes the believer from the simple repentance, belief and profession of faith into a mysterious identification with Christ, in which He is the vine, and we are the branches, in which we die with Him so that we might rise to new life. Baptism is not simply the addition of a meaningful symbol to the act of faith: It's an action which takes the believer's whole body, soul, and spirit into a new relationship with God. As Paul says in Galatians 3:27, we are "being clothed with Christ."

Bobby: But what happens to people who, for various reasons, can't be baptized?

Sonny: There are two types of baptism that apply in this case: Baptism of blood which applies to the thief on the cross and baptism of desire which applies to a profession of faith for people who have no access to water.

Peter: No access to water? You're kidding, right? Now I've heard everything!

Darrel: No, you haven't, Peter. He's just getting started. They have an answer for everything because they know their followers expect them as their sole religious authority to have all the answers. Remember the CCC, the Catholic Claims Crutch, is 752 pages long.

Peter: I'm still confused. Do Catholics believe baptism is necessary for salvation or not?

Sonny: In John 3:3-5, Jesus says that "No one can enter the kingdom of heaven unless he is born of water and the Spirit." From the earliest days of the Church, this passage has been understood to refer to baptism. Protestants of course will tell you that the water refers to the amniotic fluid of the mother's womb which breaks at the point of physical birth.

John: In its context, this more literal interpretation could very well be a correct understanding. After all, the previous verses referred to a man entering again into his mother's womb. That said, as a member of a Lutheran church, I was instructed that baptism is indeed necessary for our salvation. Luther wrote, "Baptism is no human plaything but is instituted by God himself. Moreover, it is solemnly and strictly commanded that we must be baptized or we shall not be saved. We are not to regard it as an indifferent matter." He goes on to say, "It is of the greatest importance that we regard baptism as excellent, glorious, and exalted." As a Calvinist though, I do not subscribe to Luther's interpretation because it raises more questions than it answers. What about those folks who cannot, for whatever reason, be baptized? What about the millions of people who have been baptized yet clearly are not believers? I think that connecting baptism with salvation is adiaphora.

Sonny: John's gospel is the most sacramental, and that means it's most credible on this subject of the meaning and necessity of baptism. Passages like John 3:3-5 are examples of how Christ's life and teachings are put together in such a way as to connect with, and support, the sacramental life of the early Church. In the verses that immediately follow Christ's words that one must be "born again of water and the Spirit," Jesus talks about "men loving darkness rather than light because their deeds are evil" and that whoever "lives by the truth comes to the light. The references to light point to the other main symbol of the baptismal ceremony, the lighted candle.

Bobby: I may not be the sharpest tool in the box so excuse my confusion about what light and darkness have to do with water and the sacramental life of the early church. I can't quite connect the dots here.

Darrel: That's' because the dots are scattered all over the page, Bobby. There may be some mystical connection which exists only in our Catholic friend's mind here, or Luther's spin off, but, I think it's another one of their attempts to support their church's traditions by symbolically interpreting Bible verses that should normally be taken literally.

Bobby: Does anyone have anything more to say about baptism? What can we conclude? Does it guarantee salvation? Obviously not. As John said, many people have been baptized and have not exhibited the behavior of a saved person, right?

Darrel: Correct. There is much more to salvation than going through some sacramental ritual.

Bobby: How is the sacrament administered in each of your denominations?

Sonny: We believe that when a person is baptized, God's saving grace, His very presence, enters into the human soul. The essential rite of baptism is very simple. The person celebrating the sacrament (usually a priest) says "I baptize you in the Name of the Father, and of the Son, and of the Holy Spirit while pouring water over the head of the person receiving the sacrament or dipping the person in water. We refer to this practice as triple immersion. As I said before, for us Catholics, baptism is the sacrament of salvation and the door to all other sacraments.

Bobby: Yeah, but I'm with what Peter said; I'm still confused. Is baptism necessary for salvation? I recall some verse in Romans for support of this belief.

Darrel: I think you may be referring to Romans 6:3, 4. "Do you not know that all of us who have been baptized into Christ Jesus were baptized into his death? We were buried therefore with him by baptism into death, in order that, just as Christ was raised from the dead by the glory of the Father, we too might walk in newness of life."

Bobby: Yeah, that one. Isn't Paul saying baptism saves?

John: It sounds that way, but Paul has clearly stated to us in Ephesians and other letters that God's grace is the only requirement for our salvation so, since God does not contradict Himself, we cannot assume this particular verse in Romans means baptism is a requirement of salvation. That said, it is obvious there is a sacramental union or spiritual relationship between the sign of the thing and the thing it stands for. When a sacrament is properly administered, there is a real and effectual promise attached to it. The effect that will be derived from the act will be only from God. This is not to say that baptism removes sin or conveys salvation, but it is to say that there is some spiritual advantage to being baptized. Similarly, there is a spiritual advantage to participating in the Lord's Supper. More than merely signifying something, baptism actually conveys something.

Because of the sacramental nature of baptism and the Lord's Supper, Reformed churches traditionally try to ensure that they are properly administered. This means that, based on the Biblical example, only church officials (pastors and elders) may administer the sacraments. They strive to ensure that only those who biblically qualify for them are included. Improper administration of the sacraments is considered to be blasphemous.

Daniel: What you just said, John, could be construed, in one sense, to mean that baptism does save; but it isn't the baptism by water in the visible church; it's the baptism we receive from the Holy Spirit in the invisible church.

Ray: There is no invisible church; there is only one visible Catholic Church!

John: So again, you're refuting what Saint Augustine told you.

Daniel: Don't take offence, Ray and Sonny, but it seems to me you guys just don't want to understand this concept of an invisible church because you see it as somehow denigrating the importance of your church. We've been through this discussion before, right?

Peter: You guys shouldn't be surprised at Ray's typical response. His premise from the get-go is that his church is like God; it can do no wrong, even though sinners govern the church. For this reason, as an objective observer, I just can't see how anyone could trust a church and delegate that much power to it as their sole authority of truth.

Darrel: Good point, Pete. The Catholic Church indeed does seem to always have the last word even over the word of your God. You may recall that Sonny has admitted that his church acts as a substitute for God himself, right?

Look, Catholic people, no one but you Catholics gives your church this authority. We believe your relationship with your church borders on being worshipful, and we know that the worship of a church, any church, is a violation of God's second commandment to have no other gods before him. The strength of your committed belief is undoubtedly why your minds appear to remain closed to whatever opinions we've presented in these discussions. If you can't open your mind to what we Protestants believe and understand our reason for our belief and at least consider what we have to say, why are you still attending these discussions? Did you really think you could just barge into an austute group like this and bully us into believing what you believe?

Sonny: I had hoped you Protestant people would listen to what I have had to say.

John: I think we all have been very good listeners, Sonny; God requires that of us. He has given us each the faith to believe in Jesus Christ, and we of course share that belief with you Catholics. We do object to what we see as your church denigrating God's sovereignty and His Word because we consider His Word to be our only source of His truth.

Ray: The Bible has its weaknesses, and it cannot save; only the Church can save.

Darrel: Baptism saves, the Catholic Church saves; according to your magisterium. God's unmerited favor isn't enough.

Sonny: The Church is a necessary aspect to our salvation in its administration of the sacraments and through obedience to its traditions. The Church is the truth.

John: We can only trust the Word of God to be the truth. I know you Catholics say that no one can understand the Word without your church as interpreter, but, as we've demonstrated, the Bible really isn't that hard to understand if we take it normally and not try to make it say what we want it to say to us; and God's plan of salvation, with His grace as the only driving force behind our salvation, isn't difficult to understand either. The Bible's message of truth is consistent as it relates the story of how God performs for His people throughout the history of His chosen people in patiently restoring the Jews through each of His covenants with them, finally culminating in the coming of Jesus Christ to fulfill His plan of salvation. No other source of truth is necessary. Augustine recognized this, why can't you people?

So, that said, I'll tell you what I think Romans 6:3, 4 really means in the normative sense. In previous verses in Romans and in some of his other letters, Paul has told us our baptism is a ceremonial washing, a sign from God which signifies inward cleansing and remission of sins. It signifies our union with Christ in His death, burial, and resurrection. This is what is explained to us when we read further on in this chapter of Romans. R. C. Sproul explains that baptism signifies our triune God's control and direction for our lives.

Bobby: Speaking of ceremonial washing, don't Baptists believe that, to be significant, baptism must be by total immersion?

John: Yes, but again, we must look to Scripture for support, and there is none. It's, by definition, adiaphora. Sproul tells us "No prescription of a particular mode of baptism can be found in the New Testament. The command of baptism may be fulfilled by immersion, dipping, or sprinkling; all three modes satisfy the meaning of the Greek verb *baptizo* and the symbolic requirement of passing under, and emerging from, cleansing water."

Sonny: Okay, back to what I was saying about how baptism saves. In John 3:5, Christ Himself tells us "I tell you the truth, no one can enter the kingdom of God unless he is born of water and the Spirit."

John: Yes, some Christian denominations also point to this verse to support their belief that baptism is required for salvation, but we must remember that Christ is speaking to Nicodemus here and any reference to baptism would obviously have been meaningless to him because the practice of Christian baptism hadn't even been established yet. So then, the "water" really can't be a reference to the act of baptism. But, more importantly, for the same reason I gave when refuting the use of Romans 6:3,4 as support for the belief that baptism is a requirement for salvation, John 3:5 really can't be used either. As I say, there are so many other verses in the New Testament which very clearly state that our actions cannot save us (including the act of baptism). Over and over again the apostles tell us only God's grace saves us and no action on our part is required. And, as I've already said, our triune God doesn't change His mind nor contradict Himself. God the Son doesn't tell us we must be baptized to be saved in John 3:5, and then later on, God the Father tells Paul He's changed His mind and only His grace is necessary for salvation and that baptism now means something else.

I'll tell you what Dr. Sproul believes John 3:5 means, and I agree with him. Sproul said that there are several explanations for what John 3:5 means. Some say the "water" refers to the release of fluid that accompanies our physical birth, and that Christ may be contrasting our natural birth to our spiritual birth. Dr. Ryrie also lists this as one of the possible explanations of this verse. Personally, I think this interpretation has some merit because in the very next verse, John 3:6, Jesus says "Flesh gives birth to flesh, but the Spirit gives birth to spirit," and He thus seems to be referring to us being born the first time by water and the second time by the Spirit. Sproul adds that Christ could also be referring to the Old Testament connection between "water" and "Spirit" which expresses the pouring out of God's Spirit in the end times. He concluded by saying this is the most probably explanation.

Ray: That's your opinion.

John: Most of what we know is based on someone else's opinion, Ray. We Protestants of course have more Christian liberty then you Catholics do and find that discussion among Christians like we're having here is a more effective way to learn the truth than having some authority express its opinion in pontificating its man-made dogma.

Sonny: But what about 1 Peter 3:21? This verse tells us that baptism now saves us, not the removal of dirt from the flesh, but an appeal to God for a good conscience through the resurrection of Jesus Christ. How do we answer someone when they point to these verses to prove their belief that baptism must be administered to ensure our salvation? Isn't that verse saying that baptism actually saves people? I genuinely want to know the answer.

John: Yes, that's what this verse seems to be saying. In fact, Dr. Sproul called this verse a "startling statement." But, as I've said before, because we know that God cannot contradict Himself, we must turn to those verses in the Bible which most clearly state we cannot save ourselves by our own works and that includes being baptized. So then, keeping this premise in mind, Sproul states Peter must only be emphasizing the close relationship between the sign and the reality it signifies. "Noah's physical salvation through the waters of the Flood prefigured the waters of baptism and the salvation they signify. Baptism symbolizes judgment on sin in the death of Christ and then also renewal of life. The floodwaters were judgment to the wicked and at the same time physical salvation for the just, Noah and his family." I agree with Dr. Ryrie when he interprets this verse to be saying that "though water itself cannot save, baptism with water is the vivid symbol of the changed life of one who has a conscience at peace with God through faith in Christ." I think we just have to leave it at that, and, in fact, most denominations do.

Bobby: Based on my recollection of what Luther said about baptism, it would seem he agreed with the Catholic Church interpretation: people must be baptized to be saved.

John: Yes, Luther actually agreed with many of the beliefs and practices of his former Roman Catholic Church, and this was one of them. He believed the grace of baptismal regeneration and justification could be lost. Augustine and Aquinas also believed this. Theologian Jaroslav Pelikan tells us that "Where he (Luther) differed was on the matter of assurance, being more confident that the Catholic tradition of his time that the believer could enjoy great certitude of his present state of grace. Whether the believer, now in a state of grace, would remain in grace to the end was for Luther an open question. On the one hand, so far as God is concerned, Luther believed that the heavenly Father desired the believer's eternal salvation in Christ. Nevertheless, from the believers' side, it's possible to turn aside from the grace of God and be lost, even after the pilgrimage has begun. Consequently, the believer must always take heed lest he fall. Based on my understanding of Article 12 of the Augsburg Confession of 1530, final apostasy is a genuine possibility for the baptized and justified believer.

On the other hand, while the contents of God's eternal decree of election are known infallibly only to God, the believer, by focusing on Jesus Christ as preached in the gospel and presented by the promises of Scripture, can find 'sweet consolation' in 'this most wholesome doctrine' of predestination,' according to the Formula of Concord of 1584. Through present and lively faith in the Christ of the gospel, >we are rendered certain that by mere grace, without any merit of our own, we are chosen in Christ to eternal life, and that no one can pluck us out of his hands.' There is paradox, then, in the Lutheran understanding of final perseverance. While the matter is theoretically uncertain, for a believer it can become existentially certain, to the extent that the believer maintains unwavering faith in the promises of the gospel and so grows in confidence that he has in fact been included in God's gracious election to salvation."

This is not to say that baptism isn't important. Scripture tells us baptism is a sacrament, a means of God's grace. This is what Lutherans stress, but that is what Presbyterians believe also. R. C. Sproul, a Presbyterian, tells us that while there's no effectual connection between baptism and regeneration, and no one who's baptized is automatically regenerated; there is a biblically supported, theological connection where the Lord communicates through baptism His promise of regeneration. This regeneration occurs in God's timing and He is certainly not obligated to regenerate us the moment we're baptized. Sproul tells us "Baptism, as the new covenant analogue to circumcision, is the sign and seal of the righteousness we enjoy only by faith." Paul tells us this in Romans 4:6 and Colossians 2:11-12. "This sacrament is God's visible confirmation to us that He wishes us clean of the filth of sin when we believe. Just as an ancient seal made with a signet ring shows a letter's origin, so baptism shows the origin of the cleansing we enjoy in regeneration and faith. By baptism, God tells us that He is the one who wishes us clean. He is the one that buries us and raises us with Christ, and He is the source of regeneration and faith, which realities are invisible and occur when He sees fit."

Bobby: We don't have time to take up the next sacrament, the Eucharist, so we're adjourned.

Week Nine

Bobby: Okay, let's talk about Holy Communion, or as Catholics refer to it, the Eucharist.

Sonny: The Mass is the Eucharist, and, as we discussed before, we believe that the Mass is exactly the same sacrifice that Jesus Christ offered on the Cross at Calvary. The priest or bishop is understood to act *in persona Christi*, as he imitates the words and gestures of Jesus Christ at the Last Supper. We believe that those who partake in the Eucharist receive the real Body, Blood, Soul, and Divinity of Jesus Christ in what appears to be bread and wine, but has actually been miraculously changed into Christ's body and blood by the priest. The Eucharist is critical for us because it directly connects us to Christ. As we have also said before, we Catholics prioritize our connection with Christ and recognize that only in observing the Eucharist in Mass can you fully experience your connection with Christ.

Darrel: You describe what I would call a tactile relationship with Christ; you physically connect with him through the elements. Your prideful implication that this can only be experienced through what theologians refer to as "transubstantiation" is not true because transubstantiation is not biblically supported. We alluded to this before.

It's just another example of the method the Catholic Church uses to unnecessarily exaggerate the gospel to enhance the connection with Christ through the co-dependency with the church. By the way, did you know that a recent Pew Poll indicated only half the Catholics surveyed even understand the process of transubstantiation? That makes an earlier point I made about the typical Catholic's ignorance of what their church believes.

Sonny: Protestants denigrate the sacrament in believing it's only a symbol. We take John 6:53 literally. Christ says it's His flesh that is being offered in the sacrament.

John: It would seem that you Catholics certainly pick and choose what you want to take in the literal sense, and what you believe is symbolic. You may recall when we talked about what Christ meant in Matthew 5:26 when He obviously meant just what He said about a criminal not being released until he has paid the last penny; He wasn't symbolically referring to purgatory. And when you wanted to presume the story of Onan in Genesis 38 was symbolic to provide support for your opposition to birth control, that was not the literal way most people would take this story; but now you want to take John 6:53 literally to support transubstantiation, and most people would take this verse symbolically because Christ can't obviously be referring to cannibalism, right? In Matthew 26:29 where Christ himself called the drink He shared with them the "fruit of the vine." Jesus said, "I say to you, I will not drink of this fruit of the vine from now on until that day when I drink it new with you in My Father's kingdom." Here we see that Jesus regarded the wine as merely a symbol of his blood, and He is saying He is looking forward to drinking it with His disciples in His Father's kingdom. There is nothing in what Christ said that substantiates this belief in transubstantiation.

Remember what we said about interpreting the Bible normally? It is normal to take these verses symbolically. That doesn't mean we believe that the elements are merely a symbol in the sense that they are only a commemorative celebration of the Last Supper; the Bible does not teach that. Lutherans believe that Christ is truly present in a unique and personal way; when the elements are administered, He is in our presence, but we surely don't need to believe that the elements are actually being chemically changed into the body and blood of Christ to relate to Him in what I referred to before as a tactile connection. I don't need to visualize that the wine is His actual blood and the wafer His actual flesh. When Protestant lips touch the wafer, we should visualize Christ is physically present or at the very least spiritually present; I am touching his body, and my tongue tastes His blood when I drink the wine. This visualization is sufficient for me to focus on being forgiven and express my gratitude in participating in Holy Communion. After all, Eucharist means "thanksgiving." The Catholic Church takes John 6:53-54 literally to mean Christ is telling us to eat His flesh and drink His blood to abide in Him; this practice seems very weird and even ridiculous to anyone but a Catholic. The CC also teaches that the Eucharist is offered in the sacrifice of the Mass as a propitiation for sins which is the opposite of everything Christ told His disciples about Himself. It means that every time the Mass is celebrated, Christ's substitutionary work, His sacrifice on the cross as reparation and appeasement for our sin is offered again and again. The flesh and blood of Christ were sacrificed once and for all on the cross and now the flesh and blood God of Calvary dwells within us. We partake of that flesh and blood as our spiritual food and drink as our spirits are restored and our minds are renewed. We approach Christ in Holy Communion the same way the woman approached Him when he was dining with the Pharisee; we touch Him in the same way she touched His feet. We thus find forgiveness, healing, strength and joy as God expresses His means of grace to us. Does what I just said sound like we Protestants are somehow missing out on an experience only you Catholics can understand? That's a rhetorical question, Ray.

Darrel: The elements need not be transformed by some priest into the body and blood of Christ, they are sanctified by the Word of God. That's what Augustine said. "You ought to know what you have received, what you are going to receive, and what you ought to receive daily. That Bread which you see on the altar, *having been sanctified by the Word of God,* is the Body of Christ. The chalice, or rather, what is in that chalice, having been sanctified by the word of God, is the Blood of Christ."

Why would any Christian not be satisfied with this explanation? Why would any church want to make something more of this sacrament than Augustine described? What's the point of transubstantiation? I'll answer my own question. The point of this practice is to dramatize the sacrament, to make it more visible to those who need that assistance to connect with Christ. The Catholic Church wants to convey that there is some sort of mystical thing going on here, and, from my conversations with Catholics, they really buy into that. One of these guys challenged me to undergo the Catholic experience of worship by spending some time inside the Church observing the trappings of the brass Tabernacle and a lit red Sanctuary candle where the Eucharistic presence of Christ resides, and just ask myself if God would give me a sign that this belief is true. He went on to say that the idea is to just quietly sit and let God minister to me. Devotions are to be recited and I was to recall Christ saying "Ask and you shall receive, seek and you will find, knock and it will be open to you." He concluded by saying that this experience would enable me to make an honest decision of conviction. Now, I'm not sure what he believed a fellow Christian needed to be convicted of, but I assume I was to be as convicted as he was of the infallibility of the Catholic Church as my sole authority to understanding God's Word and sole path to salvation.

So then, we can see how Catholicism appeals to the emotions, as Mormonism and tent evangelism does, and this can be a powerful tool God does utilize in drawing the elect to him, but it can also be utilized by Satan to distract us from knowing the truth. From a personal perspective, I was engaged to a Catholic girl and had actually considered Catholicism many years ago. The priest I talked to pushed the history of course, but he played to my emotions in stressing the value of the Eucharist and how once I understood its meaning, I would join the Catholic Church and never leave it, not because the Church binds me to it, but because my heart wouldn't let me leave. But reason is more important to me than emotion, and I found Catholic theology to be intellectually indefensible, full of superstition that has absolutely no grounding in the Bible or in reason. I didn't marry the girl and have never looked back.

Daniel: I know of some Protestants who have actually converted to Catholicism because they were sold on transubstantiation so it seems to be an effective evangelical tool for them. They believe the Eucharist represents a miracle and gives them a big emotional lift when they participate in this sacrament. As John said before, we Protestants don't need to believe the bread and wine are actually physically changed for us to experience a connection with Christ. Maybe one of you Catholics can tell me why you people insist that transubstantiation is the only way to understand the sacrament of Holy Communion.

Our pastors administer Holy Communion by repeating Christ's words to His disciples at the Last Supper, but this practice is to remind us of what the sacrament is doing for us, not going through the whole process of what was to happen the next day when Christ was crucified by pretending to change bread into flesh and wine into blood. Personally, I don't see the point of understanding the sacrament the way Catholics seem to understand it when Hebrews 7:27 clearly states that Christ's sacrifice was a one-time event.

Sonny: At the actual last supper, Christ provided support for transubstantiation; that's why we do it the way we do it. We do it because it's the truth.

Darrel: We've already questioned why anyone but some indoctrinated soul would take John 6:53 literally. Are you saying you really believe the priest performs a miracle in chemically changing bread into flesh, a carbohydrate into a protein?

Sonny: That's right. Of course, it requires infusion of power from Christ, the High Priest.

Darrel: But you're inferring the priest actually performs the miracle through some special power God has given to him. Your priests get to play God, right? This concept is consistent with your church's claim to be Christ. By the way, is it true that, at one time in your history, the priest was the only person who could even take communion?

Sonny: Yes. The Catholic Church forbade the cup to the laity when it instituted the Eucharist in the Council of Constance in 1414. But now all Catholics who have not committed a mortal sin can participate in the Eucharist.

Darrel: More unraveling revelation, I suppose. Someone in your leadership must have read the Bible and discovered that God commands all believers to partake of the elements to celebrate the Lord's Supper; and that the Bible makes no mention of the procedure you Catholics initiated in 1414. First Corinthians 10:16 makes the point that the cup of thanksgiving and the bread represent a participation in the blood and body of Christ for all believers. In relating the story of the Last Supper, Matthew 26:26, 27, we learn that Jesus tells His disciples to "'take and eat; this is my body. Then he took the cup, gave thanks and <u>offered it to them</u>, saying, 'Drink from it, <u>all of you</u>.'"

Daniel: You say only Catholics who have not committed a mortal sin (like not participating in Penance, another of your sacraments) can take communion. I won't get into the ramifications of that rule, but I will say that many Protestant churches place a limit on participation in Holy Communion as well. It is called close communion.

Sonny: Yes. Only members in good standing can participate in the Eucharist.

Darrel: Personally, in theory, it's the only way to practice this sacrament, but in reality, I don't like a close or closed communion. Paul said in 1 Corinthians 10:17, "Because there is one bread, we who are many are one body, for all of us share that one bread. To me, "body" means all believers, not just Lutherans or Catholics. It's not necessary or appropriate for any Christian denomination to deny communion to a fellow Christian based on what the church presumes the participant believes about its significance; but, that's just me.

John: You both should know that in the not-too-distant past, most churches practiced some form of close communion, and the majority of Christian churches still do. These pastors of these churches understand they are obligated to explain to the congregation their job is to fence the table whenever the Lord's Supper is celebrated. To Lutherans, particularly WELS Lutherans, this means no one who isn't a member of our church or another WELS church can take Holy Communion with us. To Baptists, it means anyone who hasn't received an adult baptism. To most other churches, it means the pastor should warn people that they should not take Holy Communion if they aren't believers or if they're under discipline from a gospel-believing church and have been barred from Holy Communion. You can see there's a big difference here.

Peter: Ah, yes, the table is not for those wretched sinners.

John: Actually it is for us sinners; but only for those sinners who have trusted Christ alone for salvation and are following Him as His disciple in a life of repentance. Only repentant sinners are welcome at the table.

Daniel: Again, as in other aspects of Catholicism, the focus is on the means and not the ends. And transubstantiation seems like just another "yeah, but." *Yeah*, Christians are to participate in the sacrament, *but,* the Catholic Church is needed because a priest (whose ordination is in itself a sacrament) must first change the elements to make it legit.

I'm curious, Sonny, since the bread and the elements have been changed to represent Christ's physical presence, what happens to any elements that are left over after the sacrament has been performed? They can't just be thrown in the wastebasket, can they?

Sonny: No, of course not. It is up to the individual priests to use the left over elements to conduct other Eucharist services, last rites, etc.

Darrel: But, after all, since the wine is considered to actually have been changed into the blood of Christ, the priest must fear that Christ's consecrated blood might be spilled in the administration of the sacrament too. Look, man, it's obviously a real possibility the elements could be dropped, and certainly there's the possibility of waste as well.

Bobby: What do Lutherans think about this sacrament, John?

John: Lutherans believe that the sacrament of Holy Communion is one of two external ways God extends His grace to us, the other being the Word. Lutherans believe that Christ is physical present as the elements are administered; He's giving us His real body and blood in the sacrament. Theologians refer to this belief as consubstantiation.

Bobby: I never understood the difference between consubstantiation and transubstantiation. I guess I really don't see much difference between the two. Maybe this is because of Luther's Roman Catholic training.

John: Actually Luther's Catholic background is exactly why he opposed transubstantiation. Lutherans don't like that term "consubstantiation" because it can create confusion with the Catholic belief of transubstantiation. Luther didn't accept the concept that in the Mass, the invisible essence of the elements miraculously becomes Christ Himself, body and soul; he objected to the idea that a priest could perform such a miracle, and of course there's no physical evidence that he does somehow effect this change. Again, this is yet another tradition which is designed to support the authority of the CC. Does such a belief place these priests on the level of Christ? Of course not, but that's what this concept of transubstantiation is intended to portray.

Ray: There is physical evidence to prove transubstantiation. Throughout history, there have been reports of apparitions of angels cutting up a small child into pieces as the priest cut up the bread, bloodstained clothes and bright lights have also been reported when the Eucharist has been administered.

Darrel: That's it? These reported delusions are your evidence? Look, man, this transubstantiation is ridiculous, but consubstantiation doesn't make any sense either. I don't need to believe blood is being spilled or Christ is actually there at the altar with me to understand the incredible significance of this sacrament. Holy Communion must obviously be understood to be symbolic. Yes, Christ said the wine was his blood and the bread was his body, but he obviously meant for the elements to merely represent his body and blood. How could we understand them to actually be his body and blood? Believing that the bread is actually in some mystical way Christ's flesh is weird and unnecessary to practice the sacrament in a meaningful manner as described in Scripture; and believing, as the Lutherans believe, that the elements are not actually physically changed but still in some way represent Christ's actual physical presence is ridiculous and unnecessary. I say that because the sacrament still communicates the means of grace whether you believe Christ is physically present or is symbolically present. The end is still the same regardless of the means.

The Lutheran belief in consubstantiation (Christ is actually physically present in the administration of the elements) has no biblical support either, and it doesn't make sense for Jesus to physically be in two places at once. His spirit is everywhere, of course, but, if we understand, as Calvin did, that Jesus can't physically be in two places at once, at the right hand of God and physically present in the church as the elements are distributed, the only option we have left to us is to understand that Holy Communion represents the belief that the elements are merely symbolic of Christ's body and blood.

Bobby: Different strokes for different folks.

Ray: You're wrong, Bobby. The difference is critical to our belief.

Bobby: There are many, many man-made up ordinances in Catholicism that you people consider to be critical to your belief that clearly aren't; that's why I left the Catholic Church.

Daniel: As we surmised before, this transubstantiation is yet another example of the Catholic Church's emphasis on making itself useful in giving the church a special role to pay by requiring a priest to transform the elements into Christ's physical blood and body.

Look, it's obvious we all should feel Christ's presence in the sacrament in some way; and this is realized through the action of the Holy Spirit within every true believer. The ceremony is symbolic in nature for both of us because the body and blood are not literally being administered. In taking it a step further to emphasize the importance of the sacrament (and, of course, the importance of the church), the sacrament is dramatized to the extent that it misrepresents its purpose. As John said before, Christ is being crucified all over again, right? That's the major error in transubstantiation.

John: Right. Jesus said in John 19:30, "It is finished;" and in Hebrews 10:12, "But this man, after he had offered one sacrifice for sins forever, sat down on the right hand of God." Even a hint that this is what they mean in observing the sacrament in this way is of course where the Catholics get it entirely wrong. This may represent an essential difference between Protestants and Catholics because it deals with our connection with Christ. This is what we call Christology, and we believe that for us to correctly understand the significance of the Lord's Supper and how it relates to our connection to Christ, we must know our Christology, and Catholics seem to be weak in this area too.

Classic, orthodox Christology is defined for us by the Council of Chalcedon in 451 AD, and Dr. Sproul explains what they concluded. "In this union, the two natures (of Christ) are joined without mixture, confusion, separation, or division, each nature retaining its own attributes. The divine nature does not become semi-human and the human nature does not become semi-divine. Christ is truly God and truly man, not a divine human hybrid who is neither truly human nor truly God." We need to have an understanding of Christ's nature and purpose to understand how we are to celebrate the sacrament of Holy Communion.

Bobby: That makes sense to me, but what does this have to do with transubstantiation?

John: Despite Sonny's attempt to talk around explaining this transubstantiation in the Roman Catholic Church, the Last Supper is indeed a repetition of the sacrifice of Christ each time it's celebrated in Mass. As we've seen, no Protestant church believes this is the way it works. Christ was sacrificed once for atonement of our sins.

Dr. R. Scott Clark, in his book *Recovering the Reformed Confessions*, tells us that "The Roman Catholic doctrine of the memorial, propitiatory sacrifice of Christ in the supper is an idolatrous assault on the finished work of Christ."

Darrel: Just like some of the other Romanist traditions which illustrate its weak understanding of God's grace and sovereignty and only serve to misdirect Christians and even result in their condemnation. In fact, the Bible tells us in Hebrews 10:10 that we've all been made holy through the sacrifice of the body of Jesus Christ <u>once for all</u>. John mentioned Hebrews 9:24-28 before; it says the same thing.

Sonny: You people have it all wrong. Please allow me to explain. We believe that Christ's sacrifice was only offered once; we believe that to repeat His sacrifice would be to imply that the original offering was defective or somehow insufficient, like the animal sacrifices of the Old Testament that could never take away sin and had to be repeated often. We believe that Jesus' offering was perfect, efficacious and eternal. We invite Protestants to consider this eternal aspect. Jesus is eternally a priest, and a priest's very nature is to offer sacrifice. In the case of Christ, the eternal sacrifice that He offers is Himself. This is why He appears in Revelation as a lamb, standing as though He had been slain. He appears in heaven in the state of a victim, not because He still needs to suffer, but because for all eternity, He re-presents Himself to God appealing to the work of the cross, interceding for us, and bringing the graces of Calvary to us.

Darrel: So, I hear you saying that you believe Christ does appear each time the Eucharist is administered, but this doesn't signify he's being crucified again, it signifies he was slain but is now alive for eternity? Like much of your dogma, this is very confusing.

Sonny: This is why we have a Magisterium and a Catechism, Darrel. Your statement is correct. The Mass is a participation in this one heavenly offering. The risen Christ becomes present on the altar and offers Himself to God as a living sacrifice. Like the Mass, Christ's words at the Last Supper are words of sacrifice. "This is my body...this is my blood, given up for you." This doesn't mean the Mass is repeating the murder of Jesus, but it is taking part in what never ends: the offering of Christ to the Father for our sake. After all, if Calvary didn't get the job done, then the Mass won't help, right? It is precisely because the death of Christ was sufficient that the Mass is celebrated. It does not add to or take away from the work of Christ; it <u>is</u> the work of Christ.

Darrel: I'm still confused; it seems we're on the same page from what you say, but why does your church need to make the celebration of this sacrament more than either the Bible or the physical evidence can support? Why does it have to dramatize the celebration with this transubstantiation procedure where a priest performs a miracle?

Sonny: For emphasis, Darrel, for emphasis. For us, the Eucharist is the most important sacrament because it represents Christ's atoning sacrifice. The Eucharist and the Holy Mass renew, make alive at any time the innocent sacrifice of Jesus Christ, as He is "the Holy One of God" and thus the unique door of salvation for our sins. Christ is present in the Eucharist and allows us to participate in His Last Supper and His crucifixion at Calvary.

Darrel: But in stating that Christ is present in the Eucharist and his presence allows communicants to participate in the Last Supper and Christ's crucifixion at Calvary, aren't you saying you're crucifying Christ again each time the sacrament is administered?

Sonny: Let me explain it this way: The Eucharist also involves the sacrifice of the Catholic Church which is the Body of Christ and participates in the offering of her Head. With Him, she herself is offered whole and entire. That's why I say the Church is the work of Christ. The Church which is the Body of Christ participates in the offering of her Head. With him, she herself is offered whole and entire (CCC 1368). The Catechism also says that in the Eucharist, the same Christ who offered himself once in a bloody manner on the altar of the cross is contained and is offered in an unbloody manner (CCC 1367).

John: Okay, once we sort through this convoluted explanation, it seems you're telling us that the Eucharist represents the sacrifice of the Catholic Church, which in turn represents the Body of Christ, and, through the priest's changing the elements into Christ's body and blood, it then somehow represents the work of Christ." I assumed that this "work" is Christ's atoning sacrifice even though, as your catechism states, He is "offered in an unbloody manner." Then you claim this is not the same sacrifice as Christ being on the cross ("in a bloody manner"). You say that this divine sacrifice is celebrated in the Mass, but it's an unbloody sacrifice. Well, whether the sacrifice isn't supposed to be confused with Christ's sacrifice on the cross, it's still a sacrifice that is being represented at each and every celebration of the Eucharist, and, to me, that means Christ is being sacrificed over and over again regardless of how you try to rationalize what's happening.

Darrel: Yes, yes, I now see what you're saying, John. I agree.

John: While I don't believe the difference between the Lutheran concept of consubstantiation and the symbolic understanding the other Protestant churches have of Holy Communion represents an essential difference, for reasons we've already discussed, I do believe the difference is essential in how Protestants and Catholics understand the meaning of this sacrament. Protestants focus on God's forgiveness of our sin, Catholics focus on Christ's sacrifice which of course occurs each time the sacrament is administered.

Sonny: That's what I've been saying all along. It is an essential difference between us.

Bobby: John, as I recall, you've been a Presbyterian and a Lutheran, and attend a Baptist church here on the Island so why don't you tell us about the symbolic way all Protestants but Lutherans believe about this sacrament, okay?

John: I would say that, according to surveys, Protestants are actually unified in their belief that Jesus is truly present in the Eucharist, Bobby. Dr. Clark stated that Protestants of both branches of the Reformation, the Lutheran and the other Protestants believe that both sacraments are "gospel sacraments, visible representations of the good news that was being preached in Protestant pulpits. Both branches agreed that in the gospel, God declares sinners to be righteous by His free favor alone (*sola gratia*) and that salvation is received through faith alone (*sola fide*). They agreed that the sacraments are means of grace by which God strengthens and encourages believers. They agreed that baptism is Christ's sign and seal of the washing away of sins by grace alone, that it is to be administered to believers and to their children (though they disagreed about its efficacy), and that the supper is Christ's institution for nourishing the faith of professing believers."

Dr. Sproul tells us that while some people have accepted reformer Zwingli's interpretation that Christ is merely symbolized in the elements of communion, <u>most Protestants believe that Jesus is truly present when we celebrate this sacrament.</u> "Most theological traditions have held that Christ is really present in the Lord's Supper, but there is no consensus as to how He is present." Only Lutherans believe He is physically present. All other denominations believe He is spiritually present. Luke 22:19-20,

John 6:35 and 1 Corinthians 11:26 are some of the biblical verses cited to support this concept.

Lutherans say that Christ is truly present "in, with, and under the elements." It's a sacramental union with Christ which actually occurs when the elements of Holy Communion are administered. Calvin objected to Luther's interpretation because he said that Christ was seated at the right hand of God and physically could not be in two places at once. As I said before, this is the only difference of opinion Calvin had with Luther.

Darrel: Calvin was right. Christ cannot physically be present each time Holy Communion is administered. His spirit is present, not his body. Lutherans seem to be trying too hard to be unique, or maybe it's because Luther used to be a Catholic. Why should Lutherans believe they understand how Christ is present in the Communion any differently than the rest of us? What's with this "sacramental union"? What are you guys, mystics? Or is this like some kind of theopathy, an intense absorption in a religious experience?

John: I never thought of it that way, but, yes, I guess you could say Lutherans believe they have a direct encounter with God in our Holy Communion. It is like a mystical experience. It's all about how we understand we're connecting with God on a "one on one" basis. Like baptism, the Last Supper is God's means of grace. Lutherans recognize Christ is giving communicants His real body and blood so that's more of a direct connection than just looking at the elements as being symbols. When the elements are administered, the pastor tells us to "take and eat; this is the true body of our Lord and Savior Jesus Christ given into death for the forgiveness of your sins." And, just as with baptism, there's power in the gift of Holy Communion. In receiving Christ's true body and blood, we recognize anew our sins are forgiven. I appreciate the emphasis on a closer connection with Christ.

When I took the membership class in my Lutheran church, the pastor did point out Lutherans practiced Holy Communion differently than

I had practiced it as a Presbyterian, but he didn't talk about some "sacramental union." He merely stressed that we should understand the elements are to be seen as Christ's actual body and blood, not just a symbol of them. He mentioned John 6:53 and Matthew 26:26 as support for this belief and stated that Luther believed the only way to understand what Christ is saying is to believe He's actually referring to his physical body. Matthew 26:26 represents the Old Testament Passover meal which signifies the redemption of God's people. It therefore indicates how each disciple, and each of us, is forgiven for our sins. The pastor also quoted First Corinthians 11:26-29 to tell us who this sacrament is supposed to be for. As often as we eat the bread and drink from the cup, we are to understand we are proclaiming Christ's death, and whoever eats the bread or drinks the cup of the Lord in an unworthy manner will be guilty concerning the body and blood of the Lord. We are pledged to examine ourselves and exercise discernment in our understanding of the sacrament or bring judgment onto ourselves. We are to examine our state of mind and heart for Christ before taking the sacrament. We are to believe that, like baptism, the Last Supper is God's means of grace; and, just as with baptism, there's power in the gift of Holy Communion. This description seemed like what I believed as a Calvinist so I had no problem in agreeing to it and was accepted for membership. As I recall from my reading, the language Luther used in the Large Catechism in *The Book of Concord* is remarkably similar to the language Calvin used in his *Institutes.*

I think the point here is that it's obviously good to feel the presence of Christ through the Holy Spirit, as I said before, but, we must be careful not to expect some deep, mystical experience from the sacrament lest we have our attention diverted from completely understanding all of what the sacrament really means to us.

Darrel: Right; never be satisfied with the sizzle when the steak is to be eaten.

I'm familiar with Dr. Clark's book too; as I recall, he stated that the Reformed branch consulted the Bible in an effort to gain a true understanding of the significance of Christ's sacrifice for us. As we know, the Bible isn't always crystal clear in explaining certain aspects of our doctrine, and I think this is one of those instances. In one of his most important writings, entitled "On the Clarity and Certainty of the Word of God," Reformer Huldrych Zwingli opined that Scripture is clear but that doesn't mean everything in the Bible is abundantly and equally clear; it does mean the main gospel message is clear.

Clark believed Lutherans place a limit on their understanding of the meaning of the sacraments. He goes on to state "In contrast to the Lutheran tradition, the Reformed branch worked out a thorough understanding of the biblical covenants as the framework within which to understand the sacraments." Zwingli was a big influence here. He seemed to have the big picture in mind when he stated, "There is one covenant of grace in redemptive history, variously administered, in which God has promised to be Abraham's God and the God of his children." So then, those who were influenced by Zwingli had a broader understanding of what the sacrament is supposed to mean to us. The Lutheran notion that Christ's body is truly present in, with, and under the elements fails "to account for the biblical teaching about Christ's ascension, the promise of the Holy Spirit, and the consubstantiality (of the same essence) of Christ's humanity with ours."

John: I think Dr. Clark makes a good point; but, as I said before, I personally don't consider the difference in how these two great reformers understood the meaning of Holy Communion to be an essential difference; all Protestants recognize we celebrate this sacrament as a reminder of Christ's sacrifice and how we have been forgiven of our sin; that's the essential issue here.

Darrel: Nonetheless, it does seem to me as though the Lutheran understanding fails to take into consideration there is not only a present aspect to the meaning of this sacrament, but also a past and future component. When Lutherans focus just on achieving some mystical, sacramental unity with Christ during the administration of this sacrament, they are ignoring how the Holy Communion relates to the past and future. They're missing Zwingli's big picture.

John: I've already told you that Lutherans understand the sacrament represents Christ's sacrifice for our sin, and God's forgiveness. That seems like a pretty big picture to me.

Darrel: Sure, but, as I say, the other reformers recognized there was a past and a future aspect of sacrament as well. In fact, they considered the past to be a central component of the Lord's Supper. It's supposed to remind us of what happened in the first Passover, where the blood of a lamb protected the first born of each Jew who smeared it on their door. Holy Communion commemorates the crucifixion of Christ, the true Lamb of God. The sacrament has a future orientation as well. Jesus told his disciples the Last Supper was his final partaking of the Passover cup until he drinks it anew in its fulfillment in the kingdom of God. In Luke 22, Christ speaks of his disciples' eating and drinking at the Lord's Table as they sit on thrones judging the 12 tribes of Israel.

Dr. Sproul tells us "that feast was yet future for the disciples, and it remains yet future for us." After all, such passages as 2 Timothy 2:12 promise believers that they will "likewise reign with Christ when the kingdom of God is finally consummated in all its fullness."

Bobby: Okay, but what did Calvin actually have to say about what he believed to be the meaning of Holy Communion?

Darrel: I'll just quote him from *Institutes*: He said, "We are instructed to take and eat the body once offered for our salvation and as we see ourselves as made partakers of it, we can safely conclude that the power of his death will be efficacious in us. The covenant which he once consecrated by his blood is renewed and continued as confirmation of our faith every time he offers his blood to us as drink...The sacrament of communion bears witness to all these things, enabling us to understand that they are revealed to us as surely as if Christ was physically present with us, to be seen and touched...In telling us to eat, he makes it clear that it is ours. In telling us to eat, he makes it clear that it becomes part of us. In stating that his body was given and his blood poured out, he shows that he laid them down, not for his own advantage, but for our salvation. We must grasp that the heart of the sacraments is in these words: it is given for you; it is poured out for you...So the bread broken and the wine outpoured accurately represent what is communicated to us by his body and blood." You can see how the two great reformers differed in their understanding to the meaning of the sacrament, can't you? Calvin is saying it's as though Christ is present; Luther said that he is present.

Okay, so picture this: We're all seated around that table at the last supper, joining with the disciples in receiving the bread and the wine. That's how we're to understand it. This is why we call it a sacramental unity with Christ. Luther himself said "In his Sacred Supper he bids me take, eat, and drink his body and blood under the symbols of bread and wine. I do not doubt that he himself truly presents them, and that I receive them." But I say again, from Calvin's quote from *Institutes*, I just don't see enough of a difference in the way these two great reformers understood the meaning of this sacrament to call it essential.

I should point out though that Calvin himself may have believed there was an essential difference in the way he and Luther understood Holy Communion. In a letter to Reformer Martin Bucer, Calvin criticized Luther's view that Christ's physical body and blood are present in the elements because it involves a localization of Christ's presence. In that same letter to Bucer written in 1538, Calvin said, "How foolishly he (Luther) erred when he stated the bread is the body itself." He also wrote to the Council of Geneva stating that he could not change his mind about Luther's view as he didn't want to betray the truth. It seems like Calvin had a "Here I stand, I can do nothing else" moment.

John: Dr. Clark tells us "John Calvin taught that in the supper, Christ feeds the believer on His true body and blood, through faith, by the mysterious operation of the Holy Spirit. Both the Belgic Confession and the Heidelberg Catechism confess this high doctrine." Calvin is affirming the presence of the living Christ in the sacrament through the action of the Holy Spirit. In *Institutes*, Calvin said that Christ is present with us in a spiritual sense, and through the mysterious intervention of the Holy Spirit, the communicant partakes spiritually of Christ's body. For the rest of their lives, neither one of these great reformers changed their positions on the meaning of this sacrament.

Look, it just doesn't seem to me as though either one of these reformers considered this difference to be essential; we've already referred to what each of them said about the other, and this would indicate they were basically on the same page in their understanding of Reformation theology until the end of their lives; and I repeat what I said before, it wasn't that big a deal to me either. By the way, I think it's important to know that this is the only aspect of Luther's understanding of Reformation theology Calvin disagreed with.

Calvin was big on God's sovereignty and piety. So, was Luther. Piety is "that reverence joined with love of God which the knowledge of his benefits induces." Piety glorifies God. It is our piety we express through the sacraments. Theologian Dr. Joel R. Beeke tells us Calvin "defines the sacraments as testimonies 'of divine grace toward us, confirmed by an outward sign, with mutual attestation of our piety toward him.' Being the visible Word, they're 'exercises of piety.' The sacraments strengthen our faith, make us grateful for God's abundant grace and help us offer ourselves a living sacrifice to God."

Darrel: Even though this is not the case today, for centuries only the Catholic priest took communion as a representative of the people. The concept is representative of the way the Catholic Church operates. The Bible does not single out super-Christians to perform any functions for believers; the word of Christ dwells in each of us richly in all wisdom, teaching and so on. In Colossians 3:16, Paul doesn't mention that we're to go to some wiser authority to find out how the Word can encourage us and teach us. The Bible was written for the common man to read and study and understand without the requirement for any intermediary whatsoever. Just look at what the Bible says about this. Deuteronomy 17:19 tells us that we are to read God's book of law all the days of our lives. Isaiah 34:16 tells us to search from the book of the Lord and read. Christ himself in Matthew 22:29 told the Pharisees that they were mistaken because they didn't know the Scriptures.

John: But today, in the Catholic mass, it is evident that the Catholic Church's practice of depriving the laity of involvement in Mass over the years is still prevalent as the clergy and the choir still perform most of the worship service required.

Ray: Doesn't your pastor perform the service? Of course he does.

John: The congregation participates in the liturgy in my Lutheran church; we all approach the altar where the sacrament is administered. Of course, this is as it should be. First Peter 2:9 tells us we are all "a chosen people, a royal priesthood, a holy nation, a people belonging to God, that we may declare the praises of him who called us out of the darkness into his wonderful light."

Darrel: Yeah, but even though the pastor doesn't change the elements, I don't see that much difference between transubstantiation and consubstantiation. In saying Christ is present in, with and under the elements of the Lord's Supper, it seems to me Lutherans are really saying the same thing as the Romanists are saying. I thought about this when you first told us about this sacramental union with Christ. It seems both Romanists and Lutherans are really saying the actual physical presence of Jesus is in the sacrament. It's just that a miracle is involved in the Catholic Eucharist whereas Lutherans experience a theopathy. Either way, it seems that, like the Catholics, Lutherans believe that Christ is actually present in human form in the distribution of the elements.

John: I disagree. I believe there's a big difference in that Catholics believe the bread is actually no longer bread and the wine is no longer wine, that the bread has become the body of Christ and the wine has become His blood, and our belief that the elements remain bread and wine but that Christ is physically present with the elements.

Bobby: But it's true that both traditions hold that the physical body of Christ becomes omnipresent in this sacrament, right?

John: Yes, you could say that. Entire books have been written discussing when this actually happens. Does it happen when the bread is touched to the tongue? Or does it happen when the bread is swallowed? Is the bread desecrated if it's dropped on the carpet of the altar? I believe this is an example of majoring in the minors.

Daniel: Yes, of course it is. But, in saying Christ is actually present, this means both Lutherans and Catholics obviously believe Christ's physical body can be present in more than one place at the same time. That's what omnipresent means, right?

John: Yes. But the concept is hard to explain, and I don't want to lose you all by going too much into it. I can only respond by saying both Catholics and Lutherans base our views on our shared understanding of the communication of properties or attributes of the two natures of Christ. For both of our traditions, the divine nature of Christ shares divine attributes such as omnipresence with His human nature; thus, Christ's physical body can be in several locations at once. This concept is called *communicatio idiomatum*.

Darrel: This just sounds like more mysticism to me. Where does Reformed theology stand on this concept?

John: Dr. Sproul tells us that "Reformed theology rejects this view of the communication of attributes as violating historic, orthodox Christology. According to the Council of Chalcedon, the two natures of Christ are inseparably united in the one divine person of the Son of God without confusion, mixture, or change. The divine nature remains truly divine and the human nature remains truly human, each retaining its own attributes. This must be so. If Christ's humanity acquires a divine attribute, Jesus is no longer truly human and cannot represent other human beings before God or atone for our sin." This is why Calvin opposed Luther's interpretation.

Daniel: This makes sense to me. What does Reformed theology believe about this *communicatio idiomatum*?

John: Dr. Sproul goes on to say, "For Reformed theology, the *communicatio idomatum* means the attributes of each of Christ's natures are communicated to the person of Christ. We can predicate what is true of each nature to Christ's person. So, the person of Christ is omnipresent, but not according to His human nature. He is omnipresent according to His divine nature because only deity is omnipresent. Likewise, the person of Christ died on the cross, but Jesus experienced death according to His human nature, for the divine nature is not subject to death and decay."

Bobby: This is all very, very confusing to me. I just don't understand this concept of the presence of Christ in the Lord's Supper.

Darrel: Join the club. All I know is what Jesus said. "Where two or three are gathered in my name, there am I among them." That explains it all to me.

John: Well, to me, that means Christ is present in the administration of the sacrament; but we are not communing with His divine nature alone. Sproul tells us "We are communing with a person, and to commune with the divine person of the Son of God, because He has a truly human and truly divine nature, means we are communing with the God-man. His human body and soul remain in heaven, but we have access to the whole Christ because we are communing in the supper with the divine person in whom both omnipresent deity and localized humanity are united. By faith, as Westminster Confession 29:7 states, we feed on Christ spiritually, and both His humanity and His deity nourish us. His presence is spiritual, but via that spiritual presence, we commune with Jesus in all His humanity and deity." That explains it all for me.

Bobby: I think I understand what you're saying, John. I'm not sure where I stand on what this sacrament means but I do know it's not what I was taught as a Catholic. I'm still wrestling with this concept of Christ's omnipresence. In saying Christ is physically present as the elements are administered in your church, you know that this is happening in many Lutheran churches in your time zone at the same time. This is why you say he's omnipresent. Or by saying he's omnipresent, does that mean communicants are actually spiritually transported back in time to the upper room, celebrating the actual last supper with Christ's physical presence at that same time they're taking communion? Is that what you mean by Christ's omnipresence in the sacrament?

John: Lutherans don't accept this semi-human, semi-God hybrid concept of Christ. Luther believed it's enough to understand that the Bible refers to Christ's physical presence.

Darrel: Pastor G. I. Williamson tells us that Lutherans believe Christ is ubiquitous. They believe He is able to be present physically in many different places at the same time. I believe Christ can only be omnipresent according to His divine nature, not his physical nature.

Bobby: That I can understand. That makes sense to me.

Okay, you guys are beginning to repeat yourselves over and over again, and I think we've exhausted what we know about the Eucharist. Our two Catholic participants appear to be nodding off. So then, let's move on. Let's talk about the sacrament of confession and penance.

John: The five additional Catholic sacraments are rites because they aren't something Christ told us to do in remembrance of Him, but this one is no exception. Catholics never even considered penance to be dogma until it was instituted by Pope Innocent III in the Lateran Council in 1215. Christ never told us to confess our sins to a priest or to receive punishment from him in remembrance of Him. By definition then, it's not a sacrament.

Sonny: The priest <u>acts as Christ</u> in forgiving sins through him. The sacrament of penance motivates us to confess our sins to a priest in the spirit of true repentance and we receive forgiveness. He absolves us in the name of the Father and the Son and the Holy Spirit. We know we are to confess our sins to God, and our catechism ((CCC 1493) states that "One who desires to obtain reconciliation with God and with the Church, must confess to a priest all the unconfessed grave sins he remembers after having carefully examined his conscience. If we do not follow this dogma, we have committed a mortal sin. Regular attendance at confession is considered to be a good work.

Darrel: Christians with a true Christian conscience understand we are to confess our sins; first John 1:9 tell us that, "If we confess our sins, He is faithful and righteous to forgive us our sins and to cleanse us from all unrighteousness." Our confession is voluntary, not coerced by some church. Confession consists of two parts: The first is our own work (as you say), and the other part is a work that God does when he declares us free of our sin through the word spoken through the mouth of man. Catholics focus more on the first part, an act of man, than on the second part, the act of God; we focus on the act of God. In Psalm 51, David states "against you (God) only have I sinned," and so we focus on our direct connection with God in confessing our sins directly to him and ask for his forgiveness. Only God can forgive us and remove our guilt; no person can act as Christ. I know you said your priest forgives in the name of the Father, the Son and the Holy Spirit, but you also said the priest acts as Christ, so that would indicate otherwise. Your belief illustrates yet another Catholic "yeah, but;" *yeah*, we know we are to confess our sins and ask for forgiveness, *but*, we must involve a priest or it won't count as a good work.

We Protestants believe that we can do nothing to earn forgiveness or to keep forgiveness. Salvation before God is not administered to us through an earthly priest in the Catholic Church by the sprinkling of water or giving of penance or recitation of formula prayers. Salvation for the Christian is not kept through the effort of the person who hopes and tries and worries about being good enough to be saved. Such a heretical belief can only lead to despair and hopelessness and a desperate and unwarranted dependence on the Catholic Church as the only means by which salvation can be attained.

Of course, that's exactly how your church wants you to think; but it's in error because it encourages good works to earn salvation by being good, by doing what the Catholic Church teaches them to do with prayers to Mary, by indulgences, by the Rosary, and by a host of other man-made works. In Catholicism, salvation is strictly through the Catholic Church and its sacraments and not through Christ alone, by faith alone. This is how the cults of Mormonism and Jehovah's Witnesses work which teach that true salvation is found only in their church membership and in following the revelation and authority of their church teachers and traditions. It's disturbing to see the similarities between the Catholic Church and the cults in regards to it being the final earthly authority, teaching non-biblical traditions, the use of images, and adding works to salvation."

Bobby: Okay, the next sacrament is anointing the sick.

Darrel: Christ of course did this many times, but again, he never told us to do the same in remembrance of him so we Protestants don't consider it to be a sacrament.

Daniel: I am confused by the Catholic Church's insistence that this is a sacrament. Why do you believe it's a sacrament? When did Christ institute this procedure?

Sonny: Anointing prepares the person for death, and only incidentally may produce physical healing. Christ gave the apostles the ability to heal the sick. James 5:14-15 tells the elder to perform this sacrament.

Darrel: Yes, this verse in James is your standard proof text, but James tells the elder to perform an act of healing, not to perform a sacrament, like a baptism or administering Holy Communion. In several instances, an apostle was able to heal the sick through the power invested in him by Christ; but he did not say that all his followers were to observe that function as we are required to be baptized and observe the last supper, the two legitimate sacraments supported in the Bible.

Sonny: Regardless, the Church tells us it's the right thing to do. Anointing the sick offers the comfort of God's grace to those who are ill. The sacrament provides spiritual and sometimes physical healing, according to God's will, but also allows the sick person to join his or her sufferings to Christ and prepare for death. The essential rite of this sacrament involves anointing the sick with oil and prayer.

Darrel: What about this sacrament of ordination of your priests? Why call this a sacrament? There is no biblical evidence to support the need for this ordinance, and Christ certainly didn't make reference to it. In fact, nowhere in the entire New Testament are priests mentioned or ordination of any special class of people in remembrance of Christ.

Sonny: Paul mentioned church organization in referring to bishops and deacons. In holy orders, priests are ordained by a bishop's laying on of hands and prayer; they are given the grace to live their lives in service to the Church and to God's people.

Darrel: Scripture says we are all priests. Of all these additional sacraments, this one bugs me the most. Christ never mentioned dividing people up into "ordinary Christians" and "truly spiritual Christians" by calling the ordination of priests a sacrament is an outrageous practice. This is all about making room for the church again. There is absolutely no biblical support for setting people aside as being uniquely accessible to God in a way he cannot connect with laypeople is NOT what Christ supports. Can't you folks see that the distinctions between clergy and laity have been eliminated in the new covenant? The new covenant specifies that only the two sacraments actually instituted by Christ are significant; these other sacraments were not directly instituted by Christ so they are simply ordinances of the Catholic Church, designed and implemented by man, not by God and thus should not be considered as sacraments.

Bobby: Next up for discussion is this "sacrament" of marriage.

Daniel: Marriage is to be understood as being patterned after the relationship we Christians have with Christ. It is to serve as a demonstration to the world of Christ's love for His people. We know that Christ ordained marriage and referred to Himself as the bridegroom, but again, He never said to do this in remembrance of Him or to experience some special means of grace from Him.

Sonny: No, but the Church wishes to emphasize the importance of the marriage relationship. Marriage, or matrimony, joins a man and a woman together in a life-long covenant of self-giving love. The two spouses give their consent to join together in marriage as the Church defines it. God indeed does give special grace to the couple that they may live out their vow.

Darrel: Again, your church wishes to emphasize something it believes is important and so your pope proclaims a rite to be a sacrament in 1439 along with the affirmation of the other four additional sacraments. Christ emphasized he was married to his church, but didn't emphasize marriage between human beings to the extent of requiring it to be performed in honor of him as we do with baptism and Holy Communion. The gospels provide absolutely no evidence for consideration of marriage to be a sacrament. God is certainly present at the joining together of a man and a woman in holy matrimony, and, because we know he considers marriage to be only between a man and a woman, he opposes gay marriage; but God's presence is not considered to be a means whereby he bestows his grace as he does in baptism and in Communion. With so many marriages of alleged Christians ending in divorce, this in itself is a bad witness for Christianity, but, is even more so if we consider it a failure of what Christ allegedly commanded in his memory.

Sonny: Marriage is representative of the relationship between Christ and His Church. This is why we call it a sacrament.

Darrel: But my point is that Christ didn't actually institute it as a sacrament; you guys did. Your church arbitrarily decides to make rites and ordinances sacraments.

Daniel: What about this sacrament of confirmation? What exactly is it, and how does it connect you to Christ in the same way you believe the Eucharist does?

Sonny: Nothing connects us to Christ like the Eucharist. Confirmation is the sealing of Christianity created in baptism and represents the completion of baptismal grace. It renders the bond with the Church more perfect in providing a special outpouring of the Holy Spirit, which helps the confirmed Catholic witness to Christ and lead a mature Christian life. The rite of confirmation, usually performed by a bishop, involves the anointing with holy oil, the laying on of hands, and the words "Be sealed with the gift of the Holy Spirit."

Darrel: But, as you say, confirmation is a rite. Jesus never told his disciples to do this, did he? So then, why do you call it a sacrament?

Sonny: Our Church interpreted the gospel as supporting confirmation as a sacrament.

Bobby: Why do you believe it is an act instituted by Christ, Sonny?

Sonny: It wasn't actually instituted by Jesus. Confirmation completes baptism by a new outpouring of the Holy Spirit and enables the Christian to embark on a mission to spread the gospel to the world. This is what happened to the apostles at Pentecost. There are a number of verses like Acts 19:2-6 in both the O.T. and N.T. that refer to this sacrament.

Darrel: Yes, yes, I'm familiar with all those verses in Isaiah, Ezekiel, Joel, John, Acts, and Hebrews which refer to God pouring out his spirit in motivating the believer to his Word. But, as you say, this is not actually a mandate instituted by Christ like baptism or to observe the Last Supper. In fact none of these five additional are instituted by Christ as he instituted baptism and Holy Communion. Your Church does not accept the biblical definition of what constitutes a sacrament; it just wants to establish its own credibility in setting itself up to administer more sacraments. These added sacraments of course gave the priests more authority and served to elevate their position as an ordained representative of the Catholic Church. It made Catholics more dependent on their church. Can't you see it from this objective perspective? This is incredibly obvious to anyone who hasn't been indoctrinated into your beliefs.

Sonny: We must trust someone in our religious life. We trust in our Church Magisterium and in their councils. At the Council of Trent, the greatest weight was given to the sacraments in their decrees because they wanted to emphasize the importance of these functions.

Darrel: Luther once said to Erasmus, "You cry up the decrees of Popes; you vaunt the authority of men; you try every means of carrying us off into these strange pastures and foisting upon us things both unscriptural and unnecessary, so that we may spoil the simplicity and sincerity of Christian piety, and disorder it with man-made additions." Christ, as you may know, said the same thing when he warned about doing what the Pharisees did.

The Council of Trent was organized to formally respond to the points of opposition the reformers confronted them with. More decrees were issued through the authority of men which were unscriptural and served to maintain the piety of the Catholic Church and retain the man-made additions (one of them being the addition of five sacraments). The reformers had exposed its heresy, and they were having none of it. It was necessary for the Catholic Church to respond to the Reformation with a Counter Reformation to preserve the integrity and influence of itself. This Counter-Reformation reinforced all their extra-biblical traditions and maintained the power and influence of the Catholic Church. The tradition of the sacraments was prioritized because through their administration the church was able to retain its power.

Sonny: Christ set up His Church with leaders He ordained beginning with Peter. A succession of special leaders is necessary for the administration of baptism, Holy Communion, hearing confession of sin and performing absolution, performing confirmation, marriages and last rites. And, as I've mentioned before, the Magisterium is required for correct biblical interpretation.

Darrel: You know, Sonny, it's interesting you refer to this "succession of special leaders," and, of course, you're referring to succession of popes, but the Bible never refers to just one man, a pope, being declared as the successor to the apostolic teachings. The word "apostolic succession" never appears in the Bible. The first chapter of Acts states that an apostle could only be a man who was with Jesus during his ministry and saw him after his resurrection. When the last original apostle died, the office of apostle ceased to exist. If there was to be some apostolic office which was to continue after the death of John, the last apostle, wouldn't it be consistent for there to be at least twelve who would be designated to hold that office and not just one? After all, there were 12 apostles, right?

Daniel: There is no biblical support claiming that Christ instituted a special procedure for confession and absolution of sins, confirmation, marriage or last rites. None. Christ was baptized and did baptize and He of course instituted Holy Communion at the Last Supper. He did of course ordain marriage and forgiveness of sins, but that's very different from instituting them as sacraments equivalent to baptism and Holy Communion.

John: I'd just like to summarize what we've discussed so far, if I may. Let's review which of these Catholic rites that were declared by their church to be sacraments and those that Protestants believe were instituted by Christ, which of course, is the Bible's definition of a sacrament. Even though we could consider all of these to be done in remembrance of Christ, only the two we Protestants recognize are referred to in Scripture as being done in remembrance of Christ; baptism and Holy Communion. Marriage is specifically performed in remembrance of Christ of course; neither is confession, confirmation, last rites, or ordination of clergy. These ceremonies are all performed by the Catholic Church to primarily remind its followers of itself in their spiritual lives. Once we understand the church's objective in elevating these practices to sacraments, it makes it easier to understand the Protestant positon on limiting them to just the two that were actually instituted by Christ. Protestant churches of the theology of the Reformation are about Christ, not about themselves.

Sonny: You people believe in *sola Scripture*, we do not. We do not rely on the Bible to define what a sacrament is. We have our own definition and every single one of the seven sacraments fits that definition.

Darrel: We'll stick with God's definition if that's alright by you, Sonny.

Sonny: God speaks through His Catholic Church. We need the Church to clear up the mystery.

John: Proverbs 25:2 says that it's the glory of God to conceal a matter. God obviously never intended for His mystery to be revealed until after this life is over for each of us. Remember Paul's famous statement that we now look through the glass darkly. God intends for some mystery to be there. He does intend for His church to point itself to that one, true mystery, however, and, instead of doing this, the Catholic Church attempts to explain as much of the mystery of Christianity for us as it possibly can. In its presumed role of Christ's substitute, the Catholic Church seeks to fill in the blanks it interprets are in the Bible with its extra-biblical tradition.

Darrel: We need to "let God be God." That means we are to understand what he wishes to tell us, and accept those aspects of his will he wishes to remain a mystery. There's no need or good purpose served for some church to try and reveal what God has determined to be kept secret in his will by creating oral traditions and church extra-biblical, man-made traditions.

Sonny: As Christ's substitute, the pope does have all the answers God wants us to have.

Peter: He speaks for Christ?

Sonny: He speaks infallibly as he understands Christ would speak, yes.

Darrel: But he's just a man, a sinner like the rest of us. This presumed role as Vicar of Christ gives him license to put words in Christ's mouth. When folks want to be assured of a second chance, the church, through its pope of the moment, gives them purgatory. When folks want to have their good deeds really count for something important, the church gives them salvation by grace and their good works. When folks want to be loyal soldiers who follow a king, the church gives them itself.

Sonny: The flock needs to be directed in how to relate to Jesus Christ; the Church fulfills this function. I've been saying this all along in these discussions.

Darrel: The church fulfills a function of self-interest. It keeps its loyal followers inside itself in a spiritual co-dependency, the likes of which history has never known before its establishment as a Christian institution. This psychologically abnormal situation prevents people from spiritually developing, from journeying outward and onward in their spiritual lives; this is not what God wants for his followers. Jesus called us to go on, to become more holy, and to come closer and closer to him until that day when we are able to share eternity with him. The Catholic Church serves as a barrier to its followers in accomplishing this necessary goal.

Daniel: The Catholic Church seeks to instruct through its tradition because it knows human beings instinctively respect traditions. I recall Jung's quote from before.Traditions give us an initial sense of our place in life, where we belong; for its followers, the Catholic Church becomes an extension of them. It keeps them safe from being misled by the devil; it is the voice of authority every man and woman wants in their life. The Catholic Church gives its followers what they want, and neglects to give them what they need.

Sonny: And what do we need?

Daniel: We need to hear the truth of the gospel; we need to be encouraged to grow in our relationship with Christ, unrestricted from a forced allegiance to a church. Catholics are encouraged to be prideful people through its church's assertion that it is in exclusive possession of God's truth and the true path to salvation. The CC seems to satisfy the need of the first fallen man, Adam, to be God, by being like God itself for its flock.

Ray: Is there any hope for us Catholics? I'm of course being facetious.

Daniel: Of course you are, but I'll answer that question anyway because it's a point I'd like to make. As we said before, these discussions are supposed to be motivating us to learn from each other, not to preach to each other. And, yes, there is hope for anyone so entrapped in a co-dependent relationship with his church to the detriment of a relationship with Christ that he can't get out of its clutches to wake up and smell the coffee. If you can just step back and open your mind to the possibility, you can recognize there is a deeper voice of God than what your bishops and popes tell you about. If you can do this, your true faith journey can begin at this point. You will be motivated to directly connect to your triune God as you have been freed from the shackles of your church. You will feel emboldened to burst out of that comfort zone your church has provided for you and take on God under your own initiative. You will pray directly to Him; you will ask forgiveness for your sins directly from Him; you will understand what it means to totally rely on His promise of your salvation without being subjected to the doubt a works-based religion rises in the believer that he hasn't quite done enough good to warrant a direct entrance into heaven with no stop in between. Your belief can become a relief; that's the joy of Christianity and the good news of the gospel.

Ray: Halleluja, brother, saved at last, I'm saved at last. I see the light, brother!

Darrel: Or you can just keep on plugging along, leaning on the arms of your mommy and dad.

Sonny: What would you have us do, Darrel, renounce our religion?

Ray: Never! I will never leave the Catholic Church.

Darrel: Look, personally speaking, my intent here isn't to convert you to Protestantism; it's just to plant the seed of awakening to leading an examined life which will enable you guys to at least think about what we've been saying here and maybe take another, more objective look at your relationship with your church. I want you to question why you need just one authority besides the actual Word of God to be your spiritual leader. But, if you do wish to get the indoctrinated baggage off your back, please don't throw the baby out with the bathwater and renounce the Christian religion as many ex-Catholics have done. Going from at least a hint of Christianity to "none of the above" is a tragedy. You could at least consider Protestantism as an alternative.

Ray: You don't know what you're talking about because you don't know our sacred tradition. It's still a mystery to you.

Darrel: The only mysterious thing about your sacred tradition is why anyone would believe it to be true. We have God's truth as he has given to us in his Word. You could understand why we believe in *sola Scriptura* instead of automatically rejecting it because your church tells you to do so. For centuries, Catholics were discouraged from reading the Bible, even after it became available to everyone who could read. That was then and this is now, and it's time for you, as a Christian, to read the book that is the only source of knowledge for our religion. Don't worry about the gaps, they're meant to be there. Christians should know that God tells us what he believes we need to know; the rest is a mystery that will one day be revealed when our faith becomes sight. The Catholic Church's emphasis on the mystery of Christianity serves its purpose as the interpreter of what a Christian should believe. It serves its objective of maintaining its influence over people's lives. Distance yourself from that life, and see your belief from an entirely different perspective, centering on God instead of just some self-serving church.

I can just hear these guys at this Council of Trent assuming that they can successfully resist those who would destroy their precious church by simply telling their followers what to believe; it's how they've always done it, right? Stretch some Bible verses to support the heresy or just come up with some continuing revelation which serves to support their traditions and call it good.

Sonny: I don't respond to such speculation, Darrel. The way I see it is that Protestantism deleted all but two of our sacraments.

Darrel: You can't delete what Scripture didn't put there, Sonny. The apostles didn't add them so how did they get there? Your Church put them there.

Bobby: I have to say that when I was learning about the sacraments in my Catechism classes, it occurred to me that they weren't in the Bible as being instituted by Christ himself, and they seemed to serve to make the church necessary. I was taught though that baptism must be performed on an infant to insure that they will be saved. That's pretty significant, right? That seemed to fit the description of a sacrament; and the Eucharist seemed to fit the bill too; but I wasn't convinced of the other five.

John: Oh, baptism's significant alright, but that's not why. I say this because there really isn't any biblical support for either baptism or communion to be considered necessary for salvation. We've already talked about this subject, but can review it if you like.

From what the Catholic catechism says, it doesn't seem as though even the Catholics believe that either. I'll just read what it says. "Those who die for the faith, those who are catechumens, and all those who, without knowing of the Church but acting under the inspiration of grace, seek God sincerely and strive to fulfill his will, are saved even if they have not been baptized."

Bobby: Maybe they say this because they also consider last rites to be a sacrament too. Of course, this only applies if a priest just happens to get there in time to administer them.

Darrel: Maybe so; but, regardless, from what you've been taught and what I just read from their catechism, it's obvious Romanists are confused about this issue. Many Christians are. Of course, since Romanists also believe works somehow figure into the salvation process and may consider baptism to be a good work they perform for their children, they may be even more confused about its significance. Whatever the reason, one thing we know for sure, they disregard what the Bible says about its true significance. Of course, as we've seen they do this for all their traditions; but that doesn't seem to present a problem for a religion whose main objective has been to place the authority of the Roman Catholic Church on the same level as the authority of God.

Sonny: Christ believed in ordaining a priesthood, in confessing sin to priests, the institution of last rites, marriage and confirming one's faith.

Darrel: We don't dispute that Christ believed in these acts; but there is no evidence in the gospels that he mandated them to be performed as a sole remembrance of him and our salvation.

Ray: Our Church is the original Christian church and whatever we say we believe about the sacraments or any other aspect of our doctrine is the truth.

Bobby: Okay, let's talk about another Catholic tradition. What about this veneration of Mary?

Darrel: I said before that this one has me stumped, but, the church may want to include it to provide an additional, more visible object of worship. Remember what I said before about how Freud speculated that man is instinctively inclined to worship something? There's definitely a psychological aspect to worship. Christians are to focus on the worship of our triune God; Protestants do this, Catholics seem to worship other entities like Mary, their Saints, the Holy Father pope, the magisterium and so on. Protestants have no distractions, no hurdles, no rabbit trails in our worship of God.

Sonny: We must not confuse veneration with worship. As I said before, we venerate Mary as the Queen over all things; we entrust our cares and petitions to her. Mary is our Advocate, Helper, Mediatrix and delivers our souls from death through her prayers on our behalf. She brings us the gifts of eternal salvation through her manifold intercession. As the mother of Christ, we consider Mary to be infallible through that umbilical connection; but she is not perfect as Christ is perfect. As with the pope, we distinguish between infallibility and impeccability. Mary must be considered to be holy and sinless because only a holy person could give birth to a sinless man.

Darrel: That's not only false, it's blasphemy. How can you say any person but Christ is sinless?

Sonny: We believe that grace is capable of making a person live a sinless life. Grace can do anything. We look at Mary as mother of the redeemer; a physical intermediary. We also believe she aided in reconciling sinners to her Son through her own witness of faith and presenting Christ to others. Mary, sinless yet knowing the suffering caused by sin, continues to call sinners to her Son. Through her example, she inspires us all to the faith, hope, and love that our Lord wants us to have. Because of her role assumption and role of mother for us all, she prays for us, interceding on our behalf just as she did at Cana, asking the Lord to bestow graces to us as He wills.

Darrel: Mary need not be sinless to birth a sinless man; it's not as though it was her DNA. God placed Christ in Mary's womb. She merely provided the physical home for the embryo to develop into a human being.

Look, man, there's nothing wrong in honoring Mary and all the other participants in the story of Christ and God's plan of salvation, but there is something wrong in elevating her status to "blessed mother" and actually believing she was sinless. That's even elevating her to the status of Christ; but, wait, I guess you do that with your popes too. And we surely don't need a mediatrix to connect with God. Mary just gets in the way of that connection. Those who are not Catholic are closer to Jesus, the real mediator.

Sonny: Mary's function as mother of men in no way obscures or diminishes this unique mediation of Christ, but rather shows its power. The Blessed Virgin's salutary influence on men originates not in any inner necessity but in the disposition of God. It flows forth from the superabundance of the merits of Christ, rests on His mediation, depends entirely on it, and draws of its power from it. We are not hindered in any way from union with Christ; our connection with Mary fosters it. We are to continually implore our Blessed Mother's prayers. May her example inspire us to strive to be full of grace, seeking forgiveness for sin, and to present Christ to others in our words and deeds. As she held Christ in her womb, may we hold Christ in our hearts. In so doing, we too may become like mediators, leading others to Christ through our own witness.

Our veneration of Mary is based on our understanding that she is the woman referenced in Revelation 12:1-2 who is "clothed with the sun, the moon under her feet, and on her head a garland of twelve stars." Luke 1:42, 48 and John 19:25-27 report that she was blessed by Elizabeth, mother of John the Baptist, and Christ also identified her from the cross. If Christ put on human nature through His mother, why can't we put on divine nature, in a mysterious way, through her? Or do we ignore her purpose and thus impede us from her Son?

Darrel: Mary is of course physically dead, man, just like all your saints. Neither she nor they know you're alive or anything about you; they don't hear your prayers; only God hears your prayers, and we need relate to God with Christ being our <u>only</u> mediator. A focus on her is not required to connect with Christ.

Ray: Oh, really? From the cross, Jesus speaks first to Mary. "Woman, behold your Son." Jesus then told John to behold His Mother, and we are to imitate the apostle and take her to be our own mother. When we do this, we begin to know Christ better. We begin to understand that everything the Bible teaches about Mary is really based on what it teaches about Christ. When we behold Mary as the new Eve, it helps us to see more clearly that He is the new Adam, who comes to triumph over sin and death and usher in the new heavens and new earth. When we behold Mary as the new Ark, it no more diminishes the glory of Christ than the Ark of the Covenant took away from the glory of God. We come to realize that Jesus is the new Bread of Life, who came down from heaven and was hidden inside the new Ark. When we behold Mary as the new Rachel, mother of the new Joseph who, against all odds, becomes the savior of the whole world, then you begin to realize that we are beloved younger brothers and sisters. Finally, when we begin to behold Mary and take her to be our own mother, we discover something amazing and precious. We discover that she is already there in heaven, waiting for us.

Daniel: With all due respect, Ray, the time you spent memorizing what you just repeated could have been spent reading the Bible. No Christian who is familiar with the Bible views Mary in the way Catholics do and for a very good reason; there is absolutely nothing in the Bible suggesting any of these connections you attribute to Mary. (The Ark, Eve, Rachel); that's all Catholic Church fantasy. It's obvious you need to believe what you just told us to better connect with Christ; we don't need to involve Mary at all to relate to her Son. As a matter of fact, we believe venerating or worshiping Mary acts as an impediment in our relationship with Christ. You say that this perception of Mary in no way diminishes the glory of Christ, but I disagree with you. Mary doesn't connect with Christ; she competes with Him for adoration.

Ray: Jesus is immaculately received; so is Mary. Jesus is born without sin; so is Mary. Jesus lived a sinless life: so did Mary. Jesus is the Son of God; Mary is the mother of God. Jesus is the King of heaven; Mary is the Queen of heaven. Christ is the only mediator; Mary is the mediatrix. Christ is the Prince of Peace; Mary is the Queen of Peace. Christ suffered on the Cross; Mary suffered at the Cross. Jesus bodily ascended into Glory; Mary bodily assumed glory. Christ is our source of grace; Mary is our channel of grace. Christ is the second Adam; Mary is the second Eve.

Darrel: You left out one, Ray. Christ is the Word of God; Mary is a Catholic heresy.

Look, it's as John has said before, Catholics apparently need another player in God's plan of salvation so Mary has been added to the mix. Her role was to birth Christ and follow him as every believer is pledged to do. That's it. Ironically, Sonny, in saying that she is not to be ignored lest your relationship to Christ is impeded, your relationship with Christ is actually being impeded by your focus on her.

We Protestants understand that Mary should of course be recognized as an integral part of God's plan of salvation and that she was certainly blessed, but we don't need her to act as a mediatrix between us and Jesus. After all, God selected her to bear His Son, and she did the will of God; but that doesn't mean she should be presumed to have a more special purpose and character in God's plan of salvation and should be venerated or worshipped by anyone.

Sonny: We don't worship Mary.

Darrel: Really? It sounds like Ray does. I recall that the one time I did attend a Mass, I noticed a separate altar was set up just for Mary. It actually was embellished with more artifacts than the main altar to Christ. That sure looks like worship to me.

Ray: Mary is worshiped because she is worthy of worship. Pope Pius X stated that "Mary is the supreme Minister of the distribution of graces. Jesus 'sitteth on the right hand of the majesty on high.' Mary sitteth at the right hand of her Son." I would add that for Mary to bear God incarnate, she had to give her full consent to doing so. And the only way that would have been possible would be if she was always in a state of cooperation with the divine will. Her will could not have been corrupted by the slightest measure of sin, else she would have been at war with the God who dwelt bodily within her. Hence she is full of grace: and has always been thus, allowing her to trust God in all things and never once allowing sin to damage that trust or corrupt her freedom.

Darrel: The Bible tells us that no one, not even the angels, are worthy of worship except God. Mary, of course, is worthy of our attention because we know she was used by God to accomplish his purpose; he accomplished this by sending the angel Gabriel to announce to Mary that she had found favor with God and that she would therefore conceive and bring forth a Son. Mary asked "How can this be, since I do not know a man? And the angel answered and said to her, The Holy Spirit will come upon you, and the power of the Highest will overshadow you...Then Mary said, 'Behold the maidservant of the Lord! Let it be to me according to your word." That's the way the story is told in Luke 1:30-38. Now, tell me again how Mary is to be honored because she somehow had to give her consent. She may be full of grace, but so is every other person God has elected to be his own. She may have played a very important role, but no more than the role anyone else played in carrying out God's plan of salvation.

Ray: Don't you love Mary, Darrel?

Darrel: Yes, I love Mary just as I love the apostles, but I love the real Mary, not what you Catholics mean to make of her. I love her role in the gospel story. We Protestants recognize that the focus should not be on Mary herself but on God and His sovereign and gracious choice of her to bear and birth His Son.

Ray: We cannot, and will not, toss her aside in order to "love" her in the "right way." No one who calls themselves a Bible-believing Christian should downplay her role.

Daniel: God assigned a role to Mary, and the Catholic Church assigned another role to her, Ray. There's no biblical support for the Catholic

Church elevating Mary and her purpose beyond what we've discussed it's supposed to be. We don't downplay her biblical role; we simply recognize her existence as reflecting the overall biblical balance in the rather modest presentation of the mother of Jesus.

John: Mary of course was not venerated during the first century. The Catholic tradition of venerating Mary and Mariology developed over the centuries and was officially declared to be dogma at the Council of Ephesus in 431. We could say that its growth has often come not from official declarations, but from Marian writings of church leaders, Catholic venerated saints, popular devotion, and at time reported apparitions of Mary occurring as far back as 1665.

Of course, we have seen that this is the way many of these traditions became part of the Catholic dogma over the centuries. Venerative and devotional practices and customs have often preceded formal theological declarations by the magisterium in Catholic Church history. Traditions typically preceded dogma sometimes over centuries.

Ray: Pope Pius IX proclaimed "The most Blessed Virgin Mary was, from the first moment of her conception, by a singular grace and privilege of almighty God and by virtue of the merits of Jesus Christ, Savior of the human race, preserved immune from all stain of original sin."

Darrel: The Bible of course tells us that we are all born sinners, and none of us are "preserved from its stain." That reality certainly includes Mary. And, when you referred to her as being that woman who is "clothed with the sun, the moon under her feet, and on her head a garland of twelve stars" in Revelation 12:1, you should have read the next verse which tells us she "then being with child, she cried out in labor and in pain to give birth." Genesis 3:16 tells us that a woman will experience pain in childbirth, so, if that woman described in Revelation 12:1-2 is Mary, she must be a sinner. Or that's not Mary being described in those verses.

Sonny: Mary is sinless because she was redeemed from the moment of her conception of Christ. In our tradition, Mariology is seen as

Christology developed to its full potential. Mary is seen as contributing to a fuller understanding of the life of Jesus.

Darrel: Sure, obviously she had a most special connection to Christ through an umbilical cord, but, when Christ was born, her role was over; just as John the Baptist's role was admittedly over after he baptized Christ. You don't venerate John the Baptist, do you?

Sonny: Look, all I can say is that we are to show Mary deep respect and adoration; we do not worship her.

Darrel: But Vatican II stated that "when Mary is the subject of preaching and worship, she prompts the faithful to come to her Son. And, this role of "Mediatrix" implies she is to be worshiped. First Timothy 2:5 proclaims that Jesus is the only mediator between God and men, and we know we are to worship Christ. In claiming the mediator status for Mary, the Church is arbitrarily including her in some divine company that is worthy of worship.

Bobby: I also had a problem understanding how the Catholic Church connects Mary's virginity to holiness and assumed she had to have remained a virgin her entire life to remain holy. I questioned that statement because Christ had a brother, right?

John: Yes, of course. In Matthew 1:25, the Bible tells us Joseph consummated his marriage after Christ was born, and the Apostle James was Christ's brother. In arbitrarily assigning holiness to Mary, Romanists place more emphasis on her virginity and holiness than focusing on the importance of the process of how Christ was born. The Bible tells us the Holy Spirit made Christ sinless, not the holiness of Mary. Mary had nothing to do with God's plan of salvation except serve in her God-appointed role as the mother of Jesus. We know from several of Christ's parables, that people are expected to do what God wills them to do and not expect any special recognition for serving God's purpose. Mary was not holy and didn't need to be holy to bear the sinless Christ.

G. I. Williamson said that Christ took on his human nature from Mary in such a way that her own sinfulness was not taken with it.

Ray: I just would like to know how you Protestants cannot understand Mary's position in our Christian religion. Saint Augustine wrote that Ezekiel 44:2 states that "this gate shall be shut, it shall not be opened, and no man shall pass through it. Because the Lord the God of Israel hath entered in by it." Mary is to ever be inviolate. What does it mean that no man shall pass through it, save that Joseph shall not know her? And what does "the Lord alone enters in and goeth out by it" except that the Holy Ghost shall impregnate her and that the Lord of Angels shall be born of her? And what does it mean that "it shall be shut for evermore," but that Mary is a Virgin before His birth, a Virgin in His birth, and a Virgin after His birth."

Darrel: I usually understand what Augustine is saying, but in somehow connecting this verse in Ezekiel with what happened to Mary and why she should be venerated, even worshiped, is a real stretch. Some traditions of the Catholic Church are easier for me to understand than others; but I have to admit that the necessity for the Catholic Church to elevate Mary's status to the infallible "Queen of Heaven" has me baffled. What is their point in doing this? Is it because the church is the father and so it's only natural for a mother to be in the family too? All I know is that their focus on Mary as an intermediary between God and man creates another unnecessary hurdle for folks to jump over to get to God, and it is clearly not biblically supported. We see again how the Catholics focus on a person, man, instead of on God.

Bobby: Along the same lines, what do you guys think about the idols present in all Catholic Church buildings?

Sonny: We do not worship idols, if that's where this is going. The idols portray the twelve Stations of the Cross and Christ on the cross serves as a graphic reminder of what he went through to save us.

Darrel: Yes, Roman Catholics display Christ as still being on the cross and we Protestants display the empty cross. What do you guys think about that? Your Catholic cross represents Christ finishing his work; the empty cross represents the finished work. We emphasize Christ's resurrection more than Catholics do.

Sonny: As I just said, Christ actually on the cross is a visually representation of the suffering servant role He played in our salvation.

Darrel: Do Catholics have any crosses with no Christ hanging on them?

Sonny: I know I don't. But this doesn't mean of course that we don't believe He died for our sin.

Darrel: It might also relate to the way Catholics understand the importance of God's grace and his sovereignty.

John: Good point, Darrel. From our discussions over the past two months, it's apparent to me that some of the beliefs of the Catholic Church like the veneration of Mary, adding works to salvation, requiring the Church be the sole authority, etc. are in their doctrine because their leaders they had to do to dumb the religion down to appeal to the lowest common denominator. It wasn't until relatively recent times in church history when people were even able to read, much less understand the more complex issues in Christianity. There are many highly educated Catholics like Dr. Kreeft and G.K. Chesterton, of course, and that indicates these people were caught in the same net as those at the lower end of the I.Q. scale. Like Dr. Kreeft said about being attracted to the rituals, these more educated people had their reasons for joining the Catholic Church; But, as Dr. Kreeft and others have admitted, they don't accept the entire dogma of the church. He's much too educated in the Christian doctrine to risk losing his intellectual integrity by embracing all the tenets of the Catholic belief.

Sonny: Really, what tenets are you referring to?

John: You may recall me stating that Kreeft said he didn't accept "grace plus works." He denied that works play a role in our salvation and he is correct.

Bobby: Okay, so, with that, I assume we've finished up our discussion of the various Catholic traditions. Are there any comments about this subject before we take up the Protestant doctrine?

Daniel: I'd like to mention that G. I. Williamson said the mark of a true Christian church is the faithful preaching of the Word, the right administration of the sacraments, and the exercise of discipline. In my opinion, Catholics miss the mark on the first two requirements, and we Protestants who subscribe to the theology of the Reformation get it right. As we have seen throughout these discussion sessions, the Catholic Church honors the Bible in preaching the gospel, but it also holds their traditions in such high esteem, it competes with the word and causes such confusion in what it presents our religion to be. Catholics are not being served by Christ's church, they are being dominated by the Catholic Church.

John: From my limited experience with Catholics and Catholicism, followers of this denomination in fact do honor the Word and the sacraments, and this should indicate they remain on point in acknowledging Christ as their Savior who died for their sin. Again, this is why I always refer to them as my brothers and sisters in Christ.

Daniel: Fine, but because we've just seen that we do have our differences, Catholics and Protestants are alike in some essential ways, and we should try and focus on those rather than dwelling on those differences. We must dash Satan's hope to divide and conquer us by gently confronting our Roman Catholic brothers and sisters with the truth of the biblical Christian doctrine and trust that God will open their eyes to how far astray their church has taken the original Christian church.

John: Personally, I don't consider even our differences over the number of sacraments, their meaning, the veneration of Mary, purgatory, and so on to be essential differences. I do believe, as Dr. Kreeft believes, that the way Catholics and Protestants understand God's plan of salvation does present an essential difference. Kreeft, for reasons he has stated, is willing to overlook this, I am not. That's why he's a Catholic and I am not.

Daniel: I know I would never say that Catholics are not Christians or that they are not saved through their faith in Christ. Would either of you Catholics be able to say the same of us?

Sonny: I don't think I can, Daniel; that would be disingenuous; but I do think Protestants are on the same page with us in our understanding of Christ's role as High Priest, King, and Savior in our religion. There can be no variation on this basic truth, and both Catholics and Protestants believe in the importance of our faith in this truth is a saving faith.

Darrel: While it may seem as though Catholics at least accept our *soli Deo gloria*, *solus Christus*, and *sola fide*, from what we've learned so far, giving the glory to God is compromised with their weak understanding of grace. Their focus on Christ alone is also compromised because their church distracts them from giving Christ their full attention.

Daniel: I don't agree with you. After examining their rich history and talking with many Catholics, I believe they do focus on Christ's character and purpose, and have a thorough understanding of His role in our salvation. I discern an obvious love of Christ, a deference to God's grace, and a basic understanding of how the biblical plan of salvation works. They don't believe in other prophets, legalism, tall tales of spirit bodies, gods of other worlds, and other fantasies, just plain faith in Christ as our Savior.

Darrel: I would expect that comment from a Methodist. Both denominations, Catholic and Methodist, lean heavily towards Arminianism. Protestants have a firmer understanding of God's grace, his sovereignty and his plan of salvation.

That's an essential difference between us. The rest is just "majoring in the minors." Satan likes to divide and conquer, and we shouldn't succumb to his temptations.

Satan likes to see us do that; he successfully creates division among us by causing us to squabble over our differences. As C. S. Lewis' illustrates in his *Screwtape Letters*, Satan causes us to ignore essential differences and focus on the non-essential differences among our various denominations. He hides his intentions better when the differences are minute. For this reason, we must not dwell on the non-essential aspects of our respective doctrines and remember to keep an open mind. God is truth, and his Word is the only truth of our doctrine. I just wish Catholics would comprehend that Christianity must always be represented in its most biblical form. No add-ons to Scripture.

Their vaunted church stifles independent thought. It's so puffed up with its own self-proclaimed self-importance that it's actually deluded itself that it's the substitute for Christ which Ray was talking about before. Such puffery indicates pride, a grievous sin. As we've seen in these discussions, these two guys act as though they're better Christians than we are. If they could just step back and examine what they believe and why they believe it and take a good look at how they are co-dependently connected with a church that stands for nothing more than hollow legalism and dogma created by itself, they would leave their church in a heartbeat.

Bobby: Okay, Darrel, with that last comment, I think it's time we adjourn. See y'all next week.

Week Ten

Bobby: Okay, which of you Protestants wants to present your doctrine?

Darrel: Since he's written so many books on the subject, I assume John probably is most familiar with the doctrine of reformed Christianity, so he's our man. I hope this presentation of the reformed Christian doctrine won't be just a waste of time though. I'd like to remind these two Catholics that the reformers had something to say about Christianity in the Reformation, and we Protestants have something to say now that should be considered relevant to anyone who wants to understand our great religion.

Throughout these discussions, these Catholic people have spoken of us as heretics whose opinions are worthless, but we should not be arbitrarily dismissed as such without a chance to tell them what we believe, and then they can make up their own minds. I believe that they will have the opportunity of being introduced to an opinion of Christianity their church has kept hidden from them so, you two, please hear us out and try to keep an open mind. As we've pointed out before, we're all on the same page in our belief of Christ as our Savior, and, when we present the reformed Christian doctrine, you will see what I mean. We'll be talking about our triune God, whom we both worship in our own respective way, but, we have the advantage of not having some church institution that demands to be recognized and stands in our path to attaining our goal: To know God, to glorify him and enjoy him forever. When we focus just on Christ, we put everything else aside. Lastly, we must keep in mind that, in all things, there must be love and charity which will bind us all together in perfect harmony.

All I can say is that, whether a person is a Roman Catholic or a follower of some Protestant denomination like Presbyterian, Lutheran, Methodist, Baptist, Episcopalian, or belongs to some non-denominational church, whenever we confess our faith in Jesus

Christ as our Savior, attend our Bible-based churches on a regular basis worshipping with fellow believers in spirit and truth, hearing the Word, confessing our sin, singing praise to God, confessing our faith, witnessing baptisms and receiving Holy Communion, taking vows, and greeting one another in fellowship, we are actively fostering Christian unity and motivating other believers to practice godly living. We need to keep that in mind.

Ray: We've taken our turn, now it's their turn. Since I consider you Protestants to be heretics and therefore to be contrarian indicators, I just might learn something from you that will strengthen my belief.

Darrel: That's the spirit, Ray-boy! You've had your say for the past nine weeks explaining your version of Christianity, and now we have this last week to present our doctrine; but, hey, who knows? You just might learn something about us Protestants too.

Bobby: Okay, John, let's get into the Protestant doctrine.

John: Fine. I'll begin by referring to the best summary of reformed theology I've come across in all my reading and research. Presbyterian theologian James Montgomery Boice utilized the Canons of Dort in listing four tenets of the Reformed faith. There is biblical support for each one of these doctrines, and they are interrelated.

Ray: The Canons of Dort are Calvinism, and our Church tells us that they are cold, harsh, and sterile. They are burdensome and fatalistic and hinder believers from enjoying their relationship with God. They destroy human responsibility, promote false security, hinder evangelism and missions, and discourage good works and genuine piety and godliness.

John: The theology of John Calvin played a pivotal role in describing reformed theology because of his doctrines of grace, so I wouldn't say the Canons of Dort are Calvinism. It seems you have some misunderstanding of what constitutes our reformed theology which is actually biblical theology since we believe in *sola Scriptura*. All I ask of you guys now is that each of you would simply take the time to read what Calvin and the other reformers had to say, and review the Canons of Dort on your own, rather than just accepting what your church says about them, you would form your own opinion.

Darrel: Yeah, while you're at it, you just might want to read Augustine too.

John: In his preface to *Institutes of the Christian Religion*, Calvin stated that his purpose in writing this systematic theology was "solely to transmit certain rudiments by which those who are touched by any zeal for religion might be shaped to true godliness (piety)." True piety is God-centered, and Calvin's theology and our reformed theology is God-centered; we exercise a Christ-centered doxology. There's no church or papacy to get in the way of this practice. As we go over these four basic tenets of Reformed theology, you will see how they express this focus on our triune God and only on God. You will see how we are armed with the whole counsel of God.

The four tenets of reformed theology are: The Doctrine of Scripture, The Sovereignty of God, The Doctrines of Grace (otherwise known by the acronym TULIP) and The Cultural Mandate. As I said before, the Doctrine of Scripture refers to *sola scriptura*, the Bible alone is our source of all knowledge about God. We've already discussed the five *solas* in depth. The Sovereignty of God refers to God's total sovereignty in governing His creation. He ordains everything that occurs in our lives. Unbelievers see this concept as a needless and frustrating entanglement; Christians see this as evidence of how much God loves us and cares for us. God's sovereignty is connected with His glory, and He shares neither with us. The Doctrines of Grace describe how God extends His grace to us in working out His plan of salvation. They are the logical result of our understanding of how God exercises His total sovereignty. The Cultural Mandate refers to our obligation to work actively in society for the transformation of the world and its cultures.

Well, there it is. It's important to know what we believe, but it isn't enough just to know our reformed Christian doctrine. Understanding our doctrine is only the first of the three aspects of what constitutes a saving faith. It is followed by acceptance of what we understand. And the third aspect is how we put our faith into action through fellowship with other Christians and by doing good for others. Our good works not only serve to help others, but they also present a good witness for our faith. This is where our cultural mandate applies. Our religion is to be lived out in this world and each of us has God given gifts we are to share with the world to glorify God. As Robert Boyd (author of *Boyd's Bible Handbook*) once said: "We're to bear poverty without complaining, popularity without pride, endure contradiction without resentment, and bestow favor on the unthankful and unworthy." The challenge is to not become a part of this world. The Apostle James warns us in James 1:27 we must be careful to keep ourselves from being polluted by the world.

The most important of these four aspects of Christianity that Boice listed is the Doctrine of the Sovereignty of God. We need to always remind ourselves of what God's absolute and total sovereignty over every aspect of His creation means in our relationship with Him. His secret decrees include every choice we will ever make. We know that we are called upon to obey His Word and spread His truth, knowing that He will accomplish His plan through His people.

Darrel: Yes, I can see the connection between the sovereignty of God and the other three tenets listed, particularly the connection with this cultural mandate. The Bible says that our choices are important to God. Our belief in his sovereignty should motivate our service to him, not out of fear or confusion, but out of love for him.

John: Sure, but we must keep in mind that fallen man treasures his own sovereignty as we have seen in our discussions with Arminians and these Catholics. Satan promised us we could be like God, and our acceptance of this lie caused our separation from God in the first place. This relates to our pride, one of our worst sins. We humans have a hard time understanding the degree of our sovereignty in relation to God's absolute sovereignty. We're inclined to want some sovereignty for ourselves. We talked about this when we discussed Catholicism's belief in "grace plus works."

Ray: How do you understand God's sovereignty, John?

John: From God's perspective, He's in absolute control of every molecule He's created. From our perspective, this means our lives are both predictable and unpredictable for us.

Bobby: Yeah, Forest Gump said that life is a combination of what seems to be structured and what seems to be random.

John: But we know there's nothing random about our existence. Everything happens for a reason. We can't know everything God knows about His creation, but we do know He's in total charge of it. We don't have the power to make everything work out the way we'd like it to work out for us. We have to trust in Him to always do what He believes is best for us from His divine perspective. Even our suffering has a good purpose.

Daniel: But God gave us free will because He doesn't want robots. We aren't to just let life happen to us, believing in some impersonal force which controls our lives. That's fatalism. That's Islam.

John: Correct. And robots can't glorify God.

Ray: Our free will is important to God or He wouldn't have given it to us in the first place. It allows us to make choices.

John: Sure, we can make choices, but there are limitations to our free will. Luther covered this subject in *The Bondage of the Will*. For example, we don't get to decide whether we choose to be saved or not or what we can do to earn our salvation. Our freedom of choice is important; in fact, the Bible tells us that the only thing more important to God than giving us freedom of choice is His own glory. In Matthew 26:39, 42, Christ states that His wish to avoid crucifixion is trumped by His wish to do God's will; and, in John 17:1-4, He refers to both the Son and the Father being glorified through His obedience to God's will.

Darrel: This is why Lutherans focus more on God's grace than on God's sovereignty, right?

John: We should focus on <u>both</u> His grace and His sovereignty because both give Him the glory. And we should recognize that God's grace is really worthless if He doesn't have the absolute power to extend it for us. He must be in charge of His creation for us to benefit from any of the blessings He bestows on us. I believe that Lutherans are more focused on how God has used that sovereignty to exercise His grace than on understanding what that sovereignty really means in relation to our free will. For this reason, I think Lutherans have a weaker concept of God's sovereignty than Calvinists have.

Darrel: I hear you saying that a belief in God's absolute sovereignty must be our premise.

John: That's a great way to put it, Darrel. How can we trust a God who had limited power? I couldn't worship Him or pray to Him. What good would it do? I wouldn't trust a God who required my cooperation to save me as Catholics believe. How could I ever be assured my cooperation was sufficient for my salvation?

Sonny: Regardless, I believe God has given us some sovereignty. We have free will; I'm not comfortable with the concept of our creator having complete control over us.

John: Of course fallen, sinful man naturally rebels against a personal God having complete control of his life. But, believers should be glad our Creator has the power to exercise His divine will in our lives. He loves us and knows what's best for us. We should take comfort in that fact. His grace is the result of His love for us. We should recognize God's providence is the only foundation on which we can find confidence to act in this unpredictable world. Knowing that God is in control actually sets us free to act on our own behalf. We know that no bad choice of ours can thwart His divine plan for our lives, but our choices do count in what reward we will one day receive in heaven and whatever we decide to do has eternal significance because our actions are incorporated into God's all-encompassing plan. The bottom line is that our actions are important, but it is God who gives meaning to them. Knowing this makes me feel content. God's sovereign act of grace provides us with the security offered by no other religion on the face of the earth.

Sonny: I like the way you put that, John.

Daniel: Personally, I tend to agree with what Sonny said. I believe God, by giving us free will, reserves some of His sovereignty for us although I'm not willing to go so far as to believe that His grace isn't sufficient to save us as the Catholics do. I've always believed though that we are free to reject His offer of salvation or renounce our belief.

John: Rejecting Christ, of course, is a bad choice, but it is surely the choice sinful man is most inclined to make. That's what the Bible tells us when Paul states in Romans 3:12,"There is no one who has done good, not even one;" and, thankfully, God doesn't let us make that bad choice; it not only makes perfect sense that God would not allow those He has chosen to fall away, our preservation of faith is biblically supported. I'll give you a list of all the verses that support the perseverance of the saints in Calvin's doctrines of grace when we begin that discussion. In short, God does not let His chosen thwart His divine will for us. God tells us in His Word that He is not willing to share His sovereignty with us in any sense that implies we are the primary cause of whatever happens to us in this life. As R. C. Sproul once said, "God is the primary cause; We are the secondary cause."

Sonny: Kierkegaard once said "Omnipotence which can lay its hand so heavily upon the world can also make its touch so light that the creature receives independence." That's a good way of explaining a difficult concept.

John: Yes, it is, except that I would add the condition that even our presumed independence falls under God's sovereign will in the way I've described before. And, as I've also said before, how God's sovereignty affects all of the other tenets Boice lists is critical to our understanding of the reformed doctrine. This is particularly true for our understanding of the Doctrines of Grace, TULIP.

Ray: What's this "cultural mandate" all about?

Daniel: The cultural mandate refers to our obligation as Christians to live actively in society and work for the betterment of the world. We are to do good for others.

John: The cultural mandate is Christianity in action. It is applied theology, not some ethereal concept. Christianity is a very practical religion. It isn't just the truth; it serves to change our everyday lives and all of our trivial activities in life with a spiritual significance. Some people even refer to this cultural mandate as the Doctrine of Vocation. Theologian Gene Edward Veith writes that "this doctrine is one of Luther's most important contributions to the Christian church, next only to his re-emphasis on the gospel and on the Word of God. Calvin and the other Reformers embraced what Luther taught about vocation, with Calvin applying it in some innovative ways." It relates to the term AProtestant work ethic," a powerful motivator for all of us to perform our jobs in the best way we can. Vieth goes on to say "It's at the heart of Luther's ethics, and is the locus for good works that are the fruits of the faith." In the spirit of evangelism, we're encouraged to do good in the world and thus serve as a good witness for our beliefs.

Darrel: Yes, of course, but we should understand the difference between such witnessing through good works and witnessing through evangelism. We witness our belief through good works, but we shouldn't assume people always make the connection between our good works and Christianity and Jesus Christ. This is where evangelism is important; only in proclaiming the gospel can we be assured we're witnessing our faith. This is Christ's mandate as expressed in Mark 16:15.

John: Sure, it's best to do good works AND evangelize the Word. God uses us as a tool for conversion. In this way He uses us to do good for Him. Works-based religions believe they do good for God trying to perfectly obey His law. Well, God doesn't need us to do good for Him in that way; but our neighbor does. We do good for our neighbor and show our love by proclaiming the truth. Evangelism is our best good work.

Ray: What does the AProtestant work ethic have to do with the doctrine of vocation?

John: The Protestant work ethic motivates us to practice the doctrine of vocation. We are motivated to be independent, industrious, productive, and even to be frugal. Christians are to practice good stewardship; that means we're to be responsible for what we do with our finances and our possessions.

Sonny: We should all be on the same page regarding this doctrine of vocation, regardless of our beliefs. Everyone wants to do good for others, right? Everyone should understand it's better to be a responsible, hard working person who doesn't depend on the government or others for help. That only stands to reason. The Christian doctrine advocates the most pragmatic way to live. After all, what kind of world would it be if we all were unproductive and irresponsible and depended on others to meet our needs? It only makes sense to practice the Golden Rule. And, a person's actions should be consistent with their beliefs. After all, when you make the talk, you should do the walk, right? As you've all said before, a religion's credibility is established when its members practice what they believe. To me, that's the major problem Islam is having today.

Peter: Yes, every human being should obviously be in unity regarding the concept of this doctrine of vocation for our self-preservation; and any religion should motivate its believers to at least behave themselves. When actions are consistent with words, the credibility of any belief system is supported. That just makes sense. A disconnect between words and actions indicates a belief system is weak and inadequate.

Darrel: Sure, but the real issue here goes to motive. Do we do good works to serve our own self-interest, to save ourselves, or do we do them because through our faith we're encouraged to glorify God? Do we believe as all works-based religions believe that we're to jump through hoops to be saved, or do we understand God's grace and know he's already saved us through Christ's redeeming sacrifice? Christians know our motive is to model our behavior after Jesus Christ, to love and to serve and to sacrifice for others. We are to get out of ourselves to help others. That's what the Christian cultural mandate or the doctrine of vocation is all about.

John: Good point, Darrel. Motive distinguishes the difference between a religion centered on God and a religion centered on man. It's the difference between Christianity and all other religions. Christians get out of self to practice the doctrine of vocation. We don't do good just to feel good about ourselves. We do good (as Christ did good) to glorify our God. For a most complete explanation of good works, I refer you all to Chapter 16 of the *Confession of Faith of the Presbyterian Church in America*. This Confession was basically taken from the Westminster Confession of Faith of 1647.

Sonny: While we believe that the Bible isn't the only source of knowledge, our Church certainly recognizes God's sovereignty.

John: Recognition can just be seen as paying lip service to the concept when a church, any church, acts as though it were sovereign as yours does. You may recall what we said about Catholics having a weak understanding of God's grace; well, according to Philip Yancey, grace is related to God's glory, and we believe man's chief purpose is to glorify God. God is glorified when we recognize His sovereign power over His creation, and that includes us. Absolute sovereignty means He gets what He wants and doesn't need our help or approval to exert His divine will on our behalf from His perspective.

So then, how do these concepts all tie together? Well, it only makes sense that God's power is necessary to extend His grace, right? If God isn't totally sovereign, extending unmerited favor to us would be meaningless for our salvation because we can't save ourselves. Even Catholics with their "grace plus works" concept accept that reality. Sonny has claimed that his church recognizes God's sovereignty, but, in my experience and from what these guys have been saying in these discussion sessions, Catholics seem to exhibit a weak understanding of God's sovereignty; this of course would be consistent with their weak understanding of God's grace. Augustine understood the power of grace. He said "What merits of his own has the saved to boast of when, if he were dealt with according to his merits, he would be nothing if not damned? Have the just then no merits at all? Of course they do, for they are the just. But they had no merits by which they were made just." (Letters 194:3:6). And again he said, "What merit, then, does a man have before grace, by which he might receive grace, when our every god merit is produced in us only by grace and when God, crowning our merits, crowns nothing else but his own gifts to us?" (Letters 194:5:19). Augustine's saying what Darrel said before when we talked about the Order of Salvation. We show our merit in the sanctification step which comes after our justification. Here is your most respected saint who gets the order right and you ignore him when you stated before that sanctification justifies us.

Can't you Catholic people see that when man reserves power for himself, as in your belief in grace plus works and the Catholic Church's assertion of its power in man's life, this belief serves to compromise the effect of God's grace. Yancey goes so far as to say that man's assumption of power is an actual trade-off for God's grace. The full effect of grace is sacrificed on the altar of power for the Catholic Church.

Darrel: Now would be a good time to begin our discussion of God's doctrines of grace.

John: I agree. When we don't fully understand God's sovereignty and want to reserve some power for ourselves, we misunderstand how salvation works. An adequate understanding of God's sovereignty is necessary to understand the doctrines of grace. As I said before, God gets what He wants; He tells us that in His Word. That means He elects people without their merit and without their consent; He preserves that faith for Christ, come hell or high water. Catholics just don't seem to really be on board with that reality, so we need to talk about the doctrines of grace, TULIP.

Bobby: What does "TULIP" stand for?

John: TULIP is an anachronism which summarizes what Reformed theology refers to as the doctrines of grace. T=Total depravity; U=Unconditional grace; L=Limited atonement; I=Irresistible grace; P=Perseverance of the Saints. We'll discuss the meaning of each of these terms.

Ray: TULIP's a Calvin thing, right?

John: Actually, TULIP isn't "a Calvin thing," as you put it. Theologian Cornelius Van Til said that TULIP is the bridge to the structure of Reformed theology. As was mentioned before, St. Augustine inspired it, according to Calvin. Of course you should know that Calvinism isn't confined to just these five points; rather, it has the many points that one finds in the *Belgic Confession* or the *Westminster Confession of Faith* we talked about before.

The discussion I had with my Lutheran pastor motivated me to research what Martin Luther actually wrote about his understanding of this doctrine, and concluded Calvin and Luther were basically on the same page in their understanding of the theology of the Reformation. They were on the same page because TULIP is derived from Scripture and both reformers of course accepted *sola Scriptura*. Luther didn't believe in adding anything to the Word, even when it didn't seem to make sense.

Here's that list I promised you before which give us the Bible verses supporting each of the five points.

Sonny: But there are so many Protestant denominations; some believe that Calvin corrupted Scripture with his doctrines of grace.

Darrel: Sure, many of our Protestant churches do not accept reformed or biblical theology; that's a reality we must accept; but, we don't need to have just one corporate institutional "Protestant Church" for the reasons we've discussed. You people need just one Catholic Church as a strong authoritative presence in your spiritual lives. We exercise our Christian liberty to choose the Christian church that meets our need to hear God's Word.

Look, we know Calvin's reputation has often been maligned and his views misrepresented, but, in saying Calvin actually corrupted Scripture, a person is calling Calvin a heretic and some denominations believe this. But, as I've said before, there is unity among those Protestant denominations that preach and teach the doctrine of the Reformation and that is best presented in the theology of John Calvin in his *Institutes of the Christian Religion.* As I said before, this is also the theology of Augustine so you should consider him a heretic too. You poor people are in the intellectually indefensible position of being at odds with one of most highly regarded saints; you have a saint in your church whose theology your church hasn't endorsed since his death in 430 AD. We can say that Augustine's Catholic Church is not your Catholic Church, and yet neither of you seems to have recognized this has happened over the centuries of your church evolution and Augustine still remains a revered saint, right? Either your masters of the magisterium are totally ignorant of what Augustine really believed or they wish to ignore the reality that he really didn't believe what they believe. But now that you and Ray know what Augustine really believed; your choice is do you choose to follow Catholic theology or Augustinian theology? One is wrong, one is right. It's your choice.

Ray: I'm a Catholic; I've always been a Catholic, and I will always be a Catholic.

Sonny: Augustine's theology is Catholic theology. What would be his opinion of these doctrines of grace of yours?

John: I said before that Calvin credited Augustine for his doctrines of grace; so let's get into TULIP. As I said before, "T" stands for total depravity. As Darrel mentioned before, R. C. Sproul prefers the use of the term "total inability" because it implies that man is sinful from birth and is unable to make himself righteous before God. "U" stands for unconditional election. This means God has chosen us to be believers before the creation of the world, and His choice is not based on anything we have done to deserve it. "L" stands for limited atonement, or particular atonement. This is the belief that Christ died only for the elect. He did not die to atone for the sins of everyone. "I" stands for irresistible grace, and it means we cannot resist the grace God extends to us to save us. "P" stands for perseverance of the saints, and that means the elect cannot renounce their belief. Protestant denominations which preach and teach the doctrine of the Reformation believe that TULIP describes exactly what the Bible tells us is God's plan of salvation.

I'll preface this discussion by pointing out that there are basically two ways of looking at how God's grace and sovereign will as they relate to our free will and our salvation. There's the Calvinistic interpretation, which, as was said before, is based on Augustine and Aquinas, and the Arminian way, which is based on the beliefs expressed by Jacob Arminius in opposition to Calvinism. You may recall our previous discussion about him.

Sonny: Sure, but you're not saying that the Catholic Church is Arminian, are you? I told you before that the Catholic Church is divided between the Augustine/Aquinas concept and the Arminian school of thought. My own Church subscribes to the Augustine/Aquinas concept. Others lean more towards Arminianism. I know it's the same with some of your Protestant denominations too. There's an Arminian influence in your churches.

Darrel: Yes, Arminianism or some version of it will be with us until the Second Coming, and I'm glad to hear you say that your particular church leans toward the Augustine/Aquinas interpretation of the Word, but, as we shall clearly see when we talk about election, the value of the atonement, whether grace can be resisted or not, and whether we can lose our faith or not, that Catholic theology is definitely Arminian.

John: Okay, so let's talk about "T," Total inability. This means that we are all born sinners and are born spiritually dead. Satan has taken captive of our free will, and we lack the ability to be perfect. We have been deprived of our perfect relationship with our Creator. As he stated in one of his writings (*Enchiridion xxx*, p. 247), Augustine certainly supported this point of the doctrines of grace. So, I assume we all agree on this point, right?

Bobby: It's hard to think of a new born infant as being a sinner.

John: You seem to have forgotten what it was like when that infant throws his or her first tantrum because they don't get what they want.

Ray: Sure. It's obvious something is wrong with us from the get-go. We Catholics believe we were born sinners. What's next?

John: So next we have "U" which stands for unconditional election. This means that God elected us before our birth to be His own people. And He based His choice strictly on His own council, not dependent on any conditions we would have had to meet. Arminians believe in conditional election; that means they believe our salvation is based on an act of positive volition on the part of man. Man's will must be exercised to choose to believe.

Ray: The Church says that God calls all of us, but some of us reject His call. We know that God calls all of us because He wants all to be saved. (1 Timothy 2:3-4). After all, what sort of a God, who wants all to be saved, would force people into Hell without giving them the chance to be saved?

John: Yes, God is loving and merciful and does want all to be saved. But, as we said before, He also is righteous, holy and just and will not save sinners in rebellion against Him. We are all sinners and we all deserve the punishment of Hell. Instead of focusing on how unfair it is for God just to unconditionally choose some and ignore others, we should focus on how grateful we should be He chose us to be saved. That's the glass half-full, eh?

Darrel: Ray's statement again proves that it's not just a faction of Catholics who are Arminians, all Catholics are Arminians in their understanding of election. When their catechism stated that "Moved by the Holy Spirit, we can merit for ourselves and for others all the graces needed to attain eternal life, as well as necessary temporal goods," the church is saying that our election is based on our merit; we do something to earn that election, and that's what Arminians and Pelagians believe. In 2 Timothy 1:9, Paul states that God has saved us and "called us with a holy calling, not according to our works, but according to His own purpose and grace which was granted us in Christ Jesus from all eternity." He is saying our election is not based on the condition of our willful acceptance or the conditions of our good works. Augustine believed that God gets what he wants (*Enchiridion* ciii, p. 271), and he has chosen to save some and not others based on nothing else but his sovereign decree.

Sonny: We understand God's grace, and we believe in predestination. But we further define predestination to apply in two ways: initial and final predestination. Those who will end up with God in heaven experience final predestination and are spoken of as the "predestined" or the "elect." Initially predestined means every person is drawn to Christ, but it's up to us to cooperate to make salvation happen either in this life or in purgatory. Our Catechism states that "To God, all moments of time are present in their immediacy. When therefore he establishes his eternal plan of predestination, he includes in it each person's free response to his grace." I refer you to John 12:32 where Christ refers to drawing all men to Himself.

John: Actually, we must assume that the "all men" in this verse must refer to all men regardless of culture, status, or nationality because Christ previously has referred to only those men drawn to Him whom the Father has given to Him (John 6:44). The John 12:32 reference really isn't as clearly stated as 6:44, so, presuming God doesn't contradict Himself, we use the more clear verse to interpret what Christ is really saying in 12:32. The two verses are consistent only if we interpret it this way; and it's important to note that Greek gentiles were in the audience Christ was speaking to.

Catholic theology seems to want to sand the hard edge of predestination by splitting it up into initial and final types to allow for man's cooperation in saving himself. Again I must remind you that this is not what Augustine believed. He saw it as it really is, God's sovereign act in his willful choice of saving some and not others, even before we were born. Augustinian theology is clearly not Catholic theology. As I said before, Pelagius is more qualified to be one of your saints than Augustine.

Darrel: This explanation of two kinds of predestination illustrates another "yeah, but" in Catholicism." *Yeah,* we believe in predestination, *but* there is one kind that isn't final. This heresy takes its place right up there with the two types of sin, two types of good works, two types of heaven, two types of baptism, two types of law, and two types of justification, and even two types of grace. None of this "further definition" is in the Bible of course, so I assume this is some more of your add-on tradition, right?

Sonny: Yes, but, as you know, we consider such tradition to be a part of Scripture.

Darrel: You just stated the ultimate "yeah, but." I know you believe your traditions trump the Bible, but are you now saying that it also trumps what Augustine believed?

Sonny: Augustine may be one of our most respected saints, but he was just a man. He wasn't right about every aspect of our doctrine. If you're familiar with his history, you know he changed his mind about his beliefs several times. Anyway, the fact that a person experiences salvation at some point does not mean he is among the predestined (those God has chosen to persevere to the end). Regardless, suffice it to say that we don't believe our election is conditioned on anything we have done for God to meet His approval, and leave it at that, okay. Exactly. As I stated before we believe our works are a natural accompaniment to our salvation. It's cooperative grace.

Darrel: Purgatory waters down predestination. Augustine recognized this, and that's why he was ambivalent in supporting the concept of purgatory.

John: Next up is "L," Limited Atonement, or "Particular Atonement." I assume we are going to spend more time talking about this point.

Limited Atonement means that Christ died only for God's elect and no one else. This concept, which some theologians also call Adefinite atonement? or Aparticular redemption,? is probably, like the concept of predestination, one of the most controversial concepts in the Reformed Christian doctrine. Of course, as we've seen, at least every Reformed denomination accepts the concept of predestination, but this is not the case with the concept of limited atonement.

Sonny: We Catholics don't accept particular redemption either. We believe that Christ died for everyone, but His sacrifice on the cross was only efficacious for the elect. There are a number of Bible verses that clearly state Christ came to save the world.

John: As in the reference to all men in John 6:44, we believe the "world" referred to in those verses means the elect all over the world, but, even if you think this seems a stretch, isn't it patently obvious that everyone in the world hasn't been saved?

Sonny: Exactly; and that's why we believe that, while Christ's death was for all, only those chosen were actually saved; His sacrifice makes it possible for all to be saved. Vatican II stated, "Since Christ died for all men, and since the ultimate calling of man is in fact one and divine, we ought to believe that the Holy Spirit in a manner known only to God offers to every man the possibility of being associated with being saved."

John: So it's up to us to choose Christ or we're damned.

Sonny: Correct. That's why God gave us free will.

John: But our free will is so enslaved to sin, isn't it logical to assume we would never choose to believe in Christ on our own accord? Fallen man is not inclined to do that. We're inclined to rebel against the God of Scripture; we want to worship a God of our own design, a more user-friendly, loving, forgiving God who can be easily manipulated.

Theologians refer to three different beliefs in the value of Christ's atonement. There is the limited or particular atonement Protestants believe in. By the way, Augustine believed in this too. (*On the Trinity* XIII:xv:19). There is also "Universal Atonement" also called Aactual universalism,? the belief that Christ died for everyone.

There is also the belief theologians call "Hypothetical Universalism," the belief that hypothetically Christ died for everyone, but His death had no saving effect without an added faith and repentance not foreseen in His death.

Sonny: We obviously don't believe everyone is saved, so this "Universal Atonement" is illogical. But we believe that Christ made salvation possible for everyone if they choose to accept Him; I assume that means we believe in this "Hypothetical Universalism."

John: Hypothetical Universalism is an Arminian belief too. Arminians believe that Christ's death made it possible for people who chose to believe in Him to be saved. Each person must exercise his free will to accept Christ. The Bible never tells us that all men will be saved; this is what we refer to as "salvation by death;" I know of no Christian denomination that believes in universalism.

Sonny: Universalism is not biblical, but hypothetical atonement is; Scripture tells us that God is merciful and loving and wishes to save everyone, right?

John: Yes, that's what the Bible says. God is of course loving and merciful, but He is also just and He cannot connect with us unless our sin is eradicated by Christ because His divine justice must be satisfied. The Bible tells us we're all sinners and so God's divine justice cannot be satisfied in granting salvation to us without the fine being paid for the crime. So, an atonement is necessary; but, as in the O.T., only the sacrifice of a perfect lamb can effectually atone for our sins before a perfect God; and, in addition, we know that Christ's death can only eradicate the sin of those who believe in Him and repent of their sin. By the way, Augustine denied that God desires to save all men "head for head." (*Enchiridion* xcvii, pp. 267-268; ciii, pp. 270-271).

I personally don't consider that the difference in the way we understand the value of Christ's atonement and the way Arminians and Catholics understand it is an essential one; I say this because although these two views differ on how we understand the purpose of Christ's death and how the process of salvation works, neither side can say for certain how we are to understand the saving effect of the atonement or on how many people will actually be saved. Both schools of thought believe they have biblical support, but the Bible just isn't crystal clear on this subject, and, in fact, some of the Bible verses used to support the Arminian/Catholic view are also used to support the Calvinistic, reformed theology view. My only comment is that I know God isn't into wasting anything; recall what Christ said when the disciples asked him what to do with the fish left over after feeding the 5,000; He said "save it." So, if we understand that general concept, wouldn't it make sense that God would not want to have one drop of Christ's blood wasted on anyone who wouldn't be saved through unbelief? Since Catholics don't want to waste the wine after the Eucharist is administered because it would be wasting Christ's actual blood, wouldn't it be consistent to think the same of the waste of Christ's blood in the concept of hypothetical atonement?

Ray: It's not the same thing, John.

John: Sure it is. Christ of course shed blood on the cross, and you people believe the wine that must not be wasted has actually been changed into that blood. Think about it.

Sonny: He's got a point, Ray.

Daniel: Hypothetical atonement is the belief that hypothetically Christ died for everyone but, in effect, He only died for those who chose Him as their Savior. I'm a Methodist and this is what we believe.

Sonny: Do you see what I mean when I say there's so much confusion among all these different Protestant denominations? Methodists are Arminians, Presbyterians and some Baptists are Calvinists.

Darrel: Whereas we know by now that all Catholics are Arminian.

John: Catholics are forced to be uniform; we Protestants of the reformed faith are united in our belief in the Bible as our sole source of knowledge of the truth. We consult the Bible in all matters like this. It would of course be easier to be like Catholics in obedience to that one authority, but, since Christ told us the Holy Spirit is all that's necessary, we have to trust in His Word and the guidance of the Holy Spirit.

Yes, the downside of doing it this way is that there can be some confusion, but none of us, not even your magisterium or pope can know with 100% certainty what God's plan of salvation is. You may trust your church, but that's logically just wishful thinking. We can accept different interpretation of Scripture, but when someone is telling us something the Bible is clearly not saying, we will not accept that as being true.

So then, in conclusion, when we consult Scripture in addressing the purpose and value of Christ's atoning sacrifice, we shouldn't allow our differences in our understanding this issue as being a problem that should divide us. I'm saying that I personally don't believe hypothetical atonement can be proven to be clearly wrong according the Bible. There are a number of verses in the Bible Arminians use to support hypothetical atonement that seem to do so. Methodists aren't pure Arminians anyway because Arminianism infers that God doesn't have the ability of foreknowledge and that our salvation is *not foreseen* in Christ's death. Wesley believed in God's foreknowledge.

Sonny: I avoid the problem of deciding what to believe among so many different interpretations by simply trusting our Church, our sole authority of the truth.

Darrel: As John said, yes, that would be ideal if any of us could trust some earthly authority to tell us what is true, and we could believe that with 100% certainty; but Catholicism's forced uniformity isn't the same as being united. All earthly authority is subject to sin, and, this side of heaven, no one person, no church, no magisterium, no prophet can know with complete certainty God's plan of salvation beyond what he has said in the Bible.

For this reason, we view just the one authority as a detriment. Our apparent diversity in Protestantism can actually be considered to be a strength not a weakness. That's the flip side of this argument you keep introducing into these discussions. I use the word "apparent diversity" because, as I've said before, we are all one church united under the theology of the Reformation, the five *solas*. The majority of our differences are non-essential and should not divide us.

John: And, as I just said, one of those five *solas* is *sola Scriptura*, and each of the points of TULIP is strictly based on what the Bible says and each point relates to the whole. Unconditional election presents us with the importance of understanding God's omniscience and that omniscience is of course displayed through His foreknowledge of who would be saved and who would not. That understanding also encompasses the purpose of Christ's death and how the process of salvation works. Salvation without at least God's foreknowledge is not biblically supported. That would be saying something the Bible is not saying to us, so we can't accept that. So then, this somewhat altered version of hypothetical atonement (with the caveat of substituting "not foreseen" with the word "foreseen") is really what Methodists believe in. Since Sonny has said that he's on board with unconditional election, it would seem as though Catholicism's understanding is similar to Methodists' understanding.

Sonny: Maybe so. I can't claim to know what the Magisterium knows about this so I can't personally say if that's a good thing or a bad thing; I just know what our Church believes. If that is what Methodists also believe, well, I think that's a good thing for them.

Darrel: Yes, what you say is consistent with what you said before about Catholic doctrine being more Arminian; but, are you aware that Augustine taught that God not only divinely elects those who will have faith in Christ but also divinely elects to grant to these individuals the faith to believe in Christ? God's election unto salvation is not based on a foreknowledge of an individual's faith, but is based on the act of a gracious God to elect his chosen to salvation. Augustine recognized God was totally in control in his plan of salvation; our salvation is an active process on God's part, not a passive one where he's relegated to a role of an observer or is just making salvation possible for us, but we have to decide to accept or reject his offer. Here again, Augustine contradicts what you people claim to believe.

Sonny: You've been trying to contrast Catholic theology with Augustinian theology for the past nine weeks, Darrel, and, while you may believe you have provided support for that belief, you should know that no theologian bats 1,000, including Saint Augustine. Due to his debate with Pelagius, he began to stress predestination more and more over free will in the heat of battle. This is exactly why the Church does not follow one single father but rather subscribers to the *consensus partum*, the broad general agreement in the Magisterium regarding the basics. We know there is much diverse opinion among the Church fathers, but an impressive consensus about certain things as well, and it is to this consensus which the Church makes its appeal and regards as authoritative. It listens for the essential melody of the patristic chorus, and charitably passes over the odd discordant note which many of the fathers occasionally sound. Like it or not, Augustine retains his place in the chorus.

Darrel: This creative rationalization sounds like something a politician might say, Sonny. It's ignores the obvious difference between Catholic theology and Augustine theology.

John: I think the basic difference in Catholic theology and reformed Protestant theology basically comes down to one's concept of what God's absolute sovereignty really means. Romans 9 covers this particular subject. Arminianism almost completely eliminates any role for God in His own plan of salvation, and of course that's exactly what it's designed to do: Give some of God's sovereignty and glory to man. I think we've illustrated how Arminian Catholicism is, and, to some, this may represent an essential difference between our theologies. Okay, next up is "I," Irresistible Grace."

Sonny: We consider grace to be resistible. I can see what you're saying, John, when you said these five points of TULIP are related to each other. "I" relates to "U" in the sense that if one is talking about predestination to initial salvation, then the fact that a person will come to God does not of itself mean he will stay with God; God's grace can be resisted. If one is talking about predestination to final salvation, then a predestined person will stay with God, but this does not mean the predestined are the only ones who experience initial salvation. Some might genuinely come to God (because they were predestined to initial salvation) and then genuinely leave (because they were not predestined to final salvation). As I said before when we talked about "Unconditional Election," those who will end up with God in heaven are spoken of as the "predestined" or the "elect." The fact that a person experiences salvation at some point does not mean he is among the predestined (those God has chosen to persevere to the end). Either way, predestination to initial salvation does not entail predestination to final salvation. This is why we believe that people can resist grace. Augustine believed that. He supported the concept that our free will can override God's sovereign will.

John: That's not exactly a correct statement, Sonny. Yes, Augustine's doctrine of baptismal regeneration did indicate that all who were baptized were regenerated, and, of course, since we know all baptized people are not believers, the logical conclusion is that some of these people lost their faith. Logic also tells us though that if we presume a different premise, that baptism, in and of itself, does not save, people who claimed to be saved by being baptized and renounced that belief were never really saved in the first place. Consistent with his God-centered theology, Augustine believed that those elected to grace and glory would persevere because they would be preserved by the omnipotent, irresistible grace of God. (On the Predestination of the Saints, xvi:33, p. 514). After all, in defining all five points of the doctrines of grace after Augustine's theology, Calvin must have believed he and Augustine were basically of the same mind.

That of course doesn't mean that there aren't some contemporary, well-educated, informed Catholic theologians. G. K. Chesterton comes to mind and so does Dr. Peter Kreeft whom I've talked about before. Dr. Kreeft is one of the world's leading authorities on Thomas Aquinas, and here's what he had to say about how free will and God's sovereignty work together. And I quote: "I do not think either truth needs to be compromised. I think we can do as much justice to the sovereignty of God as a Calvinist and as much justice to the free will of man as a Baptist (or a Catholic). Yet it would not compromise the very essence of God to deny predestination. Arminianism, the theological viewpoint that denies predestination and emphasizes the role of man's free will in receiving grace from God, may be wrong. But it is wrong at a relatively technical, theoretical level. Denying human free will, on the other hand, would cut out something immediately essential to the Christian life: personal responsibility. If I am a robot, even a divinely programmed robot, my life no longer has the drama of real choice and turns into a formula, the unrolling of a pre-written script. God loves me too much to allow that. He would sooner compromise his power than my freedom. Actually, he does neither. It is precisely his power that gives me my freedom. Aquinas reconciles freedom with predestination by saying that God's love is so powerful that he not only gets what he wants but he also gets it in a way that he wants. Not only is everything done that God' wills to be done, but it is also done in the way he wants it to be done."

In recognizing God's absolute sovereign will, Dr. Kreeft is correct in saying God doesn't compromise His will in giving us freedom; but he doesn't go as far as he should in this quote to make sure we thoroughly understand that our free will is compatible with God's will for us because He will not compromise His sovereignty in allowing us to share in His power; yes, that seems deterministic, but, as I said before, it's "soft determinism." Just remember what I said about God's glory being most important to Him. We must not forget what Dr. Sproul said though about God prioritizing our free will over everything except His glory.

Darrel: In focusing on Aquinas theology, Kreeft seems to gloss over Augustine' focus on God's sovereignty over all. Kreeft is like many Catholics I've communicated with who seem to have a misunderstanding of not only what the Bible tells us, but what Augustine believed.

The belief that God's grace, which he effectually gave to us, can be resisted is Arminian and inconsistent with what we know about God's character and purpose. The belief attempts to elevate man's sovereignty to a level God has not intended for it to reach. Luther said that we must recognize "the clear cut distinction between God's power and ours and God's work and ours if we are to live a godly life." He said that he could not worship, praise, give thanks or serve God if he did not know how much he should attribute to himself and how much to God. If you take the time and effort to read all the Bible verses in the doctrines of grace handout I gave you, you will see the biblical support for grace being absolutely irresistible.

John: Okay, lastly, there is "P," Perseverance of the Saints." Does it not make logical sense that if God has the power to draw us to Him, would He not have the power to keep us? Again, I point out how each of the five points in TULIP relate consistently to each other.

Sonny: God treasures our free will; this means that our election need not be considered a guaranty of our perseverance in the faith. The idea that a person can be predestined to come to God and yet not be predestined to stay the course may be new to you Protestants, but it did not sound so strange to Augustine or Aquinas.

Darrel: Look, there's no doubt that Augustine succeeded in defining for us the omnipotent, sovereign Lord who is above time and space, maintaining his creation with his power and will and yet at the same time is always near us, preserving us, directing and guiding us in the truth and administering his grace through his Word and the two sacraments of baptism and Holy Communion. Augustine and even Aquinas gave God his due.

Sonny: You have implied that Augustine and Aquinas were Calvinists before Calvin, right? Well, while they did hold high views of predestination, they did not draw Calvin's inference that all who are ever saved are predestined to remain in grace. Dr. Sproul's attempt to redefine Calvinism as the "Augustianian" view notwithstanding, while Calvin's view of predestination might be a variation of Augustine's view, the two are not the same. Augustine did not believe in Calvin's view of the perseverance of the saints, and neither did the Augustianian tradition; and neither did Aquinas.

In summary, I propose an Aquinas version of TULIP.

T= total inability to please God (without special grace);

U= unconditional election;

L= limited intent (for the atonement's efficacy);

I= intrinsically efficacious grace (for salvation);

P= perseverance of the elect (until the end of life).

Darrel: I'm confused. How is Aquinas' TULIP different than Calvin's?

Sonny: Yeah, well, there are other ways to construct a Thomist version of TULIP, but I'm trying to point out that a Calvinist like yourself wouldn't have to repudiate his understanding of predestination and grace to become Catholic. It seems we are that close, I think. A Calvinist would simply have to do greater justice to the teaching of Scripture and would have to refine his understanding of perseverance and understand what Christ is saying in Mark 13:13, "the one who endures to the end will be saved." This is why I've said before that Catholicism is mature Christianity.

Darrel: We can interpret this verse to mean that when a person endures to the end, that's a sure sign he possesses a true, saving faith. And, it's ironic you should mention maturity because it's not mature, by definition, for a person to need a parent to explain everything to you the way your church does.

Sonny: We know God values our free will; that's why we believe we have the freedom to resist His grace if we wish to do so.

Darrel: Your understanding of what actually constitutes free will is as weak as your understanding of God's grace and glory. Believing you can resist God's calling compromises the effect of his grace, and that limits his glory; as John said before, God's glory is the only thing he places above our free will. And I ask you this, what free will are you talking about? You're indoctrinated to believe what your church tells you to believe so what do you know about free will? That means you can't think outside your indoctrination box your church has placed you in. You are bound, not free. And of course we already know we're bound by our sin.

Sonny: We are bound to believe in our freedom to resist God's grace. How's that?

John: I think it's critical to this discussion that I remind you of what I said before about God's emphasis on His glory over our free will He has given to us. When we can really grasp what His total sovereignty means to Him and to us, we will understand that our premise must be that God will glorify Himself, first and foremost. To God be the glory. Amen. End of discussion. I'm good with that; I'm sorry you're not.

But, as I said before, God doesn't rule over us with hard determination; He's not a dictator. His will considers our will; that's why I called it "soft determination." And, as also mentioned before, our free will must be compatible with His will; we are the secondary causes and He is the primary cause. I can accept this; as a matter of fact, I wouldn't have it any other way. Those who can't accept this are illustrating their inability to focus on God's glory over their own. Fallen man instinctively wants to be in control; he wants to be God; we don't want to give God the glory; we want to be in charge of every aspect of our existence and to participate in our own election, justification and eventual salvation. We've seen that Catholicism isn't true Arminian; its focus is more on God than on man, but, again, as with God's grace and sovereignty, your understanding is to a lesser extent than Protestantism's focus on God; Catholicism therefore is closer to being man-centered than Protestantism. I say this because Catholicism asserts some human freedom or cooperation in salvation. This is what Arminianism implied and it is what Luther and the other reformers recognized and rebelled against in a successful attempt to bring us back to believing in a more God-centered Christianity.

Sonny: I understand what you're saying, and I agree with you about what Catholicism believes about salvation, but, for your information, recent studies of Arminius' work have concluded that he was motivated more by his desire to defend the goodness of God than he was in making man's sovereignty more important in God's plan of salvation.

Darrel: From what I know of what Arminius believed, he was motivated by both this desire to belay the suggestion that God was a tyrant or the author of sin and his desire to elevate man's sovereignty in the salvation process.

Ray: What about your vaunted Luther? He didn't accept perseverance of the saints.

John: Luther didn't believe the biblical support was clear enough on whether we can maintain our belief or reject it. He was adamant, however, about the Romanists intentionally confusing their parishioners on this matter of perseverance of their faith.

Maybe this quote from Pelikan will help us understand Luther's position on AP." ALuther's understanding of perseverance clearly bears marks of the Roman Catholic tradition and yet differs from it on the key point of the believer's present certitude of the experience of grace. In the context of the late medieval Church whose theology and practices mitigated against such certitude, Luther is horrified that the pope >should have entirely prohibited the certainty and assurance of divine.' The preacher's essential task is to make the hearers sure of their salvation.>If you want to preach to a person in a comforting way,' urged Luther in a midweek sermon on Matthew 18:21-22, >then do it so that he who hears you is certain that he is in God's favor, or be silent altogether.' Preachers who make their hearers doubt are >good for nothing.' Assurance that one is presently in a state of grace is foundational to the Christian life. 'I must be able to say,' stated the great reformer, 'I know that I have a gracious God and that my works, performed in this faith and according to this Word, are good fruits and are pleasing to Him.'" All I can add to that is that I personally think that Lutherans are more wishy-washy on several of these points in TULIP than I am. That's because I'm a Calvinist, and Calvinists (it would seem) have no problem conceding all the glory to God.

I personally believe that how each person wants to understand the doctrines of grace and God's plan of salvation has a lot to do with their own self esteem. Those who don't do well with accepting gifts in real life have a problem accepting God's free gift of grace in saving us. Psychologists tell us the people who have a problem in accepting a gift act that way because they have lower self-esteem and don't want the giver to presume they need something from them or are somehow in some way dependent on them. People with a strong sense of self don't have any problem at all in accepting a gift. Of course, as Christians who know we are God's chosen people, that knowledge alone should give us good self-esteem.

Ray: That's psycho-babble, John.

John: It's just a personal belief I strongly hold, that's all.

Bobby: Okay, it's time to summarize what each of you believes.

John: I'd like to prove to both Sonny and Ray that I've been listening to what they've had to say in describing their Catholic belief in all these discussion sessions. By way of summary, I'll just go through my notes and the handouts Sonny provided to describe briefly what I think Catholics believe, and offer my comments in rebuttal:

First, let's discuss baptism. The Catholic Church proclaims that salvation is by baptismal regeneration and is maintained through the sacraments unless a willful act of sin is committed that breaks the state of sanctifying grace. We believe baptism is always practiced after a saving faith in Christ. That's what Augustine's predestination is all about. The Church teaches baptismal regeneration of infants. That's not in Scripture.

Next up is how Catholics understand the way God's plan of salvation works. The Catholic Church claims that Christians are saved by meritorious works (beginning with baptism) and that salvation is maintained by good works (receiving the sacrament, confession of sin to a priest, etc.). Biblical verses refuting this particular notion are too numerous to mention. Catholics therefore believe that their salvation cannot be guaranteed or assured. They throw in purgatory to try and moderate the uncertainty, but Catholics will still have to undergo penance in purgatory to perfect them for heaven. There's no biblical support for this belief, and, in fact, 1 John 5:13 refutes it. Personally, as I think I said before, I find this belief based on a weak understanding of God's grace, is the most objectionable. Shame on any Christian church for creating doubt in the mind of the true, Christian believer as to whether they've been saved or not!

Next up is the Eucharist. Catholics believe in transubstantiation. The Eucharist connects believers with Christ through partaking in what they believe to be His physical body and blood. There is no support for this practice in the Bible. The bread and wine have to obviously symbolize Christ's body and blood. There's absolutely no evidence that any chemical change takes place, supernatural or natural.

Then there is the veneration of Mary whom Catholics believe is the Queen of Heaven, a perpetual virgin, and the co-redemptress who ascended into heaven. First Timothy 2:5 refutes this belief. Catholics are to not only pray to God, but also to petition Mary and the saints for their prayers. The Bible teaches we are only to pray directly to God. Christ is our only mediator. (Matthew 6:9, Luke 18:1-7).

I object to the Catholic Church's distinction between the clergy and the lay people. First Peter 2:9 refutes this concept. Neither Mary nor any other special, devout, saintly people were to be venerated either.

The Catholic Church states that the believer is infused with grace upon reception of the seven sacraments. Nowhere in Scripture are five additional sacraments supported.

Unless a believer is hindered from doing so, the only way to receive the forgiveness of sins is by confessing them to a priest. The Bible teaches that confession of our sin is made directly to God. (1 John 1:9). There is no support for the Catholic Church's claim that confession is not acceptable to God if it isn't made to a priest. The inference is consistent with what you've said about your Church believing it's a substitute for God. There is no biblical support for this concept.

In addition, there are all those other traditions and rituals listed on the handout Sonny provided which have been added to the Catholic Church's doctrine of belief over the centuries. In the handout Darrel provided, we see when these various traditions were actually made a part of the Catholic dogma beginning in 310 AD through 1950 when the last dogma was proclaimed by Pope Pius XII, the assumption of the Virgin Mary.

I don't mind the rituals like incense burning, the use of candles, a rosary for prayer, holy water, images like the crucifix and statues of Mary and

Christ on the cross because God's people need such signs to remind them of Christ's purpose and character, and this "window dressing" can enhance the experience of connecting with Christ; and, as I've said before, some folks need this visibility more than others; but I do object to the majority of the traditions which I believe are unbiblical and can and does distract people from connecting to Christ. I know why the traditions are there: For reasons we've already discussed, the traditions are in your doctrine because the Catholic Church wanted them to be there, and of course knew they weren't biblically supported so it had to establish their credibility and the credibility of its church government, the papacy, that produced them for reasons we've also discussed in these sessions.

Sonny also gave us a list that includes various distinctions within the Christian doctrine like three different Spirits, two types of sin, two types of revelation, and so forth, which we believe are unnecessary and unbiblical and only serve to confuse Catholics in their understanding of Christian beliefs. We suspect this exercise in "over-thinking" is intended to create and encourage dependence on the Catholic Church for assurance of the right understanding of Scripture, its extra-biblical traditions, and the proper practice of Church dogma.

It's obvious we Protestants differ doctrinally from Catholicism, but, as we've seen when we discussed Augustine's and Aquinas' theologies, the Catholic Church dogma of today differs from the beliefs of two of their most important saints; I think reality should be recognized by every Catholic who's capable of leading an examined life. Their church of today is a mere shadow of what it once was, and only someone indoctrinated into its dogma would refuse to see that. But, that said, the Catholic Church of today still maintains its teaching that Christ is our Savior, and this is why we are all still brothers and sisters in Christ; but I should add that we not only need to believe Christ is our Savior, we need to believe what He tells us in the gospel accounts, and I believe Protestantism best inspires us to do that.

Darrel: There is what God tells us in his Word, and then there's what the Catholic Church tells us through its extra-biblical mantra and dogma which is considered to be equal or superior to God's Word. No one but indoctrinated members bow down to this powerful church organization as it substitutes for Christ for a very good reason: It's heresy.

Ray: That opinion is heresy, Darrel.

Darrel: I'm just telling you what I've gleaned from our discussions, Ray. From these discussions, I have learned that the Catholic Church is a visible Christian church institution which falsely appropriates unto itself the prestige of the original church founded by Jesus Christ and based on the teachings of the apostles; it arbitrarily appoints one of those apostles, Peter, as its first pope and falsely assumes apostolic succession in its leaders from that time forward. Don't you know that Peter never appointed a successor? So where did all your popes come from? I'll tell you where they came from, they were elected by your church organization, and the bishops of Rome often exercised a great deal of control over who would be pope; in other words, the pope is a secular-like, political appointment.

Ray: I have given you chapter and verse to support our assertion, Darrel.

Darrel: And we have addressed every single one of those biblical verses, and concluded your church has appropriated the Christian religion to support its objective to be God to you.

Ray: You're dead wrong, Darrel! Where's your evidence for this conclusion?

Darrel: I firmly believe we have presented sufficient evidence to prove this conclusion, Ray, and only someone as indoctrinated in your beliefs as you are ignores the evidence. If you can't see by now that your Catholic Church doesn't practice "sola Catholic Church" in prioritizing its own self-interest, you are deaf, dumb and blind. We have seen evidence of your indoctrinated blind faith time and time again as you and Sonny have responded to our questions and comments in these discussions.

Can't you see that every time you turn around, you bump into your church? Are you so indoctrinated you can't understand how this all looks from a more objective perspective?

Ray: Your perspective is wrong, Darrel.

Darrel: You will never know whether my view is right or wrong because you are incapable of having an open mind. This is the horror of indoctrination; it slams the door shut on the learning. It seems that even if you had the intelligence to think about what we have been saying about your Catholic Church in these discussions, you wouldn't allow yourself to entertain any other opinion but the opinion of your church. It's a damn shame that a church that claims to have the keys to the Kingdom, won't open the door to the truth.

Ray: And let a bunch of heretics like you to come barging into the room with all your heretical, unfounded, unsupported opinions? No thanks.

Sonny: From your tone in these ten weeks of discussions, Darrel, it's obvious to me that you don't think much of our Church and us Catholics in general. You seem to infer we aren't as educated in the biblical doctrines of the Christian religion as you think we should be; that many of us are in fact even illiterate, but that those of us who are literate don't read our Bibles because our Church discourages us from doing that on our own for fear we won't understand what it wants us to know. You've claimed that our Church has intentionally created a dumbed-down version of Christianity that plays to those of lesser intelligence who tend to be lazy followers who need spiritual parents and bells and whistles to aid us in relating to Christ. You conclude in saying that those of us who are articulate and educated in the Christian religion should leave the Catholic Church but we're too indoctrinated to see this all from your perspective. Am I right?

Darrel: You left out what I said about your confusion over what Catholics believe. In arbitrarily answering that your church subscribes to the Augustine/Aquinas theology, and don't recognize how the theologies of two of your greatest saints is in opposition to what your vaunted church believes, you show your confusion about what you really do believe; and here I thought your church was supposed to straighten things out for all of you followers, not confuse you with contradictions.

Sonny: Well, of course, that's just your opinion and you're entitled to think of us in that way. But, when you said that our Church wants to be God, you went too far. That's a ridiculous presumption.

Darrel: Many Catholics I've spoken with actually believe that, Sonny. As with your confusion over what you believe, you seem confused about how you're supposed to connect with your church. You ignore the obvious indication that your church has become more of an institution than a shepherd of sheep. In reiterating what Daniel said before, I will say again that, based on what both you Catholics have said in these ten weeks of discussions in implying your church is a substitute for our triune God, and what we said about your pope being your prophet, priest and king, I think we can infer that your Catholic Church has declared itself to be Christianity and that every other Christian church is a heretical spin-off from the Reformation.

Daniel: I sure can second what you just said, Darrel. The popes haven't been very good kings either. Over the centuries, many of them have demonstrated an abuse of its power as they have led the Catholic Church away from the original church to pursue worldly wealth, power and influence. It has ingrained in the minds and hearts of its followers that it is THE connection with our triune God, even to the extent we might infer it usurps that position. This is a gesture in futility of course because, as Darrel said before, the position of God in our lives is already taken, and the Catholic Church has demonstrated over the years it wouldn't be any good at it anyway. Witness the pedophile scandals and the liberal pope going around the world telling people we all worship the same God. Nonetheless, the Catholic Church as it grew in size, power, influence and wealth has seized the opportunity to attain this divine objective and offers us a version of Christianity that is designed to address the basic desires of man listed in these discussions. Man's instinct is to follow and lead an unexamined life; he instinctively desires to worship something that is visible, authoritative and influential. The Catholic Church caters to these instincts in representing itself to be THE authority of the Christian religion. You really can't be more authoritative than representing yourself as God's actual substitute on earth.

As Darrel said before, it would seem as though the Catholic Church wants to be the head of one, big happy family. It purports to be God *the Father* by teaching that its sacred tradition is equal or greater in authority to the Word of God, the Father. It even calls its leader, "Holy Father" and assumes he speaks infallibly "ex cathedra" just as God speaks to us in his Word. The Church acts in the place of Christ, *the Son*, in its belief that its priests are necessary to forgive sin, to accept prayer, and to change the bread and the wine into the flesh and blood of Christ. It even calls the pope "The Vicar of Christ." It also acts as a substitute for the *Holy Spirit* in its belief that the will and guidance of the Holy Spirit cannot be revealed to individual believers to guide them in their understanding of God's Word, but can only revealed to its magisterium which presumes sole authority for doctrinal and biblical interpretation. Followers are not encouraged to study the Bible on their own and express private opinions on doctrine.

Bobby: Sonny and Ray, do you want to summarize what you believe Catholicism is in rebuttal?

Sonny: I have nothing more to add except that I will be praying you Protestants recognize God's one true Church on earth.

Ray: There is no invisible church. The over 2,000 year old, Catholic Church is visible. It is not a denomination, it is the Christian Church. You Protestants present a confused, even contradictory collection of heretical doctrines attached to over 30,000 different denominations that no follower of Christ should trust as an authority to convey God's truth. God established the Catholic Church to insure that the teaching of the apostles would remain intact through a succession of leaders of the Church who alone were given the keys to the Kingdom.

Darrel: That's your summary, Ray? A repeat of what you have mechanically been spouting since the second week of our sessions?

Ray: I won't waste any more words or time speaking to heretics.

Darrel: I'll say again, what you claim is a weakness is actually our strength. The existence of our different denominations can be a good thing because our independence and the lack of an intrusive and demanding authority in our spiritual life, which dictates what we must believe, encourages a dialogue on theology and motivates us to have an intelligent faith, not the blind faith of indoctrination. We yearn to learn, and that's a good thing, is it not?

Ray: It depends on whether your teachers are telling you the truth. The Catholic Church alone has been given the authority by Christ Himself to bind and loose on earth as it is in heaven. It is truly sad for people who seem to want to be followers of Christ yet ignore the most fundamental institution Christ founded which is a singular, apostolic teaching authority that protects us from the heretical beliefs of self-proclaimed theologians because it is under the charism of the Holy Spirit to teach infallibly. The worst of it is that many people are led astray, the unity of the Church, the Body of Christ, is fractured, disoriented and misled by false teachers; the bad fruit of the Reformation.

Darrel: Well, Luther certainly had something to say about how the Catholic Church binds men through its ordinances and traditions and thus interferes with the loosing of God's truth which he expresses in his Word. He said that these Catholic ordinances "bind the conscience of men which the Gospel pronounces free."

Ray: Who cares what this heretic had to say? The question before us is whether the Catholic Church's assertion that she is the sole authority of truth is actually true or not. To believe that she is not is to ignore reality.

Protestants attack the credibility of the Church in its assertion that she is the spotless Bride of Christ. You are wrong.

Darrel: Luther also said that the authority of the pope and the Catholic Church "must therefore be held null and void, and any erroneous decisions they made (as all are in conflict with the Word of God) must be torn up and thrown away; for Christ is a higher authority than the Church."

Bobby: I'm glad we're into our summarizing now because each side is beginning to repeat itself.

Darrel: Really? Ya think? Isn't that what summaries are supposed to be all about, Bobby? Besides repetition is a proven method of communicating knowledge.

Bobby: That may be, Darrel, but we're running short of time, and anyway. I feel it's time to bring these discussions to a close.

John: Sure, but before we head back to our condos, I'd like to add to my summary, if I may.

Bobby: The floor, excuse me, the sand, is yours, John; but, please try to be brief.

John: When we began these discussions, I began by saying that every human being is naturally inclined to want to believe something, even to worship something, and we call that our theology. I said then, as I say now, <u>the challenge is to have the right one.</u>

You may recall when I talked about the three options we have in deciding on a theology: the choice not to believe in God at all; the choice to believe in a personal God of our own design and lastly, the choice to believe in the God of the Bible; that's Christianity. We know we are to not only believe the Bible is God's Word, but we are to believe Him when He tells us how we are to relate to Him in His Word, and how He has insured our salvation. That's the purest form of Christianity, the

Christianity as taught by the apostles, and continued on with such truly inspired teachers as Augustine. I believe these discussions have revealed that Catholicism is a variation of that pure belief, and I believe we have offered evidence to support our conclusion that the Catholic Church is clearly not what it claims to be, that one, true church that represents the apostolic tradition because it has added some traditions of its own over the centuries. We've discussed the most important of these traditions and proved that they the majority of them are not supported in God's Word and can therefore conclude that this is not the church Christ intended for His church to be. I believe we have proved my presumption that, just as man designs his own God, the men of the Catholic Church have designed their own church which has evolved over the centuries into the corporate institution it is today. Lord Acton's maxim is proved when we see how power has corrupted the original Christian church and turned it into this business whose objective is to attain power, influence and wealth under the guise of Christianity. As Daniel said before, Augustine's City of God has transitioned into the City of Man; the Catholic Church has achieved success in substituting itself for Christ in the hearts and minds of its followers.

That is not to say that its association with the Christian religion has produced no good results; we can certainly conclude that the Catholic Church does indeed provide a certain clarity to our shared Christian doctrine through its dogma and catechism, and I will say that, in my mind, there's no question that Catholics don't love Christ as much as I do. However, that said, I believe Catholics do so in spite of, not because of, Catholicism and their church because I believe it teaches, preaches and practices the wrong theology. And although those Catholic rituals that are biblically supported can and do serve a good purpose, and, along with the relics, help the believer to focus on Christ in a more visibly and dramatic connection, in the RCC's emphasis on the visible church and disregard for the existence of the invisible church, its proclaimed dogma in its 752 plus page catechism (some of which contradicts the basic tenets of Christ's invisible church of believers as Augustine pointed out and which were taught by the apostles) the basic doctrines of the

Christian religion (as presented in the various creeds we all follow) are minimized and even compromised. In representing itself as the sole authority in the lives of its followers, the Catholic Church actually compromises the authority of God, the Father, God, the Son, and God, the Holy Spirit. I agree with what Darrel said about that, and believe the evidence presented in these discussions has supported that conclusion. I believe that when a church, any church, assumes this position in the lives of its followers, it interferes with their walk of faith and their sanctification. Throughout these discussions, some of us Protestants have challenged you Catholics to see the obvious self-serving interest in your church taking this position in your spiritual lives.

Protestants of course should recognize the purpose and importance of their church in their spiritual life, but we surely don't require our church to be the one authority in interpreting God's Word and certainly don't believe it plays any role in our salvation except to guide us in our growth as Christian. The Reformation played a necessary role in bringing the church back to the original church of the apostolic tradition, the Catholic church of Augustine and Aquinas.

Regardless, we must not allow our differences to divide us; that's what the devil wants to accomplish. As I've stated a number of times in these discussions, I think that many of our differences are non-essential and consider Catholics to be my brothers and sisters in Christ. We must all stay focused on our chief purpose in this life: To glorify God and enjoy Him forever.

Daniel: Well said, John. My summary consists of one word: "Ditto." I affirm Reformed theology for these reasons: It best represents scriptural revelation; it best represents God's sovereignty, giving Him the greatest glory and majesty and emphasizing His attributes of omniscience, omnipotence, and omnipresence; it best explains the nature and extent of Christ's atonement; it exalts God's precision in His decrees and will; it best represents man's fallenness, helplessness, and enslavement to sin; it best explains the paradox of how God's sovereignty is related to our free will; it best explains how God's grace works in our salvation; it exposes and refutes the man-centered ideology that all people deserve salvation; it best explains the sovereign right of God to elect whom He desires to save; it provides comfort in knowing that our salvation does not depend on good deeds; it best provides me with an understanding of our close direct connection with our Creator and know that my prayers have the power to save because it is God who hears them.

John: I can only say that it's a shame the Catholic Church didn't take Luther up on his offer to discuss certain important issues that he believed had served to separate him from his church. Had they done this, they might have recognize how far they had strayed from the church's original purpose, how worldly they had become in their pursuit of materialistic objectives of power, influence and wealth, and this great awakening would have eliminated the need for the split the Reformation created in Christendom. I wish we had been able to go back to the future, to revert to being the church of the apostolic tradition and only the apostolic tradition, to embrace the five *solas*, and then proceed into the future as the church Christ intended for us to be.

Peter: As the only completely objective person in these discussions, would you like to hear my opinion of Catholicism and Protestantism?

Ray: Not really, but I get the feeling you're going to tell us anyway.

Peter Okay, I'll shut up.

Bobby: I'm curious, Peter. Go ahead.

Peter: Personally, I think that Protestants and Catholics are basically on the same page. You both subscribe to a religion that is designed to serve your wish for security and knowledge. You both believe Jesus Christ is your savior, for whatever that's worth. Like all other religions that involve a God, Christianity gave people what they wanted. It also gave the governing authorities a great tool to use to make people compliant.

The indoctrination of these two Catholics is obvious to me, and I agree with what you Protestants have said about how it's almost impossible to debate with an indoctrinated person because indoctrination stifles the use of reason in examining a belief system. I don't see a unified Christian church in the future, and of course to serve my atheistic cause, I believe that's a good thing. I really do believe a religion like yours causes more harm than good through its divisiveness; our objective is to implement one, unified, global belief system.

Darrel: Catholics and Protestants at least are unified in our opposition to your atheistic religion of secular humanism. The enemy of my enemy is my friend. It's God's world and he's in charge, not man. Your atheistic religion of secular humanism causes more harm than good; you have no firm ethical foundation, and you lack the power to do any real good to accomplish what you say is your objective.

You're right about unification though; we want the unity under Christ within the Christian church that Luther wanted his Catholic Church to represent; but it was having none of it then and, as evidenced in these discussions, Catholics are having none of it now. When Luther nailed those 95 theses on the door and told them he did this out of love for the truth and a desire to elucidate it, they ignored his plea for dialogue on his issues of concern because they correctly surmised they would have to change their ways and they were not going to give up that power and influence and share the wealth; they intended to remain in the position as the sole authority in the spiritual lives of their followers. If they conceded even one point to Luther's requests, they believed this would be a slippery slope to reform, and it would mean the demise of the Catholic Church as they knew it.

Ray: What would you have us Catholics do? Renounce our religion and join up with one of your 30,000 denominations?

John: Sure. Do what others have done, come back to what the original Christian church was intended to be; consider affiliating with a Bible-believing, Protestant denomination.

Ray: No thanks. After hearing from each of you Protestants, I've not only learned more about your heresy, I've also acquired even more knowledge and understanding of the truth that I believe. I believe we do share that primary belief that Christ is our Savior, our redeemer, our King, our High Priest and our Prophet. I am best connected with that relationship with Christ through the traditions and rituals of my Church. I do not consider myself to be bound by any of the rituals and traditions because I believe in the sole authority of my Church to interpret doctrine for me through my pope, my bishops and priests who also act to connect me to Christ through the teaching and preaching of the Word, and acting as mediator between us and God. I am content with my belief.

Bobby: Yes, some people do prefer tradition and organization and want their church to be a strong influence in the spiritual lives, and some don't feel they need that. Different strokes for different folks, eh? All other things being equal that is.

Ray: But they aren't equal, Bobby; we Catholics believe our sacred traditions are true and that God meant for His Church to be sole authority in conveying the truth of His Word. There is only one God and there is only one truth. Every other belief is heresy.

Darrel: As a Protestant, of course, I believe some of what the Catholic Church teaches about Christianity to be heretical, and I think we've offered evidence to support that conclusion during these discussions. There indeed is only one God, one truth, and one apostolic church, and it isn't the Catholic Church.

John: When we began these discussions, I related the story of my friend who told me he converted to Catholicism because it was the original church. Actually, I think he converted to please his Catholic wife, and it didn't make any difference, one way or the other to him. I mentioned why Dr. Kreeft converted as well. In essence, he converted because he believed the Catholic Church signified the original roots of our religion and he identified with its add-on rituals and traditions and church architecture even though he couldn't accept its version of God's plan of salvation or strongly supported some of its traditions.

According to a Catholic TV survey, the number one reason for conversion to Catholicism is that people want a singular authority, unifying doctrine, beliefs and practices. The most important practice is adherence to the seven sacraments, particularly the Eucharist, and the Catholic Church binds itself most successfully to its converts through this sacrament in particular. Catholics are taught to believe the Catholic Church was established by Christ as an instrument of salvation through which the faithful are able to receive the sacraments. In sum, converts were attracted to Catholicism through its assertion of being the only Christian Church and sole authority, and with its various traditions and rituals (particularly its belief that the elements in the Eucharist represent the true physical blood and body of Christ), it offered them a more visible version of the Christian religion than Protestantism could offer.

There's irony in that conclusion. During these discussions, we've exposed a number of ironies in the Catholic Church and in its theology, and I'd like to summarize those, if I may. Ironically, as the "catholic church" (little "c's") has transitioned into the "Catholic Church" (capital "c's") over the centuries in adding to the content of the Bible with all its papal and council declarations which invent new doctrines contrary to the apostolic teachings presented in Scripture, it has strayed from Christ's intent for His church to teach in the apostolic tradition. In its claim to be the original and only Christian Church, the Catholic Church has successfully persuaded its followers that it is indeed a substitute for Christ Himself and usurped the role of the Holy Spirt as well in dissuading believers from individually relying on the Holy Spirit to read and interpret the Bible. To round out the trinity, they call their leader "Holy Father." The sad irony here is that the church that claims a patent on God's truth has served to lead people away from the only written evidence we have of God's truth by minimizing the importance and credibility of the Bible. Ironically, its heretical doctrine designed to meet man's basic wants, has neglected its responsibility to correctly communicate God's plan of salvation which is supposed to meet man's need to rest in contentment that he is surely saved by the grace of God and only by the grace of God. With the addition of all these extra-biblical, unbiblical and unnecessary traditions which were declared to be church dogma for members to obey, the Catholic Church has become legalistic which minimizes the importance of God's grace and serves to complicate the Christian biblical doctrine. We have seen this complexity in the handouts Sonny gave us and the reliance on their 752 page Catechism which presents page after page of these dogmatic pronouncements such as defining two types of sin, two kinds of faith, two types of assurance, two degrees of predestination, seven sacraments, which have mainly served to give the church a purpose as the required interpreter of the Christian doctrine. This perception of legalism in the church dogma is given as one of the primary reasons folks have left it. It's also ironic that in its claim to be the original church, the Catholic Church motivates some people to take a good, hard look at the apostolic teachings and see how different the original church was from what the Catholic Church is today.

There are several other ironies discussed in these sessions. It's ironic that: **1**. Augustine, the man Catholics revere as one of their most important saints is actually the elephant in the room for them because his theology was the basis for Calvin's doctrines of grace. **2**. Catholics trust their church as sole authority of truth and trust that they can perform good works to earn their salvation by following its dogma, but don't trust in their ability to read and understand God's Word without total reliance on their church to do it for them. **3**. Catholics curse people who oppose their church who are simply following Paul's opposition to people who don't believe in justification by faith alone. **4**. Peter, whom they claim to be their first pope, is the man who actually warned people not to follow false traditions like the ones imposed by the Catholic Church. **5.** Their emphasis on the worship of Mary as a mediatrix to better connect with Christ actually serves to substitute for the Christ, our only mediator. Two alters in a church is one too many. **6.** Its insistence on a co-dependent, family relationship with its members is in direct opposition to what Christ said in Luke 14:25-33 when he said His disciples are to leave their families to follow Him. 7. Its unbiblical opposition to birth control has actually resulted in more abortions, which, of course, it also rightly opposes.

Protestants, like Dr. Kreeft, who have converted to Catholicism have much to tell us, but I also believe that Catholics who convert to Protestantism have much to tell us in support of my conclusion. Their stories are more interesting than the mechanical responses of the indoctrinated members they have left behind. In recognizing the irony of the Catholic Church, they are coming from a type of blindness into the light and their joy in discovering the true meaning of the gospel is evident.

It's true that the opposite of truth can best reveal the truth, and an ex-Catholic's previous perspective permits them to have a greater insight to compare what they used to believe to what they now believe. For this reason, it is these Catholic converts who are the ones leading in many areas of the Protestant church today such as Christian apologetics (not Catholic apologetics, defending the Church) and awakening some Catholics to their indoctrination and closed minded concept of Christianity. Some of these indoctrinated Catholics, who have never given their denomination's beliefs a second thought, have seen the light and have jumped off the wagon that is leading them astray of God's truth as the Bible presents it to us.

Then there are those people who leave the Catholic Church and never find a new church home, and that is tragic. Their experience with leading the Christian life was confined to going through the motions a Catholic goes through in staying the course, and they made the mistake of assuming this was Christianity.

Ray: These pathetic people should have stayed a Catholic and learned their Catholic faith better and they would have been just as good for it. They're missing the Eucharist which is the body, blood, soul and Divinity of Jesus Christ. They're missing the teaching of the truth the Church provides; they're missing out on salvation.

John: I'm concerned about what Catholics really know about God's grace and His plan of salvation, Ray. Our theologies are different primarily because of the way we understand God's grace and His sovereignty, and our source of authority is different. We both hold Scripture in high regard and try to argue from God's Word, but we disagree on the truth of doctrine and dogma that isn't in the Bible, and we differ on our understanding of verses in the Bible. It is difficult, if not impossible, to use logic and reason with people who cannot even understand that it's obviously best for a believer to be simply joined directly to the Savior who bought us with His blood and guaranteed our salvation, and not have to defer to some church authority to accomplish this purpose. Is it not enough for believers to be content with our membership in Christ's invisible church and rely only on the visible church to act as our guide as it has been hopefully guided by the Holy Spirit, and rely on it to direct us through its teaching, preaching and practicing God's truth? That same Spirit also guarantees the success of Christ's visible church that it serves and preserves it until Christ returns. Our Christian church is to be our guide, not our king, our priest or our prophet. Christ fulfilled that purpose and we're done with that now. The kingdom of God is not to be considered as a part of some church with all its various traditions and rituals, it is within each of us. We need no middle man but Christ and the Holy Spirit to connect us with God the Father. Our Christian church should represent that invisible church within us; it should be in us not over us. Again, it's all about the focus on "mere Christianity."

It is best, and most true, to focus on our belief in "mere Christianity" and understand we are Christians first and (fill in the denomination) second. So many Catholics defend the inerrancy and infallibility of Catholicism rather than Christianity. You never hear a Protestant talk about the infallibility and inerrancy of Protestantism, do you?

I will close my summary remarks by reminding you of my old friend's proud statement of belief, "I'm not a Christian, and I'm a Catholic." I thought it an odd and misinformed statement at the time, but, after enduring these discussion sessions with you and Sonny, I'm not so sure my friend's statement didn't precisely reflect the way most Catholics understand their relationship with Christianity and with their church. The Catholic Church has become their religion.

Ray: Your friend of course was misinformed. I'm a member of the Catholic Church and a believer in Catholicism, the only true Christian Church. Its rich history, the traditions and the little rituals of the Church serve to connect me better with Christ.

Darrel: You may recall our discussion about the vertical relationship we have with Christ and the horizontal relationship we have with our church and how we were to always make sure we're prioritizing the most important one. From the tone and content of our discussions over the past nine weeks, I get the distinct impression you have your priorities confused; you focus on the sizzle when you should be focused on the steak.

Sonny: That's a funny way of putting it, Darrel, but, using your analogy, I would say that the sizzle better prepares us to enjoy the steak; sizzle whets the appetite, right?

Look, all of us should admit that the vertical relationship cannot be defined as clearly as the horizontal relationship; we need the clarity our Church provides in our relationship with it to continue to remain firmly connected to our faith in Christ. Yes, the horizontal relationship is imperfect, particularly in this challenging time for our Church with the pedophile scandals and Pope Francis' liberal bent, but it is also a difficult time for Christianity in general as each of your denominations is challenged by its liberal faction. I'm concerned for the survival of Christianity.

Ray: I will always be a Catholic.

John: I will always be a Christian, and if you're saved, you'll always be one too. That's what Jesus meant when he said the gates of Hell will not prevail against His church of elect believers.

I can summarize my opposition to Catholicism by referring to what theologian John D. Feinberg expressed in *Five Views on Apologetics.* Darrel alluded to these tests before. Feinberg described seven tests of truth which are to be applied to any belief system to determine its authenticity. Christianity in general passes all the tests, but I believe Catholicism fails the last test, the "Test of Conservation."

The test presumes that when we are confronted with some anomaly in what we believe, our first inclination is to address it by choosing the least radical revision to explain away the anomaly. If a radical change is necessary, the belief system fails this test of truth, and we are motived to switch out our belief system for another. An anomaly, by definition, is "something that is contrary to the general rule or to what is expected." Christianity is a religion of the book; believing the Bible to be our source of knowledge of our beliefs is the rule in our religion. Catholicism, as we've seen in these discussions, presents us with the three-legged stool concept where the Bible is only one of three sources of knowledge, the other two being the Catholic Church and its sacred oral tradition. The rule in the Christian religion is clearly stated by Christ in John 14:6, "No one comes to the Father, but through Me." No oral tradition, no Catholic Church, just Jesus Christ; so then, by definition, the three-legged stool concept is an anomaly.

Then there are a number of these "yeah, but" traditions that we talked about throughout these discussions; they too offer a good example of what an anomaly looks like because the rule is what the Bible clearly states, and the "yeah, buts" in the extra-biblical traditions of the Catholic Church serve to create more anomalies. *Yeah*, the Bible teaches predestination, *but* the Catholic Church teaches there are two kinds; *yeah,* we believe in sin, *but* there are two kinds of sin; *yeah,* Paul tells us in Ephesians 2:8 that we are saved by grace and not by works, *but* there are two types of works; *yeah*, Paul teaches we are justified by faith, *but* there are two types of justification; *yeah*, we believe in God's grace, *but* there are two types of grace. This is evidence that the rule of Scripture is creatively enhanced by the church through the "yeah, buts" thus creating the anomaly, by definition.

Now then, the recognition of these anomalies should send up a red flag for you folks because the oral sacred traditions of the CC are, by definition, not in the Bible; but the church modifies the anomaly by telling you that the Bible isn't the only source of truth, that the oral tradition it claims to know is God's word too even though it wasn't presented in the Bible. And, after all, it was the Catholic Church that gave Christianity the Bible which really represents the first example of an oral tradition since the canon was not specified in the Bible. And the "claim game" begins. From what Ray just said, his vaunted church got away with the modification, because he and all the other devout, loyal Catholic apologists I've communicated with over the past several years on *Facebook* still cling to the belief the church can do no wrong because (using circular logic) it tells you in its sacred tradition that it is infallible. Catholics buy into that and the modification technique used by their church has been successful in retaining its loyal following.

In these past ten weeks, we've offered evidence of the ironies in Catholicism and the "yeah, buts," and pointed out the dogma that is contrary to what we know Augustine believed, and that your church has no basis for its various outrageous claims; but, according to what Ray just said, all our efforts have been in vain. We have not been able to penetrate the wall your blind faith has constructed. You Catholics have been unable or unwilling to see the obvious difference between your church's theology and the theology based on the teachings of the apostles; you've ignored the reality that the added traditions of the CC are not sacred, but man-made and should never be considered as the word of God equal to, or greater than, the Bible; you continue to believe that the Holy Spirit only connects with the Catholic Church and not you as an individual, that your magisterium is your only teaching authority, and their opinions are infallible (as are your pope's when he speaks "ex cathedra"); you believe that your church's dogma must be obeyed or you are cursed; you believe that your church is the only path to salvation, and you'll go to Hell if you leave it. You accept the Catholic Church's modification of these obvious anomalies. When will you two see the light and join up with those Catholics who have left your church to join up with a Protestant Bible-believing church because they have not accepted the modification of the anomaly and made the radical shift? My objective in these sessions is to motivate you Catholics to think about what you believe and why you believe it; to apply the Test of Conservation to your Catholicism and either stay the course as you seem to indicate you'll do, or consider switching your allegiance to a Bible-believing Protestant church.

Ray: I don't see any anomalies in the Catholic Church or its theology. We are the rule, not the anomaly. Do you think Christ would promise His Spirit to a wide variety of sects and denominations that encourage members to read without the guidance of an ecclesiastical authority to insure infallible interpretation of God's Word? The result is that each of these denominations has come to very different view on what constitutes the Christian religion. Your lack of coherence and unity is the anomaly of Protestantism, and you all should consider returning to the mother church.

Darrel: Christ didn't leave us with a church to be the Holy Spirit; he left each of us with the Holy Spirit. In stating "We are the rule in Christianity," you believe your church has taken the role of the Holy Spirit, and you have said, for all intents and purposes, the Catholic Church is Christ and you call your pope Holy Father. You believe your church is our triune God; this is the ultimate claim in your church's claim game.

As we've said several times before, we Protestants are unified in our belief in the theology of the Reformation, but you Catholics just can't see how your church has become disconnected from the unity of the church based only on the teachings of the apostles. Can't you see that Catholicism is a shadow of its former self? Are you blind to that too? The

Christian doctrine based solely on the teachings of the apostles has been contaminated by your Church dogma. Like that *Brita* commercial where the guy says that the mercury level in Denver's water supply is acceptable, but is just being acceptable good enough? Shouldn't we want our water to be as pure as we can make it? Shouldn't we want a water filter to make it as clean as possible from debris? Shouldn't we all aspire to a belief in "mere Christianity" without the frills of tradition, habit, rituals, and added extra-biblical dogma?

I've got a "yeah, but" for you guys. *Yeah*, Catholics may be Christians, *but* the impurity created through their added traditions is what needs to be filtered out. Because of your focus on the rituals and traditions, their vision of the meaning of the gospel is clouded. Your faith isn't an intelligent faith, it's a blind faith. You miss a complete understanding of the true message of the gospel that we have been saved solely through God's grace and Christ's atonement was sufficient for our salvation. The church based solely on the teachings of the apostles is the rule in Christianity, not some man-made, self-proclaimed Catholic Church. Your church's many unsupported claims are the anomaly, and the only modification that should be accepted is the radical modification exemplified in the Reformation where so many Catholic Christians had had enough and left the church.

John: In summarizing, I'd like to refer again to 2 Corinthians 1:15-20. Paul says that "Our word to you has not been Yes and No." Verse 20 states, "For all the promises of God in Him are, yes, and in Him Amen, to the glory of God through us."

Daniel: Again I quote Dr. Leonardo De Chirico: "In Roman Catholicism, it cannot be said that the "yes" is totally missing, but the problem stems from the fact that it is not a "yes, yes." It is a "yes and no at the same time."

In the Roman Catholic view, Christ is told "yes" but also "no" because the prerogatives of the church end up arrogating what belongs exclusively to Jesus Christ. Divine grace is told "yes" but also "no" because Roman

Catholicism teaches that nature holds the capacity to be elevated in spite of sin. Faith is told "yes" but also "no" because Roman Catholicism teaches that in order to receive God's grace, there is the need for sacramental instrumentality of the church, which ends up prevailing over the Bible. The church worship rendered to God is told "yes" but also "no" because the veneration of Mary and a host of others is encouraged, ultimately detracting from the worship of the one and only God.

While reformed theology presents the five *solas*, Scripture alone, Christ alone, grace alone, faith alone, to the glory of God alone, Roman Catholicism adds its sacred tradition to Scripture; Christ and church, grace and merits, faith and works, God and Mary and the saints. We are all tempted to compromise the gospel with our "yes" and "no" answers to the gospel, but the biblical faith is expressed with the "amen" to the glory of God." To God be the glory, all the glory.

Ray: I say "no" to what you heretic Protestants believe.

Darrel: I will go to my grave in wondering why God gives Catholic Christians a good brain (Chesterton and Kreeft come to mind) if he expects them to just put it in neutral and motivate them to solely rely on a Catholic ecclesiastical authority to do all their thinking for them. It makes me wonder why Jesus would promise his Spirit to a few just to control millions of mind-numbed, indoctrinated robots who appear to be just going through the motions of belief, habitually observing their little rituals and traditions, focusing on the church over Christ. Catholicism, by William James' definition, is a "second-hand religion." Is that what we want our Christian religion to be? Of course not. I quote Calvin again, "A true faith is an intelligent faith."

We are to trust only in God to interpret his Word for us, not on some church institution that claims the divine right to invent new dogma which is to be an indisputable article of faith. The relationship between Catholics and their church reminds me of the situation in first century Jerusalem when the majority of Jews were so committed to their legalistic religion, they were blinded to the truth when Christ walked among them.

I can summarize what a Protestant believes in saying that my church is governed by elders acting in concert, some of whom specialize in teaching the Bible just like those churches founded and guided by Paul. My church believes that God is absolutely and completely sovereign in all things, including our salvation just like that church founded and instructed by Peter. My church believes that confession with no human intermediary other than Christ himself is rewarded by God's forgiveness just like those churches to whom John wrote in Revelation. This is how the apostles connect with us; not a one of them is greater than another and is labeled a pope. It's not the label, it's the substance.

I can only add that it really is a pity we didn't spend more time talking about our shared Christian theology and doctrine in these discussion sessions instead of discussing Catholicism and the Catholic Church. I wish we had spent more time talking about Christianity and less time talking about Catholicism because, as we have seen from these discussions, they're not exactly the same thing. Based on my notes and reviewing the actual recordings of these conversations over the past ten weeks, I can conclude that, if it weren't for Protestants being engaged in these discussions, we wouldn't have spent much time talking about these core beliefs of Christianity at all. For example, instead of discussing Pauline theology, our discussions have been misdirected by you Catholics to focus on how the Christian church was formed. With his tongue firmly implanted in his cheek, Luther once said, "No, no, Paul, you are altogether unprofitable; such blessings as you ascribe to Scripture must be sought from the (church) fathers, who have found acceptance down the long line of the ages, and from the see of Rome."

The Catholic Church has been successful in motivating you people to focus more on it, the City of Man, than on the gospel, the City of God, as it became more entrenched in the former. We Protestants focus on Christianity from God's perspective; our Bible-believing Protestant churches of the theology of Augustine and the Reformation serve only to preach, teach and witness the gospel message in all its fullness, retaining none of God's glory for themselves. That's what a Christian should expect from his church. We don't need a church to add to God's Word; we believe his Word is all-sufficient. Peter said that the Word of God is a lamp shining in a dark place. We say "yes" to receiving that light. No "yeah, buts" for us. C. S. Lewis challenged us to believe in 'mere Christianity," biblical Christianity; that's the unity Christ intended for his church.

I can only conclude with this observation: You Catholics have demonstrated during these discussions (which are meant to encourage open-minded discourse) that you haven't been able to play well with us other Christians, and my *Facebook* discussions have been no different. You take any criticism, no matter how constructive it is, to be an insult to your own spiritual self-esteem. Spiritual growth is thus stifled in Catholicism. Under the heavy hand of the church, believers are discouraged from thinking on their own and relying on the Holy Spirit to guide them in their understanding and practice of the gospel. The spiritual growth of Catholics has been stifled as your Catholic Church has grown in influence, power and wealth, corrupted by its own power as it has made Christianity more about itself than about Jesus Christ. The Protestantism of the theology of the Reformation is the straight biblical truth; no rituals, no traditions, no papacy, no embellishments designed to appeal to immature Christians, no additional and continuing revelation, just God's truth as expressed in his Word. You have to be a mature Christian who thoroughly understands what he believes and why he believes it to understand the critical importance of what I just said. A true faith is indeed an intelligent faith. I had hoped these discussions would have made you aware of the obedient "yes" of our faith to the "yes" of the promises fulfilled by Christ as presented in the gospel. As Paul stated, in Christianity, it's always "Yes." "Amen to God for his glory."

Ray: You Protestant people are sure a windy bunch of heretics. You may all think you have the last word, but you don't; God does.

Darrel: Right you are, Ray-boy; and I can tell you with a 99% certainty that you will never hear God say to you one day when this life is over, "Well done, good and faithful Catholic."

Bobby: Okay, boys, we've gone into overtime in today's session, but everyone had a lot of good things to say. I hope to see you all next year. Have a safe trip back to your homes. Adios.

Appendix

Doctrines of Grace

It is important for us to understand and embrace the core doctrines of the Christianity of the Reformation, its orthodoxy as expressed in the Apostles Creed, the Nicene Creed and the various confessions of faith such as the Presbyterian Westminster Confession, and the Lutheran Augsburg Confession.

An important aspect of the core doctrine is the Doctrines of Grace (known by the acronym TULIP). These doctrines were developed at the Synod of Dort in 1618 from the theology of John Calvin as expressed in his *Institutes of the Christian Religion* in opposition to the Remonstrance of 1610, a summary of the five points of Arminianism listed by the followers of Jacob Arminius. Arminianism was subsequently judged to be heresy by the Synod in 1619 just as, centuries before, the Church had rejected the Pelagian doctrine and supported the Augustinian doctrine.

I have listed below the scriptural verses utilized in support and in opposition to the Doctrines of Grace.

TOTAL INABILITY

Verses opposing: John 3:16, Acts 16:31, Romans 5:19, 10:9, 1 John 3:23.

Verses supporting: Romans 3:11, 5:12, Jeremiah 17:9, Proverbs 20:9, Psalm 51.5, 58.3, John 3:3, 3:19, Genesis 8:21, Ephesians 2:2-3, 3:8, 2 Timothy 2:25-26, 1 Corinthians 2:14, 1 John 1:8.

UNCONDITIONAL ELECTION

Verses opposing: Mark 1:15, John 1:12, 5:24, Matthew 19:29, Rev 2:23, Ephesians 2:8, Romans 8:29, James 2:14.

Verses supporting: John 6:37-39, 44, 65, 10:3-5, 10:11, 10:14-18, 25-28, 15:16, 25-28, 17:1-5, 20, Acts 13:48, Psalm 65:4, Philippians 2:13, Ephesians 1:11, 2 Timothy 1:9, Romans 8:28, Matthew 11:27, Hebrews 12:2, Luke 10:22, 12:49-53, 17:5, Isaiah 55:11, Exodus 33:16-19, 1 Corinthians 1:26-31, 12:3, Ephesians 2:9, 1 John 3:23-24, Ephesians 1:4, Romans 9:6-26, 11:5, 7, 28, 16:13, Colossians 3:12, 1 Thessalonians 1:4, 2 Thessalonians 2:13, Titus 1:1, James 2:18.

LIMITED ATONEMENT

Verses opposing: Matthew 6:14-15, John 1:12, 29, 3:16, 6:37, 51, 2 Peter 3:9, Acts 10:43, 1 Timothy 2:4-6, 4:10, 2 Corinthians 5:14, 19, 1 John 2:2, 4:14, Hebrews 2:9, 1 Timothy 4:10, Philippians 2:12, Romans 5:19, Titus 2:11, 1 Corinthians 8:11, 15:22.

Verses supporting: John 6:37, 44, 10:11, 14-15, 17:9, 20, Romans 5:8, 10, 8:32-34, Galatians 1:3-4, Matthew 1:21, 2 Peter 3:9, Colossians 1:12-24, 1 Thessalonians 1:4, 2:13, Colossians 3:12, Matthew 20:28, Ephesians 1:7, 5:25, Acts 20:28, 2 Corinthians 5:21, 15:23, Galatians 1:4, 3:13, Hebrews 2:10,

Mark 10:45, Revelation 12:11.

IRRESISTABLE GRACE

Verses opposing: John 1:12, 3:36, 3:18-21, 5:40, 8:45.

Verses supporting: Daniel 4:35, Isaiah 46:9,10, 55:11, John 6:37, 6:44, 6:65, 1:13, 5:21, James 1:18, Ephesians 2:4-5, Acts 11:18, Titus 3:5, Romans 9:11.

PERSEVERANCE OF THE SAINTS

Verses opposing: Galatians 5:4, Hebrews 3:12, 14, 6:4-6, 10:26-27, 2 Peter 2:1, 1 John 5:16, 2 Timothy 2:17-18, Matthew 24:10, Romans 11:20-22, 14:14-15, 1 Timothy 1:19, 4:1, 6:10, Philippians 2:12, Colossians 1:23, Revelation 3:5, 3:11, 1 Samuel 16:14, Psalm 51:11, 1 Corinthians 8:11, 9:27, 10:12, Psalm 95:8, Luke 8:13.

Verses supporting: Jude 1: 24, Ezekial 11:19, 36:27, Deuteronomy 30:6, 1 Peter 1:4-5, 2 Timothy 1:12, 2:19, 4:18, Psalm 37:28, 1 Thessalonians 5:24, Philippians 1:6, 1 John 2:19, 5:4, 13, John 3:36, 5:24, 6:4-7, 37-40, 10:27-29, 17:11-15, Romans 8:1, 31-39, 11:29, Jeremiah 23:3-4, 32:40, Luke 22:32, Hebrews 7:25, 10:10, 13-14, 23, 1 Corinthians 1:8-9, 10:13, 2 Corinthians 1:22, 5:5, Revelation. 3:5, Ephesians 1:14, 6:11, Hebrews 6:4-6.

In reviewing the verses included in this comparison, the first thing we can observe is that the number of verses in support of the Doctrines of Grace outnumbers the opposing verses by almost 3:1. We can also note that sometimes the same verse is listed in support of both views. Examples of this occurring are Revelation 3:5, Hebrews 6:4-6, John 6:37. We can assume these verses are therefore too ambiguous to use in support of either view, pro or con. Lastly, we will note that sometimes a verse listed in support of Arminianism is actually supporting TULIP, and in some cases, the opposite is true.

I believe we can conclude that not all these biblical verses are clear enough to support either side, and so we should seek out those verses that are most clear and use them to interpret the meaning of the less clear verses. When we do this, we will note that most of the verses listed in support of TULIP clearly support TULIP, while the majority of the verses listed in support of Arminianism are either ambiguous or are actually more supportive of TULIP. There are also other verses that seem to support both points of view. This seems to be particularly the case in the last point of the Doctrines of Grace, P, Perseverance of the Saints." Hebrews 3:12 says ASee to it that none of you turns away from God" and John 10:29 says AThey shall never perish. No one can snatch them out of my hand.? These verses appear to contradict each other. Calvinists reconcile the two verses by stating that the author of Hebrews 3:12 is offering simple reinforcement of principals clearly expressed in John 10:29 and other verses in the gospel accounts. On the other hand, Lutherans would address this apparent contradiction between these two verses by taking each verse as it stands and making no attempt to reconcile them. Of course, this is an illogical stand because the verses appear to contradict one another. In response, Lutherans claim that no one can fully understand God's mind and intent and that the truth must exist somewhere in the middle of the two interpretations.

Since Christians should presume from Scripture the premise that God is not a God of contradiction or confusion, they conclude that all of the verses must either support TULIP or support the Arminian view. Since most of the verses listed on both sides clearly support TULIP, we should conclude that Calvin's Doctrines of Grace accurately summarize biblical doctrine. As a caveat, Calvinists also take the position that where an apparent contradiction exists, the paradox can be explained by assuming that anyone who claims to have lost his or her faith, or who has rejected God's grace enabling them to believe in Christ has never actually been elected or possessed a true, saving faith. Their rejection of God's grace in electing them or their renunciation of their faith is evidence of their unbelief. One cannot lose something one never had. Those who claim to have chosen to believe in Christ as an act of their free will without acknowledging God's election as the cause of their belief, do not actually possess a true, saving faith.

www.ingramcontent.com/pod-product-compliance
Lightning Source LLC
Chambersburg PA
CBHW021208090426
42740CB00006B/162
9780996152099